# PRINCIPLES

OF

# SOCIAL SCIENCE.

# PRINCIPLES

OF

# SOCIAL SCIENCE.

BY

H. C. CAREY.

IN THREE VOLUMES.

VOL. I.

PHILADELPHIA:
J. B. LIPPINCOTT & CO.
LONDON:—TRÜBNER & CO.
PARIS:—GUILLAUMIN & CO.
1858.

# PREFACE.

THE work now offered for consideration, will speak for itself; but its readers will, perhaps, excuse its author, if, for a few moments, he asks their attention to matters of little interest to any but himself.

Of the principles here enunciated, some now make their appearance for the first time; whereas, others were first published, twenty years ago.* Since then, the latter have reappeared in another work, by a distinguished French economist,† which — its circulation having been extensive — has been read by thousands, who have never seen the volumes, in which the same ideas had previously been published. Finding, here, a repetition of what they had read elsewhere, and given without acknowledgment, those persons would, most naturally, be disposed to suspect the present author of having wrongfully appropriated the property of another; when, in point of fact, he was, himself, the real owner. This would be an unpleasant state of things; and, as the only mode by which it can be avoided, he deems it well to make, on this occasion, a brief statement of the order of discovery, of the various new ideas contained in the following pages.

The theory of value, as now given, was first published in 1837. Being very simple, it was very comprehensive — embracing every commodity, or thing, in reference to which the idea of value could exist — whether land, labor, or their products. This was one step towards establish-

* CAREY: *Principles of Political Economy.* Philad., 1837–1840.

† BASTIAT: *Humaines Économiques.* Paris, 1850.

ing the universality of natural laws — the value of land having been ascribed, by all previous economists, to causes widely different from those which gave value to its products.*

Consequent upon this, was the discovery of a general law of distribution — embracing all the products of labor, whether that applied to cultivation or conversion — to change of place or form. According to the theories then most generally received, the profit of one, was always attended with loss to another — rents rising, as labor became less productive, and profits advancing, as wages retrograded — a doctrine that, if true, tended to the production of universal discord; and that, too, as the natural consequence of a great law, instituted by the Deity for man's government.†

* "Carey, and after him Bastiat, have introduced a formula, *à posteriori*, that I believe destined to be universally adopted; and it is greatly to be regretted that the latter should have limited himself to occasional indications of it, instead of giving to it the importance so justly given by the former. In estimating the equilibrium between the cost to one's self and the utility to others, a thousand circumstances may intervene; and it is desirable to know if there be not among men a law, a principle of universal application. Supply and demand, rarity, abundance, etc., are all insufficient, and liable to perpetual exceptions. Carey has remarked, and with great sagacity, that this law is the labor saved, *the cost of reproduction* — an idea that is, as I think, most felicitous. It appears to me that there cannot arise a case, in which a man shall determine to make an exchange, in which this law will not be found to apply. I will not give a quantity of labor or pains, unless offered in exchange an utility equivalent; and I will not regard it as equivalent, unless I see that it will come to me at less cost of labor than would be necessary for its reproduction. I regard this formula as most felicitous; because, while on one side it retains the idea of cost, which is constantly referred to in the mind, on the other it avoids the absurdity to which we are led by the theory, which pretends to see everywhere a value equivalent to the cost of production; and, finally, it shows more perfectly the essential justice that governs us in our exchanges." — FERRARA: *Biblioteca degl' Economista*, vol. xii. p. 117.

† "Low wages, as a consequence of competition for the sale of labor, reduce the prices of the things to the production of which that labor is applied; and it is the consumers of those products, the whole society, that reap the profit. If, then, as a consequence of low wages, the latter find themselves obliged to contribute to the support of the poor workman, they are indemnified therefor by the reduced prices at which they obtain his products." — J. B. SAY: *Traité d'Économie Politique*, t. 11, p. 292.

It is here supposed that society profits by a state of things, that impoverishes the workman, and sends him to the hospital. The interests of the employer and his workmen being the same, such a state of things could not exist.

Directly the reverse of this, however, was the law that was then published, and now is reproduced — proving, as it did, that both capitalist and laborer profited by every measure tending to render labor more, while losing by every one that tended to render it less, productive — and thus establishing a perfect harmony of interests.

Thoroughly persuaded of the truth of the laws then presented for consideration, the author felt not less certain, that the really fundamental law remained yet to be discovered; and that, until it could be brought to light, many of the phenomena of society must continue unexplained. In what direction, however, to seek it, he could not tell. He had already satisfied himself, that the theory presented for consideration by Mr. Ricardo — not being universally true — had no claim to be so considered; but, it was not until ten years later, that he was led to remark the fact, that it was universally false. The real law, as he then saw, was directly the reverse of that propounded by that gentleman — the work of cultivation having, and that invariably, been commenced on the poorer soils, and having passed to the richer ones, as wealth had grown, and population had increased. Here was the great fundamental truth, of which he before had thought, and the one, too, that was needed for the perfect demonstration of the truth of those he previously had published. Here, too, was further proof of the universality of natural laws — the course of man, in reference to the earth itself, being thus found to have been the same that we see it to have been, in reference to all the instruments into which he fashions parts of the great machine itself. Always commencing with the poorest axes, he proceeds onward to those of steel: always commencing with the poorer soils, he proceeds onward to those richer ones which yield the largest return to labor — the increase of numbers being, thus, proved to be essential to increase in the supply of food. Here was a harmony of interests, directly opposed to the discords taught by Mr. Malthus.

This great law was first announced now ten years since.* While engaged in its demonstration, the author found himself constantly impelled to the use of physical facts, in illustration of social phenomena, and hence was led to remark the close affinity of physical and social laws. Reflecting upon this, he soon was brought to the expression of the belief, that closer examination would lead to the development of the great fact, that there existed but a single system of laws — those instituted for the government of matter, in the form of clay and sand, proving to be the same by which that matter was governed, when it took the form of man, or of communities of men.

In the work then published, the discoveries of modern science, proving the indestructibility of matter, were, for the first time, rendered available to social science — the difference between agriculture and all other of the pursuits of man, having then been exhibited in the fact, that the farmer was always employed in *making* a machine, whose powers increased from year to year; whereas, the shipmaster, and the wagoner, were always *using* machines, whose powers as regularly diminished. The whole business of the former, as there was shown, consisted in making and improving soils — his powers of improvement growing with the growth of wealth and population. To fully develop the law of the perpetuity of matter, in its bearing upon the law of population, was, however, reserved for the author's friend, Mr. E. Peshine Smith, numerous extracts from whose excellent little Manual, will be found in the present volume.

The great and really fundamental law of the science — the one required for the demonstration of the identity of physical and social laws, still, however, remained to be

* *The Past, the Present, and the Future.* Philad., 1848.

discovered; but, it is now, as the author thinks, given in the second chapter of the present volume. In the third, will be found the law developed by Mr. Smith. The fourth gives that of the occupation of the earth, as published ten years since — those of value and distribution, published ten years earlier, following, in chapters five and six. The order here required for their proper exhibition, is thus, as the reader sees, precisely the inverse one of their discovery — thus proving the truth of the idea, that first principles are always last to be discovered.

It remains now to say a few words, in regard to the course of investigation hitherto pursued by the author, and here continued. The most cursory glance at the several portions of the world, enables us to see, that all the stages of civilization in the past, may be found existing in the present; and that, if we would understand the former, we can do so only by studying the latter — thus following in the path that has so long been trodden by the teachers of physical science. Doing this, it has, of course, been necessary to examine carefully the movements of various leading European communities, and especially those of France and England — the first being the one in which originated the doctrine of over-population, and the last, that of the European nations by which the peace of the world has most frequently been disturbed. As a consequence of this, it has been, that he has been charged with hostility to both — his motives being thus impugned, by those who have found it inconvenient to undertake to show, that his facts could not be received as true, or, that his reasoning was not warranted by the facts. The charge, however, carries with itself its refutation. Had he been so injudicious, as to permit himself to be led to misstate the facts, or to draw from them inferences they did not warrant, he would thereby have laid himself so entirely at the mercy of his reviewers, as wholly to free the latter from any necessity for inquiring into the motives by which he had been actuated.

If he knows himself at all, he has been prompted by a single motive, the desire to find the truth; and that he really has been so, would seem to be proved by the fact, that, not only has he never been charged with any misrepresentation of the arguments of his opponents, but, on the contrary, has, on more than one occasion, been complimented, on the perfect accuracy with which they have been given. Widely different, he regrets to say, has been the course pursued by those to whom he has been opposed — his views having, most generally, been first misstated, as preparation for their refutation. In future, however, he hopes that a different course will be pursued, and that his reviewers will bear in mind, that, "notwithstanding the pretensions so frequently put forward by politicians and economists, some of the most interesting portions of the sciences they profess, are still imperfectly understood;" while "the important art of applying them to the affairs of mankind, so as to produce the greatest amount of permanent good, has made but little progress, and is hardly, indeed, in its infancy." *

Doubting the accuracy of the view that is thus presented, of the present state of economical science, let them next turn to the work of one of the most eminent of modern economists, to find him asking, if it is matter for surprise that, "amid such conflicting claims, such opposing exigencies, such an inextricable mass of truth and error, the science has halted — that it has only felt its way — that its gait has been tottering and doubtful?"† To him, it was not. Seeing the mists in which the science was enveloped, he declared his determination to try "not to add darkness" to the exceeding darkness that, as he declared, so obviously existed. These are the acknow-

* McCulloch: *Principles.* Preface. Third edition.
† Rossi: *Cours d'Économie Politique,* t. ii, p. 14.

ledgments of men who have earned high positions among the teachers of social science; and yet, among their followers, there are men of comparatively small experience, who treat with supreme contempt the suggestion of any new idea!*

To all such persons, the author would desire to suggest consideration of the fact, that, in every department of knowledge, the orthodoxy of the existing generation is but the heresy of that which is past—most of the ideas now held by themselves, and regarded as undeniably true, having been, and that but recently, treated as most absurd.† The disciples of Ptolemy—seeing the sun revolve around the earth, and finding in the Scriptures proof that such was the fact—had the strongest reason for believing that the accuracy of his doctrines was beyond the reach of question. Copernicus was, therefore, regarded as a heretic, and Galileo was compelled to recantation; and yet, it is now the established doctrine of the schools, that "the earth it is, that moves." Such having been the case in the past, it may be so in the present—the economical doctrines now most generally believed, passing into oblivion, there to take their places by the side of the Ptolemaic system.

It has been well said, by an eminent writer of our time, that "every one must of course think his own opinions

* That, in this respect, the present is but a repetition of the past, is proved by Newton's declaration, "that a man must either resolve to put out nothing new, or to become a slave to defend it."

† "So strong has been the belief that the sun cannot be a habitable world, that a scientific gentleman was pronounced by his medical attendant to be insane, because he had sent a paper to the Royal Society, in which he maintained that the light of the sun proceeds from a dense and universal aurora, which may afford ample light to the inhabitants of the surface beneath, and yet be at such a distance aloft as not to be among them; that there may be water and dry land there, hills and dales, rain and fair weather; and that, as the light and seasons must be eternal, the sun may easily be conceived to be by far the most blissful habitation of the whole system. In less than ten years after this apparently extravagant notion was considered a proof of insanity, it was maintained by Sir William Herschel as a rational and probable opinion, which might be deducible from his own observations on the structure of the sun."—Sir David Brewster.

right; for, if he thought them wrong, they would no longer be his opinions: but" that "there is a wide difference between regarding ourselves as infallible, and being firmly convinced of the truth of our creed. When," he says, "a man reflects on any particular doctrine, he may be impressed with a thorough conviction of the improbability, or even impossibility of its being false; and so he may feel in regard to all his other opinions, when he makes them objects of separate contemplations. And yet, when he views them in the aggregate; when he reflects that not a single being on the earth holds collectively the same; when he looks at the past history and present state of mankind, and observes the various creeds of different ages and nations, the peculiar modes of thinking of sects, and bodies, and individuals, the notions once firmly held which have been exploded, the prejudices once universally prevalent which have been removed, and the endless controversies which have distracted those who have made it the business of their lives to arrive at the truth; and when he further dwells on the consideration, that many of these his fellow-creatures have had a conviction of the justness of their respective sentiments equal to his own, he cannot help the obvious inference, that in his own opinions it is next to impossible that there is not an admixture of error; that there is an infinitely greater probability of his being wrong in some than right in all." *

All that the author of the present work desires, is, that his arguments may be fairly weighed, and that, to that end, the reader will "strengthen himself, by something of an effort and a resolve, for the unprejudiced admission of any conclusion which shall appear to be supported by careful observation and logical argument, even should it prove of a nature adverse to notions he may have previously formed for himself, or taken up, without examination, on the credit of others. Such an effort is, in

* *Essay on the Publication of Opinions*, Section V.

fact," says Sir John Herschel, "a commencement of that intellectual discipline which forms one of the most important ends of all science. It is the first movement of approach towards that state of mental purity which alone can fit us for a full and steady perception of moral beauty as well as physical adaptation. It is the 'euphrasy and rue' with which we must 'purge our sight,' before we can receive and contemplate as they are the lineaments of truth and nature." *

In the attempt here made, to demonstrate the universality of natural laws, the author has profited much of suggestions by two of his friends—the one above referred to, and Dr. Wm. Elder, of this city; and to both of them, he now desires to return his thanks.

PHILADELPHIA, February 10th, 1858.

# CONTENTS

OF

# VOL. I.

## CHAPTER I.

### OF SCIENCE AND ITS METHODS.

## CHAPTER II.

### OF MAN — THE SUBJECT OF SOCIAL SCIENCE.



## CHAPTER III.

### OF INCREASE IN THE NUMBERS OF MANKIND.

## CHAPTER IV.

### OF THE OCCUPATION OF THE EARTH.



## CHAPTER V.

### THE SAME SUBJECT CONTINUED.



## CHAPTER VI.

### OF VALUE.

## CHAPTER VII

### OF WEALTH.



## CHAPTER VIII.

### OF THE FORMATION OF SOCIETY.

## CHAPTER IX.

### OF APPROPRIATION.

## CHAPTER X.

### OF CHANGES OF MATTER IN PLACE.

## CHAPTER XI.

### THE SAME SUBJECT CONTINUED.



## CHAPTER XII.

### THE SAME SUBJECT CONTINUED.



## CHAPTER XIII.

### THE SAME SUBJECT CONTINUED.



## CHAPTER XIV.

### THE SAME SUBJECT CONTINUED.

## CHAPTER XV.

### OF MECHANICAL AND CHEMICAL CHANGES IN THE FORMS OF MATTER.



## CHAPTER XVI.

### THE SAME SUBJECT CONTINUED.

## CHAPTER XVII.

### THE SAME SUBJECT CONTINUED.



## CHAPTER XVIII.

### THE SAME SUBJECT CONTINUED.

## CHAPTER XIX.

### THE SAME SUBJECT CONTINUED.

# PRINCIPLES OF SOCIAL SCIENCE.

## CHAPTER I.

### OF SCIENCE AND ITS METHODS.

§ 1. THE first man, when he had day after day, even for a single week, witnessed the rising and setting of the sun, and had seen that the former had invariably been accompanied by the presence of light, while the latter had as invariably been followed by its absence, had acquired the first rude elements of positive knowledge, or science. The cause—the sun's rising—being given, it would have been beyond his power to conceive that the effect should not follow. With further observation he learned to remark that at certain seasons of the year the luminary appeared to traverse particular portions of the heavens, and that then it was always warm, and the trees put forth leaves to be followed by fruit; whereas, at others, it appeared to occupy other portions of the heavens, and then the fruit disappeared and the leaves fell, as a prelude to the winter's cold. Here was a further addition to his stock of knowledge, and, with it came foresight, and a feeling of the necessity for action. If he would live during the season of cold, he could do so only by preparing for it during the season of heat, a principle as thoroughly understood by the wandering Esquimaux of the shores of the Arctic Ocean, as by the most enlightened and eminent philosopher of Europe or America.

Earliest among the ideas of such a man would be those of space, quantity, and form. The sun was obviously very remote, while of the trees some were distant and others were close at hand. The moon was single, while the stars were countless. The tree was tall, while the shrub was short. The hills were high, and tending towards a point, while the plains were low and flat. We have here the most abstract, simple, and obvious of all conceptions. The idea of space is the same, whether we regard the distance between the sun and the stars by which he is surrounded, or that between the mountains and ourselves. So, too, with number and form, which apply as readily to the sands of the sea-shore as to the gigantic trees of the forest, or to the various bodies seen to be moving through the heavens.

Next in order would come the desire, or the necessity, for comparing distances, numbers, and magnitudes, and the means for this would be at hand in machinery supplied by nature, and always at his command. His finger, or his arm, would supply a measure of magnitudes, while his pace would do the same by distance, and the standard with which he would compare the weights would be found in some one among the most ordinary commodities by which he was surrounded. In numerous cases, however, distances, velocities, or dimensions, are found to be beyond the reach of direct measurement, and thus is produced a necessity for devising means of comparing distant and unknown quantities with those that being near can be ascertained, and hence arises mathematics, or The Science—so denominated by the Greeks, because to its help was due nearly all the positive knowledge of which they were possessed.

The multiplication table enables the ploughman to determine the number of days contained in a given number of weeks, and the merchant to calculate the number of pounds contained in his cargo of cotton. By help of his rule, the carpenter determines the distance between the two ends of the plank on which he works. The sounding-line enables the sailor to ascertain the depth of water around his ship, and by help of the barometer the traveller determines the height of the mountain on which he stands. All these are *instruments* for facilitating the acquisition of knowledge, and such, too, are the formulæ of mathematics, by help of which the philosopher is enabled to determine the magnitude and weight of bodies distant from him millions of millions of miles, and is thus enabled to solve innumerable questions of the highest interest to man. They are the key to science, but are not to be confounded with science itself, although often included in the list of sciences, and even so recently as in M. Comte's well-known work. That such should ever have been the case has been due to the fact that so much of what is really physics is discussed under the head of mathematics; as is the case with the great laws for whose discovery we are indebted to Kepler, Galileo, and Newton. That a body impelled by a single force will move in a right line and with a velocity that is invariable, and that action and reaction are equal and opposite, are facts, at the knowledge of which we have arrived in consequence of pursuing a certain mode of investigation; but when obtained, they are purely physical facts, obtained by help of the instrument to which we apply the term mathematics—and which is, to use the words of M. Comte, simply "an immense extension of natural logic to a certain order of deductions."*

Logic is itself, however, but another of the instruments devised by man for enabling him to obtain a knowledge of nature's laws. To his eyes the earth appears to be a plane, and yet he sees the sun rising daily in the east and setting as regularly in the west, from which he might infer that it would always continue so to do—but of this he can feel no certainty until he has satisfied himself why it is that it does so. At one time, he sees the sun to be eclipsed, while at another, the moon ceases to give light, and he desires to know why such things are—what is the law governing the movements of those bodies; having obtained which he is enabled to predict when they will again cease to give light, and to determine when they must have done so in times that are past. At one moment ice or salt melts; at another gas explodes; and at a third, walls are shattered and cities are hurled to the ground; and he seeks to know why these things are—what is the relation of cause and effect? In the effort to obtain answers to all these questions, he observes and records facts, and these he arranges with a view to deduce from them the laws by virtue of which they occur—and he invents barometers, thermometers, and other instruments to aid him in his observation—but the ultimate object of all is that of obtaining an answer to the questions: Why are all these things? Why is it that dew falls on one day and not on another? Why is it that corn grows abundantly in this field and fails altogether in that one? Why is it that coal burns and granite will not? What, in a word, are the laws instituted by the Creator for the government of matter? The answers to these questions constitute science—

* *Positive Philosophy*, Martineau's Translation, Vol. i. 33.

and mathematics, logic, and all other of the machinery in use are but instruments used by him for the purpose of obtaining them.

In discussing the subject of rational mechanics, under the head of mathematics, M. Comte informs his readers that we here "encounter a perpetual confusion between the abstract and the concrete points of view; between the logical and the physical; between the artificial conceptions necessary to help as to general laws of equilibrium and motion, and the natural facts furnished by observation, which must form the basis of the science."* This, however, is only saying that as "the natural facts," furnished by observation, increase in number, there arises a necessity for endeavoring to perfect the machinery by the help of which they are to be studied, and that this is the case in the instance referred to by M. Comte, is shown in his admission that the science of which he treats is "founded on some general facts, furnished by observation, of which we can give no explanation whatever."† As we pass from gate to gate of science, we pass from simple to compound locks, requiring additional wards in the keys by which they are to be opened; but the key still remains a key, and can never become a lock, even though the wards should become fifty-fold more numerous than those of any yet constructed by Bramah, Chubb, or Hobbs, and might require years of study before its proper management could be acquired. There might then arise what would be called the science of the key, but it would constitute no part of true science. When D'Alembert made, to use the words of Comte, "a discovery, by help of which all investigation of the motion of any body or system might be converted at once into a question of equilibrium," he merely opened a new ward in the key by which we were to unlock the cabinet of nature, and thus enlarge the boundaries of that department of knowledge which treats of the properties of matter and the laws by which it is governed, and known as physical science.

§ 2. The abstract mathematics necessarily took precedence of the more concrete physics, because they were the sole product of logic, and dependent upon those first principles which are in their

* *Positive Philosophy*, Martineau's Translation, Vol. i. p. 107.
† Ibid.

elements so nearly intuitive that when the boy commences the study of geometry, he finds that he had already acquired a knowledge of much that is now being given to him as science. Hence, too, it was that moral science, poetry, the fine arts, and metaphysics were so far advanced in Greece, while mechanical science had scarcely an existence.

In default of observation, men of speculative habits looked inwards to their own minds and invented theories that were given to the world as laws, but, as has well been said: "Man can *invent* nothing in science or religion but falsehood, and all the truths that he *discovers* are but facts or laws that have emanated from the Creator." The men of the Middle Ages—the philosophers of the schools—taught the theories that had been invented by their Grecian predecessors, and it was left for Bacon to teach the philosophy that leads to the search for truth among the facts of nature and not among the speculations of men. From his day to the present there has been a perpetual tendency towards the substitution of careful observation and induction for the dreams of theorists, and as the Cartesian doctrine of Vortices gave way to the discovery of gravitation, so the imaginary phlogiston of Stahl, and the Plutonian and Neptunian cosmogonies have yielded to the discoveries of modern science. The former was early displaced by the oxygen of Lavoisier, while the latter held their ground until disproved by the observations of geologists, whose branch of science dates its existence but little beyond the present century.

In physics, as has everywhere been the case, the more abstract and general has, in its development, taken precedence of that which is concrete and special. Astronomy, the science of the laws governing bodies exterior to our own planet, was studied at an early period, the shepherds of Chaldea having carefully noted the movements of the celestial bodies, and Babylonians having calculated eclipses thousands of years before the commencement of the Christian era. From a well of Syene, Eratosthenes obtained the observations required for determining the terrestrial meridian; and many centuries before Copernicus, Archimedes taught the double motion of the earth around its axis and around the sun. The precise length of the solar year was determined by Hipparchus, while Mexican and Etrurian observation led in this respect so nearly to the same result, that the difference between them was but ten minutes.

The motions of the celestial bodies were thus early studied and comprehended, yet was it left to Newton to discover the reason why the apple falls to the earth; to Franklin to discover the identity of lightning and electricity; to Cavendish to discover the composition of the air we breathe; to Black to discover the existence of latent heat; and to philosophers, even of our own day, to discover the laws in virtue of which we see and hear. Laplace's great work of Celestial Mechanics, was the product of the same period that witnessed the birth of a new science, having for its object to determine the composition of the globe on which we live and move, and from which we derive our daily bread. It is thus, that as we approach nearer to man, his uses and purposes, we find the greatest retardation of that positive knowledge so early attained in reference to the method to be pursued in the effort for its attainment. The study of the history of science leads inevitably to an agreement with Buffon in the opinion that, "however great may be our interest in knowing ourselves," we probably "understand better all that is not ourselves"—and with Rousseau in the belief that "much philosophy is required for observing the facts that are very near to us."

Passing from the more abstract and general laws governing the movements of distant bodies towards those determining the composition of the matter by which we are immediately surrounded, we find new laws, but all subordinate to, and in harmony with, those first obtained. Chemistry, following physics, which deals with masses, deals with the elements of which they are composed, all of which are, however, subject to the same laws by which the masses themselves are governed. The atoms produced by the analysis of Cavendish, were as obedient to the law of gravitation as were the earth, the satellites of Jupiter, and Jupiter himself. "The distinction between physics and chemistry," says M. Comte, "is much less easy to establish" than between chemistry and astronomy, and, as he continues, "it is one more difficult to pronounce upon from day to day, as new discoveries bring to light closer relations between them."* That such is the case, will readily be seen by the reader who reflects how much of the present great development of physical knowledge has been due to the labors

* *Positive Philosophy*, Martineau's Translation, vol. i. p. 216.

of Cavendish, Priestley, Black, Davy, Lavoisier, Fourcroy, Gay-Lussac, and other eminent chemists.

On another occasion, in the course of his admirable review of the progress and gradual development of science, M. Comte thus shows the intimate relation between physics on one side of chemistry, and physiology on the other :—

"By the important series of electro-chemical phenomena chemistry becomes, as it were, a prolongation of physics : and at its other extremity, it lays the foundation of physiology by its research into organic combinations. These relations are so real that it has sometimes happened that chemists, untrained in the philosophy of science, have been uncertain whether a particular subject lay within their department, or ought to be referred either to physics or to physiology."*

As yet, he is of opinion that "the direct dependence of chemistry on astronomy" is very slight, but "when the time shall come for the development of concrete chemistry, that is, the methodical application of chemical knowledge to the natural history of the globe, astronomical considerations will no doubt enter in where now there seems no point of contact between the two sciences. Geology, immature as it is, hints to us such a future necessity, some vague instinct of which was probably in the minds of philosophers in the theological age, when they were fancifully and yet obstinately bent on uniting astrology and alchemy. It is, in fact, impossible to conceive of the great intestinal operations of the globe as radically independent of its planetary conditions."†

Passing thus from the masses of physics through the atoms into which they are resolved by chemistry, we next find those atoms arranging themselves in organized and living forms, and constituting the still more special subjects of vegetable, animal, and human physiology, whose connection with chemistry is thus described :—

"Physiology depends upon chemistry both as a point of departure and as a principal means of investigation. If we separate the phenomena of life, properly so called, from those of animality, it is clear that the first, in the double intestinal movement which

* *Positive Philosophy*, Martineau's Translation, vol. i. 298.
† Ibid., vol. i. 299.

characterizes them, are essentially chemical. The processes which result from organization have peculiar characteristics; but apart from such modifications, they are necessarily subjected to the general laws of chemical effects. Even in studying living bodies under a simply statical point of view, chemistry is of indispensable use in enabling us to distinguish with precision the different anatomical elements of any organism."*

Again, in treating of biology, he says :—

"It is to chemistry that biology is, by its nature, most directly and completely subordinated. In analyzing the phenomenon of life, we saw that the fundamental acts which, by their perpetuity, characterize that state, consist of a series of compositions and decompositions; and they are therefore of a chemical nature. Though in the most imperfect organisms, vital reactions are widely separated from common chemical effects, it is not the less true that all the functions of the proper organic life are necessarily controlled by those fundamental laws of composition and decomposition which constitute the subject of chemical science. If we could conceive throughout the whole scale the same separation of the organic from the animal life that we see in vegetables alone, the vital motion would offer only chemical conceptions, except the essential circumstances which distinguish such an order of molecular reactions. The general source of these important differences is, in my opinion, to be looked for in the result of each chemical conflict not depending only on the simple composition of the bodies between which it takes place, but being modified by their proper organization; that is, by their anatomical structure. Chemistry must clearly furnish the starting-point of every rational theory of nutrition, secretion, and, in short, all the functions of the vegetative life, considered separately; each of which is controlled by the influence of chemical laws, except for the special modifications belonging to organic conditions."†

It is not, however, with chemistry alone that physiology is connected. Remote from astronomy as that department of knowledge appears to be, the relation between them "is more important," says M. Comte, "than is usually supposed. I mean," continues he,

* *Positive Philosophy*, Martineau's Translation, vol. i. p. 300.

† Ibid., vol. i. p. 379.

"something more than the impossibility of understanding the theory of weight, and its effects upon the organism, apart from the consideration of general gravitation. I mean, besides, and more specially, that it is impossible to form a scientific conception of the conditions of vital existence without taking into the account the aggregate astronomical elements that characterize the planet which is the home of that vital existence. We shall see more fully, in the next volume, how humanity is affected by these astronomical conditions; but we must cursorily review these relations in the present connection.

"The astronomical data proper to our planet are, of course, statical and dynamical. The biological importance of the statical conditions is immediately obvious. No one questions the importance to vital existence of the mass of our planet in comparison with that of the sun, which determines the intensity of gravity; or of its form, which regulates the direction of the force; or of the fundamental equilibrium and the regular oscillations of the fluids which cover the greater part of its surface, and with which the existence of living beings is closely implicated; or of its dimensions, which limit the indefinite multiplication of races, and especially the human; or of its distance from the centre of our system, which chiefly determines its temperature. Any sudden change in one or more of these conditions would largely modify the phenomena of life. But the influence of the dynamical conditions of astronomy on biological study is yet more important. Without the two conditions of the fixity of the poles as a centre of rotation, and the uniformity of the angular velocity of the earth, there would be a continual perturbation of the organic media which would be incompatible with life. Bichat pointed out that the intermittence of the proper animal life is subordinate in its periods to the diurnal rotation of our planet; and we may extend the observation to all the periodical phenomena of any organisms, in both the normal and pathological states, allowance being made for secondary and transient influences. Moreover, there is every reason to believe that, in every organism, the total duration of life and of its chief natural phases depends on the angular velocity proper to our planet; for we are authorized to admit that, other things being equal, the duration of life must be shorter, especially in the animal organism, in proportion as the vital phenomena succeed each other more rapidly. If the earth were to rotate much faster, the course of physiological phenomena would be accelerated in proportion; and thence life would be shorter; so that the duration of life may be regarded as dependent on the duration of the day. If the duration of the year were changed, the life of the organism would again be affected: but a yet more striking consideration is that vital existence is absolutely implicated with the form of the earth's orbit, as has been observed before. If that ellipse were to become, instead of nearly circular, as eccentric as the orbit of a comet, both the medium and the organism would undergo a change fatal to vital existence. Thus the small eccentricity of the earth's orbit is one of the main conditions of biological phenomena, almost as necessary as the stability of the earth's rotation: and every other element of the annual motion exercises an influence, more or less marked, on biological conditions, though not so great as the one we have adduced. The inclination of the plane of the orbit, for instance, determines the division of the earth into climates, and, consequently, the geographical distribution of living species, animal and vegetable. And again, through the alternation of seasons, it influences the phases of individual existence in all organisms; and there is no doubt that life would be affected if the revolution of the line of the nodes were accelerated; so that its being nearly immovable has some biological value. These considerations indicate how necessary it is for biologists to inform themselves accurately, and without any intervention, of the real elements proper to the astronomical constitution of our planet. An inexact knowledge will not suffice. The laws of the limits of variation of the different elements, or, at least, a scientific analysis of the chief grounds of their permanence, are essential to biological investigation; and these can be obtained only through an acquaintance with astronomical conceptions, both geometrical and mechanical.

"It may at first appear anomalous, and a breach of the encyclopedical arrangement of the sciences, that astronomy and biology should be thus immediately and eminently connected, while two other sciences lie between. But, indispensable as are physics and chemistry, astronomy and biology are, by their nature, the two principal branches of natural philosophy. They, the complements of each other, include in their rational harmony the general system of our fundamental conceptions. The solar system and Man are the extreme terms within which our ideas will forever be included. The system first, and then Man, according to the positive course of our speculative reason : and the reverse in the active process : the laws of the system determining those of Man, and remaining unaffected by them. Between these two poles of natural philosophy the laws of physics interpose, as a kind of complement of the astronomical laws ; and again, those of chemistry, as an immediate preliminary of the biological. Such being the rational and indissoluble constitution of these sciences, it becomes apparent why I insisted on the subordination of the study of Man to that of the system, as the primary philosophical characteristic of positive biology."

Passing now towards the more concrete and special department of knowledge treating of the relation of man with his fellow-man and with the earth from which he derives his means of support, we find chemistry laying the foundation for it when "abolishing the idea of destruction and creation,"* and thus establishing the facts that the consumption of food is but a necessary step towards its reproduction—that in all the processes of agriculture man is but making a machine which supports him while engaged in making it—that the more time and mind he devotes to the development of the powers of the earth, the greater must be his power of consumption, and that the more rapidly the consumption of food follows its production the greater will be the reproduction of the elements required for new supplies thereof. These views of the effect of the principle thus established do not appear to have occurred to M. Comte, but he shows clearly the direct connection of chemical and social science when telling his readers that "before anything was known of gaseous materials and products, many striking appearances must inevitably have inspired the idea of the real annihilation or production of matter in the general system of nature. These ideas could not yield to the true conception of decomposition and composition till we had decomposed air and water, and then analyzed vegetable and animal substances, and then finished with the analysis of alkalies and earths, thus exhibiting the fundamental principle of the indefinite perpetuity of matter.

* *Positive Philosophy*, Martineau's Translation, p. 305.

In vital phenomena, the chemical examination of not only the substances of living bodies, but their functions,—imperfect as it yet is,—must cast a strong light upon the economy of vital nature by showing that no organic matter radically heterogeneous to inorganic matter can exist, and that vital transformations are subject, like all others, to the universal laws of chemical phenomena."

It is scarcely possible to study these facts without arriving at a belief in the universality of the laws governing matter, whatever form that matter may take, whether that of clay, coal, iron, wheat, or man—whether aggregated in the form of systems of mountains, or in that of vast communities of men. We can conceive of no body without weight, nor would it be possible to imagine any one not in subjection to the law of the composition of forces. Chemistry and physiology, more concrete and special than physics, furnish additional laws, but always in subordination to those governing the masses from which had been derived the atoms treated of in those departments of human knowledge. Chemistry aids in the development of physics, while the researches of physiologists are steadily making new demands upon, and thereby promoting the growth of, chemical science. Each helps, and is helped by, the other.

The root, the stem, the branches, the leaves, and the blossoms of the tree are obedient to the same system of laws. Colored water applied to the root changes the color of the blossom, and stoppage of nourishment to the root destroys the tree. It is but a single tree, and so it is with the tree of science, whose root is found in physics, while its stem branches into those divisions which are based upon observation and experiment, leaving us to find the leaves, the blossoms, and the fruit in the less demonstrable departments of knowledge.

That this is true as regards the more abstract and general portions of science to which reference has thus far been made, can scarcely now be doubted. Wherefore, then, should we doubt that it would be found equally so in relation to those more concrete and special ones treating of man in his relation with the material world—of man in his relations with his fellow-man—of man as a being capable of acquiring power over the various natural forces provided for his use, and responsible to his fellow-men, and to his

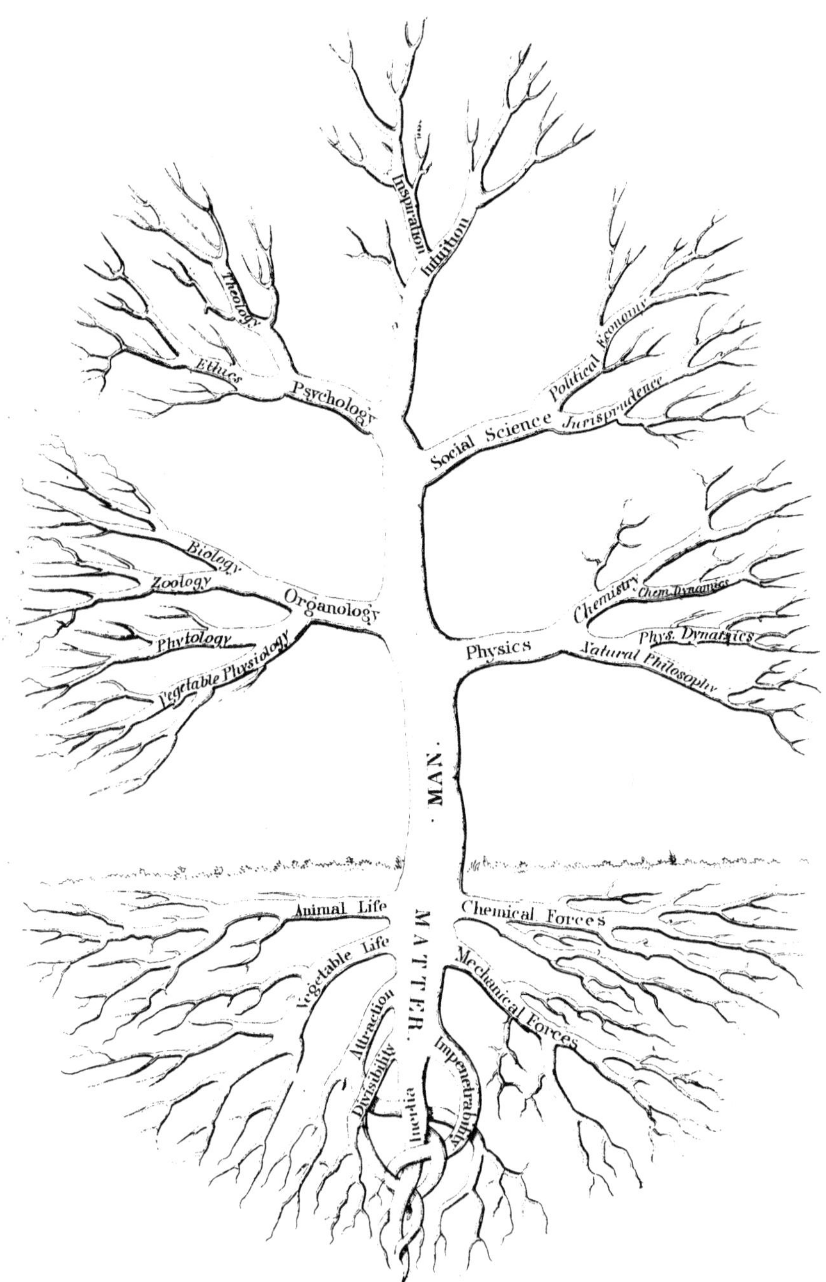
Inspiration
Intuition
Theology
Ethics
Psychology
Political Economy
Jurisprudence
Social Science
Biology
Zoology
Organology
Phytology
Vegetable Physiology
Chemistry
Chem. Dynamics
Phys. Dynamics
Physics
Natural Philosophy
MAN.
Animal Life
Vegetable Life
Chemical Forces
Mechanical Forces
MATTER.
Attraction
Divisibility
Inertia
Impenetrability

Creator, for the proper use of the faculties with which he has been so wonderfully endowed? If the root, the stem, and the branches obey the same laws, should we not find the blossoms and the fruit of the tree of science equally obedient to them, and will not the diagram opposite represent with considerable accuracy the relation of the various departments of knowledge and the order of their development?

§ 3. "The distributions and partitions of knowledge," says Lord Bacon in his *Novum Organum*, "are not like several lines that meet in one angle, and *touch but in a point;* but are like branches of a tree that meet in a stem, which hath a dimension and quantity of entireness and continuance before it comes to discontinuance and break itself into arms and boughs; therefore," as he continues, "it is good before we enter into the former distribution, to create and constitute one universal science by the name of Philosophia Prima, or Summary Philosophy, as the main or common way, before we come where the ways part and divide themselves."

Concerned as he was with the order and division of the sciences, and pledged as he was in the introduction to his work to furnish it, he failed to do so, "the first part of the Introduction which comprehends the division of the sciences" being, says his editor, "wanting." A study, so far as the idea of the text appeared to the latter to require elucidation, rather than an attempt to supply the deficiency, is submitted in its stead.

The several *branches* of natural science are commonly spoken of, but the figure has a larger parallelism with the subject, a tree having not only branches but also roots. These latter are properly underground branches, constituting the structural support, and furnishing the vital subsistence of the tree, which grows from its roots and with them. Its stem, branches, flowers, and fruits, being converted aliment supplied by and through the roots, the allusions of the figure are in good keeping with the natural history of the subject intended to be illustrated.

The central or taproot, as the reader sees, represents matter, with its essential properties of inertia, impenetrability, divisibility, and attraction. The lateral ones stand, on one side, for mechanical and chemical forces, and on the other, for vegetable and animal ones—and from these substantive roots of being rises the stem man, so composed as to his natural constitution. The soul, being the occult life of the structure, is incapable of representation, though manifested by its proper evidence in the flowers and fruits, the emotions and thoughts of his faculties.

We have now the stem—the man—"having dimension and quantity of entireness and continuance before it came to discontinue and break itself," branching off into his diverse activities. These branches are his functions, ramifying into all their specific differences of application. The first branch on the material side is Physics, as represented in the drawing. Its ramifications are into natural philosophy and chemistry—masses and atoms—and the shoots from these are mechanics and chemical dynamics—the one being the action of masses and the other that of atoms.

The main branch on the vital side of the tree, rising a little above Physics, must necessarily be Organology, branching first into the science of vegetable beings, Phytology, and sending off the shoot, Vegetable Physiology; and second, into that of animal beings, Zoology, leading to Biology, or the science of life.

Following the stem in the natural order of rank and successive development, it is seen next giving off Social Science, which divides itself into Jurisprudence and Political Economy, while on the corresponding side the main branch, Psychology, ramifies itself into Ethics and Theology—and the tree finally tops out with Intuition as the material branch and Inspiration as the vital one. These highest and last named, are rightly the source of the other science or sciences to which Bacon alludes as standing above Metaphysics, when he says that, "as for the vertical point, the summary law of nature, we know not whether man's inquiry can attain unto it"—that is, so as to order and methodize its teachings.

In this scheme of the sciences of things, there is no place for either Logic or Mathematics, the respective regulative sciences of mind and matter. Neither of these belongs to Natural History, being both alike mere instruments to be used in the study of nature.

Historically, the top branches of the tree of knowledge, as of all other trees, are first produced, and the branches next below are soon put forth, but mature later, the instincts of religion and reason appearing in their vigor in the childhood of the race. Social science, necessarily, and metaphysics, spontaneously, extend themselves as early as societies take form, and speculation is awakened—and they bring forth quickly the flowers and fruits of music, poetry, the fine arts, logic, mathematics, and those generalities of speculative truth which are the products of imagination and reflection. The correspondence between the figure chosen and the facts to be illustrated would seem to be complete.

In time, the branches nearer to the earth, more material in their substance and more dependent upon observation, obtain development in their larger diversity of use. The sciences of substance, of natural objects, grow and ramify themselves almost indefinitely—physical philosophy and organology, in their dependencies, shooting out in every direction of observation and experiment, at first overshadowed by the speculative branches above them, but always vivified by them; while in their turn repaying this service by affording substantive strength and corrective modification as they grow into maturity.

Such is the history of science, and such the illustration of its orderly divisions, succession, and co-ordination; it represents the compound nature of man, the sources of his powers, and the order of their development.

§ 4. Man seeks to obtain power over matter, and therefore is it that he desires to obtain a knowledge of the laws that have been instituted for its government. To become the subject of law it is required that there should be a regular and uniform succession of causes and effects, the nature of which may be expressed in several propositions—so that when we observe the former we may be enabled to predict the latter, or when the latter are observed we may safely assume the former to have pre-existed.

In the early ages of society theories abound, and they do so because, in default of knowledge, almost every occurrence is "regarded as accidental, or is attributed to the direct interposition of mythological powers, whose qualities are so vaguely conceived as to make the idea of the events depending upon their action scarcely one remove from that of its being absolutely fortuitous and irreducible to order and rule"[1]—and thus it was that the Greeks of the days of Homer were seen soliciting the aid of imaginary deities, who were moved to action by the same feelings and passions that influenced their worshippers; precisely as does now the poor African who makes his oblations of palm-wine or rum, corn or oil, to the stock or stone, the alligator, or the bundle of rags, he has chosen for his idol.—With time, however, the regular succession of effects and causes comes to be understood, and with every stage of the progress, theory tends to pass away, yielding place to knowledge—and with the latter comes the power of man to direct the forces of nature to his service. With each such stage he obtains new evidence of the universality of natural laws—new proof that where exceptions appear to exist they are but appearances and will, when carefully analyzed and fully understood, but prove the rule; as does the smoke when rising in apparent opposition to the great law in virtue of which all the matter of which the earth is composed tends towards its centre.*

To prove the universality of law, and thereby to establish the unity of science, seemed at first to be the intention of M. Comte, from whose work preliminary to, and intended as the basis of, the one that was to be specially devoted to social science, the above extracts have been made. The promised work has since appeared, but in it, as well as in all the parts of his previous one treating of man and his operations, he has intentionally ignored the mathematical method to which the earlier and more developed departments of science had so largely been indebted. That he should so have done would seem to have been a consequence of regarding mathematics as a science, and not as a mere instrument for the acquisition of scientific knowledge. Thus, in treating of chemistry, he tells us that "every attempt to refer chemical questions to mathematical doctrines must be considered, now and always, profoundly irrational, as being contrary to the nature of the phenomena."† What, however, are those doctrines? Are they anything beyond simple formulæ adapted to the peculiar circumstances of the case under consideration? Certainly not. The geometer tells us that every whole is equal to all its parts, and that things which are

* "We ought to conceive the study of nature as destined to furnish the true rational basis of the action of man upon nature; because the knowledge of the laws of phenomena, of which the invariable result is foresight, and that alone, can conduct us in active life to modify the one by the other to our advantage. In short, SCIENCE WHENCE FORESIGHT, FORESIGHT WHENCE ACTION, such is the simple formula which expresses the general relation of Science and Art."—*Comte.*

† Ibid., vol. i. p. 299.

halves of the same thing are equal, axioms of universal application, and equally true in relation to all bodies, whether those treated by the chemist, the sociologist, or the measurer of land, but involving no question of doctrine whatsoever.

Occasionally, M. Comte speaks of mathematics as what it clearly is, an "instrument of admirable efficacy," but being an instrument it can no more be a science than can a key become a lock. That instrument, the mathematical method, is always applicable, whatever may be the subject of investigation. That method is analysis —the study of each separate cause tending to produce a given effect. To that method we owe all the discoveries of Copernicus, Kepler, Newton, and their successors—but such too is the method of the chemist, who commences by ascertaining the separate force of each of his various ingredients, and ends by deducing the law of the effect. The physiologist analyzes what is known, in hopes to be able to deduce that which remains as yet unknown, and uses always the formulæ belonging to the particular class of subjects of which he treats. When engaged in the study of the skeleton, he uses those of the physicist; but when studying the composition of the blood, he resorts necessarily to those of the chemist, in which is embodied all the knowledge derived from the observation of the philosophers by whom he has been preceded. This method, however, is discarded by M. Comte in treating of social science, as will be seen by the following passage :—

"There can be no scientific study of society, either in its conditions or its movements, if it is separated into portions, and its divisions are studied apart. I have already remarked upon this, in regard to what is called political economy. Materials may be furnished by the observation of different departments; and such observation may be necessary for that object: but it cannot be called science. The methodical division of studies which takes place in the simple inorganic sciences is thoroughly irrational in the recent and complex science of society, and can produce no results. The day may come when some sort of subdivision may be practicable and desirable; but it is impossible for us now to anticipate what the principle of distribution may be; for the principle itself must arise from the development of the science; and that development can take plaee no otherwise than by our formation of the science as a whole."*

"In the organic sciences, the elements are much better known to us than the whole which they constitute: so that in that case we must proceed from the simple to the compound. But the reverse method is necessary in the study of man and of society; man and society as a whole being better known to us, and more accessible subjects of study, than the parts which constitute them. In exploring the universe, it is as a whole that it is inaccessible to us; whereas, in investigating man or society, our difficulty is in penetrating the details. We have seen, in our survey of biology, that the general idea of animal nature is more distinct to our minds than the simpler notion of vegetable nature; and that man is the biological unity; the idea of man being at once the most compound, and the starting-point of speculation in regard to vital existence. Thus, if we compare the two halves of natural philosophy, we shall find that in the one case it is the last degree of composition, and, in the other, the last degree of simplicity, that is beyond the scope of our research."†

This would seem to be going back to what M. Comte is accustomed to denominate the metaphysical stage of science. The philosopher of old would, in like manner, have said: "These masses of granite are better known to us than the parts of which they are composed, and therefore we will limit our inquiries to the question as to how they came to have their existing form and occupy their present position." Without the analysis of the chemist it would have been as impossible that we should be enabled to "penetrate into the details" of the piece of stone, and thus to acquire a knowledge of the composition of the distant mountain from which it had been taken, as it would now be for us to penetrate into those of the communities that have passed away, were we not in the midst of living ones, composed of men endowed with the same gifts and animated by the same feelings and passions observed to have existed among the men of ancient times; and were we not, too, possessors of the numerous facts accumulated during the many centuries that since have intervened. It is the details of

* *Positive Philosophy*, Martineau's Translation, vol. ii. p. 81.
† Ibid., vol. ii. p. 82.

life around us that we need to study, commencing by analysis and proceeding to synthesis, as does the chemist when he resolves the piece of granite into atoms, and thus acquires the secret of the composition of the mass. Having ascertained that it is composed of quartz, feldspar, and mica, and having fully satisfied himself of the circumstances under which it appears in the country around him, he feels entire confidence that wherever else it may be found, its composition, and its position in the order of formation, will be the same. He is constantly going from the near and the known, which he can analyze and examine, to the distant and the unknown, which he cannot; studying the latter by means of formulæ obtained by analysis of the former. Thus it was that by study of the deposits of Siberia and California, the geologist was enabled to predict that gold would be found among the mountains of Australia.

If we desire to understand the history of man in past ages, or in distant lands, we must commence by studying him in the present, and having mastered him in the past and present, we may then be enabled to predict the future. To do this, it is required that we should do with society as the chemist does with the piece of granite, resolve it into its several parts and study each part separately, ascertaining how it would act were it left to itself, and comparing what *would be* its independent action with that we see *to be* its action in society; and then by help of the same law of which the mathematician, the physicist, the chemist, and the physiologist. avail themselves—that of the composition of forces—we may arrive at the law of the effect. To do this would not, however, be to adopt the course of M. Comte, who gives us the distant and the unknown—the societies of past ages—as a means of understanding the movements of the men by whom we are surrounded, and of predicting what will be those of future men. With great respect for M. Comte, we must say that to pursue this course appears to us to be equivalent to furnishing his readers with a telescope by which to study the mountains of the moon for the purpose of understanding the movements of the laboratory.

The necessary consequence of this inverse and erroneous method is that he is led to arrive at conclusions directly the reverse of those to which men's natural instincts lead them; and directly opposed, too, to the tendencies of thought and action in all the times of advancing civilization, whether in the ancient or modern world; and, as a necessary consequence, he leaves his readers as much at a loss to understand the causes of disturbance that now exist, or the remedy required to be applied, as would a physician who should limit the study of his patient to an examination of the body in a mass, omitting all inquiry into the state of the lungs, the stomach, or the brain. His system of sociology does not explain the past, and cannot therefore be used to direct the future; and the reason why it does not and cannot is, that he has declined to use the method of physics, the philosophy which studies the near and the known for the purpose of obtaining power to comprehend the distant and the unknown—which studies the present to obtain knowledge by help of which to understand the causes of events in the past, and predict those which are bound to flow from similar causes in the future.

§ 5. Turning from France to Britain, we find ourselves in the home of Adam Smith, whose most essential doctrines have, however, been wholly repudiated by his successors of the modern school, which had its origin in the teachings of Messrs. Malthus and Ricardo. "Social science," as we are there taught by one of the most distinguished teachers, and in opposition to the views of Mr. Comte, "is a deductive science; not indeed," as he continues, "after the model of geometry, but after that of the highest physical sciences. It infers the law of each effect from the laws of causation upon which the effect depends; not, however, from the law merely of one cause, as in the geometrical method, but by considering all the causes which conjointly influence the effect, and compounding those laws with one another." *

Such is the theory. What is the practice under it, we may now examine. "Political economy," says the same author, "considers mankind as occupied solely in acquiring and consuming wealth, and aims at showing what is the course of action into which mankind, living in a state of society, would be impelled, if that motive, except in the degree in which it is checked by the two perpetual counter motives above adverted to—aversion to labor and the desire of the present enjoyment of costly indulgences—were absolute ruler of all their actions. Under the influence of this desire,

* J. S. Mill. *System of Logic*, Book vi. ch. 8.

it shows mankind accumulating wealth, and employing this wealth in the production of other wealth; sanctioning by mutual agreement the institution of property; establishing laws to prevent individuals from encroaching on the property of others by force or fraud; adopting various contrivances for increasing the productiveness of their labor; settling the division of the produce by agreement, under the influence of competition, * * and employing certain expedients * * to facilitate the distribution. All these operations, though many of them are really the result of a plurality of motives, are considered by political economy as flowing solely from a desire of wealth. * * * * Not that any political economist was ever so absurd as to suppose that mankind are really thus constituted, but because this is the mode in which the science must necessarily be studied."*

"For the sake of practical utility," however, the principle of population is required to be "interpolated into the exposition," and this is done, although to do so involves, as we are told, a departure from "the strictness of purely scientific arrangement."†

That having been done, we have the politico-economical man, on one hand influenced solely by the thirst for wealth, and on the other so entirely under the control of the sexual passion as to be at all times ready to indulge it, however greatly such indulgence may tend to prevent the growth of wealth.

What, however, is this thing in the quest for which he is so assiduously engaged? What is wealth? To this question political economy furnishes no reply, it having never yet been settled in what it is that wealth consists. Were it suggested that land constituted any part thereof, the answer would at once be made that by reason of a great law of nature, the more of it that was brought into use, and the larger the quantity of labor given to its improvement, the less must be the return to human effort, the poorer must the community become, and the greater must be the tendency towards poverty and death—and that such must certainly be the case could readily be proved by passages from writers of high authority. Were it next assumed that wealth might be found in the development of the individual faculties, proof sufficient could be furnished that not only would any search in that direction be

* J. S. Mill. *System of Logic*, Book vi. ch. 8.
† Ibid.

vain, but that it would result in the establishment of the fact that any increase in the number of teachers must be attended with diminution of the quantity of wealth at the command of the community. Foiled thus in all his efforts, the inquirer, after having studied carefully all the books, would still be found repeating the question —What is wealth?

Turning next to the being so sedulously engaged in the pursuit of an undefined something that seems to embrace so much, and that yet excludes so large a proportion of the things usually regarded as wealth, he would desire to satisfy himself if the subject of political economy was really the being known as man. He might perhaps ask himself, has man no other qualities than those here attributed to him? Is he, like the beasts of the field, solely given to the search for food and shelter for his body? Does he, like them, beget children for the sole gratification of his passions, and does he, like them, leave his offspring to feed and shelter themselves as they may? Has he no feelings or affections to be influenced by the care of wife and children? Has he no judgment to aid him in the decision as to what is likely to benefit or to injure him? That he did possess these qualities he would find admitted, but the economist would assure him that his science was that of material wealth alone, to the entire exclusion of the wealth of affection and of intellect held by Adam Smith in such high esteem—and thus would he, at the close of all his search, discover that the subject of political economy was not really a man, but an imaginary being moved to action by the blindest passion, and giving all his energies to the pursuit of a thing in its nature so undefinable that all the books in use might be searched for a definition that would be admitted by a jury of economists as embracing all that should be included, and excluding all that should not.

The law of the composition of forces requires that we should study *all* the causes tending to produce a given effect. That effect is MAN—the man of the past and the present; and the social philosopher who excludes from consideration his feelings and affections, and the intellect with which he has been endowed, makes precisely the same mistake that would be made by the physical one who should look exclusively to gravitation, forgetting heat; and should thence conclude that at no distant day the whole material of which the earth is composed would become a solid mass, plants, animals and men having disappeared. Such is the error of modern political economy, and its effects are seen in the fact that it presents for our consideration a mere brute animal, to find a name for which it desecrates the word "man," recognized by Adam Smith as expressing the idea of a being made in the likeness of its Creator.

It was well asked by Goethe—"*What is all intercourse with nature, if by the analytical method, we merely occupy ourselves with individual material parts, and do not feel the breath of the spirit* which prescribes to every part its direction, and orders or sanctions every deviation by means of an inherent law?" And what, we may ask, is the value of an analytical process that selects only the "material parts" of man—those which are common to himself and the beast—and excludes those common to the angels and himself? Such is the course of modern political economy, which not only does not "feel the breath of the spirit," but even ignores the existence of the spirit itself, and is therefore found defining what it is pleased to call the natural rate of wages, as being "that price which is necessary to enable the laborers, one with another, to subsist and perpetuate their race, without either increase or diminution"*—that is to say, such price as will enable some to grow rich and increase their race, while others perish of hunger, thirst, and exposure. Such are the teachings of a system that has fairly earned the title of the "dismal science"—that one the study of which led M. Sismondi to the inquiry—"What, then, is wealth everything, and is man absolutely nothing?" In the eyes of modern political economy he *is* nothing, and can be nothing, because it takes no note of the qualities by which he is distinguished from the brute, and is therefore led to regard him as being a mere instrument to be used by capital to enable its owner to obtain compensation for its use. "Some economists," said a distinguished French economist, shocked at the material character of the so-called science, "speak as if they believed that men were made for products, not products for men;"† and at that conclusion must all arrive who commence by the method of analysis, and close with exclusion of all the higher and distinctive qualities of man.

§ 6. In the progress of knowledge we find ourselves gradually passing from the compound to the simple; from that which is

* Ricardo. † Droz. *Economie Politique.*

abstruse and difficult to that which is plain and easily learned. That "all simple ideas are true," we have been assured by Descartes, and evidence of the fact may everywhere be found in the beautiful simplicity, and wonderful breadth of propositions in science, themselves the result of a long induction, leading to the knowledge of great truths not at first perceptible, but when announced so conclusive as to close, almost at once and forever, all discussion in reference to them. The falling of the apple led Newton to the law of gravitation, and to the discovery of that law we owe the astonishing perfection of modern astronomy. The establishment of the identity of lightning and electricity laid the foundation of a science, by help of which we have been enabled to command the services of a great power in nature, that has superseded all the contrivances of man. Kepler and Galileo, Newton and Franklin, would have failed in all their efforts to extend the domain of science, had they pursued the method of M. Comte in his attempt to establish a system of social science.

Does this method, however, supersede entirely the *à priori* one? Because we pursue the method of analysis, are we necessarily precluded from that of synthesis? By no means. The one, however, is the indispensable preparation for the other. It was by the careful observation of particular facts that Le Verrier was led to the grand generalization that a new and unobserved planet was bound to exist, and in a certain part of the heavens, and there it was almost at once discovered. To careful analysis of various earths it was due that Davy was led to the announcement of the great fact that all earths have metallic bases—one of the grandest generalizations on record, and one whose truth is being every day more and more established. The two methods were well described by Goethe, when he said that synthesis and analysis were "the systole and diastole of human thought," and that they were to him "like a second breathing process—never separated, ever pulsating." "The vice of the *à priori* method," says the writer from whom this passage is taken, "when it wanders from the right path, is *not* that it *goes before* the facts, and anticipates the tardy conclusions of experience, but that it rests contented with its own verdicts, or seeking only a partial, hasty confrontation with facts—what Bacon calls '*notiones* temerè à rebus abstractas.'"*

* *Westminster Review*, Oct. 1852: Article, *Goethe as a Man of Science.*

If science be one and indivisible, then must the method of study be one. That this is so, with regard to all the departments of knowledge that underlie social science—physics, chemistry, and physiology—cannot now be doubted, yet it is but recently that there has been reason to believe in any such connection. With each new discovery the approximation becomes more close, and with each we see how intimately are the facts of all the earlier and more abstract departments of knowledge connected with the progress of man toward that state of high development for which he seems to have been intended. From hour to hour, as he acquires further control over the various forces existing in nature, he is enabled to live in closer connection with his fellow man—to obtain larger supplies of food and clothing—to improve his own modes of thought and action, and to furnish better instruction to the generation destined to succeed him. The knowledge that leads to such results is but the foundation upon which we are required to build, when undertaking to construct that higher department denominated social science, and the instrument that has been so successfully used in laying the foundation cannot but be found equally useful in the construction of the building itself.

Mathematics must be used in social science, as it is now in every other branch of inquiry, and the more the former is used, the more the latter takes the form of real science, and the more intimate are shown to be its relations with other departments of knowledge. The Malthusian law was the first instance of its application, and had it proved a true one, it would have given a precision to political economy, of which before it had been utterly incapable, making the progress of man directly dependent upon the presence or absence of certain powers in the soil on which he lived. So, too, with Mr. Ricardo's celebrated theory of rent, by which was established what he deemed to be the natural division of the products of labor among the men who labored, and those who superintended the work, or those who owned the land by which they were yielded. The *method* of both these great laws was right, and the fact of their having adopted that method has properly placed their authors in the front rank of economists, and has given to their works an amount of influence never before exercised by any writers on economical science. That they fell into the error above described, of "seeking only a partial, hasty confrontation with facts," and, therefore, furnished the world with theories directly the reverse of truth, does not prevent us from seeing of what infinite advantage to the progress of science it would have been to have had the facts brought under these relations, if true, nor of how great importance it must be to have the real facts brought under such relations whenever possible.

Let us, for example, take the following proposition :—

In the early period of society, when land is abundant and people are few in number, labor is unproductive, and of the small product, the land-owner or other capitalist takes a large *proportion*, leaving to the laborer a small one. The larger proportion yields, however, but a small amount, and both laborer and capitalist are poor—the former so poor that he is everywhere seen to have been a slave to the latter. Population and wealth, however, increasing, and labor becoming more productive, the land-owner's share diminishes in its *proportion*, but increases in its *amount*. The laborer's share increases not only in its amount, but also in its proportion, and the more rapid the increase in the productiveness of his labor, the greater is the *proportion* of the augmented quantity retained by him; and thus, while the interests of both are in perfect harmony with each other, there is a constant tendency towards the establishment of an equality of condition—the slave of the early period becoming the free man of the later one.

Admitting this to be true—and if so, it establishes directly the reverse of what was propounded by Messrs. Malthus and Ricardo—we have here the distinct expression of a mathematical relation between the concomitant variations of power of man and matter—of the man representing only his own faculties, and of the man representing the accumulated results of human faculties upon matter and its forces. The problem of social science, and the one attempted to be solved by those writers, is, what are the relations of man and the outside material world. They change, as we see, men becoming, in some countries, from year to year more and more the masters, and in others, the slaves of nature. In what manner is it that changes in one tend to produce further changes in itself, or to effect changes in the other? To this question we need a mathematical answer, and until it shall be furnished—as it is believed to be in the above very simple proposition—political economy can bear only the same relation to social science that the observations of the Chaldean shepherds bear to modern astronomy.

Social science can scarcely be said to have an existence. That it might exist, it was required that we should first possess the physical, chemical, and physiological knowledge enabling us to observe how it is that man is enabled to obtain command over the various forces provided for his use, and to pass from being the slave, to becoming the master of nature. "Man," says Goethe, "only knows himself in as far as he knows external nature," and it was needed that the more abstract and general departments of knowledge should acquire a state of high development, before we could advantageously enter upon the study of the highly concrete and special, and infinitely variable science of the laws by which man is governed in his relations with the external world, and with his fellow-man. Chemistry and physiology are both, however, of recent date. A century since, men knew nothing of the composition of the air they breathed, and it is within that period that Haller laid the foundation of the physiological science that now exists. In physics, even, the Aristotelian doctrine of the four elements had yet possession of many of the schools, and still probably remains in some of those on the outer borders of civilization. In this state of things there could be but little progress towards the attainment of the knowledge how far it was in the power of man to compel the earth to yield the supplies required for a steadily increasing population; and without that knowledge there could be no such thing as social science.

Science requires laws, and laws are but universal truths—truths to which no exceptions can be found. Those obtained, harmony and order take the place of chaos, and we are led in every department of knowledge as much to recognize effects as having been the natural results of certain definite causes, and to look for the reappearance of similar effects when like causes shall again occur, as did the first man when he had definitely connected the presence and absence of light with the rising and setting of the sun.

Where, however, is there in social science a proposition whose truth is universally admitted? There is not even a single one. A century since, the strength of a nation was regarded as tending to increase with augmentation of its numbers, but now we are taught that increase of numbers brings with it weakness instead of strength. From year to year we have new theories of the laws of population, and new modifications of the old one—and the question of the laws governing the distribution of the proceeds of labor between the owner and occupier of land, is now discussed as vigorously as it was fifty years since. Of the disciples of Messieurs Malthus and Ricardo, scarcely any two are agreed as to what it was that their masters really meant to teach. On one day we are told that the Ricardo-Malthusian doctrine is dead, and on the next we learn that it is an evidence of want of knowledge to doubt its truth; and yet the parties to whom we are indebted for all this knowledge, belong to the same politico-economical school.* The strongest advocates for the removal of all restrictions on trade in cloth are found among the fiercest opponents of freedom in the trade in money; and among the most enthusiastic friends of competition for the sale of merchandise, are to be found the most decided opponents of competition for the purchase of the laborer's time and talents. Teachers who rejoice in everything tending to increase the prices of cloth and iron, as leading to improvement in the condition of man, are found among the foremost of those who deprecate advance in the price of the laborer's services, as tending to diminution of power for the maintenance of trade. Others who teach non-interference by government when it looks to the diffusion of knowledge among the people, are among the most decided as to the propriety of such interference when it looks to measures leading to war and waste. All is therefore confusion, and nothing is settled; as a necessary consequence of which the world looks quietly on, waiting the time when the teachers shall

* "We believe it (the Ricardo principle of rent), dominates in the long run, and is the main cause of the decline of nations. * * We believe the law of population to which Malthus first directed public attention, to be founded in fact."—London *Spectator*, Nov. 18, 1854.

"Nobody, except a few mere writers, now troubles himself about Malthus on population, or Ricardo on rent. Their error may yet indeed linger in the universities, the appropriate depositories for what is obsolete."—London *Economist*, same date.

"In fact, this phenomenon, the announcement of which caused so much clamor against Malthus, appears to me incontestable."—Bastiat. *Harmonies Economiques.*

"The theory of rent, given by Ricardo, appears to me to remain untouched."—Chevalier. *De la Monnaie.*

"The Essay on the Principle of Population was really, and we must acknowledge it, a revelation."—*Journal des Economistes*, Oct. 1854.

arrive at some understanding among themselves as to what it is that is to be believed.

That they may do so, it is essential that they arrive at some such understanding as to the meaning of the various terms in common use, no approach towards which has yet been made. "The great defect of Adam Smith, and of our economists in general," says Archbishop Whateley, "is the want of definitions," and in proof of this he gives his readers the numerous and widely different ones furnished by the most distinguished teachers in relation to the highly important terms, Value, Wealth, Labor, Capital, Rents, Wages, and Profits, and shows that, for want of clear conceptions, the same word is used by the same writer at one time in a manner totally inconsistent with that in which he uses it at another. To that list, he might, as he most truly says, add many others "which are often used without any more explanation, or any more suspicion of their requiring it, than the words "triangle," or "twenty"*—and as a consequence of this it is that, as will be hereafter shown, words of the highest importance are used by distinguished writers as being entirely synonymous, when really expressing not only different, but directly opposite ideas.

§ 7. The causes of the existence of this state of things are readily explained. Of all others, social science is the most concrete and special—the most dependent on the earlier and more abstract departments of science—the one in which the facts are most difficult of collection and analysis—and therefore the last that makes its appearance on the stage. Of all, too, it is the only one that affects the interests of men, their feelings, passions, prejudices, and therefore the one in which it is most difficult to find men collating facts with the sole view to deduce from them the knowledge they are calculated to afford. Treating, as it does, of the relations between man and man, it has everywhere to meet the objection of those who seek the enjoyment of power and privilege at the cost of their fellow-men. The sovereign holds in small respect the science that would teach his subjects to doubt the propriety of his exercise of power by the grace of God. The soldier cannot believe in one that looks to the annihilation of his trade, nor can

* *Elements of Logic.*

the monopolist readily be made to believe in the advantages of competition. The politician lives by managing the affairs of others, and he has small desire to see the people taught the proper management of their own concerns. All these men profit by teaching falsehood, and therefore frown upon those who would desire to teach the truth. The landlord believes in one doctrine and his tenant in another, while the payer of wages looks at all questions from a point of sight directly the opposite of the one occupied by him to whom the wages are paid.

We here meet a difficulty with which, as has been already said, no other science has had to contend. Astronomy has wrought its way to its present prodigious height with but temporary opposition from the schools, because no one was personally interested in continuing to teach the revolution of the sun around the earth. For a time the teachers, secular and spiritual, were disposed to deny the movement of the latter, but the fact was proved, and opposition ceased. Such, too, was the case when geology began to teach that the earth had had a longer existence than previously had been believed. The schools that represented by-gone days did then as they had done in the days of Copernicus and Galileo, denouncing as heretics all who doubted the accuracy of the received chronology, but short as is the time that has since elapsed, the opposition has already disappeared. Franklin, Dalton, Wollaston, and Berzelius prosecuted their inquiries without fear of opposition, for their discoveries were unlikely to affect injuriously the pockets of land-owners, merchants, or politicians. Social science is, however, still to a great extent in the hands of the schoolmen, backed everywhere by those who profit by the ignorance and the weakness of the people.

The occupants of academic chairs in Austria or Russia may not teach what is unfavorable to the divine rights of kings, or favorable to increase in the powers of the people. The doctrines of the schools of France vary from time to time as despotism yields to the people, or the people yield to it. The landed aristocracy of England was gratified when Mr. Malthus satisfied it that the poverty and misery of the people resulted necessarily from a great law emanating from an all-wise and all-benevolent Creator; and the manufacturing one is equally so when it sees, as it thinks, the fact established that the general interests of the country are to be promoted by measures looking to the production of an abundant supply of cheap, or badly paid, labor.

The system of this country being based upon the idea of entire political equality, we might, perhaps, be warranted in looking to our teachers for something different, even if not better, but if we should do so we should, in general, be disappointed. With few and slight exceptions, our professors teach the same social science that is taught abroad by men who live by inculcating the divine rights of kings; and they teach self-government by aid of books from which their pupils learn that the greater the tendency towards equality the greater is the hatred among the several classes of which society is composed. Social science, as taught in some of the colleges of this country and of Europe, is now on a level with the chemical science of the early part of the last century; and there it will remain so long as its teachers shall continue to look inwards to their own minds and *invent* theories, instead of looking outwards to the great laboratory of the world for the collection of facts with a view to the *discovery* of laws. In default of such laws, they are constantly repeating phrases that have no real meaning, and that tend, as Goethe most truly says, to " ossify the organs of intelligence," not only of themselves but of their hearers.*

The state in which it now exists is what M. Comte is accustomed to denominate the metaphysical one, and there it must continue to remain until its teachers shall waken to this fact, that there is but one system of laws for the government of all matter, whether existing in the form of a piece of coal, a tree, a horse, or a man—and but one mode of study for all departments of it. " The leaf," says a recent writer, "is to the plant what the microcosm is to the macrocosm—it is the plant in miniature—a common law governs the two, and therefore whatever disposition we find in the parts of the

* "The pagan, the idolater, the ignorant even of the Catholic church, worship their stocks and stones; and instead of regarding these as signs only shadowing forth what in its intellectual state, the human mind cannot otherwise express of its religious sentiments, takes the signs for the things they represent, and worships them as facts. We, too, worship our signs—our words. Let any man set himself to the task of examining the state of his knowledge on the most important subjects, divine or human, and he will find himself a mere word-worshipper; he will find words without ideas or meaning in his mind venerated, made idols of—idols different from those carved in wood or stone only by being stamped with printer's ink on white paper."—Laing, *Chronicle of the Sea Kings*, *Introd. Dissertation*, chap. ii.

leaf, we may expect to find in the parts of the plant, and *vice versa*." So is it with the tree of science, with its many branches, what is true of its root cannot be otherwise than true of the leaves and the fruit. The laws of physical science are equally those of social science, and in every effort to discover the former we are but paving the way for the discovery of the latter. "The entire succession of men," said Pascal, "through the whole course of ages, must be regarded as one man, always living, and incessantly learning;" and among the men who have most largely contributed towards the foundation of a true social science are to be ranked the eminent teachers to whose labors we have been so largely indebted for the wonderful development of physical, chemical, and physiological science in the last and present centuries.

The later man is, therefore, the one possessing the most of that knowledge of the operations of society required for comprehending the causes of the various effects recorded in the pages of history, and for predicting those which must result in future from causes now existing. The early man possessed little of science but the instrument required for its acquisition, and what of it he did acquire was purely physical in its character and most limited in its extent. The existing one is in possession not only of physical science to an extent that is wonderful compared with what existed a century since, but to this he has added the chemical and physiological sciences then scarcely known, and has proved that the laws of the former and more abstract are equally those of the latter more concrete and special ones. If, then, there is truth in the suggestion of Pascal that we are to consider the endless succession of men as one man, may it not be that the laws of all the earlier and more abstract departments of science will be found to be equally true in reference to the highly concrete and special one which embraces the relations of man in society—and that, therefore, all science will prove to be but one, its parts differing as do the colors of the spectrum, but producing, as does the sun's ray, undecomposed, one white and bright light? To show that such is the case is the object of the present work.

# CHAPTER II.

## OF MAN—THE SUBJECT OF SOCIAL SCIENCE.

§ 1. MAN, the molecule of society, is the subject of social science. In common with all other animals he requires to eat, drink, and sleep, but his greatest need is that of ASSOCIATION with his fellow-men. Born the weakest and most dependent of animals, he requires the largest care in infancy, and must be clothed by others, whereas to birds and beasts clothing is supplied by nature. Capable of acquiring the highest degree of knowledge, he appears in the world destitute even of that instinct which teaches the bee and the spider, the bird and the beaver, to construct their habitations, and to supply themselves with food. Dependent upon the experience of himself and others for all his knowledge, he requires language to enable him either to record the results of his own observation, or to profit by those of others; and of language there can be none without association. Created in the image of his Maker, he should participate in his intelligence; but it is only by means of ideas that he can avail himself of the faculties with which he has been endowed, and without language there can be no ideas—no power of thought. Without language, therefore, he must remain in ignorance of the existence of powers granted to him in lieu of the strength of the ox and the horse, the speed of the hare, and the sagacity of the elephant, and must remain below the level of the brute creation. To have language there must be association and combination of men with their fellow men, and it is on this condition only that man can be man; on this alone that we can conceive of the being to which we attach the idea of man. "It is not good," said God, "that man should live alone," nor do we ever find him doing so; the earliest records of the world exhibiting to us beings living together in society, and using words for the expression of their ideas. Whence came those words? Whence came language? With the same propriety might we ask—Why does fire burn? Why does man see, feel, hear, or walk? Language escapes from him at the touch of nature herself, and the power of using words is his essential faculty, enabling him to maintain commerce with his fellow men, and fitting him for that association without which language cannot exist. The words society and language convey to the mind separate and distinct ideas, and yet by no effort of the mind can we conceive of the existence of the one without the other.

The subject of social science then is man—the being to whom have been given reason and the faculty of individualizing sounds so as to give expression to every variety of idea—and who has been placed in a position to exercise that faculty. Isolate him, and with the loss of the power of speech, he loses the power to reason, and with it the distinctive quality of man. Restore him to society, and with the return of the power of speech he becomes again the reasoning man.

We have here the great law of molecular gravitation as the *indispensable* condition of the existence of the being known as man. The particles of matter having each an independent existence, the atom of oxygen or of hydrogen is as perfect and complete as it could be were it in connection with millions of others like itself. The grain of sand is perfect whether flying alone before the wind or resting with its fellows on the shores of the broad Atlantic. The tree and the shrub, brought from distant lands and standing alone in the conservatory, produce the same fruits and yield the same odors as when they stood in the groves from which they had been transplanted. The individual dog, cat, and rabbit possess all their powers in a state of entire isolation. Such, however, is not the case with man. The wild man, wherever found, has always proved to be not only destitute of the reasoning faculty, but destitute also of the instinct that in other animals takes the place of reason—and therefore the most helpless of beings.

Man tends of necessity to gravitate towards his fellow-man. Of all animals he is the most gregarious, and the greater the number collected in a given space the greater is the attractive force there exerted, as is seen to have been the case with the great cities of the ancient world, Nineveh and Babylon, Athens and Rome, and as is now seen in regard to Paris and London, Vienna and Naples, Philadelphia, New York, and Boston. Gravitation is here, as everywhere else in the material world, in the direct ratio of the mass, and in the inverse one of the distance.

Such being the case, why is it that all the members of the human family do not tend to come together on a single spot of earth? Because of the existence of the same simple and universal law by means of which is maintained the beautiful order of the system of which our planet forms a part. We are surrounded by bodies of various sizes, and some of these are themselves provided with satellites, each having its local centre of attraction, by means of which its parts are held together. Were it possible that that attractive power could be annihilated, the rings of Saturn, the moons of our earth and of Jupiter, would crumble to pieces and fall inward upon the bodies they now attend, a mass of ruins. So, too, with the planets themselves. Small as are the asteroids, each has within itself a local centre of attraction enabling it to preserve its form and substance, despite the superior attraction of the larger bodies by which it is everywhere surrounded.

So it is throughout our world. Look where we may we see local centres of attraction towards which men gravitate, some exercising less influence, and others more. London and Paris may be regarded as the rival suns of our system, each exercising a strong attractive force, and were it not for the existence of the counter attraction of local centres like Vienna and Berlin, Florence and Naples, Madrid and Lisbon, Brussels and Amsterdam, Copenhagen, Stockholm, and St. Petersburg, Europe would present to view one great centralized system, the population of which was always tending towards those two cities, there to make all their exchanges, and thence to receive their laws. So, too, in this country. It is seen by all how strong is even now the tendency towards New York, and that, too, in despite of the existence of local centres of attraction in the cities of Boston, Philadelphia, Baltimore, Washington, Pittsburg, Cincinnati, St. Louis, New Orleans, Augusta, Savannah, and Charleston, and in the numerous capitals of the States of which the Union is composed. Were we to obliterate these centres of attraction and place a centralized government like that of England, France, or Russia, in the city of New York, not only would it grow to the size of London, but soon would far exceed it, and the effect would be the same as would be produced in the astronomical world by a similar course of operation. The local governments would fall to pieces, and all the atoms of which they had been composed would tend at once towards the new centre of gravity that had been thus produced. Local and voluntary association for the various purposes of life, throughout what would then be the provinces of a great centralized State, would be at an end, but in its place would be found the forced association of dependents on one hand and masters on the other. Every neighborhood that required to have a road or a bridge, to establish a bank, or to obtain a redress of grievances, would be required to make its application therefor at the great city, distant many hundreds of miles, and to pay innumerable officers before it could obtain the desired permission, as is now the case in France. Every community that found itself suffering from heavy taxes, or from other oppressions from which it desired to be relieved, would be found seeking to make itself heard, but its voice would be drowned by those of the men who profited by such abuses, as is now the case with the complaints to Parliament of Ireland and of India. Instead of going, as now, to the little capital of the State, close at hand, and obtaining without cost the required laws, they would find themselves compelled to employ agents for the negotiation of their business, and those agents would then, as now in England, accumulate enormous fortunes at the cost of the poor and distant suitors. Much of this is already seen at Washington, and yet how trivial is it compared with what it would be were all the various business transacted by State Legislatures and by County Boards brought within the sphere of Congress, as it now is within that of the British Parliament.

The centralizing tendency of the State capital is, in its turn, greatly neutralized by the existence of opposing centres of attraction at the various county seats, and in the numerous towns and cities of the Union, each managing its own affairs, and each presenting places at which the people of the various districts, and of the whole country itself, are brought into connection with each other, for the exchange of the products of physical or mental effort. Obliterate these—centralize the powers of towns and counties in the State Legislatures—and the power of local association throughout the States would be in a great degree annihilated. The State capital, or that of the Union, would grow rapidly, as would the sun were the local attraction of the planets destroyed.

The splendor of both might be greatly increased, but in the space now traversed by the planets motion would cease to exist, as would be the case throughout this country, were it made dependent on a single centre—and without motion there can be neither association nor force, nor consequently progress.

Further, with the growth of centralization there would be seen a diminution in the counteracting force by which families are held together, despite the attractions of the capital. Whatever tends to the establishment of decentralization, and to the production of local employment for time and talent, tends to give value to land, to promote its division, and to enable parents and children to remain in closer connection with each other—and the stronger the ties that bind together the members of the various families of which the community is composed, the more perfect will be their revolution on their own axes, and the greater the attraction within the bosom of the communities which constitute the State. Whatever tends, on the contrary, to the diminution of local employment, tends to the consolidation of land, the breaking up of families, and the building up of great cities at the expense of the country, as we see to have been the case in Italy, Ireland, India, and Britain, and as is at this moment seen in the rapid growth of our own cities, accompanied, as it always is, by the expulsion of our people to distant lands, with constant diminution of the power of association and combination.

The pages of history furnish throughout evidence that the tendency towards association—without which the human animal cannot become the being to which we apply the denomination of man—has everywhere grown with increase in the number and strength of local centres of attraction, and has declined with their diminution. Such centres were found in nearly all the Grecian Islands, while Laconia and Attica, Bœotia and Argos, Arcadia and Elis, Megara and Corinth, were enabled each to rejoice in its own. Local association existed there to an extent that had until then been unequalled in the world, yet the tendency towards general association was exhibited in the foundation of the Isthmian and Nemean, and the yet more celebrated Olympic games, which drew together all that were distinguished for physical or intellectual power, not only in the States and cities of Greece itself, but in the distant Italy and Asia. In the Amphictyonic league we find further evidence of the tendency to general as a consequence of local association; but here, unhappily, the idea was not fully carried out. The attractive power of this sun of the system was not sufficient for the maintenance of order in the movements of the planets, which frequently, therefore, shot madly from their spheres and jostled against each other.

To the equal action of opposing forces it is due, that the celestial world is enabled to exhibit such wonderful harmony and such unceasing motion—and to the same principle, here carried out to a greater extent than elsewhere in the world, it is due that the history of the Union has presented no case of civil war, while exhibiting an amount of peaceful motion far exceeding what has elsewhere been exhibited. Destroy the State governments and centralize power in the hands of the general government, and the result would be found in a steady diminution of the power of voluntary association for the purposes of peace, and increase in the tendency towards involuntary association for the purposes of war. Destroy the central government, and conflicts among the States would become inevitable. The people of Greece had all this yet to learn, and the consequences were found in frequent war among the states and cities, resulting in the establishment of a highly centralized government, controlling the disbursements of a treasury filled by the contributions of a thousand subject cities. Thenceforward, the people of those cities lost the power of association for the determination of their respective rights, and had to seek for justice among themselves in the courts of Athens. To that city resorted all who had money to pay to, or to receive from, the State—all who had causes to try—all who sought places of power or profit—all who found themselves unable to obtain a living at home—and all who preferred the work of plunder to that of labor; and with every step in this direction, decentralization gave way to centralization, until at length Athens and Sparta, Samos and Mitylene, and all the other states and cities of Greece were involved in one common ruin—Attica herself becoming, to a great extent, the property of a single individual, surrounded by hosts of slaves, the disposition for voluntary association, and the power to exercise it, having wholly passed away.

Looking to Italy, we see a similar course of things. In its early days, Etruria and the Campagna, Magna Græcia and the Samnite

Hills, presented to view numerous cities, each the centre of a district throughout which existed in a high degree the habit of local and voluntary association. With time, however, we see that habit gradually disappearing, and first among the people of Rome itself, perpetually engaged in disturbing their peaceful neighbors. The central city growing by help of plunder, with every step in that direction the local centres of attraction diminished in importance, and it became more and more necessary to resort to the arbitration of Rome itself. As power became more and more centralized within her walls, her people became more and more dependent on the public treasury, and the power of voluntary association gradually disappeared—while Italy throughout presented the spectacle of great landlords occupying palaces, and surrounded by troops of slaves. So long as the opposing forces were in equal balance, Italy furnished the world with men, but with her decline she is seen more and more to have presented it with slaves, sometimes attired in the beggar's rags, and at others in the imperial purple.

Studying the history of the Republic and the Empire, we see that their long duration is to be attributed to the fact that to so great an extent the people of the provinces were left to govern themselves, subject only to the performance of certain duties to the central power. Local association for almost every purpose was for centuries left untouched, and the towns and cities imposed their own taxes, determined their own laws, and selected the magistrates by whom they were to be carried into effect.

Modern Italy, from the days of the Lombards, presented during many centuries the most remarkable case of the connection between local attraction and the power of voluntary association. Milan, Genoa, Venice, Florence, Rome, Naples, Pisa, Sienna, Padua, and Verona, were each centres of attraction such as had existed once in Greece, but in default of a sun with attractive force sufficient to maintain the harmony of the system, they were perpetually at war with each other, until at length Austria and France centralized within themselves the government of the peninsula, and the habit of voluntary association entirely disappeared.

India had numerous centres of attraction. In addition to its various capitals, each little village presented a self-governing community in which existed the power of association to an extent scarcely elsewhere equalled—but with the growth of central power in Calcutta, the habit and the power of exercising it have almost altogether disappeared.

Spain had numerous local centres. Association there existed to a great extent, not only among the enlightened Moors, but among the people of Castile and Arragon, Biscay and Leon. The discovery of this continent, of which the government became the absentee landlord, greatly increased the central power, with corresponding decline in local activity and local association, and the consequences are visible in the depopulation and weakness that have since ensued.

In Germany we find the home of the decentralization of Europe —of jealousy of central power—and of the maintenance of local rights—as a consequence of which the tendency towards association has always been strong among her people, and has now been followed up by the union of her communities in the *Zoll-Verein*, one of the most important events recorded in the history of Europe. Like Greece, Germany has always been deficient as regards the sun around which the numerous planets might peacefully revolve, and as in Greece, powers exterior to her system have been enabled to use one community against another to an extent that has greatly retarded the progress of civilization at home, although as a rule, she has interfered little with its progress abroad.* Strong for defence, she has, therefore, been weak for offence, and has exhibited no tendency towards wars for conquest, or towards the levying of contributions upon her poorer neighbors, as has been so much the case with her highly centralized neighbor, France. Abounding always in local centres of attraction, it has been found impossible to create a great central city to direct the modes of thought and action, and to that it is due that Germany is now so rapidly taking the position of the great intellectual centre, not only of Europe, but of the world at large.

Among the states of Germany there is none whose policy has so much tended to the maintenance of local centres of action, as advantageous to the best interests of the people and the state, as Prussia. All the ancient divisions, from the communes to the provinces, have been carefully preserved, and their constitutions as

* Austria is a compound of numerous bodies, a large portion of which is entirely exterior to Germany. Her wars in Italy have mostly been Austrian and not Germanic.

carefully respected, as a consequence of which it is that here we find the people advancing towards freedom with great rapidity while the state is rapidly advancing in wealth and power. The peaceful effects of decentralization are here fully exhibited in the fact that, under the lead of Prussia, Northern Germany has been brought under a great federal system, by help of which internal commerce has been placed on a footing almost precisely corresponding with that of these United States.

Nowhere in Europe had decentralization more existed, and nowhere had the tendency to peaceful association, or the strength of resistance to attacks from without consequent upon union, been more fully exhibited than in Switzerland, notwithstanding the existence of the widest religious differences. The wars and revolutions of the period ending in 1815, and the constant revolutions and growing centralization of France, have here, however, produced their usual effect in the establishment of increased centralization, under which the weaker cantons have been deprived of rights they had for ages enjoyed, and tyranny and oppression are gradually taking the place of the freedom and exemption from taxation that before existed.

The French Revolution annihilated, when it should have strengthened the local governments—and thus was centralization increased when it should have been diminished, the consequences of which are seen in a perpetual succession of wars and revolutions. Much was done towards decentralization when the lands of absentee nobles and of the church were divided among the people, and to the counteracting effect of this measure it is due that France has grown in strength notwithstanding the extraordinary centralization of her system.

Belgium and Holland present remarkable instances of the power of local action to produce habits of association. In both, the towns and cities were numerous, and the effect of combined action is seen in the wonderful productiveness of what was originally one of the poorest countries of Europe.

In no part of Europe was the division of land so complete, or its possession so secure, as in Norway, at and before the date of the Norman conquest of England; and in none, consequently, was the power of local attraction so fully exhibited. The habit of association, therefore, existed to an extent then unknown in France and Germany, developing itself in the establishment of "a literature in their own language, and living in the common tongue and minds of the people."* Elsewhere, the languages of the educated and uneducated classes have differed so widely as to render the literature used by the former entirely inaccessible to the latter; and, as a necessary consequence, there has been "a want of that circulation of the same mind and intelligence through all classes of the social body, differing only in degree, not in kind, in the most educated and most ignorant, and of that circulation and interchange of impressions, through a language and literature common to all, which alone can animate a population into a nation."† They were in advance of other nations, too, in the fact that employments were diversified, affording further proof of the existence of the habit of association and combination. "Iron," continues Mr. Laing, "is the mother of all the useful arts; and a people who could smelt it from the ore, and work it into all that is required for ships of considerable size, from a nail to an anchor, could not have been in a state of such utter barbarism as they have been represented to us. They had a literature of their own, and laws, institutions, social arrangements, a spirit and character, very analogous to the English, if not the source from which the English flowed; and were in advance of all Christian nations in one branch of the useful arts, in which great combinations of them are required—the building, fitting out, and navigating large vessels."‡

The same habit of local association has ever since existed, accompanied by a tendency to union whose effects were fully exhibited in the establishment, forty years since, of a system of government, in which the centralizing and decentralizing forces are balanced to an extent not exceeded in the world; and, as a consequence, this little people has exhibited a force of resistance to centralization, sought to be introduced from abroad, to which it would be difficult to find a parallel in history.§

* Chronicle of the Sea-Kings of Norway. Introductory chapter by S. Laing, p. 33.

† Ibid., p. 36.

‡ Ibid., p. 146.

§ The reader who may desire fully to appreciate the strength of resistance of free governments, can scarcely fail to derive advantage from Mr.

The attraction of local centres, throughout the British islands, formerly so great, has, for a long time past, tended steadily to diminish—Edinburgh, once the metropolis of a kingdom, having become a mere provincial city; and Dublin, once the seat of an independent Parliament, having so much declined, that were it not for the fact, that it is the place at which the representative of majesty holds his occasional levées, it would scarcely at all be heard of. London and Liverpool, Manchester and Birmingham, have grown rapidly; but with those exceptions, the population of the United Kingdom was stationary in the period from 1841 to 1851. Everywhere, there is exhibited an increasing tendency towards centralization, accompanied by diminution in the strength of local attraction, increase of absenteeism, and decline in the power of voluntary association—the diminution of the latter wonderfully exhibited, in the few past years, in the emigration from its shores. With every step in that direction, there is witnessed a steady increase in the necessity for involuntary association, manifested by an increase of fleets and armies, and an increase in the amount of contributions required for their support.

The Northern States of the Union present, as has been already shown, a combination of the centralizing and decentralizing forces to an extent that has never elsewhere been equalled; and there, accordingly, we find existing in a high degree, the tendency to local action for the creation of schools and school-houses, the making of roads, and the formation of associations for almost every imaginable purpose. The system of laws that maintains harmony throughout the Universe is here exactly imitated—each State constituting a body perfect in itself, with local attraction tending to maintain its form, despite the gravitating tendency towards the centre, around which it, and its sister States, are required to revolve.

As a consequence of this it is, that the course of the North has been always peaceful—there having been, at no period, the smallest manifestation of a desire for the acquisition of territory, or for interference with the rights of neighboring States. Annex-

Laing's account of his residence in Norway during the period of the several conflicts between the Swedish and Norwegian governments, in the period from 1830 to 1840.

ation of the British provinces, with their millions of free inhabitants, would add largely to the northern strength; and yet, while co-operating with the South for the purchase of Florida and Louisiana, and for the acquisition of Texas, the question of incorporating Canada into the Union, can scarcely be regarded as having ever, seriously, been considered.

Looking to the Southern States, the reverse of the picture is presented to our view. Masters, there, own men who are denied all power of voluntary association, and may not even sell their own labor, or exchange its product for that of the labor of others. This is centralization, and hence it is, that we see throughout the South, so strong a tendency towards disturbance of the power of association elsewhere. All the wars of the Union have here had their origin. War tends to increase the number of human machines that carry muskets, and require for their support large contributions, that might be better employed in the construction of roads or mills, by help of which association would be promoted.

Barbarism is a necessary consequence of the absence of association. Deprived of this, man—losing his distinctive qualities—ceases to be the subject of social science.

§ 2. The next distinctive quality of man is INDIVIDUALITY. Each rat or robin, fox or wolf, is the type of his species wherever found, possessing habits and instincts in common with all his race. Not such is the case with man, in whom we find differences of tastes, feelings, and capacities, almost as numerous as those observed in the human countenance. In order, however, that these differences may be developed, it is indispensable that he be brought into association with his fellow man; and where that has been denied, the individuality can no more be found, than it would be, were we searching for it among the foxes, or the wolves. The wild men of Germany, and those of India, differ so little, that in reading the description of the one, we might readily suppose we were reading that of the other. Passing from these, to the lower forms of association, such as exist among savage tribes, we find a growing tendency to the development of the varieties of individual character; but, desiring to find their highest development, we must seek it in those places in which there exists the greatest demand for intellectual effort—those in which there is the greatest variety of employment—those in which, therefore, the power of association most perfectly exists, in towns and cities. That this should be the case, is perfectly in accordance with what is everywhere else observed.

"The more imperfect a being is," says Goethe, "the more do its individual parts resemble each other, and the more do these parts resemble the whole. The more perfect a being, the more dissimilar are the parts. In the former case, the parts are more or less a repetition of the whole; in the latter case they are totally unlike the whole. The more the parts resemble each other, the less subordination is there of one to the other; subordination of parts indicates a high grade of organization."*

This is as true of societies as it is of the plants and animals in reference to which it was written. The more imperfect they are—the less the variety of employments, and the less, consequently, the development of intellect—the more do the parts resemble each other, as may readily be seen by any one who will study man in the purely agricultural countries of the earth. The greater the variety of employments—the greater the demand for intellectual effort—the more dissimilar become the parts, and the more perfect becomes the whole, as may readily be seen on comparing any purely agricultural district with another in which agriculture, manufactures, and commerce are happily combined. Difference is essential to association. The farmer does not need to associate with his brother farmer, but he does need to do so with the carpenter, the blacksmith, and the miller. The mill operative has little occasion to exchange with his brother operative, but he does require to exchange with the builder of houses, or the seller of food; and the

* The same idea is thus given in a recent work of great ability: "The differences are the condition of development; the mutual exchanges, which are the consequences of these differences, waken and manifest life. The greater the diversity of organs, the more active and superior is the life of the individual. The greater the variety of individualities and relations in a society of individuals, the greater also is the sum of life, the more universal is the development of life, the more complete, and of a more elevated order. But it is necessary, not only that life should unfold itself in all its richness by diversity, but that it exhibits itself in its utility, in its beauty, in its goodness, by harmony. Thus we recognize the proof of the old proverb, 'Variety in unity is perfection.'"—Guyot's *Earth and Man*, p. 80.

more numerous the shades of difference in the society of which he is a part, the greater will be the facility for, and the tendency to, that combination of effort required for developing the peculiar qualities of its individual members. It is frequently remarked to what an extraordinary extent, when a demand arises, peculiar qualities are found whose existence had before been unsuspected. Thus, in our own revolution, blacksmiths and lawyers proved themselves distinguished soldiers, and the French revolution brought to light the military abilities of thousands of men that otherwise might have passed their lives at the tail of the plough. It is the occasion that makes the man. In every society there exists a vast amount of latent capacity waiting but the opportunity to show itself, and thus it is that in communities in which there is no diversity of employment, the intellectual power is to so great an extent wasted, producing no result. Life has been defined as being a "mutual exchange of relations," and where difference does not exist, exchanges cannot take place.

So is it everywhere throughout nature. To excite electricity, two metals are required to be brought together; but in order that they may combine, they must first be reduced to their original elements, and this can be done only by help of a third body differing totally from both. That done, what was before dull and inert becomes active and full of life, and capable at once of entering into new combinations. So, too, with the lump of coal. Break it up into pieces, however small, and scatter them in the ground, and there they will remain, still pieces of coal. Let them, however, be decomposed by the agency of heat—let the several parts be *individualized*—and at once they become capable of entering into new combinations, forming parts of the trunks, branches, leaves, or blossoms of trees, or of the bones, muscles, or brain of man. The wheat yielded to the labors of man, might remain, as we know it to have remained for numerous centuries, undecomposed and incapable of entering into combination with any other matter; but let it pass through the stomach, and at once it is resolved into its original element, part of which becomes bones, blood, or fat, and then again passes off in the form of perspiration—while another is ejected in the form of excrement, and ready to enter instantly into the composition of new vegetable forms. The power of association thus exists everywhere throughout the material world in the ratio of individualization. So, too, has it everywhere been with man—and the development of individuality has, at all times, and in all countries, been in the ratio of his power to act in obedience to that prime law of his nature which imposes upon him a necessity for association with his fellow-men.

That power, as has already been seen, has always existed in the ratio of the equal action of the centralizing and decentralizing forces, and where that action has most been found we should most find individuality, and that such has been the case can readily be shown. In no country of the world has it ever existed to so great an extent as was the case in Greece in the period immediately anterior to the invasion of Xerxes, and then and there it is that we find the highest development. To the men produced in that period it is that the age of Pericles owes its illustration. The destruction of Athens by Persian armies brought with it the conversion of citizens into soldiers, with steady tendency to increase of centralization and decline of the power of voluntary association and of individuality, until the slave alone is found cultivating the lands of Attica, the free citizens of the earlier period having entirely disappeared.—So, likewise, was it in Italy, where the highest individuality was found when the Campagna was filled with cities. Following their decline the great city grows, filled with paupers, the capital of a land cultivated by slaves.—So it is now throughout the East, where society is divided into two great parts—the men who toil and slave on the one side, and, on the other, those who live by the labors of the slave. Between two such masses there can be no association, and among the members there can be but little, because there is wanting among them that *difference* of pursuits which is required for producing an exchange of relations. The chain of society being there deficient in the connecting links, there is no motion among the parts, and where motion does not exist there can be no more development of individuality of character than could be found in the pebble-stone before it had been subjected to the action of the blowpipe.

The numerous towns and cities of Italy of the Middle Ages were remarkable for their motion, and for the development of individuality. So, likewise, was it in Belgium, and in Spain prior to the centralization which followed close upon the expulsion of the Moors, and the discovery of the gold and silver deposits of this continent.—Such was the case, too, in each of the kingdoms now composing the united kingdom of Great Britain and Ireland. If we take Ireland separately, we find her at the close of the last century giving to the world such men as Burke, Flood, Grattan, Sheridan, and Wellington; but since then centralization has greatly grown, and individuality has passed away. So, likewise, has it been in Scotland since the union. A century since that country presented to view a body of men occupying positions as distinguished as any that could be found in Europe, but her local institutions have decayed, and there are now, as we are told, "fewer individual thinkers" in that country than at any period "since the early part of the last century."* The mind of the whole youth of that country is now, as the same journal tells us, required to be "cast in the mould of English universities," which exercise upon it "an influence unfavorable to originality and power of thought."

In England herself, centralization has made great progress, and the consequence among her people has been witnessed in the steady increase of pauperism, a condition of things adverse to the development of individuality. The little landed proprietors have gradually disappeared to make way for the farmer and his hired laborers, and the great manufacturer, surrounded by hosts of operatives, of whose names even he is ignorant—and with every step in this direction there is diminished power of voluntary association. London grows to an enormous size, at the cost of the country at large, and thus does centralization produce the disease of over population, to be cured by a colonization tending at every step further to diminish the power of association.

Looking to France, we may see the steady decline of individuality attending the growth of centralization. In the highly centralized days of Louis XIV., almost the whole land of the kingdom was in the hands of a few great proprietors and of the dignitaries of the church—nearly all of whom were mere courtiers whose faces but reflected the expression apparent on that of the sovereign they were bound to worship. The right to labor was then held to be a privilege to be exercised at the pleasure of the monarch, and men

* North British Review, Aug., 1853.

were forbidden, on pain of death, to worship God according to their consciences, or even to leave the kingdom.

Passing to this country, we find in the Northern States individuality developed to an extent elsewhere entirely unknown, and for the reason that centralization exists in a very limited degree, while decentralization facilitates the rapid growth of the associative power. All the links of the chain are here to be found, and as every man feels that he can rise if he will, there is the strongest inducement to strive for intellectual development. In the Southern States power centralizes itself in the hands of the few, and association among the slaves can take place only through the master, as a consequence of which there is little individuality.

It is in variety there is unity, and this is quite as true of the social as it is of the material world. Let the reader watch the movements of a city and study the facility with which men, so various in their qualities, combine their movements—and the number required to work in combination for the production of a penny newspaper, a ship, a house, or an opera—and then compare it with the difficulty experienced throughout the country, and particularly in the purely agricultural portions of it, of combining for even the most simple purposes, and he will see that it is difference that leads to association. The more perfect the organization of society—the greater the variety of demands for the exercise of the physical and intellectual powers—the higher will be the elevation of man as a whole, and the stronger will be the contrasts among men.

Individuality thus grows with the growth of the power of association, and prepares the way for further and more perfect combination of action.

The more perfectly the local attraction tends to counterbalance that of the centre—the more society tends to conform itself to the laws we see to govern our system of worlds—the more harmonious will be the action of all the parts, and the greater will be the tendency towards voluntary association, and to the maintenance of peace abroad and at home.

§ 3. Next among the qualities by which man is distinguished from all other animals, is that of RESPONSIBILITY before his fellow-man, and before his Creator, for his actions.

The slave is not a responsible being, for he but obeys his master.

The soldier is not responsible for the murders he commits, for he is but an instrument in the hands of his superior officer, and he in turn but obeys the irresponsible chief of the State. The pauper is an irresponsible being, though often held by man to be responsible. Responsibility grows with the growth of individuality, and the latter grows, as we have seen, with the growth of the power of association.

The savage slays and robs his fellow-men, and proudly exhibits their scalps, or the plunder he has acquired, as evidence of his cunning or his courage. The soldier boasts of his prowess in the field, and gladly enumerates the men who have fallen by his arm, and this he does in a community whose laws award fine and imprisonment as the punishment for even the smallest violation of personal rights. The warlike nation prides itself upon the glory acquired in the field, at the cost of hundreds of thousands of lives, and decorates its galleries with pictures plundered from their rightful owners, while generals and admirals live in affluence upon their respective shares of the spoils of war. With growing individuality men learn to denominate such acts by their true and only legitimate titles—robbery and murder.

The savage is not responsible for his children, nor is the slave, who regards them as only his master's property. With every step towards perfect individuality—always the result of increase in the power of voluntary association—men learn more and more to appreciate their severe responsibility towards society at large, and towards their Creator, for the careful preparation of their children for the performance of their duties to both. To that feeling, more than to any other, are due the vigorous efforts made for acquiring the mastery over the forces of nature by which the associated man is distinguished from the isolated one—and thus it is that each of the distinguishing characteristics of man aids, and is aided by, each and every of the others. The savage is indolent, and he destroys his female children. The farmer extends his cultivation that he may provide more fully for the moral and physical training of his sons, and so fit them better than he himself had been for the performance of their duties to their fellow-men. The artisan improves his machinery, that he may call to his aid the power of electricity or of steam, and every step in this direction develops more fully his own peculiar powers. He thus becomes more individualized with great increase in the feeling of responsibility both for himself and his children, and in the disposition for combination of his efforts with those of his fellow-men—whether for the purpose of increasing the productiveness of their common labor, or for administering the affairs of the community of which he is a part.

Here again we find the correspondence between the development of the essential qualities of man to be in the ratio of the equal action of the centralizing and decentralizing forces. The Spartans permitted no responsibility for their children, and they endeavored to prevent the growth of wealth, while surrounding themselves with slaves, to whom all individuality was denied. The helot had no will of his own. In Attica, on the contrary, although slaves were numerous, labor was held in much higher respect, and diversity of employment caused great demand for intellectual effort. There, consequently, the rights of parents were respected, while those of the child were fully cared for under the laws of Solon.

In the East, and in Africa, where individuality has no existence, parents kill their children, and children expose their parents when unable to support themselves. In the highly centralized France, foundling hospitals abound, and it is but quite recently that any effort has been made to diffuse the blessings of education among the masses of the people. The growth of centralization in the United Kingdom, has been accompanied by a growing disregard for the rights of children, and child-murder now occupies the place that in France is filled by the foundling hospital. No provision exists for the general education of the people, and the feeling of responsibility declines with the decline of individuality that has attended the consolidation of the land, and the substitution of day laborers for small proprietors.

In decentralized Germany, on the contrary, there is a steady increase in the provision for education. It is, however, in the highly decentralized Northern States of the Union that we see the most conclusive evidence of a growing feeling of responsibility in this regard. The system of universal education commenced in Massachusetts by her earlier settlers has made its way gradually through New England, New York, Pennsylvania, and all the Western States, aided in all these latter by grants of land from the general government expressly devoted to this object. New York, unaided, exhibits, in her public schools 900,000 students, with school libraries containing 1,600,000 volumes. The public schools of Pennsylvania contain 600,000 students, while Wisconsin, youngest of the States, manifests a disposition to place herself, in this respect, in advance of her elder sisters.

In no part of the world is the subject of education studied with so much care as throughout the Northern States, whereas the highly centralized ones of the South stand alone in the fact that all instruction of the laboring population is by law prohibited. As a natural consequence of this, schools of any kind are few, and the proportion of uninstructed among the white population is extremely great.

Responsibility, individuality, and association grow thus together, each helping and helped by the other, and everywhere they are seen to grow in the direct ratio of the approach of social government to the system under which the wonderful harmony of the heavens is maintained.

§ 4. Lastly, man is distinguished from all other animals by his CAPACITY FOR PROGRESS. The hare, the wolf, the ox, and the camel are the same as those that existed in the days of Homer, or in those of the monarchs of Egypt, who left behind them, in the pyramids, evidence of the absence of individuality among their subjects. Man alone records what he has seen and learned, and man alone profits by the labors of his predecessors. To do this, he requires language, and that he may have that he must have association.

That there may be progress, there must be motion. Motion is itself a result of the incessant decomposition and recomposition of matter, and the work of association is but the incessant decomposition and recomposition of the various forces of man. In a heap of penny newspapers we find portions of the labor of thousands of persons, from the miner of iron and lead ores and of coal, and the collector of rags, to the makers of the types and paper, the engine-makers and engineer, the compositor, the pressman, the writer, editor, and proprietor, and finally to the boys by whom they are distributed; and this exchange of services goes on from day to day, without intermission, throughout the year, each contributor to the work receiving his share of the pay, and each reader of the paper receiving his share of the work.

To have motion there must be heat, and the greater the latter the more rapid will be the former, as is seen in the rapidity with which, in the tropical regions, water is decomposed and returned again in the form of rain, and in the rapid growth and development of their vegetable products. Vital heat is the result of chemical action, the fuel being food, and the solvent some of those juices which result from its consumption. The more rapid the process of digestion, the more healthful and perfect is the motion of the machine. Social heat results from combination, and that the latter may be produced there must be *difference*. "Everywhere," says a writer already referred to, "a simple difference, be it of matter, be it of condition, be it of position, excites a manifestation of vital forces, a mutual exchange of relations between the bodies, each giving to the other what the other does not possess"*—and the picture thus presented of the movements of the inorganic world is just as true in reference to the social one.

The more rapid the consumption of either material or intellectual food, the greater will be the heat that must result, and the more rapid the increase of power to replace the quantity consumed. That consumption may follow closely on production there must be association, and that there cannot be without variety in the modes of employment. That such is the fact will be obvious to all who see how rapid is the spread of ideas in those countries in which agriculture, manufactures, and commerce are combined, compared with that observed in those which are purely agricultural—Ireland, India, the West Indies, Turkey, Portugal, Brazil, and others. Nowhere, however, is the difference more strongly marked than in the Northern States of the Union as compared with the Southern ones. In the one there is great heat and corresponding motion, and the more motion the greater is the force. In the other there is little heat, but little motion, and very little force.

Progress requires motion. Motion comes with heat, and heat results from association. Association brings with it individuality and responsibility, and each aids in the development of the other while profiting by the help received from them.

* Guyot. *Earth and Man*, p. 74.

§ 5. The laws here given are those which govern matter in all its forms, whether that of coal, clay, iron, pebble stones, trees, oxen, horses, or men. If true of communities they must be equally so of each and every individual of which they are composed—as are those relating to the atmosphere at large in reference to all the atoms of which it is composed. That they are so will be obvious to every reader who reflects to how great an extent he profits, physically and intellectually, by association with his fellow-men—and that the severest of all punishments is universally recognized as being deprivation of the intercourse he is accustomed to obtain by means of that association. Further reflection will satisfy him that the more perfect his individuality—the greater his material or intellectual wealth—the more perfect is his power to determine for himself what shall be the extent of his association with his neighbor men. Again, he will see that his responsibility for his actions increases in the ratio of the increase of his power to determine for himself what shall be his course in life—that if he be poor and perishing for want of food, he cannot be held to the same rigid responsibility that might with propriety be exacted were he in affluent circumstances. Lastly, he will be satisfied that his power of progress is in the direct ratio of his ability to combine his efforts with those of his fellow-man, and that, materially and intellectually, the power of production tends to increase with every increase in the demand for either commodities or ideas resulting from the increased ability of others to furnish commodities or ideas in exchange for them.

Were the reader now to ask himself to what it was that he had been indebted for being the man he is, his answer would be that it had been to his power of association with his fellow-men of the present, and with those of the past who have left behind the records of their experience. Were he to extend his inquiry with a view to determine what it was of which he would least desire to be deprived, he would find that it was the power of association. Next, and only second to that, he would desire perfect volition—the right to determine when, how, and with whom he would labor and what disposition he should make of the product. Deprived of volition he would feel himself an irresponsible being. With it, knowing that it depended upon himself what should be his future, he would feel responsible for the proper use of the advantages that he possessed—and would have every inducement so to strengthen his faculties as to qualify himself for rising in the world himself, and for providing for his wife and children—and every step in this direction would be but the preparation for further progress.

Social science treats of man in his efforts for the maintenance and improvement of his condition, and may now be defined to be *the science of the laws which govern man in his efforts to secure for himself the highest individuality, and the greatest power of association with his fellow-men.*

# CHAPTER III.

## OF INCREASE IN THE NUMBERS OF MANKIND.

§ 1. THAT the power of association may increase, and that there may be increased motion among men, accompanied by an increase of ability to command the forces of nature, there must be increase in the numbers occupying a given space—or in other words, population must increase in density. That it has done so, is shown in the fact that the population of France has doubled since the commencement of the last century—that that of Great Britain has doubled in the present one—and that New York and Massachusetts, which sixty years since had but 700,000 inhabitants, now contain more than four millions.

The quantity of matter has not, however, grown, nor is it susceptible of increase. Man can make no addition to it, his power over it being limited to effecting changes of place and of form. Such being the case, it is evident that a portion of that which had previously existed, has taken upon itself new and higher forms, passing from the simple ones of granite, shale, clay, or sand, to the complex and heterogeneous ones exhibited in the bones, muscles, and brains of men.

With this increase in the number of persons requiring to be fed, there has been required a corresponding one in the quantity of animal and vegetable food—and, that it might be furnished, it has been necessary that other portions of the rocks, or of the clays and sands resulting from their decomposition, should take upon themselves the forms of wheat and rye, of oats and grass, while others still have passed into the forms of sheep and calves, hogs and oxen. That this change must have taken place is obvious from the fact that large as has been the increase in the number to be fed, the facility of obtaining food is greater now than at any former period. What, however, we may now inquire, has been the agency of man in bringing about these results?

"The phenomena of the visible universe are resolvable into Matter and Motion. These in conjunction make Force; and Matter itself has been regarded, in a metaphysical analysis, as the result and the evidence of an equilibrium of forces. They are in perpetual flux and circulation. Man can neither create nor destroy a particle of matter, nor can he affect the quantity of force in the world. His power is limited to altering the mode of its manifestation, its direction and distribution. It is latent in matter, and he can set it free by destroying the equilibrium of other forces that hold it bound in quiescence. He may do this by giving the appropriate direction to some independent force existing in the storehouse of Nature, which, after accomplishing its mission, enters into a new equilibrium with one or more of the liberated forces, to remain at rest until again evoked for fresh labor. Every development of force, however, involves a consumption of matter—not its destruction, but its change of form. To generate in the battery a given amount of light or heat, to produce a certain amount of electro-magnetic motion, for the purpose of transmitting a message upon the telegraph wires from New York to Buffalo, a certain quantity of zinc must be burned by an acid and converted into an oxide. To propel a steamboat a hundred miles, a given quantity of coal must be decomposed into gas and cinders, and a given quantity of water turned into steam. To effect a muscular action of the human body, the brain—the galvanic battery of man's frame—must send its message along the animal telegraph wires, the nerves, and in doing so part with a portion of its own substance; and the muscle, in obeying the command, undergoes a change by which a portion of its substance loses its vital properties and separates from the living part, uniting with oxygen and being transformed into unorganized matter, to be thrown out of the system. The gymnoti, or electrical eels of South America, by being stimulated to give repeated shocks, become exhausted, so that they may be safely handled. Long repose and abundant food are required to replace the galvanic force which they have exhausted. It is no otherwise, except in degree, with man.

"The electro-magnetic telegraph has made the action of its battery familiar to most of our readers. A number of plates of zinc and copper are arranged alternately in a vessel containing an acid. When the extremities of the apparatus are joined by means of a wire, however long, a chemical action begins upon the surface of the zinc, and a force is propagated along the wire, by which we can raise weights, set wheels in motion, and decompose compounds the elements of which have the strongest affinity for each other. The moment the continuity of the wire is interrupted and the circuit broken, the force disappears, and the action between the acid and the zinc immediately stops. When the communication is restored, the action of the acid upon the zinc is renewed, and the force which had vanished reappears with all its original energy. The substance of the wire, however, is merely the conductor of force, and does not contribute the slightest share to its manifestations. Something analogous to this is the office of man in regard to matter and the forces of nature. He serves merely to give them circulation, without adding to or detracting from their quantity. His person is but a scene in the theatre of their action, in which they have their exits and their entrances, and each one in his time plays many parts, sustaining transmutations of force, and causing them ; but they are immortal in their essence, and run in an endless vicissitude through a round of various utilities, for the maintenance of life, and the means of life."*

We have here perpetual circulation, and the more rapid the motion the greater is the force produced. That circulation has endured from all time, but with every step in the progress of the earth towards its present condition, there has been seen an increase of the machinery of decomposition and recomposition, with steadily increasing tendency towards the development of those forces always latent in matter, and waiting until man shall come to set them free. Geologists inform us that in the Silurian period, the present continent of Europe was represented by little more than a few islands, marking the places now occupied by England, Ireland, France, and Italy. Russia and Sweden were then somewhat more defined, but neither Spain nor Turkey yet existed, and what there was of vegetable or animal life was uniform of character, and lowest in development. Later, we reach the period of the coal formation, when vegetable life abounded, but still of the most monotonous character. The English coal measures, and those of Belgium and of this country, presented then everywhere the same description of

* *Manual of Political Economy*, by E. Peshine Smith, p. 24.

plants, all exhibiting a total absence of true flowers, always the characteristic of a state of low development.

What now, we may inquire, was the object of all this vegetation? To produce decomposition, and thus set free the latent forces of matter. "It is in the stomach of plants," says Goethe, "that development begins." Without that stomach—without that process of digestion—the process of change from the angular forms of the inorganic world to the oval and beautiful ones of the highly developed organism could never have even been begun, nor could the earth have ever become the residence of man, who requires for his support both animal and vegetable food.*

"The animals he consumes are," to quote again from the same writer, "themselves nourished by vegetable aliment. The vegetables, in their turn, digest the inorganic elements supplied by the soil and the air. Modern chemistry has proved that the ultimate constituents of all are carbon, oxygen, nitrogen, and hydrogen, the four principal elements of the organic creation, and sulphur, phosphorus, chlorine, lime, potassium, sodium, iron, and a few other inorganic substances. These must be introduced into the vegetable or animal body, in order that it may live and grow. From these few elements, combined in different numbers and proportions, are formed air and water, the rocks and the earths, which are the result of their decomposition.

"That the elements incorporated into the frame of vegetables and animals, are derived from air, water, earth, and rock, has been demonstrated by repeated experiments, exhibiting the fact that the precise quantities of the identical elements gained by the former had disappeared from the latter, under circumstances artificially arranged so as to exclude the possibility of their being drawn from other contributories than those whose loss was to be examined. For detailed accounts of the experiments and reasoning by which these conclusions are demonstrated, we refer the student to the works of Liebig, and other writers on organic chemistry, who have pursued the path of inquiry which he opened and so successfully wrought.

* "In every given moment is the plant the ruin of the past, and yet at the same time the potentially and actually developing germ of the future; still more, it also appears a perfect, complete, and finished product for the present."—Schleiden. *The Plant*, p. 90.

"The fundamental property of vitality, common to all organized bodies, consists in their constant material renovation; an attribute which distinguishes them from the inert or unorganized bodies, whose composition is always fixed. The latter may be artificially constructed by putting together their constituent parts; while no chemical skill is adequate to the production of wood, sugar, starch, fat, gelatine, flesh, &c., whose elements, though equally simple and equally well known, refuse to combine in organized compounds, otherwise than under the operations of that mysterious power which we call vital force. The growth of a crystal—the highest inorganic process we are acquainted with, involving but one action, that of accretion—may be conducted artificially by the chemist; while the growth of a simple cell, such as compose the yeast fungus, and the minute *algæ* which color the waters of stagnant pools, though the lowest organic process, involves the double action of accretion and disintegration, and defies the power of science to produce. The meanest and least complex form of life it is beyond man's reach to fashion.

"While the ultimate elements of vitality are profusely furnished in the natural world, vegetables alone have sufficient assimilative power to compose their tissues directly from inorganic matter, the liquid and gaseous materials, and the earthy particles, which are minerals decomposed. Not only so, but no part of an organized being can serve as food to vegetables, until, by the process of putrefaction and decay, it has assumed the form of inorganic matter. It is this capacity which renders vegetable organization the essential base of all other. In the absence of vegetation all animals must be carnivorous, and subsist by mutual destruction, which would soon exterminate their species. For this reason it must necessarily precede animal life. That such has been the fact is abundantly proved by geological research, which, reading the history of buried ages in the rocks, shows us that a period of long duration intervened, after the growth of lichens and ferns in the primitive world, before the lowest order of animals made its appearance on the earth.

"Animal organism, on the contrary, requires for its support and development highly organized atoms. The food of animals, in all circumstances, consists of parts of organisms. While some of them feed directly upon vegetation, others, requiring that matter should have taken on a higher order of life before it can support their own, prey upon other and inferior animals. Having a lower assimilative capacity, it is necessary that their food should have been brought by intermediate agents, into combinations agreeing more nearly with those of their own tissues than even vegetable organization. Without some arrangement and gradation of this character, the higher natures must either perish for lack of food, or consume all their activity in chemical transformations, without reserving any for locomotion or other muscular effort. We may remark here, that with this necessity of overcoming and capturing prey, arises a degree of mental power, enabling the carnivorous animals to devise plans, and to compass by association with their fellows, ends beyond their unassisted power. The spider spins an artful web to catch flies, and wolves hunt their game in packs. The superior functions are everywhere united with less energy in the inferior. Those beings in whom the latter prevail are self-sufficing and independent, but have little reach and power beyond the satisfaction of the low primary wants. As we rise in the scale up to man, the crown and roof of things, we find him, of all, the most dependent, the most prone to association, for which, by the faculty of speech, he is most adapted; and by means of association, though *alone* the least self-sufficing of all beings, he wins the dominion over nature and her forces, whether animate or inanimate.

"Another distinction between animal and vegetable life is this: The growth and development of vegetables depend upon the *elimination* of oxygen from the other component parts of their nourishment. They are perpetually exhaling this gas from the surfaces of their leaves into the air. The life of animals exhibits itself in the continual *absorption* of the oxygen of the air, and its combination with certain component parts of the body. Its office is to generate animal heat by burning the combustible substances of the frame. It combines with the carbon of the food, and in so doing precisely the same quantity of heat is disengaged as if it had been directly burned in the air. The result is carbonic acid gas, which is thrown out of the lungs and the skin; this is absorbed by the leaves of plants, the carbon separated and incorporated into their substance, and the oxygen again exhaled into the atmosphere, to resume its round of circulation.

"To trace the cycle a little further—the carbon uniting with water in the plant, forms, among other things, starch, which the sap conveys to the part requiring it. It is found largely in the seeds. Starch exists in wheat to the extent of one-half the weight of the grain, and it consists of carbon and water only. Man eats the wheat, but we find no starch in the human body. When it enters our frames it undergoes a chemical change, a slow burning, in fact, in which the carbon of the starch combines with oxygen, forming carbonic acid gas, which, together with the liberated water in the shape of vapor, is thrown out of the human system into the atmosphere, to be again converted in the laboratory of the plant into the starch from which they were derived. Having served our purpose in keeping up the internal warmth upon which animal life depends, the disengaged elements are recomposed by the plants into part of their substance, which when completed again serve as fuel in the animal economy.

"The instances we have given, will, so far as relates to their *organic* constituents, suffice to exemplify the law that animals and vegetables are mutually convertible one into the other, and depend on each other for existence. The interchange of their elements is accomplished through the medium of the atmosphere from which plants derive far the greatest portion of their nutriment. It is found by burning any form of vegetable matter, in a dry state, that the organic part, which is combustible and disappears in the air, is by far the largest. It ordinarily constitutes from ninety to ninety-seven pounds in every hundred. This part of the plant can only have been formed from air at first, if not directly, yet from compounds whose elements were themselves derived from air, existing in the soil, and taken up by the roots. In the language of Professor Draper, in his *Chemistry of Plants*, 'Atmospheric air is the grand receptacle from which all things spring and to which they all return. It is the cradle of vegetable, and the coffin of animal life.'

"About one pound in ten, upon an average, of the dry weight of cultivated plants, including their roots, stems, leaves and seeds, is formed of matter which existed as a part of the solid substance of the soil in which the plant grew. Every organ in the stalk, stems, and leaves of the plant has a reticulated framework of inorganic matter, the base of which is either silex or lime. Silex, familiar to us in the various shapes of white sand, flint, and crystal of quartz, constitutes more than sixty per cent. in quantity of the soil, sometimes forming as much as ninety-five per cent.* It gives porosity to the soil, in order that water and air may be admitted into its texture. Alumina, the base of clay, on the contrary, renders it compact and retentive. The office of silex in plants is to give strength—to the straw of wheat for example; it serves as the *bone* of all the grass family. From ninety-three to one hundred and fifty pounds of soluble flint are required to form an acre of wheat."†

§ 2. Development thus beginning in the stomach of vegetables is continued in that of animals, until the earth is, by degrees, prepared to serve the purpose of man—and with his coming we find the important difference that whereas all other animals were bound to continue forever the slaves of nature, he alone was gifted with the faculties required for enabling him to become her master, and to make her do his work.

Casting our eyes at the present moment over the earth, we see the same forces everywhere in action, producing new combinations for the support of vegetable life, as a preparation of land as a residence at first of the lower animals, but ultimately for that of man. The amount of heat by which the sea water is raised in the form of vapor is estimated as being equal to the power of 16 billions of horses. Condensed again, that vapor reassumes the form of water,

* "Two hundred pounds weight of earth was dried in an oven, and afterwards put into an earthen vessel. The earth was then moistened with rain water, and a willow-tree, weighing five pounds, was placed therein. During the space of five years the earth was carefully watered with rain water, or pure water; the willow grew and flourished, and to prevent the earth being mixed with fresh earth or dust blown to it by the winds, it was covered with a metal plate perforated with a great number of small holes suitable for the free admission of air only. After growing in the air for five years, the tree was removed and found to weigh 169 pounds and about three ounces; the leaves which fell from the tree every autumn not being included in this weight. The earth was then removed from the vessel, again dried in the oven and afterwards weighed when it was discovered to have lost only about two ounces of its original weight: thus 164 pounds of woody fibre, bark and roots, were certainly produced, but from what source? The air has been discovered to be the source of solid element at last. This statement may at first appear incredible, but on slight reflection its truth is proved, because the atmosphere contains carbonic acid, which is the compound of 714 parts by weight, of oxygen, and 338 parts by weight, of carbon."

† Smith. *Manual of Political Economy*, p. 25.

which descending in rain, has again to seek the ocean, and in its passage carries with it large quantities of soil, resulting from the decomposition of the rocks of which the earth is formed—and that decomposition is in its turn a consequence of the ever-varying temperatures, themselves consequences of motion among the particles of which the water and the air are composed. "The frost," says Dr. Clarke, "is God's plow which he drives through every inch of the ground, opening each clod, and pulverizing the whole," and fitting all the parts for readily entering into new combinations.

The particles of earth thus yielded are, by means of the moving waters, brought into close connection with each other, and here again we find difference leading to combination and producing motion. The greater the variety of the particles, the greater will be the ability of the compound to yield support to vegetable life, as is seen to be the case in the deltas of the Mississippi, the Amazon, and the Ganges, all furnishing trees of gigantic size, surrounded by shrubs of every description, growing in the rankest luxuriance. Here we find the lower forms of animal life, but the impurity of the air forbids that they should, during a long period of time, become the residence of man, or even of the higher order of brute animals.

Vast quantities of this earth pass into the ocean, and here it is taken up and passed through the stomach of myriads of animated beings, of which the ocean is the residence. The recent deep sea soundings of the Atlantic have brought to light the fact that no earth is found to attach itself to the lead, while hosts of microscopic animals are brought by it from the bottom of the great deep.

"Within its bosom," says a recent writer, "tiny insects are at work, upon which nature has imposed, in addition to the quest for food and the care for their offspring, the perpetual labor of building new houses. For defence as well as for shelter, the shell-fish toils continually, repairing, enlarging, and renewing his own dwelling-place; and dying at last, he leaves it as a contribution to the growing thickness of shelly limestone. For thousands of miles, in more southern seas, still humbler insects erect their massive coral walls, which, now skirting long coastlines, and now encircling solitary islands, bid defiance to the angriest waters; and, as they die, generation after generation, they leave, in rocky beds of coralline limestone, an imperishable memorial of their exhaustless labors. These rocks contain, chained down in a seemingly everlasting imprisonment, two-fifths of their weight of carbonic acid. This has been derived either directly or indirectly from the atmosphere, and thus the sea must ever be drinking in carbonic acid from the air. The labors of marine animals, therefore, like the burying of vegetable matter, should cause a yearly diminution of the absolute quantity of this gas contained in the atmosphere, were no other natural operation to compensate for the constant removal.

"But the earth herself breathes for this purpose. From cracks and fissures, in the crust, which occur in vast numbers over the surface of the earth, carbonic acid gas issues in large quantities, and daily mingles itself with the ambient air. It sparkles in the springs of Carlsbad; rushes as from subterranean bellows on the table land of Paderborn; chinks in the pockets of the Prince of Nassau; astonishes innocent travellers in the Grotto del Cane; interests the chemical geologist in the caves of Pyrmont; and is terrible to man and beast in the fatal 'Valley of Death,' the most wonderful of the wonders of Java. And, besides, it doubtless issues still more abundantly from the unknown bottom of the expanded waters which occupy so large a proportion of the surface of the globe. From these many sources, continually flowing into the air, or rising into the sea, carbonic acid is daily supplied in place of that which is daily withdrawn, to be buried in the solid crust. Did we know after what lapse of time the earth would again breathe out what is thus daily entombed, we should be able to express in words how long this slowly revolving secular wheel requires fully to perform one of its immense gyrations.

"Thus, like the watery vapor of the atmosphere, its carbonic acid also is continually circulating. While that which floats in the air, during one generation, circles many times, it may be, from the atmosphere to the plant, from the plant to the animal, and from the animal to the air again—never really the property of any, and never lingering long in one stay—the whole created carbon is slowly moving in a greater circle between earth and air. It rises from the earth at one end of the curve in the state of an elastic gas; it amuses itself by the way in assuming for brief intervals many successive varieties of plant-form and animal-form, till it is finally buried in the earth again, at the other end of the curve, in the state of solid limestone and fossil plants."*

The beds of limestone resulting from the labor of these little beings, who thus absorb carbonic acid from the atmosphere, become in their turn nuclei of islands, destined to furnish places of abode for the lower orders of animals, and ultimately for man. What is the process by which the work of preparation is accomplished, is well described in the following passage :—

"The coral islands of the tropical seas present the most remarkable examples of the rapid clothing of a naked rock with vegetable life, and its preparation for the habitation of human beings. The creatures which build up these islands from unknown depths in the ocean partake, as is indicated by the name of their species, zoophyte, or animal plant, in the characteristics of both orders of vitality. They fulfil their functions without a heart or system of circulation—the several polypi in a group have separate mouths and tentacles, and separate stomachs ; but beyond this there is no individual property—and form a living sheet of animals, fed and nourished by numerous mouths and stomachs, but coalescing by intervening tissues. They possess no more power of motion than is sufficient to thrust out their arms to seize the food that drifts past them, and they propagate by buds, the bud commencing as a slight prominence on the side of the parent ; the bud enlarges, a circle of tentacles grows out, with a mouth in the centre, and the enlargement goes on till the young equals the parent in size, when it begins to protrude buds itself—and the group thus continues to grow. They secrete the coral as the quadruped secretes its bones, until single reefs are formed and attain the surface of the water. But it is essential to the life of these submarine builders that they should be covered by the waves, and when they have reached low water mark they die. A new process now begins, in the accumulation of loose materials upon its summit, from coral boulder—broken off from the reef by the waves, thrown up from below, and gradually ground into fragments—coral gravel and sand. Agassiz states that all that portion of Florida known as the Everglades is only a vast coral bank, composed of a series of more or less parallel reefs, which have successively grown from the bottom of the sea up to the surface, and have been added to the main land,

* Dr. Johnston, in *Blackwood's Magazine*, May, 1853.

by the gradual filling of the intervals which separate them with deposits of the coralline sand, and debris brought thither by the action of the tides and the currents.

"The cocoanut, with its husk, being well adapted to be wafted by the waves, it takes root upon the naked sand of the coral island, just lifted above the level of the ocean, and, washed by the spray, grows luxuriantly. Nourished at first by only so much of organic aliment as the remains of the zoophytes, who build the island, supply, the decay of its leaves soon furnishes a mould which suffices for other vegetable growth. Its uses are manifold: the inhabitants, when they come, find in it material for the scanty dresses which the climate requires, drinking-vessels from the shell of its nut, and other utensils, mats, cordage, fishing-lines, and oil, besides food, drink, and building materials. In every stage, from its first formation after the fall of the blossom, to the hard, dry, and ripe nut, that has almost begun to germinate, the fruit may be seen *at the same time, on the same tree.* The pandanus, or screw-pine, another tree which soon roots itself in the scanty soil, throwing out props from the trunk, which plant themselves in the ground, and widen the supporting base as it grows, furnishes a sweetish, husky fruit, 'which, though a little bitter,' says Mr. Dana, in his Geology of the Exploring Expedition, from which these facts are drawn, 'admits of being stored away for food when other things fail.' Fish and crabs from the reefs, and the large fish caught with wooden hooks from the deep waters, eke out the subsistence of the natives. 'From such scanty resources,' says Mr. Dana, 'a population of 10,000 persons is supported on the single island of Taputeouea, whose habitable area does not exceed six square miles.'

"The process in this case, by which the emerging peak of the submarine mountain is fitted by the germination of vegetation for a human abode, is rapid. That by which the peaks of the land mountain have crumbled into soil involves more intermediate stages, and a much greater variety of results. Some of the rocks, such as slates and shales, decompose with such facility, that the whole process may be observed within a brief period, and we have constant opportunities of watching its progress. The granitic rocks, however, which, constituting in the view of geologists the lower and earlier strata, have been made, upon the disruption and upheaving of the crust of the earth, to occupy the highest place, are of a less frangible character. But their chemical composition is such as to favor their speedy disintegration under the action of the elements. The presence of alkalies in the feldspar and mica, which are combined with silex in granite, exerts a powerful influence in this change. Carbonic acid, the great solvent for the hardest materials, decomposes the potash with which silica is combined in the feldspar, and it is made soluble. The intensity of the frost, and the length of time during which rocks on the mountain tops are exposed to it, the suddenness of the changes of temperature to which they are subjected, and which, from their being poor conductors of heat, involve an inequality in the contraction and expansion of the surface and the interior, which induces flaking and cracking, the dampness of the air during the summer, when watery vapors condense upon their summits, are among the circumstances which hasten the destruction of rocks in these places. As disintegration is accomplished by the process of weathering, the decomposed particles fall by their own weight, and are washed by the rains into the valleys beneath, which receive in the same manner the contributions of the intermediate rocks. During this process, the rocks are not merely mechanically broken into small fragments, but from their insoluble constituents, soluble salts, as those of lime, soda, &c., are generated, which may be absorbed by the root of plants. In the decomposition of feldspar, the silicate of potassa is gradually removed by the water, and while the sand remains upon the sloping surfaces, the fine alumina or clay accumulates in the valleys, and forms a mixture of clay and sand, which is more favorable to the support of grass and grain. Thus every gradation is presented, from the naked granite of the hill-tops through the thin, porous soils of the slopes, to the rich meadow lands of the valleys.

"Vegetation of some kind, however, can find nourishment even on the surface of the rock.* Lichens and algæ grow high above

* "Look at a recently exposed surface of a block of granite for instance, on the summit of the Brocken; there we find that vegetation is soon developed, in the form of a little delicate plant, which requires the microscope for its recognition; and this is nourished by the small quantity of atmospheric water impregnated with carbonic acid and ammonia. This, the so-called violet-stone, a scarlet, pulverulent coating over the bare stone, which on account of the peculiar smell of violets which it emits when rubbed, has become a curiosity, industriously sought by the thoughtful wanderer on the Brocken. By the gradual decay and decomposition of this little plant,

the line of perpetual snow; and in bleak northern climes, upon the bare face of the granite rock, a species of lichens flourishes, which the hunger-pinched Canadian voyageur seeks for food, and gives the appetizing name of '*tripe de roche.*' Decaying vegetable matter of such kinds is swept by every shower down hill, to accumulate at the base with the deposits of mineral origin. After a sufficient period, a soil is thus formed at the bottom of the slopes, which is capable of sustaining heavy timber. The first tree sheds its leaves and branches to feed the fattening soil, in a circle around its trunk, whose area is measured by the spread of its branches. The probable process from this starting-point is this: Upon the outer circumference of the first circle thus nourished, and that edge of it, which, lying between the trunk and the hill-top, upon the ascending slope, is inferior to the lowest point in the collected elements of vegetable nutrition, it becomes possible for another tree to grow. This, in its turn, becomes the centre of a circle of fertilized ground, upon whose upper exterior the material to support a new growth is accumulated, by the droppings of its stem and branches. Each new plant thus manures the ground for its successor, and vegetation creeps up the hill-side, along a soil of constantly diminishing richness, and which, though made more fat and tenacious by its growth, is always parting with some portion of its mineral and vegetable elements to fatten the valley beneath it. The process, like so many others in the operations of nature, is one of action and reaction, of a disturbance of equilibrium which sets at work the machinery for its own restoration. The elemental forces, gravitation, and the wash of running water, carry to the

a very thin layer of humus is by degrees produced, which now suffices to procure from the atmosphere food sufficient for a couple of great blackish-brown lichens. These lichens, which densely clothe the heaps of earth round the shafts of the mines of Fahlun and Dannemora in Sweden, and through their gloomy color, which they impress on all around, make those pits and shafts look like the gloomy abysses of death, have been appropriately called by the botanists the Stygian and Fahlun lichens. But they are no messengers of death here: their decay prepares the soil for the elegant little Alpine moss, the destruction of which is speedily followed by the appearance of greener and more luxuriant mosses, until sufficient soil has been formed for the whortleberry, the juniper, and finally for the pine. Thus, from an insignificant beginning, an ever-increasing coating of humus grows up over the naked rock, and a vegetation, continually stronger and more luxuriant, takes up its position, not to be nourished on that humus, which increases instead of decreasing with every decaying generation, but by its means to be supplied with nourishment from the atmosphere."—Schleiden, *The Plant*, p. 162.

lowest levels the mineral and organic nutriment for vegetation; and vegetation, thus originated, carries them back again up the slopes, preparing a soil for its own progress as it goes. The slimmest and scantiest vegetation is always in the advance, like the pioneers and light troops who clear the ground for the heavy columns of an army."*

The plant is thus, as we see, a manufacturer of soil, and what, in this respect, is true of it, is equally so of all the living and moving beings that walk the face of earth. The development commenced in the stomach of the plant is continued and carried out in that of the man, who has been well compared to a locomotive engine. Into the stomach of the latter we introduce fuel under circumstances tending to promote its decomposition, or motion of the elements of which it is composed—and this motion gives force. The man takes into his stomach, as fuel, the various products of the vegetable and animal kingdom, and there they are subjected to the process of decomposition, whence result vital heat and force. The manner in which plants and animals combine to produce this increasing motion, is well exhibited in the following passage:—

"Man himself, and other animals, assist in the same conversion. They consume vegetable food with the same final result as when it perishes by actual decay, or is destroyed by the agency of fire. It is conveyed into the stomach in the form in which the plant yields it; it is breathed out again from the lungs and the skin, in the form of carbonic acid and water. We can follow out this operation, however, more closely, and it will be both interesting and instructive to do so.

"The leaf of the living plant sucks in carbonic acid from the air and gives off the oxygen contained in this gas. It retains only the carbon. The roots drink in water from the soil, and out of this carbon and water the plant forms starch, sugar, fat, and other substance. The animal introduces this starch, sugar or fat, into its stomach, and draws in oxygen from the atmosphere by its lungs; and with these materials it undoes the previous labors of the living plant, delivering back again from the lungs and the skin both the starch and the oxygen in the form of carbonic acid and water. The process is clearly represented in the following scheme:—

* Smith. *Manual of Pol. Econ.* p. 38.

| | Takes in | Produces |
|---|---|---|
| THE PLANT, | *Carbonic acid* by its leaves; *Water* by its roots. | *Oxygen* from its leaves; *Starch, &c.*, in its solid substance. |
| THE ANIMAL, | *Starch and fat* in the stomach; *Oxygen* into the lungs. | *Carbonic acid and water* from the skin and the lungs. |

"The circle begins with carbonic acid and water, and ends with the same substances. The same material—the same carbon, for example—circulates over and over again, now floating in the invisible air, now forming the substance of the growing plant, now of the moving animal, and now again dissolving into the air, ready to begin anew the same endless revolution. It forms part of a vegetable to-day—it may be built into the body of a man to-morrow; and, a week hence, it may have passed through another plant into another animal. What is mine this week is yours the next. There is, in truth, no private property in ever-moving matter."*

§ 3. In the early periods of society the changes of form are very slow, and thus we see that, in the days of the Plantagenets, and for centuries afterwards, the yield of an acre of land was but six or eight bushels of wheat. Small as it was, it was, nevertheless, attended with constant improvement in the form of matter resulting from the motion that thus far had been obtained. The rocks had been decomposed, and the clays and the sands had taken upon themselves a higher form—and the beautiful green of the wheat had replaced the sombre brown of the earth. Step by step, however, man is seen obtaining higher command of the various forces provided for his use, and passing onward until at a later period he obtains thirty, forty, and fifty bushels to the acre; while of other commodities they count by hundreds.

Without vital heat this command could not be obtained, and without fuel there could be no heat. That fuel, as we see, is food, without which there can be no vital action—and thus it is that we reach the point at which man and other animals stand upon a level with each other. In common with them all, he eats, drinks, and sleeps, and in common with them he must obtain supplies of food.

Looking around, he sees vast bodies of matter held in a quies-

* Blackwood's *Magazine*, May, 1853.

cent state, by reason of the force of gravitation, and therefore unproductive. It is a magazine of power, latent, waiting help to set it free. The hard soil yields scanty herbage, but he now loosens it so as to expose its particles to the action of the sun and the rain, and, that done, he places therein a seed ready to receive into its stomach the food required for its nourishment. It sprouts, and the plant grows by aid of earth and atmosphere, yielding the oats, the rye, or the corn required for his support, or that of the animals on which he feeds. In all this, however, he has done no more than is done by the man who feeds the locomotive, placing matter in a situation to become decomposed, and thus giving individuality to its atoms, by help of which they are enabled to combine with other atoms. The act of combination is one of motion, and that motion gives force.

To accomplish this, he has ploughed deeper, and has enabled a larger quantity of soil to become presented to the action of the rain and the sun. He has dug drains, and has thus enabled the water to run off, that otherwise would have remained stagnant and would have destroyed his seed; and precisely as he has thus facilitated the motion of matter he has found himself rewarded by a more rapid increase in the quantity that has taken upon itself the form required for his purposes.

The greater the motion, the more rapid is the improvement in the form. The stiff pine gives way to the graceful barley, while beautiful fields of clover replace the rank weeds of the swamp, and the gaunt wolf disappears from the land that now maintains the high-bred horse and well-formed man.

With increased control over the natural forces, he is thus enabled to obtain a constant increase of food from any given surface, with steady increase in the power to live in connection with his fellow man. Association grows, giving in its turn power to bring into activity other forces that thus far have remained dormant and waiting the help of man. He turns up the limestone and subjects it to the process of decomposition, furnishing carbonic acid to the air, and giving quicklime to the earth. He digs the coal, and that in its turn is decomposed, furnishing to the atmosphere new supplies of the material that is to be recomposed in the form of vegetables for his nourishment. He mines the iron ore, to be decomposed by help of coal, and here again are new supplies of the materials required for the support of organic life; and furnished, too, by the very process required for giving him instruments needed for the work of cultivation. The matter thus decomposed continues in motion, and must so continue while men increase in the power of association. The various ores never again return to their original form, nor does the lime become again limestone, after it has entered into the composition of food. Eaten, it returns again to the atmosphere, or to the earth, and the man himself at length dies and is buried, and thus repays the debt he owes to nature. Even, however, while still living, he is constantly absorbing and giving out again to the earth and atmosphere the atoms of which his system is composed, as is well explained in the following passage:—

"In natural forests, where the leaves are annually shed and the trees periodically die, the mineral matter quits the soil for the plant, and again, in the decaying plant, returns to the soil, thus making but a short stage up and down from earth to plant, and from plant back to the earth again. And it is so also in natural meadows, where yearly in autumn the grass ripens, withers, and returns its mineral matter to the soil, and yearly again in spring the young herbage springs up and feeds on the relics of the previous year. But it is different when the vegetable produce is consumed by animals. It then enters into their stomachs, is dissolved or digested, and its several parts taken up by vessels provided for the purpose, to be conveyed to the parts of the body where their services are required. The saline matter we need not at present follow further than the blood and the tissues. The phosphoric acid and the lime—in the form of phosphate of lime—are chiefly deposited in the bones.

"The importance of this phosphate of lime to the animal economy will be apparent, when we mention that ordinarily dry bones leave, on burning, half their weight of a white ash, which consists for the most part of phosphate of lime.

"But, as we have already explained, all the parts of the body, even the most solid, are in a constant course of renewal. To this law of change the bones are subject equally with the soft parts, and the phosphoric acid carried in to-day is in a few days carried out again, mixed up with the other refuse and excretions of the body; and finally the body itself dies, and all its material parts are at once returned to the earth from which it came. There they undergo, through the agency of the air, a complete breaking-up or decomposition, by which their mineral matter itself is brought into a condition in which it can enter usefully into the roots of new plants. There are other minutiæ in reference to the revolution of this mineral matter which are full of interest, but we will not try the patience of our readers by insisting upon them in this place. The general changes we have indicated are represented briefly as follows:—

| | Taken in by | Produced |
|---|---|---|
| The Plant, | Phosphoric acid, lime, common and other salts from the soil. | Perfect substance of plants. |
| The Animal, | *a.* Parts of plants. | Perfect bone, blood, and tissues. |
| | *b.* The bone and tissues, with oxygen from the lungs. | Phosphates and other salts in the excretions. |
| The Soil, | Excretions of animals, dead animals and plants. | Phosphoric acid, lime, &c. &c. |

"It may be that a careful hunter after human earth might scrape together as much as would 'stop a hole to keep the wind away.' But our science teaches us that the earth is not the kind of stuff that clay is made of, and such vile uses are, after all, only imaginary slights to which our cherished ashes can never be subjected. They have another appointed use, from which, treat them as they may, they cannot long be kept. The plant is wonderfully framed, so as not to grow without the phosphoric acid, &c., which it is bound to gather up and supply to the growing animal. And the soil is so poorly provided with these and other necessary substances, that plant and animal are both ordained to return without fail their borrowed material to mother earth when the term of life has come. Thus a constant circulation of the same comparatively small quantity of mineral matter is secured, and a duty is laid upon each particle zealously to prepare for a new service, as soon as each earlier commission is performed. As we have no property in, so we ought to have no foolish affection or reverence for dead ashes; and certainly we ought to have no fear that they can ever long be withheld from connecting themselves, in some form or other, with new phases of vegetable and animal life."*

"Plant and animal are both," as we here see, ordained to return

* Ibid.

their borrowed materials to mother earth," and it is *upon this condition only that motion can be increased, or even maintained.* Our great mother, Earth, *gives* nothing, but she is willing to *lend* everything, and the larger the demand made upon her the larger will be the supply, provided, that man always recollects that he is but a borrower from a great bank, in which punctuality is as much required as it is in the banks of America, France, or England.

That this condition may be complied with, there must be association, and difference is in the social, as well as in the material world, indispensable to association. The man whose land yields corn does not require to associate with his brother corn grower; the sugar planter does not need to exchange with his neighbor planter—nor does the wool grower require to meet his brother farmer who also has wool to sell—but they, each and all, find it advantageous to exchange labor and its products with the carpenter, the blacksmith, the mason, the sawmiller, the miner, the furnace man, the spinner, the weaver, and the printer, as all of these require to purchase food, and to give in pay for it their services, or the various commodities with which they have to part. Where there is diversity of employment, the producer and the consumer take their places by the side of each other, and there is rapid motion among the products of labor, with constant increase in the power to repay to mother earth her loans, and to establish with her a credit for larger ones in future. Where, on the contrary, there are none but farmers or planters, and where consequently there is no motion in society, the producer and the consumer are so widely separated that the power to repay the loans from the great bank dies away, and motion gradually ceases among the particles of the earth itself—as we see to be the case in all the purely agricultural countries. Virginia and the Carolinas have been steadily engaged in exhausting the elements of fertility originally contained in the soil, because of the absence of consumers, and the necessity for dependence on distant markets; and such, to a great extent, is the case throughout this country, and particularly in the Southern States. The farmer who commences on rich prairie land, obtains at first forty or fifty bushels of corn to the acre, but the quantity declines from year to year, and finally falls to fifteen or twenty bushels. A century since, the farmers of New York were accustomed to obtain twenty-four bushels of wheat, but the average now is but little more than half that quantity, while the rich State of Ohio has fallen to an average of only eleven bushels, and with every step in the progress of decline there is a diminution of ability to associate; the power of the soil to yield support being always the measure of the power of men to live together. That this state of things must certainly arise when the consumer and the producer are widely separated, is clearly shown in the remarkable emigration at this moment going on from Ohio, whose settlement commenced but little more than half a century since; from Georgia, with a population of 900,000, and with a territory capable of supporting half the people of the Union; and from Alabama, that but forty years since was a wilderness occupied chiefly by a few bands of straggling Indians.*

"The plant," says Professor Johnston, in the article already so largely quoted from, "is the servant of the animal." "Man," as he continues, "placed upon the earth, without the previous existence of the plant, were utterly helpless. He could not live either upon earth or upon air, and yet his body requires a constant supply of the elements contained in each. It is the plant which selects, collects, and binds together these indigestible materials, and manufactures them into food for man and other animals. And these appear *only to throw back again to their toiling slaves the waste materials which they cannot further use, to be again worked up into palatable food.* In this aspect, the plant appears only the appointed bond-servant of the animal; and yet, how willing, how

* "True it is that thorns and thistles, ill-favored and poisonous plants, well named by botanists *rubbish plants*, mark the track which man has proudly traversed through the earth. Before him lay original Nature in her wild but sublime beauty. Behind him he leaves the desert, a deformed and ruined land; for childish desire of destruction, or thoughtless squandering of vegetable treasures, has destroyed the character of nature, and, terrified, flies man himself from the arena of his actions, leaving the impoverished earth to barbarous races or to animals, so long as yet another spot in virgin beauty smiles before him. Here again in selfish pursuit of profit, and, consciously or unconsciously, following the abominable principle of the great moral vileness which one man has expressed, '*après nous le déluge*,' he begins anew the work of destruction. Thus did cultivation, driven out, leave the East, and perhaps the deserts formerly robbed of their coverings; like the wild hordes of old over beautiful Greece, thus rolls this conquest with fearful rapidity from east to west through America, and the planter now leaves the already exhausted land, the eastern climate become infertile through the demolition of the forests, to introduce a similar revolution into the far West."—Schleiden, *The Plant*, p. 306.

beautiful, how interesting a slave it is. It works for ever, yet it is self-tasked. It toils itself to death, yet, punctually as spring comes round, it rises, young, beautiful, and willing as ever, rejoicing to resume its destined work."* It can do so, however, only on the condition that "the waste materials" which man can no further use be returned to the place from whence they had been drawn.

Those materials, as we have seen, come chiefly from the atmosphere; but, in order that they may be drawn from thence, it is indispensable that the earth itself should contain the ingredients required for combination with them.† The atmosphere that now rests upon the worn-out tobacco fields of Virginia contains the same elements with that which rests upon the finest farms of Massachusetts, of Belgium, or of England ; yet the power of combination has no existence, because certain other elements have been withdrawn and sent abroad, in the absence of which there can be no motion in the soil. While they existed there, men could live together on the land; but with impoverishment of the latter the former have disappeared. That the power of association among men may increase, there must be a constantly increasing interchange—motion—between the earth and the atmosphere, and that there cannot be in any country where there is no diversity of employment; and in which, consequently, the place of consumption being remote from that of production, the farmer is limited to the cultivation of such commodities only as will bear transportation to distant countries. Hence it is that we should see a great decline in

* Blackwood's *Magazine.*

† "All the nitrogenous components of plants, which we use as food, consist, it is true, of merely carbon, hydrogen, oxygen and nitrogen. But the presence of these substances alone does not help the plant in the least; it cannot form from them a granule of albumen or gluten, unless it contains, at the same time and in the proper relative condition, salts of phosphoric acid. The useful starch, the sweet sugar, the cooling citric acid, the aromatic oil of oranges, are indeed composed solely of carbon, hydrogen and oxygen; but the plant cannot prepare those gifts for us, out of ever so great an abundance of these elements, if it does not possess also alkaline salts. The slender stalk of the wheat could not lift itself to ripen its grain in the sun's rays, unless the soil furnished it with silex, through which it gives its cells that solidity necessary to enable it to maintain an erect position."—Schleiden, *The Plant*, p. 206.

"The conclusion is therefore simple: that we must in future never cultivate the potato as the first crop, as has generally been hitherto done throughout the greater part of Europe, but we must begin with rye, and allow the potato to follow it, or perhaps still better, to come two years later, after the productive powers of the land in those countries of the eastern continent in which there are few or no manufactures—Ireland, Portugal, Turkey, India, and others. Hence, too, it is that with declining population and diminished motion in society, we see the difficulty of obtaining food increasing with diminution of the numbers requiring to be fed. Famines are now more frequent in India than they were a century since when the population was far more numerous, and when combination of action existed throughout that country. Looking to past ages, we see everywhere facts of a similar kind. The valley of the Euphrates once exhibited millions of well-fed men; but as they passed away motion ceased, and its few straggling occupants now obtain with difficulty the means of supporting life. When the African province was well peopled, its people were well fed, but the few who now remain perish for want of food. So has it been in Attica and in Greece generally, in Asia Minor, in Egypt, everywhere in fact. Association, combination of action, is required to enable man to obtain control over the various forces existing in nature—and that combination can never take place except when the loom and the spindle take their natural places by the side of the plough and the harrow. The consumer must take his place by the side of the producer, to enable man to comply with the condition upon which he obtains loans from the great bank of mother Earth—the simple condition that when he has done with the capital furnished to him he will return it to the place from which it had been taken.

In all those countries in which this condition is complied with, we see a steady increase in the motion of the matter destined to furnish man with food, and equally steady increase in the number of persons requiring to be supplied, with constant improvement in the quantity and quality of food to be divided among an increasing population. In the days of the Plantagenets and Lancasters, when the population of England but little exceeded two millions, an acre of land yielded but six bushels of wheat, and, small as

clover, if we would raise a healthy produce, and in future be rid of the plague to which we have recently been subject. The fundamental proposition will henceforward stand firmly established, that the nutrient matter which the plant itself takes up from the soil consists essentially only of the inorganic constituents of the same, and that these, and not the organic substances, constitute the peculiar richness of a soil."—*Ibid.*, p. 181.

were the numbers to be fed, famines were frequent and severe. In our day, we see eighteen millions occupying the same surface, and obtaining greatly increased supplies of very superior food.

Looking to France, we meet precisely similar facts. In 1760, the population was 21,000,000, and the total produce of grain was 94,500,000 hectolitres; whereas, in 1840, the former had risen to 34,000,000, and the latter to 182,516,000 hectolitres, giving to each person twenty per cent. more in quantity in the latter than in the earlier period, with great improvement in the quality of the grain itself; and yet the surface appropriated to the cultivation of the cereals has scarcely at all increased. In the same time the potato culture has been introduced, and green crops of various kinds now furnish supplies of food that themselves alone are two-thirds as great as the whole quantity produced but eighty years before.* The total product has been trebled in that time, while the numbers to be fed have increased but 60 per cent. The French peasant now pays his debts to mother earth, returning to her the manure yielded by his crops, and he is enabled so to do, because of the growing diversity of employment; whereas, at an earlier period, when manufactures had scarcely an existence in that country, famines were so numerous and sometimes so severe as to sweep off a large proportion of the very scattered population.

So it is in Belgium, in Germany, and in every other country in which diversity of employment—difference—facilitates the work of association; while precisely the reverse is observed in all those purely agricultural countries that are steadily employed in exhausting the soil, and diminishing the power of association, as we see to have been so uniformly the case in Virginia and Carolina on this side of the ocean, and Portugal and Turkey on the other.

With every step in the progress towards increased power to associate resulting from increased motion among the elements of

* The facts are thus stated by *M. de Jonnés*, in his *Statistique de l'Agriculture de France.*

| | 1760. | 1840. |
|---|---|---|
| Wheat . . . | 150 | 208 litres. |
| Inferior grains . . | 300 | 333 |
| Potatoes and green crops . | | 291 |
| Total per head . . . | 450 | 832 |

which food is composed, man is enabled to call to his help other forces to be employed in grinding his grain and transporting its product to market—in converting his trees into planks and preparing them for the construction of houses—in converting his wool into cloth—and finally, in carrying his messages with such rapidity that time and space seem almost annihilated. With each, he is enabled more and more to economize his own labors, and to devote his time and mind with increased force to the production of the grain that is to be ground, the trees that are to be sawed, or the wool that is to be converted, and thus to make provision for increased association with his fellow-man, and increased correspondence with the distant ones, each step being but the preparation for a new and greater one.

With the development of the latent powers of the earth there is thus a daily increasing tendency towards increase in the movement of matter, and improvement of the form in which it exists, passing from the inorganic to the organic, and terminating in its highest one—that of man. The more that matter tends to take upon itself this highest form, the more rapidly does the power of association grow, with constantly increasing power on the part of man to direct the great forces of nature, accompanied by an equally rapid growth of individuality, or power of self-government—warranting us in holding him to a constant increase of responsibility.

§ 4. The law of the relative increase in the numbers of mankind, and in the supply of food and other commodities required for their support, will now be found in the following propositions :—

Motion gives force, and the more rapid the motion the greater is the force obtained.

With motion matter takes upon itself new and higher forms, passing from the simple ones of the inorganic world and through the complex ones of the vegetable world to yet more complex ones of the animal one, and ending in man.

The more rapid the motion the greater the tendency to changes of form, to increase of force, and increase of power at the command of man.

The more simple the forms in which matter exists the less is the power of resistance to gravitation ; the greater the tendency to centralization, the less the motion, and the less the force.

The more complex the form, the greater becomes the power of resistance to gravitation—the greater the tendency to decentralization—the greater the motion—and the greater the force.

With every increase of power on one side, there is diminished resistance on the other. The more the motion produced, the greater must, therefore, be the tendency to further increase of motion and of force.

The most complex and highly organized form in which matter exists, is that of man, and here, alone, do we find that capacity for direction required for producing increase of motion and of force.

Wherever man most exists we should, therefore, find the greatest tendency to the decentralization of matter—to increase of motion—to further changes of form—and to that higher development which commences in the vegetable world, and ends in the production of further supplies of men.

With every increase in the extent to which matter has taken upon itself the form of man, there should consequently be found an increase of his power to guide and direct the forces provided for his use—with constantly accelerating motion, and constantly accelerating changes of form—and constant increase in his power to command the food and clothing required for his support.

---

That, in the material world, the resistance to gravitation is in the direct ratio of organization, will be obvious to the reader on a moment's reflection. Inorganic matter rising in obedience to the influence of heat, with the slightest reduction of temperature it is again condensed, and falls as rain. In the organic world, the lower forms of vegetable life are found in the little plants that return annually to the dust from whence they came; whereas, the higher ones are found in the oak, that, for centuries, spreads its arms to the wind—furnishing, year after year, leaves, flowers, and fruits, despite the force of gravitation. In the animal one, the mollusca, the coral insects, and the polypes—standing lowest in organization—are most obedient to the control of forces by which they are chained to earth; but the obedience diminishes, as we pass upward to the horse, the bee, and the bird. Coming next to man, we find him making his home upon the living waters, or, at his pleasure, diving into the recesses of the ocean—at one time circumnavigating the globe, and at another providing himself with machinery, by means of which he is enabled to descend within the bosom of the great deep, and not only to return from thence himself, but to bring back with him, in opposition to gravitation, such inorganic matter as suits his purposes.

So is it with the races of men. The lower they stand in moral and physical condition, the greater is their subjection to the centralizing forces—and hence it is, that in the early stages of society, when they have little power over nature, we see it to have been so easy for the Attilas and Alarics to collect together hundreds of thousands of men, for the purpose of robbing and murdering those who chanced to be better provided than themselves with worldly goods. Hence, too, it is, that we see the great cities of the world exercising such strong attractive force upon those who are dissolutely disposed, and those who would live by plunder rather than by honest industry.

The direct ratio between motion, force, and function, above affirmed in regard to all organized beings, is fully illustrated in the individual life of man. From birth to manhood his vital functions—digestion, circulation, and assimilation—being rapid and vigorous, greatly overmatch the physical and chemical laws which are in direct antagonism with vitality—and thus do they "make increase of the body" until the term of development is reached. The circulation—the commerce of his system—which represents all the activities of assimilation, ranges from 130 pulsations in a minute to 60, in the ages of decline. The history of his youth is a series of triumphs over the resistance of surrounding agencies, until his grand climacteric is attained; and in all the process of emancipation from the dominion of the opposing forces of nature, the rapidity of the motion within his structure is the measure, and the exponent, of his proper power, life, and liberty. When, however, the scale begins to turn—when motion and its attendant sensibility begin to decline—when the conversion of digestion, the commerce of circulation, and the appropriation of nutrition, begin to abate in celerity and force—he is beginning to die. Thenceforth, the balance of power against him grows steadily, while the resistance of his vital organism as steadily loses motion and force, until at length his frame is forced to obey the laws of decomposition and gravitation.

In the material world, motion among the atoms of matter is a consequence of physical heat. It is therefore greatest at the equator, and it diminishes until, as we approach the poles, we reach the region of centralization and physical death.

In the moral world, motion is a consequence of social heat—motion, as has been already shown, consisting in "an exchange of relations" resulting from the existence of those differences that develop social life. Motion is greatest in those communities in which agriculture, manufactures, and commerce are happily combined, and in which, consequently, society has the highest organization. It diminishes, as we approach the declining despotisms of the East, the regions of centralization and social death. It increases, as we pass from the purely agricultural States of the South, towards the regions of more diversified industry in the Northern and Eastern ones, and there, accordingly, we find decentralization and life.

Centralization, slavery, and death, travel hand in hand together in both the material and the moral world.

§ 5. The view thus presented, differs totally from that now most commonly received, and known as the Malthusian law of population, which may be briefly given in the following words:—

Population tends to increase in a geometrical ratio, while the supplies of food can increase in an arithmetical one only. The former is, therefore, perpetually outstripping the latter, and hence it is, that there is everywhere seen to arise the disease of overpopulation, with its accompaniments, poverty, wretchedness, and death—a disease requiring for its remedy wars, pestilences, and famines on the one hand, or, on the other, the exercise of that "moral restraint," which shall induce men and women to refrain from matrimony, and thus avoid the danger resulting from further addition to the numbers requiring to be fed. Reduced to distinct propositions, the theory may now be given as follows:—

1. Matter tends to take upon itself higher forms, passing from the simple ones of inorganic life to the complex and beautiful ones of vegetable and animal life, and finally terminating in man.

2. This tendency exists in a small degree as relates to the lower forms of life—matter tending to take upon itself the forms of potatoes, turnips, and cabbages, herrings, and oysters, in an arithmetical ratio only.

3. When, however, we reach the highest of all the forms of which matter is capable, we find the tendency to assume that form augmenting in a geometrical ratio; as a consequence of which, while man tends to increase as 1, 2, 4, 8, 16, and 32—the potatoes and cabbages, the peas and turnips, the herrings and the oysters, increase as 1, 2, 3 and 4 only—producing the result that the highest form is perpetually outstripping the lower ones, and causing the disease of over-population.

Were such things asserted in regard to anything else than man, they would be deemed in the highest degree absurd, and those by whom they were asserted, would be required to explain why it was, that an universal law had here been set aside. Everywhere else, the increase in number is in the inverse ratio of development. The little coral insects are required, in quantity innumerable, to build up islands, for animals and men that count by thousands, or by millions. Of the *clio borealis*, thousands are required to furnish a mouthful for the mighty whale. The progeny of a pair of carp would, in a single decade, as we are told, amount to millions. The countless ferns prepare the soil for the single oak; and the progeny of a pair of rabbits would, in twenty years, count by millions—whereas, that of a pair of elephants, would not amount to dozens. When, however, we reach the highest condition of which matter is capable, we learn the existence of a new and greater law, in virtue of which man increases in a geometrical ratio, while the increase of herrings, rabbits, oysters, potatoes, turnips, and all other commodities required for his use, is limited to the arithmetical one! Such is the extraordinary law propounded by Mr. Malthus, as existing in reference to the only being on whom has been impressed the desire for association, as necessary for compliance with the sole condition of his existence; the only one, to whom has been given an infinite variety of capacities fitting him for association with his fellow men, and requiring it for their development; and the only one, too, that—having been gifted with the power to distinguish right from wrong, and thus been made responsible for his actions—might with reason have required, that he should be exempt from any law requiring him to make his election between abstinence from that association which, of all others, tends most to the improvement of his head and heart, on one hand, and starvation on the other. Such, however, according to the generally received doctrines of modern political economy, is the law of population instituted by an all-wise, all-powerful, and all-benevolent Creator, in reference to the being made in his own likeness, and gifted with power to control and direct all the forces of nature to his use—and, strange as it appears, no proposition ever offered for consideration has exercised, or is now exercising, upon the fortunes of the human race a greater amount of influence. That such should have been the case has, in part, resulted from the fact that it has been buttressed up by another one, in virtue of which man is supposed everywhere to have commenced the work of cultivation on rich soils—necessarily those of swamps and river bottoms—with large return to labor; and to have found himself compelled, with the growth of population and of wealth, to have recourse to poorer ones, with constant decline in the return to all his efforts—a theory that, if true, would fully establish the correctness of that of Mr Malthus. What are its claims to being received as true, will now be shown.

# CHAPTER IV.

## OF THE OCCUPATION OF THE EARTH.

§ 1. Look where we may, we see man to have commenced his career as a hunter, subsisting upon the spoils of the chase, and dependent entirely upon the voluntary contributions of the earth; and thus to have everywhere been the slave of nature. Later, we find him in the shepherd state, surrounded by animals that he has tamed, and upon whom he is dependent for supplies of food, while deriving from them the skins by which he is protected from the winter's cold.

In this state of things there can exist but little power of association, eight hundred acres of land being estimated to be required for enabling a hunter to obtain as much food as could be obtained from half an acre under cultivation. Why this is so is thus explained by Liebig :—

"A nation of hunters on a limited space is utterly incapable of increasing its numbers beyond a certain point, which is soon attained. The carbon necessary for respiration must be obtained from the animals, of which only a limited number can live on the space supposed. These animals collect from plants the constituents of their organs and their blood, and yield them in turn to the savages who live by the chase alone. They again receive this food, unaccompanied by those compounds destitute of nitrogen, which, during the life of the animals, served to support the respiratory process. In such men, confined to an animal diet, it is the carbon of the flesh and of the blood which must take the place of starch and sugar. But fifteen pounds of flesh contain no more carbon than four pounds of starch; and while the savage, with one animal and an equal weight of starch, could maintain life and health for a certain number of days, he would be compelled, if confined to flesh, in order to procure the carbon necessary for respiration during the same time, to consume five such animals."—*Animal Chemistry*, Part I, § 14.

That the power of association may increase, it is, then, indispensable that man should be enabled to obtain increased supplies of vegetable food, and they can be obtained only by the help of cultivation. That, however, implies an approach to individuality which, in such cases, can have no existence. The lands are common stock, and so are the flocks; and when, by reason of any failure of supplies, it becomes necessary to effect a change of place, the tribe moves bodily, as is seen to have been the case with those of Asia and of the north of Europe—and as it is now with those of the Western Continent. Under such circumstances, there can be no approach to that individuality which consists in the power of determining for themselves, whether they will go or remain where they are. If the majority determine to remove, all must do so, for the few who might remain would be butchered by other tribes, greedy for additions to the territory over which they had been accustomed to roam, and from which they had derived but a miserable subsistence. In this stage of society, man is, therefore, not only the slave of nature, but also of his neighbor men, bound to yield to the tyranny of the majority.

Absence of power in the individual man, to determine his own course of action—or, in that of a minority to judge and act for themselves—is thus a necessary consequence of inability to call to their aid the natural forces by which they are everywhere surrounded, and by whose aid larger supplies of food might be obtained from diminished surfaces—enabling them to live in closer connection with each other. In what manner, however, can the hunter or the shepherd compel nature to work for him? "His implements are of the rudest description, such as nature offers ready-made to his hand, like the shell that the South Sea Islanders use for a hoe. All the arms and tools that his forefathers had used, while the tribe was passing through its stages of hunter and shepherd life, were of this description. A flint had served for an arrow-head, and its sharp edge gave the only cutting instrument they had been able to construct. A bow fashioned by such a knife, the string of which was a thong cut from a deer-skin, was his chief weapon for the chase, or for combat at a distance—a club hardened by the fire, armed sometimes with a sharp stone, fastened to it by thongs, was the weapon for close strife. A pointed bone, from the leg of the deer, furnished his wife with a needle, and its sinews with the thread, by which she sewed together the skins that clothed her household. It is with such tools only that experience or the traditions of his tribe have made him acquainted. One has but to walk into the nearest museum that contains a collection of savage implements, to see how imperfect they are, and, at the same time, to observe with some astonishment how fully they meet the limited wants of those who use them, and through what a long tract of time generations of men made no sensible improvement upon their primitive stock."*

What, under such circumstance, is his course of operation, is exhibited in the following sketch of that of a single supposed individual and his descendants, during a period of time that the reader may, if he will, extend from years to centuries. By thus taking a supposititious case, and placing the settler on an island, we are enabled to eliminate the causes of disturbance that have, everywhere in real life, resulted from the vicinity of other individuals equally deficient in the machinery required for the subjugation of nature—and therefore driven, by fear of starvation, to robbery and murder of their fellow-men. Having thus, by aid of the system pursued by the mathematician, studied what *would be* the course of man left undisturbed, we shall then be prepared to enter into an examination of the disturbing causes to which it is due that his course *has been*, in many countries, so widely different.

The first cultivator, the Robinson Crusoe of his day, provided, however, with a wife, has neither axe nor spade. He works alone. Population being small, land is, of course, abundant, and he may select for himself, fearless of any question of his title. He is surrounded by soils possessed in the highest degree of qualities fitting them for yielding large returns to labor; but they are covered with immense trees that he cannot fell, or they are swamps that he cannot drain. To pass through them, even, is a work of serious labor, the first being a mass of roots, stumps, decaying logs, and shrubs, while, into the other, he sinks knee deep at every step. The atmosphere, too, is impure, as fogs settle upon the lowlands, and the dense foliage of the wood prevents the circulation of the air. He

* Smith's Manual of Political Economy, p. 43.

has no axe, but had he one he would not venture there, for, to do so, would be attended with risk of health, and almost certain loss of life. Vegetation, too, is so luxuriant, that before he could, with the imperfect machinery at his command, clear a single acre, a portion of it would be again so overgrown that he would have to recommence his Sisyphean labor. The higher lands, comparatively bare of timber, are little fitted for yielding a return to his exertions. There are, however, places on the hill, where the thinness of the soil has prevented the growth of trees and shrubs—or there are spaces among the trees that can be cultivated while they still remain; and, when pulling up by the roots the few shrubs scattered over the surface, he is alarmed by no apprehension of their speedy reproduction. With his hands he may even succeed in barking the trees, or, by the aid of fire he may so far destroy them that time alone will be required for giving him a few cleared acres, upon which to sow his seed, with little fear of weeds. To attempt these things upon the richer lands would be loss of labor. In some places the ground is always wet, while in others, the trees are too large to be seriously injured by fire, and its only effect would be to stimulate the growth of weeds and brush. He therefore commences the work of cultivation on the higher grounds, where, making with his stick holes in the light soil that drains itself, he drops the grain an inch or two below the surface, and in due season obtains a return of twice his seed. Pounding this between stones, he obtains bread, and his condition is improved. He has succeeded in making the earth labor for him, while himself engaged in trapping birds or rabbits, or in gathering fruits.

Later, he succeeds in sharpening a stone, and thus obtains a hatchet, by aid of which he is enabled to proceed more rapidly in girdling the trees, and in removing the sprouts and their roots, a very slow and laborious operation, nevertheless. In process of time, he is seen bringing into activity a new soil—one whose food-producing powers were less obvious to sight than those at first attempted. Finding an ore of copper, he succeeds in burning it, and is thus enabled to obtain a better axe, with far less labor than had been required for the inferior one he has thus far used. He obtains, also, something like a spade, and can now make holes four inches deep, with less labor than, with his stick, he could make those of two. Penetrating to a lower soil, and being enabled to stir the earth and loosen it, the rain is now absorbed where before it had run off from the hard surface, and the new soil thus obtained proves to be far better, and more easily wrought, than that upon which his labor has heretofore been wasted. His seed, better protected, is less liable to be frozen out in winter, or parched in summer, and he now gathers thrice the quantity sown. At the next step, we find him bringing into action another new soil. He has found that which, on burning, yields him tin, and, by combining this with his copper, he has brass, giving him better machinery, and enabling him to proceed more rapidly. While sinking deeper into the land first occupied, he is enabled to clear other lands upon which vegetation grows more luxuriantly, because he can now exterminate the shrubs with some hope of occupying the land before they are replaced with others equally useless for his purposes. His children, too, have grown, and they can weed the ground, and otherwise assist him in removing the obstacles by which his progress is impeded. He now profits by association and combination of action, as before he had profited by the power he had obtained over the various natural forces he had reduced into his service. Next, we find him burning a piece of the iron soil which surrounds him in all directions, and now he obtains a real axe and spade, inferior in quality, but still much superior to those by which his labor has been thus far aided. With the help of his sons, grown to man's estate, he now removes the light pine of the hill-side leaving still untouched, however, the heavy timber of the river bottom. His cultivable ground is increased in extent, while he is enabled, with his spade, to penetrate still deeper than before, thus bringing into action the powers of the soils more distant from the surface. He finds, with great pleasure, that the light sand is underlaid with clay, and that, by combining the two, he obtains a new one far more productive than that he first had used. He remarks, too, that by turning the surface down, the process of decomposition is facilitated, and each addition to his knowledge increases the return to his exertions.—With further increase of his family, he has obtained the important advantage of increased combination of action. Things that were needed to be done to render his land more rapidly productive, but which were to himself impracticable, become simple and easy when now attempted by his numerous sons and grandsons, each of whom obtains far more food than he alone could at first command, and in return for far less severe exertion. They next extend their operations downwards, towards the low grounds of the stream, girdling the large trees, and burning the brush—and thus facilitating the passage of air so as to fit the land, by degrees, for occupation.

With increase of numbers there is now increased power of association, manifested by increased division of employments, and attended with augmented power to command the service of the great natural agents provided for their use. One portion of the little community now performs all the labors of the field, while another gives itself to the further development of the mineral wealth by which it is everywhere surrounded. They invent a hoe, by means of which the children are enabled to free the ground from weeds, and to tear up some of the roots by which the best lands—those last brought into cultivation—are yet infested. They have succeeded in taming the ox, but, as yet, have had little occasion for his services. They now invent the plough, and, by means of a piece of twisted hide, are enabled to attach the ox, by whose help they turn up a deeper soil, while extending cultivation over more distant land. The community grows, and with it grows the wealth of the individuals of which it is composed, enabling them, from year to year, to obtain better machinery, and to reduce to cultivation more and better lands. Food and clothing become more abundant, while the air on the lower lands is improved by the clearing of the timber. The dwelling, too, is better. In the outset, it was a hole in the ground. Subsequently, it was composed of such decayed logs as the unaided efforts of the first settler could succeed in rolling and placing one upon the other. As yet, the chimney was unknown, and he must live in perpetual smoke, if he would not perish of cold, as a window was a luxury then unthought of. If the severity of the weather required him to close his doors, he was not only stifled, but passed his days in darkness. His time, during a large portion of the year, was therefore totally unproductive, while his life was liable to be shortened by disease produced by foul air within, or severe cold without, his miserable hut. With increase of population all have acquired wealth, resulting from the cultivation of new and better soils, and from a growing power to command the services of nature. With this increase of power there has been a further increase in the power of association, with steady tendency to the development of individuality, as the modes of employment have become more and more diversified. They now fell the heavy oak and the enormous pine, and are thereby enabled to construct additional dwellings, each in regular succession better than the first. Health improves, and population increases more rapidly. A part of it is now employed in the field, while another prepares the skins, and renders them more fit for clothing—and a third set makes axes, spades, hoes, ploughs, and other implements calculated to aid the labors of the field, and in those of construction. The supply of food increases rapidly, and with it the power of accumulation. In the first years, there was perpetual danger of famine, but now there being a surplus, a part is stored to provide against failure of the crops.

Cultivation extends itself along the hill-side, where deeper soils, now laid open by the plough, yield larger returns—while down the slope of the hill each successive year is marked by the disappearance of the great trees by which the richer lands have heretofore been occupied—the intermediate spaces becoming meanwhile enriched by the decomposition of the enormous roots, and more readily ploughed because of the gradual decay of the stumps. A single ox to the plough can now turn up a greater space than in the outset could be done by two. A single ploughman can now do more than on the ground first cultivated could have been done by hundreds of men armed with pointed sticks. The community being next enabled to drain some of the lower lands, copious harvests of grain are obtained from the better soil now first cultivated. Thus far the oxen have roamed the woods, gathering what they could, but the meadow is now granted to their use, the axe and the saw enabling the family to enclose them, and thus to lessen the labor attendant upon obtaining supplies of meat, milk, butter, and hides. Heretofore their chief domestic animal has been the hog, which could live on mast, but now they add beef, and perhaps mutton, the lands first cultivated being abandoned to the sheep. They obtain far more meat and grain, and with less labor than at any former period; a consequence of their increase in numbers and in the power of association. Numerous generations having already passed away, the younger ones now profit by the wealth they had accumulated, and are thus enabled to apply their own labor with daily increasing advantage—obtaining a constantly increasing return, with increasing power of accumulation, and decreasing severity of exertion. They now bring new powers to their aid, and the water no longer is allowed to run to waste. Even the air itself is made to work, windmills grinding the grain, and saw-mills cutting the timber, which disappears more rapidly; while the work of drainage is in course of being improved by help of more efficient spades and ploughs. The little furnace makes its appearance, and charcoal being now applied to the reduction of the iron yielding soil, it is found that the labor of a single day becomes more productive than before had been that of many weeks. Population spreads itself along the faces of the hills and down into the lower lands, becoming more and more dense at the seat of the original settlement; and with every step we find increasing tendency to combination of action for the production of food, the manufacture of clothing and of household utensils, the construction of houses, and the preparation of machinery for aiding in all these operations. The heaviest timber—that growing on the most fertile land—now disappears, and deep marshes are now drained. Roads are next made to facilitate the intercourse between the old settlement and the newer ones that have been formed around it, and to enable the grower of corn to exchange for wool, or perhaps for improved spades or ploughs, for clothing or for furniture.

Population again increases, with still further development of wealth and power, and therewith is acquired leisure for reflection on the results furnished by the experience of themselves and their predecessors. From day to day, mind becomes more stimulated into action. The sand in the neighborhood being found to be underlaid with marl, the two are, by aid of the improved machinery now in use, brought into combination; thereby producing a soil of power far exceeding that of those heretofore in cultivation. With increased returns to labor all are better fed, clothed, and housed, and all are incited to new exertions, while with improved health and with the power of working in-doors and out-of-doors, according to the season, they are enabled to apply their labor with greater steadiness and regularity. Thus far, however, they have found it difficult to gather their crops in season. The harvest time being short, the whole strength of the community has been found insufficient to prevent much of the grain remaining on the ground until, over ripe, it was shaken out by the wind, or in the attempt to gather it. Not unfrequently, indeed, it has been totally ruined by changes of weather after it had been fit for harvesting. Labor has been superabundant during the year, while harvest produced a demand for it that could not be supplied. The reaping-hook, however, now takes the place of the hand, while the scythe enables the farmer to cut his hay. The cradle and the horse-rake follow, all tending to increase the facility of accumulation, and thus to increase the power of applying labor to new soils, deeper or more distant, more heavily burdened with timber, or more liable to be flooded—and thus requiring embankment as well as drainage. New combinations, too, are formed. The clay is found to be underlaid with the soil called lime, which latter, like the iron yielding soil, requires decomposition to fit it for the task of combination. The road, the wagon, and the horse facilitate the work by enabling the farmer readily to obtain supplies of the carbon-yielding soil, called coal, and he now obtains, by burning the lime and combining it with the clay, a better soil than at any former period—one yielding more corn, and requiring less severe labor from himself. Population and wealth again increase, and the steam-engine assists the work of drainage, while the railroad and the engine facilitate the transportation to market of his products. His cattle being now fattened at home, a large portion of the produce of his rich meadow-land is converted into manure, to be applied to the poorer soils that had at first been cultivated. Instead of sending food to fatten them *at* market, he now obtains *from* market their refuse in the form of bones, by help of which to maintain the powers of his land.—Passing thus, at every step, from the poor to the better soils, there is obtained a constantly increasing supply of food, and other necessaries of life, with corresponding increase in the power of consumption and accumulation. The danger of famine and disease now passes away. Increased returns to labor and daily improving condition rendering labor pleasant, he is seen everywhere applying himself more steadily as his work becomes less severe. Population further increases, and the rapidity of its increase is seen to be greater with each successive generation—while with each is seen an increase of the power of living in connection with each other, by reason of the power of obtaining constantly increasing supplies from the same surface. With every step in this direction the *desire* for association and for combination of action is seen to grow with the growth of the *power* to satisfy it, and thus are their labors rendered more productive and the facilities of commerce augmented—with constant tendency to the production of harmony, peace, and security of person and property, among themselves, and with the world—accompanied by constant increase of numbers, wealth, prosperity, and happiness.

Such has been everywhere, where population and wealth have been permitted to increase, the history of man. With growth of numbers there has been increased power of combination among men for obtaining control over the great forces existing in nature—setting them free and then compelling them to aid him in the work of producing the food, the clothing, and the shelter required for his purposes, and to facilitate him in obtaining power to extend the sphere of his associations. Everywhere he is seen to have commenced poor and helpless in himself, and unable to combine his efforts with those of his fellow-men—and everywhere, consequently, the slave of nature. Everywhere, as numbers have increased, he is seen to have become, from year to year, and from century to century, more and more her master—and every step in that direction has been marked by rapid development of individuality, attended by increased power of association, increased sense of responsibility, and increased power of progress.

That such has been the case with all nations and in all parts of the earth, is so obvious that it would seem almost unnecessary to offer any proof of the fact, nor could it be so but that it has been asserted that the course of things has been directly the reverse—that man has always commenced the work of cultivation on the rich soils of the earth, and that then food has been abundant—but that, as population has increased, his successors have found themselves forced to resort to inferior ones, yielding steadily less and less in return to labor; with constant tendency to over-population, poverty, wretchedness, and death. Were this so, there could be no such thing as universality in the natural laws to which man is subjected, for in regard to all other descriptions of matter, we see him uniformly commencing with the inferior, and passing, as wealth and population grow, to the superior—with constantly increasing return to labor. He is seen to have commenced with the axe of stone, and to have passed through those of copper, bronze, and iron, until he has finally arrived at those of steel—to have passed from the spindle and distaff to the spinning-jenny and the power-loom—from the canoe to the ship—from transportation on the backs of men to that in railroad cars—from rude hieroglyphics painted on skins to the printed book—and from the wild society of the savage tribe, where might makes right, to the organized community in which the rights of those who are weak in numbers, or in muscular power, are respected. Having studied these facts, and having satisfied ourselves that such has been his course in reference to all things other than the land required for cultivation, we should be disposed to believe that it must there also prove to have been the case, and that the theory referred to—by virtue of which man is rendered more and more the slave of nature as wealth and population grow—must be untrue.

§ 2. Forty years have now elapsed since Mr. Ricardo communicated to the world his discovery of the nature and causes of rent, and of the laws of its progress,* and during nearly all that time it

* The theory is thus stated by its author:—

"On the first settling of a country in which there is an abundance of rich and fertile land, a very small portion of which is required to be cultivated for the support of the actual population, or, indeed, can be cultivated with the capital which the population can command, there will be no rent; for no one would pay for the use of land when there was an abundant quantity not yet appropriated, and, therefore, at the disposal of whomsoever might choose to cultivate it. * * * * * If all land had the same properties, if it were boundless in quantity and uniform in quality, no charge could be made for its use, unless where it possessed peculiar advantages of situation. It is only, then, because land is not unlimited in quantity and uniform in quality, and because, in the progress of population land of an inferior quality, or less advantageously situated, is called into cultivation, that rent is ever paid for the use of it. When, in the progress of society, land of the second degree of fertility is taken into cultivation, rent immediately commences on that of the first quality; and the amount of that rent will depend on the difference in the quality of these two portions of land. * * * When land of the third quality is taken into cultivation, rent immediately commences on the second; and it is regulated as before by the difference in their productive powers. At the same time the rent of the first quality will rise, for that must always be above the rent of the second, by the difference between the produce which they yield with a given quantity of capital and labor.

"The most fertile and most favorably situated land will be first cultivated, and the exchangeable value of its produce will be adjusted in the same manner as the exchangeable value of all other commodities, by the total quantity of labor necessary in various forms, from first to last, to produce it and bring it to market. When land of inferior quality is taken has been received by a large portion of the economists of Europe and America, as being so unquestionably true, that doubt of its truth could be regarded only as evidence of incapacity to comprehend it. Furnishing, as it did, a simple and easy explanation of the poverty existing in the world—and by help of a law emanating from an all-wise, all-powerful, and all-beneficent Creator—it relieved the governing classes from all responsibility for the wretchedness with which they were surrounded, and was therefore at once adopted. From that time to the present it has been the established doctrine of a considerable portion of the schools of this country and of Europe; and yet no two of its teachers have ever quite agreed as to what it was that their master had really meant to teach. Having studied the works of the most eminent among them, and having found an almost universal disagreement, the student turns, in despair, to Mr. Ricardo himself, and there he finds in his celebrated chapter on rent, contradictions that cannot be reconciled, and a series of complications such as scarcely ever before was found in the same number of lines. The more he studies the greater is his difficulty, and the more readily does he account for the variety of doctrines taught by men who profess to belong to the same school; and who all agree, if in little else, in regarding the new theory of rent as the great discovery of the age.

Looking around, he sees that all the recognized laws of nature are characterized by the most perfect simplicity, and the greatest breadth—that they are of universal application—and that those by whom they are taught are freed from any necessity for resorting to narrow exceptions to account for particular facts. The simplicity of Kepler's law of "equal areas in equal times" is perfect. Its truth is, consequently, universal, and all to whom it is explained feel assured not only that it *is* true, but that it must continue to be so in relation to all the planets that may be discovered, numerous though they may be, and however distant from the sun and from us. A child may comprehend it, and the merest novice may so fully master it as to fit himself for teaching it to others. It needs

into cultivation, the exchangeable value of raw produce will rise, because more labor is required to produce it."—*Ricardo's Political Economy*, chap. ii.

no commentary, no modification, and therein it differs greatly from that to which the reader's attention now is called. Whatever else may be the merits of the latter, it cannot be charged with either simplicity or universality.

At first sight it looks, however, to be exceedingly simple. Rent is said to be paid for land of the first quality, yielding a hundred quarters in return to a given quantity of labor, when it becomes necessary, with the increase of population, to cultivate land of the second quality, capable of yielding but ninety quarters in return to the same quantity of labor; and the amount of rent then paid for No. 1 is equal to the difference between their respective products. No proposition could be calculated to command more universal assent. Every man who hears it sees around him land that pays rent, and sees, too, that that which yields forty bushels to the acre pays more rent than that which yields but thirty; and that the difference is nearly equal to the difference of product. He becomes at once a disciple of Mr. Ricardo, admitting that the reason why prices are paid for the use of land is that soils are different in their qualities; when he would certainly regard it as in the highest degree absurd if any one were to undertake to prove that prices are paid for oxen because one ox is heavier than another—that rents are paid for houses because some will accommodate twenty persons and others only ten—or that all ships command freights because some ships differ from others in their capacity.

The whole system is based, as the reader will perceive, upon the assertion of the existence of the fact, that, in the commencement of cultivation, when population is small and land consequently abundant, the richest soils—those whose qualities fit them for yielding the largest return to any given quantity of labor—alone are cultivated. This fact exists or it does not. If it has no existence, the system falls to the ground. That it has none, and that it is contrary to the nature of things that it should have had, or can ever have it, it is proposed now to show.

The picture presented by Mr. Ricardo differs totally from that which has above been presented for the consideration of the reader. The former, placing the settler on the lands of highest fertility, requires that his children and his children's children should, each in regular succession to the others, find themselves driven, by sad necessity, to the occupation of those capable of yielding smaller returns to labor—and that they should thus become, from generation to generation, more and more the slaves of nature. The latter, placing the early settler on the poorer soils, exhibits his successors exercising constantly increasing power to pass to the cultivation of the richer soils—and becoming, from generation to generation, more and more the masters of nature, compelling her to do their work, and pressing steadily onward from triumph to triumph, with constant increase in the power of association, in the development of individuality, in the feeling of responsibility, and in the power of further progress. Which of these pictures is the true one, is to be settled by the determination of the fact, what it is that men in times past have done, and what it is they are now doing, in regard to the occupation of the earth. If it can be shown that, in every country and at every age, the order of events has been in direct opposition to that it is supposed by Mr. Ricardo to have been, then must his theory be abandoned as wholly destitute of foundation. That it has been so, and that everywhere, in both ancient and modern times, cultivation has commenced on the poorer soils—and that it has been with the growth of population and wealth alone that man has been enabled to subdue to cultivation the richer ones, will now be shown by a brief examination of the facts as presented in the history of the world.

That examination will be commenced with the United States; and for the reason that, their settlement having been recent, and being, indeed, still in progress, the course to which the settler has been and is prompted, can readily be traced. If we find him invariably commencing on the high and thin lands, requiring little clearing and no drainage—those capable of yielding but small return to labor—and as invariably passing from the higher to the lower ones, requiring both clearing and drainage, then will the view presented to the reader as the true one be confirmed by practice—at least by the practice of America. If, however, we can then follow the settler into Mexico, and through Brazil, Peru, and Chili—into Britain, and through France, Germany, Italy, Greece, and Egypt, into Asia and Australia—and show that such has been his invariable course of action, then may it be believed that when population is small, and land consequently abundant, the work of cultivation is, and always must be, commenced upon the poorer soils—that with the growth of population and wealth, the richer ones are always brought into activity, with constantly increasing return to the efforts of the laborer—and that, with the progress of population and wealth, there is a steady diminution in the proportion of those efforts required for obtaining the necessaries of life, with constant increase in the proportion that may be applied to adding to its comforts, conveniences, luxuries, and enjoyments.

§ 3. The first settlers of the English race are seen to have established themselves on the barren soil of Massachusetts—founding the colony of Plymouth. The whole continent was before them, but, like all other colonists, they had to take what, with their means, they could obtain. Other settlements were formed at Newport and New Haven, and thence they may be traced, following the courses of the rivers, but occupying in all cases the higher lands, leaving the clearing of timber and the draining of swamps to their more wealthy successors. Were the reader desired to designate the soils of the Union least calculated for the production of food, his choice would fall upon the rocky lands first occupied by the hardy Puritans; and were he now to place himself on Dorchester heights, near Boston, and look around him, he would find himself surrounded everywhere by evidences that poor as was in general the soil of Massachusetts, the richest portions of it remain even yet uncultivated; while of those in cultivation the most productive are those that have been subdued to the uses of man in the last half century.

Looking now to New York we see that the process has been the same. The unproductive soil of Manhattan island and the higher lands of the opposite shores, claimed early attention, while the lower and richer ones close at hand remain, even to the present moment undrained and uncultivated. Following the population, we find them passing along the course of the Hudson to the Valley of the Mohawk, and there establishing themselves near the head of the stream on lands requiring but little of either clearing or drainage. Passing further west, we see the early railroad following the course of the higher lands upon which are found the villages and towns of the earlier settlers; but if we follow the new and straight road we find it passing through the richest lands of the State, as yet undrained and uncultivated.

Looking next into the history of even those towns and villages we find that they themselves came late in the order of settlement. Sixty years since Geneva had scarcely an existence, and the road thence to Canandaigua was but an Indian path, upon which but two families as yet had settled—but looking thence south, towards the high lands bordering on Pennsylvania, we meet everywhere with evidence of occupation. The great purchase of Mr. Pulteney was there made, and a settlement was formed on the Coshocton creek, the lands around being described as very valuable because of their "total exemption from all periodical disorders, particularly the fever and ague"—from which, as is so well known, the later settlers on the rich lands of the lower Genesee country so severely suffered.*

In New Jersey, we find them occupying the higher lands towards the heads of the rivers, while neglecting the lower grounds that cannot drain themselves.† That State still abounds in fine timber, covering rich lands requiring only to be cleared to yield larger returns to labor than any of those cultivated a century since, when land was more abundant, and population small. On the banks of the Delaware, we find the Quakers selecting the lighter soils which produce the pine, while avoiding the richer and heavier ones of the opposite shore of Pennsylvania. Every settler selects, too, the higher and drier parts of his farm, leaving the meadows, many of which remain even now in a state of nature, while others have been drained within the last few years. The best portions of every farm are, invariably, those which have been most recently brought into cultivation, while the poorest lands of the various neighborhoods are those on which are seen the oldest farm-houses. Passing further through the sandy lands of the State, we find hundreds of little clearings, long since abandoned by their owners, attesting the character of the soil that men cultivate when population is small, and fertile land most abundant. Having cleared the lands that produce the oak, or drained those which yield the white cedar,

* On the map of the Genesee tract published in 1790, the settled townships are marked, and they are found at and near the junction of the Canisteo, Cahoctin, and Tioga rivers, where Corning is now situated—around Hornellsville and on the head waters of the Canisteo—&c., &c.—See *Documentary History of New York*, vol. ii. (octavo edition), p. 1111, &c.

† The reader may see this by reference to the map of East Jersey in 1682, recently republished.

they abandon those which produce the pine of that State, the poorest of all the pines.

The Swedes settled Lewistown and Christiana, on the sandy soil of Delaware. Crossing the State towards the head of Chesapeake Bay, we find, in the little and decaying towns of Elkton and Charlestown, once the centres of a somewhat active population, further evidence of the poverty of the soils first occupied, when fine meadow-land, on which are now the richest farms in that State, was abundant, but held as worthless. Penn follows the Swedes, and, profiting by their expenditure and experience, selects the high lands on the Delaware, about twelve miles north of the site which he afterwards chooses for his city, near the confluence of that river and the Schuylkill. Starting from this latter point, and tracing the course of settlement, we find it not at first extending downwards towards the rich meadow-lands, but upwards along the ridge between the two rivers, where many miles of early settlements remain to mark the tendencies of early colonists. Passing, right or left, to the river banks, we see, in the character of the buildings, evidences of later occupation and cultivation. On the maps of that early day, the fertile lands in the vicinity of the Delaware, from New Castle almost to the head of tide-water, a distance of more than sixty miles, are marked as held in large tracts, and dotted over with trees, to show that they are still uncleared—while all the upper lands are divided into little farms.* Passing northward and westward, we see the oldest habitations always most distant from the river; but later times, and increase of population and wealth, have carried cultivation to the water's edge. With every additional mile, we find increasing evidence of the recent cultivation of the best soils. Everywhere we now meet farms on the hill-sides, while the lower lands become more wild and rough. Further on, cultivation almost leaves the river bank, and if we would seek it we must pass outward, where, at a distance, we may find farms that have been cultivated for half a century or more. If now, following the old road, winding about, and seeking, apparently, hills to cross, we inquire the cause of thus lengthening the distance, we learn that it was made to suit the early settlers; but, if we follow the new roads, they are found keeping near the stream,

* See Holmes's Map, published in 1681, and recently republished.

on the low and rich lands last brought into cultivation.* Returning to the river, and passing on our course, the trees become more and more numerous, and the meadow-land less and less drained or occupied; until, at length, as we pass up the little branches of the river, cultivation disappears, and the original woods remain untouched, except so far as the wants of the recently established coal trade have tended to their extermination. If we desire to see the land chosen by the early settlers, we have but to ascend the hill-side, and on the flat above will be found houses and farms, some of them half a century old, many of which are now abandoned. Crossing the mountains, we see, near their tops, the habitations of early settlers, who selected the land of the pine, easily cleared; and whose pine-knots afforded at one time tar, and, at another, substitutes for candles that they were too poor to buy. Immediately afterwards, we find ourselves in the valley of the Susquehanna, on meadow-lands whose character is proved by the great size of the timber by which they are covered; but upon which neither the spade nor the plough has yet made its mark. Rich lands thus abound, but the settler prefers the poorer ones, as the

* "In the regions sufficiently advanced to admit the construction of canals and railroads, every one has it in his power to verify the fact, by observing the contrast in the aspect of the lands bordering their course, and those which line the old highways. The latter will generally be found ascending every hill-top which lies in the neighborhood of their general direction, even when nothing is saved, in point of distance, by going over the hill instead of going round it. It is usually found, indeed, that the length of a railroad connecting two towns at any considerable distance from each other, is less than that of the old roads which formed the route of travel before it was built; although the former is necessarily under restrictions which prevent attempts to save distance at the expense of elevations in the grade, much more than the ordinary carriage-road. But the highway is lined with cultivated fields, and with houses. It was made to facilitate communication between them, its track worn by the footsteps of men before it was run out by the surveyor, and its purposes compelled it to go where population went, with small regard to the labor which its steep grades would impose upon the beasts of draught that were to toil over it. The railroad, on the contrary, is constructed by engineers, whose problem it is to reduce the power to be expended in drawing heavy loads to a minimum, regard being had both to distance and to elevation. It plunges through swamps and forests, as if to hide itself from the habitations of men. They will grow up upon its edge in due season, for the road has drained the swamps, and let in the sunlight to the gloomy depths of the woods; but, upon the first opening of a railroad, we ordinarily are struck with the juxtaposition of this work of highest art with those of rudest nature.—(Smith, *Manual of Political Economy*, p. 52.)

cost of clearing the former would be more than they were worth when cleared. Descending the little stream, we reach the Susquehanna; and, with every step of our progress, cultivation is seen descending the hills, the valleys becoming more cleared of timber, and meadows and cattle appearing—the most certain signs of increasing wealth and population.

Passing west up the Susquehanna, the order is again inverted. Population diminishes, and cultivation tends to leave the river bottom, and to ascend the hill-sides. If, leaving the river and ascending the bank, we pass to the foot of the Muncy hills, our road will cross fine limestone land whose food-producing qualities being less obvious to the early settlers, whole tracts of it, containing hundreds of acres, passed from hand to hand in exchange for a dollar, or even for a jug of whiskey. They preferred the oak-producing soils, whose trees they could girdle, and afterwards destroy by fire. With increasing population and wealth, they are seen returning to the lands at first despised, combining the inferior and superior soils, and obtaining greatly increased returns to labor. Could we now take a bird's-eye view of the country, we might trace with perfect accuracy the course of every little stream, by the timber still standing on its banks, conspicuous among the higher and cleared lands of the neighborhood. Attaining the head of the stream, we are again in the midst of cultivation, and see that, here, as everywhere else, the settlers have selected the high and dry lands upon which they might commence with the plough, in preference to the more fertile soils that required the axe. If, instead of turning southward towards the older counties, we look northward to the newly settled ones, we shall find the centre of population always occupying the highest lands, near the head of the several little streams which there originate. Passing westward, and crossing the ridge of the Alleghany to the head-waters of the Ohio, the order of things is again inverted. Population at first being scattered, occupies the higher lands, but as we descend the river, the lower ones become more and more cleared; until at length we find ourselves at Pittsburg, in the midst of a dense population, actively employed in bringing into connection the coal, the limestone, and the iron ore with a view to the preparation of machinery for enabling the farmer of the west to sink deeply into the land of which heretofore he has but scratched the superficial soil; and to clear and drain the fertile lands of the river bottoms, instead of the higher and drier ones from which he has heretofore derived his supplies of food.

The early settlers of the West uniformly selected the higher lands, leaving the lower and richer ones for their successors. The immediate valleys of streams, fertile as were the soils, were and still are avoided on account of danger to be apprehended from the fevers which even now sweep off so many of the emigrants to the newer States. The facility of getting some small crop, always prompted to the selection of the land most readily brought under cultivation, and none so well answered the purpose as that which was slightly clothed with timber, and clear of undergrowth. The constant fall of leaves had by their decay kept the ground covered with a light mould, and prevented the growth of grass; and by deadening the trees to let in the sun, they could obtain a small return to labor. The first great object was to have a dry place for the dwelling, and therefore the settler was always found selecting the ridges—the same reason which prevented him from commencing the work of artificial drainage to secure a place for his dwelling, operating with equal force in regard to land required for cultivation.*

* The following extract from an article in the *Merchant's Magazine* furnishes so many facts illustrative of the course of operation throughout this country that it can scarcely fail to be read with interest:—

"The proposition proclaimed by Carey in opposition to the long received theories of Ricardo and Malthus, and recently sustained by Mr. Smith in his Manual of Political Economy, that the inferior lands are first occupied by the pioneers, is a fact that strikes one throughout the whole West—at the South and the North. The oldest settlements are always found upon the thinly-wooded and comparatively barren hill lands, upon the dry and upland prairies. The sandy plains and pine barrens of Georgia, Alabama, Florida, and Mississippi, received the first emigrants. The first homes of Texas were built on the upland prairies—studded with their islands of timber, that gave illimitable ranges to stock, and sustained here and there small patches of corn. The smoke from the first log cabins on the Mississippi River ascended from the high clay and rocky bluffs on its shores, around which are now the poorest soils. In Arkansas and Missouri the first settlers are found among the pine lands and hills, still in the hunter state, their civilization and their lands but a little more, if any, advanced or improved than they were the day they became squatters thereon. On the Ohio, the truth of the position is more apparent. The original pioneers selected Wheeling, Marietta, Limestone, North Bend, and Vevay, as the first town sites, in the poorest agricultural regions on the river; and the first population along the whole river spread itself over the hills, and cleared their first fields and patches on the oak knobs and thin soil of the

Passing into Wisconsin, the traveller finds the first white settler of the State placed on its highest land, known by the title of "The Big Mound"—and he follows the early roads along the ridges upon which are found the little towns and villages created by the men who have had there to commence the work of cultivation. Occasionally he crosses a "wet prairie," in which may be found the richest land of the State, and "the terror of the early emigrant."*

uplands, where twenty acres are not worth one acre of the rich bottoms which the first settlers rejected at a price a little more than the surveyor's fees for locating. And now along the whole extent of the Lower Ohio, the deserted and falling log cabin of the first settler is found by the side of some gushing spring among the hills—his little patch grown up to briers and bushes, and surrounded by a forest as desolate and silent as when it was first disturbed with the stroke of the woodman's axe. Or, if it be still inhabited, it is encompassed by a sickly patch of corn, the soil of which is too poor to tempt the speculators to enter it over the squatter's head, which is still covered with a coon-skin cap, and his feet with moccasons.

"This country has on its rugged hill-sides hundreds of these crumbling and deserted memorials of the early pioneers. George Ewing, brother of the Hon. Thos. Ewing, of Ohio, was among the first settlers in this region, and located himself on a tract of land—when he had the selection of all the richest bottom lands in the country—which, at this day, is worth but little more than he paid the government for it, forty years ago; and the field where he buried the father and mother of one of the most eminent men of his country, is fast returning to its wilderness state. And yet George Ewing was a man of intelligence, and of sound judgment and sagacity, and though less cultivated, was in native powers not inferior to his brother. He with his father cut the first wagon path into Wheeling, and was among the first white men that crossed the Ohio. He lived first near the rich valley of the Muskingum, then in sight of the teeming lands of the Scioto, and removed successively through the richest regions of Ohio, Kentucky, and Indiana, always in advance of the tide of emigration, having the first choice of all the lands on the river, and yet, at his death, there was not an acre of any of the lands he had possessed worth double the price he had paid the government for it. These are remarkable facts in the history of the first settlers, and difficult to be accounted for except on the grounds assigned by Carey and Smith."

* "Many small tracts, known as 'wet prairie' fifteen years ago, and *rejected by the first settlers*, have become dry by being annually resown, and fed down by domestic animals, without any other than its natural drainage, and exposure to the sun and air, by the destruction of the impervious screen of tall 'slough grass.'

"The 'dry prairies' are generally very similar in appearance, so far as surface is concerned. Small portions of 'level prairie' are found everywhere, but to constitute dry prairie it must be 'rolling.' Between the waves on this great ocean of God's own beautiful sod are the 'sloughs,' *the terror of the early emigrant, and the most valued possession of his successor*, as often affording water, and always an unfailing and most luxuriant natural meadow. These sloughs are the drains of the dry prairie. They are in

Descending the Ohio, and arriving at the confluence of that river and the Mississippi, we lose sight of all signs of population, except that of the poor wood-cutter, who risks his health while engaged in providing wood for the numerous steamboats. Here, for hundreds of miles, we pass through the most fertile land, covered with timber of gigantic size; but, with all its powers of production, it is valueless for all purposes of cultivation. Unembanked, it is liable to overflow from the river, and its neighborhood is destructive of life and health; and millions of acres possessed of qualities fitting them to yield the largest return to labor, remain uncleared and undrained, while the higher and poorer lands are under cultivation.*

Descending further, we meet population and wealth in the act of ascending the Mississippi, from the shores of the Gulf of Mexico.

general nearly parallel, and oftenest at about a right angle with the course of the rivers; they are from 140 to 160 rods asunder, and sometimes of many miles in length. The soil of the dry prairie is from 12 to 18 inches deep in this region; the wet prairie in general much deeper: and the alluvion (of the river bottoms), as in all countries, of irregular and often astonishing depth."—*Proceedings of Pomological Convention*, Syracuse, 1849.

* "The Lower Mississippi is bordered upon each side by a broad belt of low land, known as "the Swamp." At Memphis, in the southwestern corner of Tennessee, the bluff touches the eastern side of the river, and then, bearing away to the eastward, approaches the river no more until it reaches a point near Natchez.

"While the hill country has become cleared and settled with that rapidity which characterizes the advance of the Western States, "the Swamp," notwithstanding its boundless fertility, has remained almost a wilderness. The enterprising planter, who, leaving the worn-out lands of Virginia or the Carolinas, seeks a location where the soil may repay more liberally the labors of the husbandman, shrinks from exposing his slaves to the deadly miasma of its stagnant lagoons, and to the toil of clearing its tangled and wiry brakes. In some places, indeed, wealthy farmers who have boldly and patiently met these dangers and obstacles, have succeeded in opening magnificent farms on which a bale to the acre is but an ordinary crop. Unfortunately, however, a rise of water occasionally overflows the whole farm, covering the fields with driftwood, sweeping away stock, and leaving the work of years a ruin.—But the swamp has other denizens, who, fortunately for themselves, are in more independent circumstances, since they owe nothing to fortune, and cannot, therefore, be expected to pay her anything. These are the wood-cutters, the lumbermen, the trappers, bee and bear hunters, and fishermen, who have made their cabins by the side of some lake or bayou, and who, secure of a subsistence while the dug-out will float, and their hands can wield axe and rifle, pay a very literal obedience to the injunction of scripture, and "take no thought for the morrow."—*Correspondence of New York Tribune.*

Embankments, or *levées*, keep out the river, and the finest plantations are seen on land, corresponding, in every respect, with the wild and uncultivated region left behind. If, now, the traveller desires to seek the habitations of the early settlers, he must leave the river bank and ascend the hills; and, with every step, he will find new proof that cultivation invariably commences on the poorer soils. Interrogating the pioneer settlers why they waste their labor on the poor soil of the hill-tops, while fertile soils abound, their answer is invariably found to be, that the one they *can* cultivate as it stands, while the other they *cannot.* The pine of the hills is small, and easily cleared, and it affords him fuel, while its knots furnish artificial light. To attempt to clear the land that bears the heavy timber would ruin him. If, instead of descending the Mississippi, we ascend the Missouri, the Kentucky, the Tennessee, or the Red River, we find, invariably, that the more dense the population, and the greater the mass of wealth, the more are the good soils cultivated—that as population diminishes with our approach to their head-waters and land becomes more abundant, cultivation recedes from the river banks, the timber and the undrained meadow-lands increase in quantity—and that the scattered inhabitants obtain from the superficial soils a diminishing return to their labor, accompanied with diminished power to command the necessaries, conveniences, and comforts of life. Crossing the Mississippi into Texas, we find the town of Austin, the centre of the first American settlement, placed high up on the Colorado, while millions of acres of the finest timber and meadow-lands in the world, totally unoccupied, were passed over, as incapable of paying the cost of simple appropriation. Looking to the Spanish colony of Bexar, we find further illustration of the same universal fact, the whole tendency of colonization being towards the head-waters of the streams.

Turning towards the Southern Atlantic States, we meet everywhere evidence of the same great fact. The richest lands of North Carolina, to the extent of many millions of acres, remain, to this time, uncleared and undrained—while men are everywhere wasting their labor on poor ones yielding three, four, or five bushels to the acre. South Carolina has millions of acres of the finest meadow and other lands, capable of yielding immense returns to labor, and waiting only the growth of wealth and population—and so is it in Georgia,

Florida, and Alabama. So entirely valueless are the richest lands of the West, South, and Southwest, that Congress has recently granted them, to the extent of nearly forty millions of acres, to the States in which they lie, and the latter have accepted them.

The facts are everywhere the same, and, were it possible to find an apparent exception, it would but prove the rule. For the same reason that the settler builds himself a log-house, to provide shelter while waiting until he can have one of stone, he begins cultivation where he can use his plough, and thus avoid the starvation that would result from endeavoring to do so where he cannot; and where fevers, followed by death, would be the inevitable result of the attempt. In every case on record, in which settlements have been attempted on rich lands, they have either failed totally, or their progress has been slow; and it has been only after repeated efforts that they have thriven. The reader who desires evidence of this fact, and of the absolute necessity for commencing with the poorer soils, may obtain it by studying the history of the French colonies in Louisiana and Cayenne—and comparing their repeated failures with the steady growth of those formed in the region of the St. Lawrence, where numerous and somewhat prosperous settlements were formed at places where the land is now held to be almost utterly valueless, because better soils can be obtained elsewhere at so little cost of labor. He may obtain additional evidence by comparing the gentle, but steady, growth of the colonies planted on the sterile soils of New England, with the repeated failures of colonization upon the richer lands of Virginia and Carolina. The latter could not be reduced to cultivation by men working for themselves; and hence it is, that we find the richer colonists purchasing negroes, and compelling them to perform the work, while the free laborer seeks the light, sandy lands of North Carolina. No man, left to himself, will commence the work of cultivation on the rich soils, because it is from them that the return is then the least; and it is upon them, throughout all the new countries of the world, that the condition of the laborer is the worst, where the work is undertaken in advance of the habit of association that comes with the growth of wealth and population. The settler who sought the high, light lands obtained food, although the return to his labor was very small. Had he undertaken to drain the rich soils of the

Dismal Swamp,* he would have perished for want of food, as did those who settled the fertile island of Roanoke.

§ 4. Crossing the Rio Grande, into Mexico, the reader will find further illustration of the universality of this law. At his left, near the mouth of the river, but at some distance from its bank, he will see the city of Matamoras, of recent date. Starting from that point, he may follow the river through vast bodies of the richest lands in a state of nature—with here and there a scattered settlement occupying the higher ones—to the mouth of San Juan, following which to its source, he will find himself in a somewhat populous country, having Monterey for its capital. Standing here, and looking towards the north, he sees cultivation advancing among the high lands of Chihuahua, but keeping, invariably, away from the river banks. The city of that name is distant twenty miles even from the tributary of the great river, and more than a hundred from the mouth of the little stream. Passing west from Monterey, through Saltillo, and thence south, his road will lie over sandy plains whose existence is evidence of the general character of the region. Arriving in Potosi, he finds himself in a country without

* There is, probably not in the world, a richer body of land than that of Lower Virginia and North Carolina, of which the Dismal Swamp forms a part, but, for that reason, it cannot, at present, be cultivated. It is thus described in a recent article of the *New York Tribune*:—

" Between Norfolk and the sea on the east is the County of Princess Ann, without a single elevation which can be called a hill, but full of swamps and lagoons. Norfolk County lies to the south of the town, and embraces the Dismal Swamp, which extends into North Carolina; and beyond that, some forty or fifty miles, lies the county around Elizabeth City, on the Albemarle Sound, all low, and cut up with creeks, lagoons, and salt-water marshes. West of Norfolk County is that of Nansemond, so low and level, that steamboats run up the Nansemond River, and, by slight cuts through the land, might run all through the county. Northwest of this, Isle of Wight County extends from James River to Black River, a branch of the Chowan; and that, as well as Southampton County, the next west, is composed of the same flat, sandy land and swamps, and sluggish streams. Sometimes the surface is sandy, and just below is a bed of fetid mud, affording well-water that it is not well to drink. This whole county is full of marl. Across the bay north of Norfolk, Elizabeth City County overlies the point of the peninsula formed by the waters of the bay, Hampton Roads and Back Bay, and is almost as level as the water. Ascending the James River, which is in places several miles wide, the water is very shoal on the shores, which are occasionally a little elevated. The timber is mostly pine and oak on the upland, with maple, ash, elm, cypress, and other swamp woods on the lowlands, with a dense growth of swamp bushes."

rivers, and almost without the possibility of irrigation, and where any failure of the periodical rains is followed by famine and death; yet, if he cast his eyes downwards towards the coast, he sees a magnificent country, watered by numerous rivers, and in which the cotton and the indigo plant grow spontaneously—a country in which the maize grows with a luxuriance elsewhere unknown—one that might supply the world with sugar, and in which the only danger to be apprehended from the character of the soil is, that the crops might be smothered by reason of the rapid growth of plants springing up in the rich earth, without aid, or even permission, from the man who might undertake to cultivate it; but there he sees no population. The land is uncleared and undrained, and likely so to remain, because those who should undertake the work, with the present means of the country, would starve, if they did not perish by the fevers that there, as everywhere, prevail among the richest soils until they have been subjected to cultivation.*

Passing on, he sees Zacatecas, high and dry like Potosi, yet cultivated. Keeping the ridge, he has on his left Tlascala, once the seat of a great and wealthy people, far removed from any stream whatsoever, and occupying the high lands from which descend little streams seeking the waters of both the Atlantic and the Pacific. On his right is the valley of Mexico, a land capable of yielding the largest returns to labor—one that in the time of Cortes, produced food in abundance for forty cities. Population and wealth having, however, declined, the remaining people have retired to the high lands bordering the valley, to cultivate the poorer soils from which the single city that still remains draws its supplies of food; as a

* "The narrow plain along the sea-coast"—such are the words of Murray's *Encylopædia of Geography*, in describing Mexico—"is a tract in which the richest tropical productions spring up with a luxuriauce scarcely to be paralleled. Yet, while the climate is thus prolific of vegetation, in the finest and most gigantic forms, it is almost fatal to animal life: two consequences which, according to Humboldt, are in this climate almost inseparable. The Spaniards, terrified by this pestilential air, have made this plain only a passage to *the higher districts, where even the native Indians chose rather to support themselves by laborious cultivation, than to descend into the plains, where every luxury of life is poured forth in ample and spontaneous profusion.*"

"Throughout Mexico and Peru, the traces of a great degree of civilization are confined to the elevated plateaux. We have seen, on the Andes, the ruins of palaces and baths, at heights between 1600 and 1800 toises (10,230 and 11,510 English feet.")—*Humboldt.*

consequence of which corn is higher in price than in either London or Paris, while wages are very low. Fertile land is here superabundant, but the people fly from it; whereas, according to Mr. Ricardo, it is that which would be first appropriated.

Passing southward, Tabasco is seen almost unoccupied, although possessing highly fertile lands. Arriving in Yucatan, a land in which water is a luxury, we meet a large and prosperous population, near neighbors to the better soils of Honduras that, when population and wealth shall have sufficiently increased, will yield returns to labor as large, if not larger, than any hitherto known—yet now they are a wilderness, affording subsistence but to a few miserable logwood and mahogany cutters.

Standing here, and looking northward, towards the Caribbean sea, we see the little dry and rocky islands of Montserrat, Nevis, St. Kitts, St. Lucia, St. Vincent, and others, cultivated throughout—while Trinidad, with the richest of soils, remains almost in a state of nature, and Porto Rico, a land excelled by none in fertility, is but now beginning to be subjected to cultivation.

Turning next southward, we mark the line of the Panama railroad, pierced through thick jungles which reproduced themselves almost as rapidly as they were cleared. Left to itself it would be overgrown again in a single year, the destruction of dead material being there in the direct ratio of the growth of that which is living. On the side of Costa Rica and Nicaragua are seen lands of incomparable fertility totally unoccupied, while Indian villages may everywhere be seen midway up the mountains, on lands that drain themselves.*

Looking further south, and marking the position of Santa Fe

* "The whole of the immense territory of Costa Rica, with the exception of the upper valleys I have mentioned, is an impervious forest, known only to the beasts of prey which rove through its sunless depths, and to a few independent Indian tribes; but this forest covers riches which will be found, when the natural resources of the country shall have been developed by a large immigration of a stronger race of men, to be inexhaustible. The soil is of a marvellous fertility, and within its bosom contains some of the richest mines. But the immigrants must remember that if this fertility is an earnest of the wealth they may attain, it is also one of the great obstacles against which they will have to contend, for it is produced by the extreme dampness of the air and by the continuous rains which last seven months in the settled parts of the country, and may be said to last the whole of the year in the districts they would have to redeem from the wilderness."—*Correspondence of the New York Tribune.*

de Bogota, and the city of Quito, centres of population, where men cluster together on the high and dry lands while the valley of Oroonoko* remains unoccupied, the reader will see exhibited on a great scale the same fact which, on a small one, has been shown to exist on the banks of rivers of Pennsylvania. That done, taking his station on the peaks of Chimborazo and looking around, he will see the only civilized people of the days of Pizarro, occupying high and dry Peru, drained by little streams whose rapid course forbade the possibility that marshes should be formed in which vegetable matter might decay; to give richness to the soil for the production of timber before the period of cultivation, or of food afterwards. Being poor it was easily cleared. Requiring no artificial drainage, it was early occupied.†

Turning now towards the East he sees before him Brazil, a land watered by the greatest rivers of the world, to this day a wilderness; yet capable of yielding in the greatest abundance sugar, coffee, tobacco, and all other of the productions of the tropics. Its fields are covered with numberless herds of cattle; and the most precious metals are found near the surface of the earth, but being "destitute of those elevated table lands which cover so much of Spanish America, it affords no eligible situation for European colonists."‡ "The largest rivers" says another writer, "are those which bear least upon their bosoms;"§ and for the reason that such rivers constitute the drains of the great basins of the world, the soil of which is only to be subjected to cultivation when

* "Floods of forty feet rise and upwards are frequent at this season in the great rivers of South America; the llanos of the Orinoco are changed into an inland sea. The Amazon inundates the plains through which it flows, to a vast distance. The Paraguay forms lagoons, which like those of Xarayes, are more than three hundred miles in length, and ooze away during the dry season."—*Guyot's Earth and Man*, p. 136.

† "On the other side of the Andes all is changed. Neither the trade-wind nor its vapors arrive at the western coasts. Scarcely do the table lands of Peru and Bolivia receive from the latter benefits, by the storms which burst out at the limits of the two atmospheres. The coast of the Pacific Ocean, from Punta Parina and Amatope to far beyond the tropic, from the Equator to Chili, is scarcely ever refreshed by the rains of the ocean. * * Drought and desert are their portion, and on the border of the seas, in sight of the waves, they are reduced to envy the neighboring countries of the centre of the Continent, the gifts which the ocean refuses to themselves, while lavishing them on others."—*Ibid*, p. 151.

‡ *McCulloch's Gazetteer.*

§ Gan Eden. *A picture of Cuba*, p. 234.

population and wealth, and the consequent power of association, shall have greatly grown. With that growth will come the development of individuality, and then men will become free; but the strong man is everywhere seen endeavoring to cultivate the rich lands in advance of both population and wealth—and therefore seizing upon the poor African, and compelling him to work for low wages, and under conditions destructive to human life. The most useful rivers of Brazil, those which bear most upon their bosoms, are not the Amazon, the Topayos, the Xingu, or the Negro, "flowing through regions which will one day"* says Murray, "be the finest in the world;" but "those between the coast chain and the sea, none of which can attain any long course"—and thus it is that we find on a comparison of the several parts of this country, the same great fact that is exhibited on so extensive a scale by the Eastern and Western sections of the continent. The short steep slope of Peru furnished the earliest civilization of that portion of the earth, and if we look now to the similar slope of Chili we see a people rapidly advancing in population and wealth—while the great valley of the La Plata, a land capable of yielding the largest return to labor, remains to this hour steeped in barbarism. Here, as everywhere, we have evidence that cultivation begins on the poorer soils.

§ 5. Crossing the ocean and landing in the south of England, the traveller finds himself in a country in which the streams are short and the valleys limited; and, as a consequence, well fitted for early cultivation. There it was that Cæsar found the only people of the island who had made any progress in the art of tillage—the habits of life among the natives becoming more rude and barbarous as they receded from the coast. The distant tribes, as he tells us, never sowed their land, but followed the chase or tended their flocks, living upon the spoils of the one or the milk of the other, and having skins for their only raiment.—Turning next his steps toward Cornwall, he finds a land noted for its barrenness, exhibiting everywhere marks of cultivation "of great and unknown antiquity"—and on the outer edge of this barren land, in a part of

* *Encyclopædia of Geography.* Article Brazil.

the country now so remote from all the thoroughfares as scarcely even to be visited, he meets with the ruins of Tintagel, the castle in which King Arthur held his court.* On his route he sees scarcely a hill-top not even now exhibiting evidences of early occupation.† Inquiring next, for the seats of early cultivation, he will be referred to the sites of rotten boroughs—to those parts of the kingdom in which men who can neither read nor write, still live in mud-built cottages, and receive eight shillings a week for their labor—and to those commons upon which, to so great an extent, cultivation has recommenced.‡ Seeking the palace of the Norman Kings, he will find it at Winchester, and not in the valley of the Thames. Inquiring for the forests and swamps of the days of the Plantagenets, he will everywhere be shown cultivated lands of the highest fertility.§ Should curiosity lead him to desire to see the country whose morasses had nearly swallowed up the army of the conquering Norman, on his return from the devastation of the north—that which daunted the antiquary, Camden, even so late as the age of James I.—he would be shown South Lancashire, with its rich fields covered with waving grain, and meadows on which pasture the finest cattle. Asking for the land most recently reduced to cultivation, he will be taken to the fens of Lincoln—to the late

* *Edinburgh Review*, Jan. 1851. Article, Devon and Cornwall.

† *The Celt, the Roman, and the Saxon*, p. 87.

‡ Such are the lands described by Eden, less than sixty years since, as "the sorry pastures of geese, hogs, asses, half-grown horses and half-starved cattle," and existing by thousands of acres, but which wanted only "to be enclosed and taken care of, to be as rich and as valuable as any lands now in tillage." In many cases, however, cultivation is shown to have been extended over lands so entirely worthless, that even now, with all the improvements of modern times they cannot be rendered productive, as will be seen by the following extract from a work above referred to:—

"In many parts of Britain we find distinct marks of former cultivation on land which is now common, and has certainly lain fallow for ages, and it is not impossible but it may have been the work of the Roman ploughshare. * * * Mr. Bruce observed similar traces of cultivation on the waste lands in Northumberland, and he is probably right in attributing them to the Romans."—*Ibid.*, p. 206.

§ "If we cast our eyes over the map of Roman Britain, we perceive considerable tracts of land which the great roads avoided, and in which there were apparently no towns. These were forest districts, represented by the medieval forests of Charnwood, Sherwood, and others, which abounded in beasts of the chase. Some of the more extensive forests were inhabited by wild boars, and some even by wolves."—*Ibid.*, p. 207.

sandy wastes of Norfolk—and to Cambridgeshire*—all of them yielding now the largest and best crops of England; but which yet were almost wholly valueless until the steam-engine, with its wonderful power, was brought to aid the operations of the agriculturist. "The expenditure of a few bushels of coal," says Porter, "places it in the farmer's power to drain his fields of superfluous moisture, at a comparatively inconsiderable expense."†

Should the traveller next desire to study the order of the occupation of the land in towns and villages, he would find, on inquiring, that those who performed the work of cultivation had sought the hill-sides—leaving the lower situations for those who required to use the water that drained from off their lands.‡ Further, should he wish to compare the present value of what was so recently regarded as poor land, he would learn that it had changed places with what was formerly considered rich land, and now paid a higher rent; thus furnishing additional proof that not only are the best soils last taken into cultivation, but that the command of them is obtained at the cost of far less labor—wages having steadily risen with the increase in the amount of rent.§

Passing north into Scotland, if we desire to find the seats of earliest cultivation, it will be required to visit remote districts, now either wholly abandoned, or in which "the grazing of a few black cattle alone tempts to the claim of property in the soil;"‖ and, if we seek the earliest dwellings, they will be found

* "The fen country of Cambridgeshire is now so well drained that almost the whole of it has become highly valuable land, bearing heavy crops of wheat. * * When contemplating it we cannot avoid being struck with the success which has attended the application of great skill and consummate energy and perseverance to the work of rendering available for agricultural purposes this extensive and once nearly worthless tract."—*Encyclopædia Britannica*; new edition.

† *Progress of the Nation*, p. 155.

‡ "In the said manner are two towns, one called Over Combe, in which reside the yeomen, who are occupied in the culture and working of the land which lies on the hill, and the other called Nether Combe, in which dwell the men who are to make cloth, such as weavers, fullers, dyers, and other tradesmen."—William of Worcester, between 1430 and 1465, quoted in Scrope's *History of Castle Combe*.

§ "Looking to the rent-rolls (land tax and other documents) of former times, it will be found that, whilst stiff (wheat and bean) land has stood still, or is rather deteriorated in value, the light, or what is called poor land, from an improved system of cropping, has risen most considerably." —*Poor Law Commissioner's Report*.

‖ "Other and scarcely less interesting evidences of ancient population in districts that in modern times remain "uninvaded by the plough."* The places at which the people of early days were accustomed to assemble—and where they have left behind them evidences of their existence, in stone circles, similar to that of Salisbury Plain, in England—will invariably be found in those portions of the kingdom now presenting the smallest inducements for occupation or cultivation.† Inquiring for the homes of the chiefs by whom the peace of the country was in former times so frequently disturbed, we find them in the higher regions of the country; but if we desire to see what has been styled the "granary of Scotland," we are referred to the light and easily cleared and cultivated soils of the Moray Frith. Asking for the newest soils, we are taken to the Lothians, or to the banks of the Tweed, inhabited but a short time since by barbarians, whose greatest pleasure was found in expeditions, for the purpose of plunder, into the adjacent English counties. Seeking the forests and swamps of the days of Mary and Elizabeth, we find the finest farms in Scotland. Desiring to find the poorest people, we are referred to the isles of the west—Mull or Skye—which were occupied when meadow lands were yet undrained; to Mona's Isle,

are still observable in remote nooks of the Western Highlands, where the Dalriadic Scots first effected a settlement in the land which has borne their name for centuries. * * In various districts of the same neighborhood, and particularly amid the scenes on which a new interest has been conferred as those in which the great Campbell passed some of his earlier years, the curious traveller may descry amid "the desolate heath" indications on the hill-side of a degree of cultivation having existed at some former period far beyond what is exhibited in that locality at the present day. The soil on the sloping sides of the hills appears to have been retained by dwarf walls, and these singular terraces occur frequently at such altitudes as must convey a remarkably vivid idea of the extent and industry of an ancient population, where now the grazing of a few black cattle alone tempts to the claim of property in the soil. *In other districts the half-obliterated furrows are still traceable on heights which have been abandoned for ages to the fox and the eagle.*" "Such evidences of ancient population" as the writer adds, "occur in many parts of Scotland, and have given rise to the superstition of "elf furrows, by which," as he says, "they are commonly known."—Wilson. *Pre-historic Annals of Scotland*, p. 74.

* "Of these primitive pit dwellings numerous traces are discernible on Leuchar moss, in the parish of Skene and in other localities of Aberdeenshire; on the banks of Loch Fine in Argyleshire; in the counties of Inverness and Caithness; and in various other districts of Scotland, *still uninvaded by the plough.*"—*Ibid.*, p. 123.

† "On one of the wildest moors in the parish of Tongland, Kirkcudbrightshire, a similar example may be seen, consisting of a circle of eleven stones, with a twelfth of larger dimensions in the centre, the summits of the whole appearing just above the moss."—*Ibid.*, p. 116.

celebrated in the days when the rich soil of the Lothians was yet uncultivated; or to the Orkneys, deemed in former times so valuable as to be received by the King of Norway in pledge for the payment of an amount far greater than the poor islands would now command, did the sale include the land itself as well as the right of sovereignty. Standing on the hills of Sutherland, we are in the midst of lands that have been, from time immemorial, cultivated by starving Highlanders; but on the flats below are rich crops of turnips growing on soil that was, but a few years since, a waste. Stand where we may—on Arthur's Seat, or Stirling's towers; or on the hills which border the great valley of Scotland—we see fertile soils, almost, even when not wholly, undrained and unoccupied, while around may be seen high and dry lands that have been for centuries in cultivation.

§ 6. Looking to France in the days of Cæsar, we see the Arverni, the Edui, and the Sequani, descendants of the earliest possessors of Gaul, and the most powerful among her tribes, seated on the flanks of the Alps, in a country now far less populous than it was then.* There however it is that we find great centres of trade

* "*Le Morvan*," a territory containing a hundred and fifty square leagues, "across which, but forty years since, there was neither a great road nor a departmental road, nor even a single local one of any importance in good condition. There were no bridges. At the most, occasional trees, scarcely squared, were thrown across the streams, but most commonly stones were disposed here and there to facilitate the passage of the traveller. Although situated in the heart of France, this country was absolutely impassable by the people of the neighboring ones—frightful by reason of the cold, the snow, the character of the soil, and the wildness of its occupants—a true *pays de loup*, in which the traveller feared to find himself involved. This country, nevertheless, then an integral portion of the State of the Œdui, had followed the progress of that people, friends and allies of the Romans and the most civilized of all the Gauls, whose capital, Autun, had merited the title of *Soror et æmula Romæ*. It was traversed by fine military roads of which we yet find the remains in a state of perfect preservation. Antique medals are there frequently discovered, and widely disseminated over the country are the ruins of ancient residences, amid which are found the fragments of sculptures and of mosaics, which reveal to us the magnificence of their ancient masters. Their great merit may be appreciated on an examination of the beautiful mosaic of *Autun*, recently exhibited in Paris and London—by that of *Villars*, near to *Chatillon-en-Bazois*—and that of *Chaigneau*—in the midst of the forests of Chastellux. The abundance and perfection of this description of works prove the existence of great opulence and exquisite taste, fruits of an ancient civilization, which perished in barbaric times, and which modern civilization is far from having equalled."—*Journal des Economistes*, December, 1852.

in the rich cities of Bibracte, Vienne, and Noviodunum—while the now rich Belgica presented to view but a single place of any note; and that at the place of passage of the river Somme, where stands the city of Amiens. Still higher, amongst the Alps themselves, we see the Helvetii, with their dozen cities and near four hundred villages. Looking west, we see in the savage Brittany, where wolves even yet abound, another portion of the early settlers of Gaul, with their wretched *oppidi* placed upon rocky promontories of the coast, or in the almost inaccessible gorges of the interior country. Everywhere around, among the highest and poorest lands, even now are seen monuments of their existence, the like of which are never found among the lower and richer lands of France. Seeking on the map for the cities with whose names we are most familiar as connected with the history of that country in the days of the founder of the Capetian race, of St. Louis, and of Philip Augustus—Chalons, St. Quentin, Soissons, Rheims, Troyes, Nancy, Orleans, Bourges, Dijon, Vienne, Nismes, Toulouse, or Cahors, once the great centre of the banking operations of France—we find them far towards the heads of the streams on which they stand, or occupying the high grounds between the rivers. Looking next for the centres of power at a later period, we meet them in wild and savage Brittany, yet inhabited by a people but little removed from barbarism—in Dijon, at the foot of the Alps—in Auvergne, but recently, if not even yet, a "secret and safe asylum of crime, amidst inaccessible rocks and wilds, which nature seems to have designed rather for beasts than men"—in the Limousin, which gave to the church so many popes that the Limousin cardinals at length were almost enabled to dictate the proceedings of the Conclave, and yet is now among the poorest parts of France—or on the flanks of the Cevennes, where literature and art were far advanced at a period when the richer soils of the kingdom remained uncultivated.*

* "These men"—the inhabitants of the country between the Mediterranean, the Rhone and the Garonne—"for the most part vassals of the Count of Toulouse, were in the twelfth and thirteenth centuries, infinitely more civilized than those of the rest of Gaul. They carried on a greater commerce with the East, where the signature of their Count had greater credit than the King of France's seal. Their towns had a municipal organization, and had even the external appearances of the Italian republics. * * Their literature was the most refined in all Europe, and their literary idiom was classical in Italy and Spain: their Christianity, ardent and even exalted—for they were naturally impassioned—did not consist in an implicit belief

Even yet, after the lapse of so many centuries, its richest soils remain undrained—marshy lands abounding throughout the kingdom, for the reclamation of which the aid of government is now invoked.*

Turning next to Belgium we see the rude and poor Luxemburg and Limburg to have been cultivated from a period far beyond the range of history, while Flanders, now so rich, remained until the seventh century an impenetrable desert. As late even as the thirteenth century, the forest of Soignies covered the site of the city of Brussels, and the fertile province of Brabant was in a great degree uncultivated; yet have we but to pass to the next adjoining province, that of Antwerp, to find, in the now almost abandoned *Campine*, evidences of cultivation dating back to the commencement of our era. There are found the ancient city of Heerenthals, with its walls and gates—and Gheel, which dates back to the seventh century; and there the traveller passes over the domain of the Counts of Merode, with its castle of Westerloo, one of the oldest in Belgium; in the ditches of which are yet found implements of war dating back to the period of the Romans. Everywhere, the oldest villages are found on the knolls, or in the sand, near the swamps with which the country was once to so great an extent covered. The wool trade of the country had its origin in the *Campine*, and it was to the necessity for communication between the people of these and other poor lands that the existence of many of the towns and cities was due. In the days of Cæsar, the site of the present Maestricht was known only as the place of passage of the Maes—and that of Amiens was then but little more than the place of passage of the Somme; while the *Broecksel* of a later period, now Brussels, came into notice because of being used by those who required to cross the Senne.

of the dogmas, and a mechanical observance of the practices of the Roman church. * * To stop this intellectual contagion, nothing less was necessary than to strike the people collectively, and annihilate the social order from which its independent spirit and its civilization proceeded." Hence the crusade against the Waldenses, and Albigeois, which resulted in the incorporation of these provinces into the Kingdom of France, the most disastrous event in the history of Southern France. "The old civilization of these provinces," continues *M. Thierry*, "received a mortal blow from their union with countries less advanced in cultivation, in manufactures, in policy, and in taste for the arts."—*History of the Conquest of England*, vol. iii. p. 324.

* *Journal des Economistes*, Nov. 1855, p. 210.

In the early history of Holland, we see a miserable people, surrounded by forests and marshes covering the most fertile lands—but living on islands of sand, and forced to content themselves with eggs, fish, and very small supplies of vegetable food of any kind. Their extreme poverty exempted them from the grinding taxation of Rome, and by slow degrees they increased in numbers and in wealth. Chief among the provinces, however, from an early period, was the narrow district lying between Utrecht and the sea, which eventually gave its name Haupt, or headland, to the entire region—and there it is we find the poorest soil, capable of yielding little beside bent, or fern. Unable by means of agriculture to obtain food, the Dutch sought it from manufactures and trade. Wealth and population continued to grow, and with their growth came the clearing of woods, the draining of marshes, and the subjection to cultivation of the rich soils in the outset so much avoided; until at length we find in it the richest nation of Europe.

§ 7. Further north, we meet a people whose ancestors passed from the neighborhood of the Don, through the rich plains of Northern Germany, and finally selected for themselves the barren mountains of the Scandinavian peninsula—as the land best suited for them in their then existing condition.* Poor as was the

* The philosophy of this is thus most accurately exhibited by one of the best travellers of our time, a gentleman who has given much attention to every portion of the Scandinavian Peninsula. "What could have induced a migratory population from the Tanais (the Don), on which traditionary history fixes their original seat, after reaching the southern shores of the Baltic, to have turned to the north and crossed the sea to establish themselves on bleak, inhospitable rocks, and in the severe climate of Scandinavia, instead of overspreading the finer countries on the south side of the Baltic? * * * We make a wrong estimate of the comparative facilities of subsisting, in the early ages of mankind, in the northern and southern countries of Europe. If a tribe of red men from the forests of America had been suddenly transported in the days of Tacitus to the forests of Europe beyond the Rhine, where would they, in what is called the hunter state, that is, depending for subsistence on the spontaneous productions of nature, have found in the greatest abundance the means and facilities of subsisting themselves? Unquestionably on the Scandinavian peninsula, intersected by narrow inlets of the sea teeming with fish, by lakes and rivers rich in fish, and in a land covered with forests, in which not only all the animals of Europe that are food for man abound, but from the numerous lakes, rivers, ponds, and precipices in this hunting field, are to be got at and caught with much greater facility than on the boundless plains, on which, from the Rhine to the Elbe, and from the Elbe to the Vistula, or to the steppes of Asia, to hem in a herd of wild animals in their flight."—Laing, *Chronicles of the Sea Kings, Introductory Dissertation*, p. 39.

general character of the soil, the poorest portions of it were those first settled. Everywhere throughout the country is found a repetition of the facts already described in regard to Scotland—the marks of early agriculture being found on high and poor lands that long since have been abandoned. To such an extent has this been the case, that it has afforded countenance to the belief that the peninsula must really have been the seat of the great "Northern Hive," the overflow from which had peopled Southern Europe —it having been supposed that no one would have cultivated these very poor soils when it rested with himself to select for his use the very rich ones that, according to M. Ricardo, are always first selected for occupation. The facts here observed are, however, only a repetition of those we see to have occurred in North and South America, in England, Scotland, France, and Belgium.

Looking next to Russia, we find a recurrence of the same great fact.* "Almost everwhere," says a recent English traveller, "we see the poorest soil selected for cultivation, whilst that of the richest description remains neglected in its vicinity; for the poorer soil is generally the higher ground, which requires no trouble in draining."†

In Germany, according to Tacitus, "but a small part of the open and level country was occupied;" the natives dwelling "chiefly in forests, or on the summit of that continuous ridge of mountains by which Suevia is divided and separated from other tribes that lie still more remote."‡ Looking now to the country watered by the Danube and its tributaries, we see the population abounding at the heads of the streams, but gradually diminishing as we descend the great river, until at length reaching the richest lands, we find them entirely unoccupied. Pausing for a moment in Hungary, we see in "the Puszta" the cradle, or rather, as we are told by a recent traveller, "the keep of Hungarian nationality"—and here

* "The government of Pskow occupies the ninth place in regard to its relative extent of arable land, whilst, in consequence of the bad quality of its soil, it is one of the poorest in regard to its productive forces. On the other hand, the governments of Podolia, Saratow, and Wolhynia, which are the most fertile portions of the empire, occupy a rank far inferior to many others, in regard to their extent of cultivated land."—*Tegoborski's Russia*, vol. i. p. 131.

† *Revelations of Russia*, vol. i. p. 355.

‡ *Manners of the Germans*, chap. xliii.

we have a wide plain extending from the Theiss to the Danube, containing 15,000 square miles—consisting of a series of sandhills that roll away like waves, until earth and sky are blended together.*

Beyond the Theiss, rich lands abound, exhibiting no signs of life except "countless flocks of wild birds, cranes, and ducks, and divers, among the reeds—there, on a bank, a vulture tearing some carrion to pieces; and now and then the bold eagle or the hawk flying heavily by, scarcely any of these stirring at our approach. A lonely, desolate scene enough, but a part of those immense marshy districts in Hungary whose drainage, under an efficient agriculture, would reclaim so much good land; and which are now the causes of such deadly fevers and diseases."†

Looking into Italy, we see a numerous population in the highlands of Cisalpine Gaul, at a period when the rich soils of Venetia were unoccupied. Passing southward, along the flanks of the Apennines, we find a gradually increasing population, with an increasing tendency to the cultivation of the better soils; and towns whose age may almost be inferred from their situation. The Samnite hills were peopled, Etruria was occupied, and Veii and Alba were built, before Romulus gathered together his adventurers on

* "The expanse, in truth, resembles the great ocean solidified. Mile after mile it stretches away in a dull, depressing uniformity, unbroken by a village, a house, or a tree. Indeed, the name by which the plain is known—the Puszta—means "empty or "void;" and it is well described by its name. It is bare, naked, and desolate, and destitute even of a stream of water. Here and there the long pole of a draw-well rises against the sky, like a spectral arm; or like the mast of a stranded ship. Occasionally a herd of cattle strays along in search of herbage, watched by mountain herdsmen. The only other sign of life is a solitary crane or stork, perched on one leg, amidst a bog white with the powder of soda; or a vulture wheeling high in the air in search of prey. A profound silence rests on the plain; and when broken by the herdsman's voice, or the bellowing of the cattle, the sound startles the ear, as it speeds, one knows not whence, on the wings of the wind. * * Its denizens are pure and unadulterated Hungarians; the same men as the Magyars, when, a thousand years ago, they wandered away in search of "fresh fields and pastures new," from the plains of distant Asia. Every man is a horseman, and every one is able and ready to become a soldier in defence of his country. The inhabitants of the Puszta are herdsmen, following great droves of horses, buffaloes, snow-white bullocks, sheep, and swine, from pasture to pasture; and remaining the whole year round beneath the canopy of heaven. The wildest amongst them are the swineherds, and their greatest distinction is to be a redoubtable fighter. They are pre-eminently the heroes of the plain. Even their very pleasures are warlike and sanguinary."

† *Brace's Letters on Hungary*, N. 12.

the banks of the Tiber; and Aquileia filled a place in Roman history that was denied to the site of the modern Pisa.

In the island of Corsica there are three distinct regions; on the lower one of which the sugar-cane, the cotton-plant, tobacco, and even indigo could be grown; and it might be made, as we are told, "the India of the Mediterranean."* The second "represents the climate of Burgundy, Morvan, and Bretagne, in France," all of which latter the reader has seen to have been the seats of early settlement; and here it is, accordingly, that "the greater part of the Corsicans live in scattered hamlets on the mountain side, or in the valleys."† Looking next to Sicily, we learn that "the natives seem to have been of rude pastoral habits, dispersed either among petty hill-villages, or in caverns hewn out of the rock, like the primitive inhabitants of the Balearic islands and Sardinia;"‡ and yet, of all the islands of the Mediterranean, none so much abounded in those rich soils which, according to M. Ricardo, should have been first appropriated.

Turning now to Greece, we meet the same great and universal fact. Earliest amongst the settlements were those of the hills of Arcadia, which long preceded those on the lands of Elis watered by the Alpheus; and the meagre soil of Attica, whose poverty was such as to have been assigned as a reason why it had escaped the desolating presence of invaders of early ages, was among the earliest occupied; while the fat Bœotia followed slowly in its rear. On the hill-tops, in various quarters, the sites of deserted cities presented, in the historical times of Greece, evidences of former occupation§ and cultivation. The short, steep slope of eastern Argolis was early abandoned as incapable of yielding a return to labor, yet there was the seat of "the Halls of Tiryns," and there now are found the ruins of the palace of Agamemnon, and of the Acropolis of Mycenæ. The place of the city, as we are told by Aristotle, "was chosen because the lower part of the plain was then so marshy as to be unproductive;" whereas, in his own time, or almost eight centuries afterwards, the plain of Mycenæ had become barren, and that of Argos well drained and fertile.|| North of the

* *Gregorovius's Corsica*, p. 143. † *Ibid.*, p. 144.
‡ Grote. *History of Greece*, vol. iii. 368.
§ Grote. *History of Greece*, vol. ii. 108.
|| Leake. *Travels in the Morea*, vol. ii. 366.

Gulf of Corinth, we see the Phocians, the Locrians, and the Etolians, clustered together on the highest and poorest lands; while the rich plains of Thessaly and of Thrace remained almost entirely unpeopled.

Crossing the Mediterranean we see the mountainous and rocky Crete to have been occupied from the earliest ages, while the Delta of the Nile remained a wilderness. Ascending that river, cultivation becomes more and more ancient as we rise, until at length far towards its head we reach Thebes, the first capital of Egypt. With the growth of population and of wealth we find the city of Memphis becoming the capital of the kingdom; but still later, the Delta is occupied, and towns and cities rise in places that to the earlier kings were inaccessible—and with every step in this direction there was increased return to labor.

Turning eastward from the Nile, we see the most civilized portion of the people of Northern Africa clustering round the mountains of the Atlas, while the richer lands in the direction of the coast remain in a state of nature. Looking next south, the Capital of Abyssinia is found at an elevation of no less than 8,000 feet above the sea, while lands of unbounded capability remain entirely uncultivated. Everywhere throughout Africa, the greatest amount of population and of wealth, and the nearest approach to civilization, are found on the elevated table lands whose natural drainage fits them for early occupation—while everywhere on the rich lands, towards the mouths of the great streams, population is small, and man is found in the lowest state of barbarism.

§ 8. Passing by the Red Sea and entering the Pacific, we see almost innumerable islands whose lower lands are unoccupied, their superior richness rendering them dangerous to life; while population clusters round the hills. Farther south, are rich valleys in Australia, uninhabited, or, where inhabited at all, it is by a people standing lowest among the human race; while on the little high-pointed islands of the coast, but a few miles distant, are found a superior race, with houses, cultivation, and manufactures. Turning our steps northward, towards India, we meet Ceylon, in the centre of which are found the dominions of the king of Candy, whose subjects have the same aversion to the low and rich lands, unhealthy in their present state, that is felt by the people of

Mexico and of Java. Entering India by Cape Comorin, and following the great range of high lands, the back-bone of the peninsula, we find the cities of Seringapatam, Poonah, and Ahmednugger; while below, near the coast, are seen the European cities of Madras, Calcutta and Bombay, the creation of a very recent day. Intermediate between the two, are seen numerous cities, whose positions, sometimes far away from the banks of the rivers, and at other times near their sources, show that the most fertile lands have not been those first cultivated. Standing on the high lands between Calcutta and Bombay, we have on the one hand the delta of the Indus, and on the other that of the magnificent Ganges. Through hundreds of miles the former rolls its course, almost without a settlement on its banks; while on the higher country, right and left, exists a numerous population. The rich Delta of the latter is unoccupied, and if we desire to find the seat of early cultivation we must follow its course until far up towards its head, we meet Delhi, the capital of all India while yet the government remained in the hands of its native sovereigns. Here, as everywhere, man avoids the low rich soils that need clearing and drainage, and seeks in the higher lands that drain themselves, the means of employing his labor in the search for food—and here, as always when the superficial soil alone is cultivated, the return to labor is small. Hence it is that we find the Hindoo working for a rupee, or two, per month; sufficient only to give him a handful of rice per day, and to purchase a rag of cotton cloth with which to cover his loins. The most fertile soils exist in unlimited quantity on land that is untouched; and close to that which the laborer scratches with a stick for want of a spade, raking his harvest with his hands for want of a reaping hook, and carrying home upon his shoulders the miserable crop, for want of a horse and a cart.

Passing northward, by Caubul and Affghanistan, and leaving on our left the barren Persia, whose weak dry soils have been cultivated through a long series of ages, we attain the highest point of the earth's surface; and here, even among the Himalayas themselves, we find the same order of cultivation—the villages being everywhere placed upon slopes upon which their people grow scanty crops of millet, maize, and buckwheat; while the bottom lands are generally a mass of jungle, unappropriated and uncultivated

vated.* Immediately around is the cradle of the human race, where head the streams that empty into the Frozen Ocean and the Bay of Bengal, the Mediterranean and the Pacific. It is the land, of all others, suited to the purpose; that which will most readily afford to the man who works without a spade or an axe, a small supply of food—and therefore the one least fitted for his uses when he has acquired power to direct the forces of nature to his service.

Here we are surrounded by man in a state of barbarism; and standing here, we may trace the course of successive tribes and nations passing towards the lower and more productive lands; but compelled in all cases to seek the route least disturbed with water-courses—and therefore keeping the ridge that divides the waters of the Black Sea and the Mediterranean from those of the Baltic. Standing here we may mark them, as they descend the slope, sometimes stopping for the purpose of cultivating the hilly land that can, with their indifferent machinery, be made to yield a small supply of food; at others marching on and reaching the neighborhood of the sea, there to place themselves, not on the rich lands, but on the poor soils of the steep hill-side—those on which water cannot stand to give nourishment to trees, or to afford annoyance to settlers whose means are inadequate to the draining of marshes and of swamps; or on little peaked islands, from which the water passes rapidly, as is the case with those of the Ægean, cultivated from so early a period. Some of these tribes are seen reaching the Mediterranean, where civilization is first found, and soonest lost under the pressure of successive waves of emigration; while others are passing farther west, and entering Italy, France, and Spain. Others, more adventurous, reach the British isles. Again, after a few centuries of rest, we see them crossing the broad Atlantic, and commencing the ascent of the slope of the Alleghany, preparatory to the ascent and passage of the great range dividing the waters of the Pacific from those of the Atlantic; and in all cases we mark the pioneers gladly seizing on the clear dry land of the steep hill-side, in preference to the rich and highly wooded land of the river bottoms. Everywhere we see them, as population gradually increases, descending the sides of the hills and mountains towards the rich lands at their feet; and every-

* See *Hooke's Himalayan Journals.*

where, with the growth of numbers, penetrating the earth to reach the lower soils, to enable them to combine the upper clay, or sand, with the lower marl, or lime—and thus to compound for themselves, out of the various materials with which they have been provided by the Deity, a soil capable of yielding a larger return than that upon which they were at first compelled to expend their labor. Everywhere, with increased power of union, we see them exercising increased power over land. Everywhere, as the new soils are brought into activity, and as their occupants are enabled to obtain larger returns, we find more rapid increase of population, producing increased tendency to combination of exertion, by help of which their powers are trebled, quadrupled, and quintupled, and sometimes fifty-fold increased; enabling them better to provide for their immediate wants, while accumulating more rapidly the machinery by means of which further to increase their power of production, and still more fully to bring to light the vast treasures of nature. Everywhere, we find that with increasing population the supply of food becomes more abundant and regular, and clothing and shelter are obtained with greater ease—famine and pestilence tend to pass away—health becomes more universal—life becomes more and more prolonged—and man becomes more happy and more free.

In regard to all the wants of man, except the single and important one of food, such is admitted to be the case. It is seen that with the growth of population and of wealth men obtain water, and iron, and coal, and clothing—and the use of houses, and ships, and roads—in return for less labor than had been at first required. It is not doubted that the gigantic works by means of which great rivers are carried through our cities, enable men to obtain water at smaller cost than was required when each man took a bucket and helped himself on the river bank. It is seen that the shaft which has required years to sink, and to discharge the water from which the most powerful engines are required, supplies fuel at far less cost of labor than has been required when the early settlers carried home the scraps of half-decomposed timber, for want of an axe with which to cut the already fallen log—that the grist-mill converts the grain into flour more cheaply than was the case when it was pounded between stones—and that the gigantic factory supplies cloth more cheaply than the little loom; but it is denied that such is the case in reference to the soils required for cultivation. In regard to every thing else, man commences with the worst machinery and proceeds upward towards the best; but in regard to land, and that alone, he commences, according to Mr. Ricardo, with the best and proceeds downward towards the worst; and with every stage of his progress finds a decreasing return to labor, threatening starvation, and admonishing him against raising children to aid him in his age; lest they should imitate the conduct of the people of India and of the islands of the Pacific,—where land, however, is abundant and food *should* be cheap,—and bury him alive or expose him on the river shore, that they may divide among themselves his modicum of food.

How far all this is so the reader will now determine for himself. All others of the laws of nature are broad and universally true, and he may now agree with us in believing that there is one law, and one alone, for food, light, air, clothing, and fuel—that man, in all and every case, commences with the worst machinery and proceeds onward to the best—and that he is thus enabled, with the growth of wealth, of population, and of the power of association, to obtain with constantly diminishing labor an increased supply of all the necessaries, conveniences, comforts, and luxuries of life.

In further proof, if proof can yet be required, it may be mentioned that almost everywhere tradition carries back the early settlement of the various portions of the world to the higher lands. The traditions of the Chinese place their ancestors at the heads of the great rivers, in the high table-lands of Asia. The Brahmins derive their origin from the Vale of Cashmere, and throughout Asia that region is recognised by a term equivalent to that of "the roof of the world." The name of Abram, father of the high land, became in time Abraham, father of a multitude; and the Northmen placed the city of Odin in Aasgard, or the castle of Aas,—"which word," says Mr. Laing, "still remains in the Northern languages, signifying a ridge of high land."*

Again: rivers never, as we are told by Agassiz, establish a line of separation between terrestrial animals; and it is as a consequence of this that "the watersheds, not the rivers," are "found

* Chronicle of the Sea Kings, Saga 1.

to constitute the demarcations of an accurate ethnographical map."* Were it possible that man could commence the work of cultivation on rich bottom lands, such would not be the case; because as population and wealth increased he would find himself irresistibly impelled towards the higher and poorer lands, as here is shown:

Mr. Ricardo places his early settlers at the point marked B, being that at which the lands are richest; and where the natural advantages of situation are greatest, because of the proximity of the river. As their numbers increase, they must ascend the hill, or fly to some other valley, there to resume their labors. Directly the reverse of this, as the reader has seen, is what has occurred in every quarter of the world—the work of cultivation having everywhere been commenced on the sides of the hills, marked A, where the soil was poorest, and where the natural advantages of situation were the least. With the growth of wealth and population, men have been seen descending from the high lands bounding the valley on either side, and coming together at their feet. Hence it is that rivers are never found to be the dividing lines of races of animals or of nations.

The doctrine of Mr. Ricardo is that of increasing dispersion and weakness; whereas under the real laws of nature there is a tendency towards a constant increase of that power of association and combination to which alone man is indebted for the ability to subjugate the more productive soils. As he descends the hills and meets his neighbor man, efforts are combined, employments are divided, individual faculties are stimulated into action, property becomes more and more divided, equality grows, commerce becomes enlarged, and person and property become more secure; and every step in this direction is but preparation for further progress.

* *Edinburgh Review*, January, 1851: article, Devon and Cornwall.

# CHAPTER V.

## THE SAME SUBJECT CONTINUED.

§ 1. POPULATION and wealth tend to increase, and cultivation tends towards the more fertile soils, when man is allowed to obey those instincts of his nature which prompt him to seek association with his fellow-men. They tend to decrease as association declines, and then the fertile soils are everywhere abandoned; and with every step in that direction the difficulty of obtaining food is increased. Population it is that makes the food come from the rich soils of the earth; while depopulation drives the unhappy cultivator back to the poorer ones.

When men are poor, they are compelled to select such soils as they *can* cultivate, not such as they *would*. Although gathered around the sides of the same mountain range, the difficulty of obtaining food compels them to remain far distant from each other; and having no roads, they are unable to associate for self-defence. The thin soils yield small returns, and the little tribe embraces some who would prefer to live by the labor of others rather than by their own. The scattered people may be plundered with ease, and half a dozen men, combined for the purpose, may rob in succession all the persons of whom the little community is composed. The opportunity makes the robber, and the most daring among them becomes the leader of the band. One by one, the people who would desire to live by their own labor are plundered; and thus are they who prefer the work of plunder enabled to pass their time in dissipation. The leader divides the spoil, and with its help is enabled to augment the number of his followers, and thus to enlarge the sphere of his depredations. With the gradual increase of the little community, he is led, however, to commute with them for a certain share of their produce, which he calls rent, or tax, or *taille*. Population and wealth grow very slowly, because of the large proportion which the non-laborers bear to the laborers. The good soils are but slowly improved, because the people are unable to obtain spades with which to cultivate the land, or axes by help of which to clear it. Few want leather, and there is no tanner on the spot to use their hides. Few can afford shoes, and there is no shoemaker to eat their corn, while making those which are required. Few have horses, and there is no blacksmith. Combination of effort has scarcely an existence.

By very slow degrees, however, they are enabled to reduce to cultivation better lands, thus lessening the distance between themselves and the neighboring settlement, where rules another little sovereign. Each chief, however, now covets the power of taxing the subjects of his neighbor, and, as a consequence, war ensues—the object of both being plunder, but disguised under the name of "glory." Each invades the domain of the other, and each endeavors to weaken his opponent by murdering his rent-payers, burning their houses, and wasting their little farms; while manifesting, perhaps, the utmost courtesy to the chief himself. The richer lands are now abandoned, and their drains fill up, while the tenants are forced to seek for food among the poor soils of the hills to which they have fled for safety. At the end of a year or two, peace is made, and the work of clearing has again to be performed. Population and wealth having, however, diminished, the means of recommencing the work have now again to be created—and that, too, under the most disadvantageous circumstances. With continued peace, the work advances, and, after a few years, population, wealth, and cultivation regain the point from which they had fallen. New wars, however, ensue, for the determination of the question: Which of the two chiefs shall collect all the (so-called) rent? After great waste of life and property, one of them being slain, the other falls his heir, having thus acquired both plunder and glory. He now wants a title, by which to be distinguished from those by whom he is surrounded. He is a little king; and as similar operations are performed elsewhere, such kings become numerous. Population extending itself, and each little sovereign now coveting the dominions of his neighbors, new wars are made, and always with the same result—the people invariably flying to their hills for safety—the best lands being abandoned — food becoming more scarce — and famine and pestilence sweeping off those whose flight had preserved them from "the tender mercies" of the invading force.

Small kings now becoming great ones, find themselves surrounded by lesser chiefs, who glorify themselves in the number of their murders and in the amount of plunder they have acquired. Counts, viscounts, earls, marquises, and dukes next make their appearance on the stage, heirs of the power and of the *rights* of the robber chiefs of early days. Population and wealth go backward, and the love of title grows with the growth of barbarism.* Wars are now made on a larger scale, and greater "glory" is acquired. In the midst of distant and highly fertile lands, occupied by a numerous population, are rich cities, whose people, unused to arms, may be robbed with impunity — always an important consideration to those with whom the pursuit of glory is a trade. Provinces are laid waste, and the population is exterminated; or, if a few escape, they fly to the hills and mountains, there to perish of famine. Peace follows, after years of destruction, but the rich lands are overgrown; the spades and axes, the cattle and the sheep, are gone; the houses are destroyed; their owners have ceased to exist; and a long period of abstinence from the work of desolation is required to regain the point from which cultivation had been driven by men intent upon the gratification of their own selfish desires, at the cost of the welfare and happiness of the people over whose destinies they have so unhappily ruled. Population grows again slowly, and wealth but little more rapidly, for almost ceaseless wars have impaired the disposition and the respect for honest labor — while the necessity for beginning once more the work of cultivation on the poor soils

* It is interesting to trace with each step in the progress of the decay of the Roman Empire, the gradual increase in the magnificence of titles; and so again with the decline of modern Italy. In France, they became almost universal as the wars of religion barbarized the people. The high-sounding titles of the East are in keeping with the weakness of those by whom they are assumed, as are the endless names of the Spanish grandee with the poverty of the soil cultivated by his dependants. The time is probably approaching when men of real dignity will reject the whole system as an absurdity, and when small men alone will think themselves elevated by the title of Esquire, Honorable, Baron, Marquis, or Duke. Extremes always meet. The son of the duke rejoices in the possession of half a dozen Christian names, and the little retailer of tea and sugar calls his daughter Amanda Malvina Fitzallan—Smith, or Pratt; while the gentleman calls his son Robert, or John.

adds to the distaste for labor. Swords or muskets are now held to be more honorable implements than spades and pickaxes; and the habit of union for any honest purpose being almost extinct, thousands are ready, at any moment, to join in expeditions in search of plunder. War thus feeds itself by producing poverty, depopulation, and the abandonment of the most fertile soils; while peace also feeds itself by increasing the number of men and the habit of association, because of the constantly increasing power to draw supplies of food from the surface already occupied, as the almost boundless powers of the earth are developed in the progress of population and of wealth.

§ 2. The views above given are not in accordance with the doctrine of Mr. Ricardo, yet, look where we may, there is furnished evidence of their truth. If to India, we may see the rich soil everywhere relapsing into jungle, while its late occupant starves among the forts of the hills. In hither Asia we see the country washed by the Tigris and the Euphrates—a land of unbounded fertility, and one that in times long past maintained the most powerful communities in the world—now so utterly abandoned, that Mr. Layard found himself compelled to seek the land of the hills when he desired to find a people at home. Hence it is that ague and fever, the constant concomitants of wild and uncultivated lands, are found to be the universal scourge of Eastern travel.

Coming west, we see the high lands of Armenia to be so well occupied as to give occasion to the continued existence of a city like that of Erzeroum; while around the ancient Sinope nothing is to be seen but forests of timber, whose gigantic size affords proof conclusive of the fertile character of the soil in which they grow. Passing farther west, and arriving in Constantinople, we find the great valley of Buyukdere—once known as "the fair land"—totally abandoned, while the city is supplied with food for its daily consumption from the hills forty or fifty miles distant; and the picture there presented is but an exhibition in miniature of the whole Turkish empire. The rich lands of the Lower Danube, once the busy theatre of Roman life and industry, furnish now but a miserable subsistence to a few Servian swineherds and Wallachian peasants. Throughout the

Ionian Islands the richest lands, once in a state of high cultivation, are now almost entirely abandoned; and must so continue until there can be again exhibited that habit of association which enables man to combine with his fellow-man for the subjugation of nature.

Coming now to Africa, we may trace the increase of that habit, and the growth of that power, in the gradual descent of population towards the Nile — bringing into activity the rich lands of the Delta; and with their decline, the abandonment of those lands, the filling up of the canals, and the concentration of the population on the higher and less productive soils. Passing thence to the Roman province, we see the rich lands of the olden time — the plains of the Metidja, of Bona, and others — almost, even when not quite, abandoned; while the yet remaining population clusters around the mountains of the Atlas. Looking next to Italy, we see a growing people subduing to cultivation the rich lands of the Campagna and of Latium, to be again gradually abandoned — and now affording miserable subsistence to men, many of whom go clothed in skins of beasts—and whose number but little exceeds that of the cities which once flourished there. Passing north, we may see the rich lands of the Siennese republic in cultivation until the sixteenth century, when the ferocious Marignan drove to the hills the small remnant of the population that escaped the sword—and gave to the world a pestilential desert, in lieu of the highly cultivated farms that before abounded. Farther north may be seen the destruction of the canals of Pisa and the abandonment of its fertile soils, while its inhabitants perish by pestilence within the city walls—or transfer themselves to the head of the Arno, to seek there the subsistence no longer afforded by the richer lands near its mouth.

In France, in the days of the English wars, we see the lower and richer countries ravaged by bands of fierce mountaineers — the wild Breton, the ferocious Gascon, and the mercenary Swiss — united for the plunder of the men who cultivated the more fertile soils — and driving them to seek refuge in the wild and savage Brittany itself. We may see the richest lands of the kingdom rendered utterly desolate — *la Beauce*, one of its most fertile portions, becoming again a forest — while from Picardy to the Rhine not a house, unprotected by city walls, is left standing, nor a farm that is not stripped. In later times, Lorraine was reduced to a desert—and fine forests but recently stood where formerly the richer soils yielded liberal returns to labor. Throughout France we witness the effects of perpetual war, in the concentration of the whole agricultural population in villages, at a distance from the lands they cultivate—there inhaling a foul atmosphere, and losing half their time in transferring themselves, their rude implements, and their products, to and from their little properties; whereas the same labor bestowed upon the land itself would give to cultivation the richer soils.

§ 3. Crossing the Atlantic, we find further evidence of the fact that as population everywhere brings the food from the rich soils, so depopulation everywhere drives men back to the poor ones. In the days of Cortes, the valley of Mexico afforded food for a numerous people, but it is now in a state of desolation—its canals choked up and its cultivation abandoned; while, from the poorer lands that border it, strings of mules bring, from a distance of fifty miles, the provisions by which the people of the city are now supplied.

Passing north and arriving in the United States, we find further illustration of the law, that to enable men to pass from the cultivation of the poor to the rich lands there must be a growing habit of association, consequent upon diversification in the modes of employment, and development of their various individualities. The State of Virginia once stood at the head of the Union, but the policy she has advocated has tended to the exhaustion of the lands first cultivated and to the abandonment of her soil—the consequences of which are seen in the constantly increasing unhealthiness of the parts first occupied—the lower counties of the State. "The entire country," says a recent writer, "is full of the ruins of gentlemen's mansions—some of them palatial in size—and noble old churches, whose solid walls were built of imported brick, but which could not hold the builders. And as for their descendants," as he asks, "where are they? The splendor, indeed, which filled all the counties of Lower Virginia has departed. Why? Because the whole country is miasmatic, and is suffered to remain so. It is dangerous for whites to spend the sickly season there; and all, accordingly, who can, abandon their homes in August and September, to seek a more healthful location.

"This miasmatic region covers all the sea-coast of Virginia, North Carolina, South Carolina, Georgia, Florida, Alabama, Mississippi, and Louisiana, except occasionally an isolated spot; and extends inland from ten to a hundred miles. It is so bad in the vicinity of Charleston, that it is death to sleep a single night outside of the city; and even riding across the infected district in the night, on the railroad, has caused all the passengers to vomit like a sea-sick company on shipboard."

As a consequence of this, Virginia and Carolina are steadily declining in their position in the Union; and so must continue to do, until increase in the power of association shall enable them to cultivate their richest lands.—Looking to Jamaica, we see the same great fact as a result of the selfsame cause—a recent return of the property on the island showing that no less than 128 sugar estates have been totally, while 71 have been partially, abandoned. If to these be added the coffee and other estates wholly or partially so, the number amounts to 413—embracing an area of more than four hundred thousand acres.

Abandonment of the soil by a portion of its inhabitants, brings with it, necessarily, a diminution of the power of combination for the maintenance of drains that are required for the preservation of health—and for the construction and support of roads; and as the burdens increase, the disposition to fly from the land is seen augmenting from year to year. The purely agricultural country must export raw produce and must exhaust its soil; and such export must bring with it a necessity for the export of man—followed by constant decline in the power of association, in the development of individuality, in the ability to maintain commerce, and in the position of the community among the communities of the world. That such is the case is proved by the experience of all antiquity; and if we would see it fully established in modern times, we have but to turn our eyes to Portugal, Ireland, and Turkey in the Eastern hemisphere, and Jamaica, Carolina, and Virginia in the Western one.

Whenever population and wealth, and the consequent power of combination, are permitted to increase, there arises a tendency towards the abandonment of the poor lands first cultivated; as is proved by the experience of France, England, Scotland, Sweden, and several of our Northern States. Whenever, on the contrary, population, wealth, and the power of association decline, it is the rich soil that is abandoned by men who fly again to poor ones, in hopes to find in their cultivation the means of subsistence for their families and themselves. With every step in the former direction, there is an increase in the value of man and a decline in that of all the commodities required for his use, accompanied by growing facility of accumulation; whereas with every movement in the latter one, he becomes more and more the slave of nature and of his fellow-man, with constant increase in the value of commodities, and as constant decline in his own.

# CHAPTER VI.

## OF VALUE.

§ 1. With the growth of numbers and increase in the power of association, man is everywhere seen passing from the cultivation of the poor to that of the richer soils — from being the slave of nature towards becoming her absolute master, and compelling her to do his bidding — from a state of weakness towards one of strength — from being a mere creature of necessity towards becoming a being of power — from poverty to wealth — and now possessed of numerous objects to which he attaches the idea of VALUE. Why he does so, and how he is accustomed to measure value, we may now examine.

Our Crusoe, on his island, found himself surrounded by fruits, flowers, and animals of various descriptions—some of them more, and others less, calculated to supply his wants; but nearly all of them beyond the reach of his unassisted forces. The hare and the goat so far excelled him in speed, that he could have no hope for success in the chase while dependent on his legs alone. The bird could soar in the air, while he was chained to earth. The fish could sink at once into the deep water, where, if he attempted to follow, he would surely perish; and he might die of hunger in the sight of endless quantities of the materials of food, while the fly and the ant were rejoicing in the superabundance of their supplies. The tree would furnish him with a house, had he an axe with which to fell it; or a saw with which to convert it into planks. Destitute of these implements, he finds himself compelled to occupy a hole in the earth, always damp and always exposed to the wind; while the humble-bee is enabled to provide for herself the most perfect habitation.

Inferior to all other beings in the physical qualities required for self-preservation—and in the instinct which prompts them to the use of the faculties with which they have been endowed — he is greatly their superior in the fact that he has been gifted with intelligence to appreciate the natural forces by which he is surrounded; and with a hand to enable him to carry into effect the ideas suggested by his brain. If a stone can be made to strike a bird, gravitation, as he sees, will bring the latter within his reach. The elasticity of wood enables him, after repeated efforts, to detach a branch from the tree, and next its qualities of weight and hardness are brought into activity as he fells to the ground wild animals of strength greatly superior to his own. Having thus learned the existence of elasticity, he bends a piece of wood, and next the tenacity of animal fibre is brought into action as he converts it into a cord, by the help of which he completes a bow. He makes a canoe, by aid of which he is enabled to float upon the waters, and to pass from point to point in pursuit of game; and thus, step by step, he is seen obtaining power over various forces always existing in nature, and waiting only his call to enlist themselves in his service. With each he finds a diminution in the labor required for enabling him to obtain the food, the clothing, and the shelter by means of which his physical powers are sustained and invigorated, while his mental ones become more and more developed.

Working, in the early days of his sojourn on the island, with his hands alone, he was compelled to depend upon the fruits spontaneously yielded by the earth—to obtain a sufficient supply of which required almost unceasing exertion in wandering over extensive surfaces of land. Obtaining occasionally a little animal food, he attached to it a high degree of value — knowing well how great he had uniformly found to be the obstacles standing in the way of its attainment—and here it is we find the cause of the existence in the human mind of the idea of value, which is simply *our estimate of the resistance to be overcome, before we can enter upon the possession of the thing desired.* That resistance diminishes with every increase in the power of man to command the always gratuitous services of nature; and hence it is that we see in all advancing communities a steady increase in the value of labor when measured by commodities, and decline in that of commodities when measured by labor.

In the outset, vegetable food could be had in return for less exertion than was required for obtaining animal food; but with the possession of the bow a supply of meat can now be obtained with less effort than would be required for one of fruit. At once there is a change of value — birds and rabbits falling as compared with fruits, and the latter rising as compared with the former. Fish, however, are still unattainable, although abounding in the sea around him; and he would give, perhaps, half a dozen rabbits for a single perch. His inventive faculties are now stimulated by the desire for change of diet, while the increased facility of obtaining supplies of food enables him to devote more time to the improvement of machinery by help of which to command the services of nature. Converting a bone into a hook, he attaches it to a cord similar to the one he had used in making a bow, and is now enabled to obtain fish at even less cost of labor than would be required for similar supplies of other kinds of food. At once the former declines in value as compared with the latter, and the latter rises as compared with the former; but man rises in value as compared with all, because of the command he has obtained over the various natural forces. At first, his whole day had scarcely sufficed to afford indifferent supplies of the least nourishing food; but now, aided by nature, he obtains it in abundance, and at the cost of only half his time — leaving him the remainder to be applied to the making of clothing, the improvement of his habitation, and the preparation of machinery required for further enlargement of his powers.

With every step in this direction, there is a diminution in the value of all previously accumulated machinery, because of the steady diminution in *the cost of reproduction*, as nature is more and more forced to labor in the service of man. In the outset, it was with difficulty he could obtain a cord with which to make a bow — but now the bow itself enables him readily to obtain birds and rabbits that furnish him with cords to a greater extent than are required for his purposes; and thus is the bow itself a cause of depreciation in its own value. So it is everywhere. The coal enables us more readily to obtain supplies of iron ore, with diminution in the value of iron; and the iron enables us to obtain larger supplies of coal, with constant decline in the value of fuel, and increase in the value of man.

Profiting by his leisure, Crusoe now avails himself of the services of the canoe to extend his knowledge of the coast, and in one of his expeditions discovers on a distant part of the island another person similarly situated; except that in some directions he has acquired more, and in others less, power over nature than himself. The latter has no boat, but his arrows are better, as he has been enabled to avail himself of the weight and hardness of the flint with which he arms them; and can, therefore, kill more birds or rabbits in a day than Crusoe could do in a week. Their value in his eyes is, therefore, less, but that of fish is far greater, because of the greater difficulties to be overcome before a supply can be obtained. Here we have the circumstances preliminary to the establishment of a system of exchanges. The first could obtain more meat in a day, by the indirect process of catching fish to be exchanged with his neighbor, than he could in a week with his inefficient bow and arrows; and the second could obtain more fish by the devotion of a day to the shooting of birds than he could in a month while deprived of the hook and line; and by the process of exchange the labor of both may be rendered more productive. Each, however — seeking to give day's labor for day's labor — refuses to permit the other to obtain a greater amount of service than he gives in return. The one has fish of various kinds—some requiring more and others less time to capture them — and he values each in reference to the resistance he has had to overcome in obtaining it; for which reason he regards a single rockfish as the equivalent of half a dozen perch. The other has animal food of various kinds; and he, in like manner, regards a turkey as the equivalent of half a dozen rabbits. Value in exchange is, therefore, determined by precisely the same rules that had governed each of the parties when working by himself.

What, now, is their position as compared with that in which they previously had been? Both have profited by calling to their aid certain natural forces, by help of which their labor has been lightened while its results have largely increased; and the whole of that increase they have retained for themselves—nature asking no compensation for her services. Again; both having profited by their power to combine their efforts for the improvement of their common condition, each is now enabled to devote himself with less interruption to the particular pursuits for which he finds himself most fitted—with steady tendency to increase in the return to labor as individuality becomes more and more developed. With both there is an increase in the time that may be appropriated to the improvement of machinery to be used in aid of further production; and thus does every step towards obtaining the command of nature prove to be merely the precursor of a new and greater one. Had our islander, instead of finding a neighbor, been so fortunate as to obtain a wife, a similar system of exchange would have been established. He would follow the chase, and she would cook the meat and convert the skins into clothing. He would raise the flax, and she would convert it into cloth. The family becoming numerous, one would cultivate the earth, while a second would supply the animal food necessary for their support; and a third would be engaged in the management of the household, in the preparation of food, and in the manufacture of clothing. Here would be a system of exchanges as complete, so far as it went, as that of the largest city.

§ 2. The idea of comparison is inseparably connected with that of value. We estimate a deer as worth the labor of a week, and a hare at that of a day; *i. e.* we should be willing to give that quantity of labor for them. The sole inhabitant of an island has thus his system of exchange established, with a measure of value precisely similar to that in use among the various members of a large community. When joined by another person, exchanges arise between them, and are governed by the same laws as when performed among nations whose numbers count by millions.

In measuring value, the first and most natural idea is to compare the commodities produced with the resistance that has been required to be overcome in order that they might be obtained—or in other words, with the labor of body and mind that has been given for them. In exchanging, the most obvious mode is to give labor for labor. The land of A yields more fruit than he can use, and that of B more potatoes. Neither possesses any value in its present state, and either party may appropriate the one or the other, at his pleasure. It being most convenient for each to gather that which is nearest to him, each is willing that the other should thus work for him, receiving work in return. Each, however, desiring to have as large a quantity as he could himself obtain with the same amount of effort, watches carefully that he does not give more labor than he receives.

Our colonists, having thus established between them a system of exchanges, desire, of course, to obtain the best aids to labor that are within their reach; and it soon becomes obvious to them that in the clearing of lands, the building of houses, and in almost every species of employment, they would be greatly assisted by the possession of an axe, or some species of cutting instrument. Having no iron, they are compelled to avail themselves of such substitute as is at their command—flint or other hard stone; and of this they at length succeed in making an instrument, which, though very rude, so materially aids their operations, that they now build a house in half the time that had been required to construct the first. This produces an immediate change in the value of all previously existing articles in the production of which an axe can be of service. The boat that had cost the labor of a whole year can now be reproduced in half that time; and as much fuel as had cost a fortnight's labor can now be cut in a week. No further improvement having yet taken place in the mode of taking deer or fish, their value, in labor, remains unchanged. If, now, one of the parties has more fish than he requires, while the other has a surplus of fuel, the latter is required to give twice as much as he would have done before the axes were made; because he can now reproduce that quantity with the same amount of effort that previously would have been required for half of it.

All previously existing accumulations, in the form of houses, boats, or fuel, now exchange for only the quantity of labor required for their reproduction, so that the acquisition of the axe—by means of which they had been enabled to command the services of nature—has increased the value of labor when estimated in houses or fuel, and lessened the value of houses and fuel when estimated in labor. The cost of production has ceased to be the measure of value, the cost at which they can be reproduced having fallen. The fall, however, having been occasioned by the improvement in the means of applying labor, the present values will continue until further changes are effected. The more slowly such improvements are made, the more steady is the value of property as compared with labor; and the more rapidly they are made, the more rapid is the growth of the power of accumulation, and the decline in the value of all existing machinery when measured by labor.

In this state of things, let us suppose a vessel to arrive, the master of which desires supplies of fruit, fish, or meat, for which he offers axes, or muskets, in exchange. Our colonists, valuing the commodities they have to part with by the amount of labor they have cost to produce, or by the quantity necessary for their reproduction—the fruit at less than potatoes, and hares and rabbits at less than deer — will not give the produce of five days' labor in venison, if they can obtain what they require for potatoes that could be obtained in exchange for that of four.

In estimating the value of the commodities offered to them in exchange, they will pursue a course exactly similar — measuring the amount of difficulty standing in the way of obtaining them by any other process. It has cost them the labor of months to make a rude axe, and if they can obtain a good one at similar cost, it will be more advantageous to do so than to employ the same time in the production of another similar to the one they already have. Such instruments, however, they can make for themselves — but muskets they cannot; and they will attach more value to the possession of a single musket, than to that of several axes. They might give the provisions obtained by the labor of several months for the one; but they would be willing to give all the accumulations of a year for the other.

Let us suppose that each is enabled to supply himself with a musket and an axe, and examine the effect. Both parties being exactly equal — each possessing the same machinery — their labor would be of equal value, and the average produce of a day of the one would continue to exchange for that of a day of the other.

The house that had cost, at first, the labor of a year, could be reproduced, with the assistance of the first rude axe, by that of half a year; but a similar one might now be built in a month. It is, however, so inferior to those that can now be constructed, that it is abandoned, and ceases to have any value whatsoever. It will not, perhaps, command the efforts of a single day. The first axe in like manner declines in value. The increased capital of the community has thus been attended with a diminution in the value of all that had been accumulated previously to the ship's arrival; while that of labor, as compared with houses, has risen—two months now providing shelter vastly superior to that which had been at first obtained in exchange for that of twelve.

The value of the provisions that had been accumulated experiences a similar fall. A week's labor of a man armed with a musket is more productive of venison than that of months without its aid; and the value of the existing stock is measured by the effort required for its reproduction—and not by what its production had cost. Labor being now aided by intellect, a smaller quantity of muscular exertion is required for the production of a given effect.

In mere brute force, a man is equal to the traction of 200 pounds at an uniform rate of four miles an hour—whereas a horse can draw 1800 at a similar rate; and, therefore, of men unaided by intellect it requires no less than nine to equal a single horse. Intelligence, however, enables him to master the horse; and now, adding the powers of the latter to his own, he can move ten times as great a weight, while the quantity of labor required for obtaining food to keep in operation this increased amount of muscular effort is not even doubled. With further knowledge he obtains the command of the wonderful power of steam; and now, with the help of half a dozen men to furnish fuel, he controls a power equal to hundreds of horses, or thousands of men. The force by which this labor is accomplished, is in THE MAN; and, as that force is brought to bear upon the matter by which he is surrounded, the value of his labors is increased, with constant increase in his power of further progress. The master of the vessel obtained for an axe, produced by a mechanic in a single day, provisions that had required months for their collection and preservation, because the labors of the mechanic had been aided by intelligence; whereas the poor and lonely settlers were, almost altogether, dependent upon that quality in which they were excelled by the horse and many other animals—mere brute force.

Throughout the operations of the world the result is the same. The savage gives skins, the product of many months of exertion, for a few beads, a knife, a musket, and a little powder. The people of Poland give wheat, produced by the labor of months, for clothing produced by that of a few days, assisted by capital in the form of machinery, and the intellect required to guide it.

Those of India give a year's labor for as much clothing or provisions as could be had in the United States for that of a month. The people of Italy give a year's exertions for less than those of England obtain in half a year. The mechanic, aided by his knowledge of his trade, obtains in a single week as much as the laborer can earn in two; and the dealer in merchandise, who has devoted his time to obtaining a thorough knowledge of his business, gains in a month as much as his neighbor, less skilled in it, can do in a year.

In order that quantity of labor may be a measure of value, there must be an equal power to command the services of nature. The product of two carpenters in New York or Philadelphia can generally be exchanged for that of two masons; and that of two shoemakers will not vary much in value from that of two tailors. The time of a laborer in Boston is nearly equal in value to that of another in Pittsburg, Cincinnati, or St. Louis; but it will not be given for that of a laborer in Paris or Havre — the latter not being aided to the same extent by machinery, and being therefore more dependent on mere brute force. The value of labor, as compared with that of the commodities required for man's support, varies to a small extent in the various portions of France, as is the case with that of the different parts of England and of India; but between the man of Paris and his competitor of Sedan, or Lille, the variation is trifling, compared with that which exists between a workman in any part of France, and one in the United States. The circumstances which affect the power of man over nature in Paris and Lille are, in a great measure, common to all the people of France; as are those which affect that of a workman in Philadelphia to all the people of the Union. Here we find the same effect at the same time, but at different places, that has before been shown to be produced at the same place, but at different times. The improved machinery of our colonists having increased their powers, their third year was more valuable than that of the two previous ones had been; and in like manner a single year's labor in the United States is worth more than that of two in France. Labor grows in value in the direct ratio of the substitution of mental for muscular force — of the peculiar qualities by which man is distinguished from the animal, for those which he possesses in common with so many animals;

and in the same precise ratio does the value of all commodities decline.

§ 3. The house and the axe, the capital that had been accumulated, fell in value when, by the aid of improved implements, labor had been rendered more productive — the necessary consequence of an increased facility of accumulation. With every step in this direction, the laborer finds an increase in the reward for bodily or mental exertion, as is seen in the fact that the clothing which, half a century since, would have purchased the labor of weeks, could not now command that of as many days. Half a century since, a steam-engine would have required the labor of a life to pay for it, but at present it could be exchanged for that of very few years of a common workman of the United States. In fact, like the house first built by the settler, so great would be found its inferiority to those now produced, that a purchaser at any price whatsoever could with difficulty be found.

The value of commodities or machinery at the time of production is measured by the quantity and quality of labor required to produce them. Every improvement in the mode of production tends to increase the power of labor, and to diminish the quantity required for the reproduction of similar articles. With every such improvement there is a diminution in the quantity that can be obtained in exchange for those previously existing; and because no commodity can be exchanged for more labor than is required for its reproduction. In every community in which population and wealth increase, such changes are taking place, and each is seen to be but preparatory to new and greater ones, with constantly increasing tendency to decline in the labor value of existing commodities, or machines, that have been accumulated. The longer, therefore, that any one, in the mode of producing which improvements have been made, has been in existence—even where there has been no change in its powers from use — the smaller is the proportion which its present value bears to that which it originally possessed.

The silver produced in the fourteenth century was exchanged for labor at the rate of sevenpence halfpenny for that of a week. Since that time it has steadily diminished in its power of commanding the services of men, until, at the present time, twelve or fifteen shillings are required to obtain as much of them as, five centuries, since could be had for $7\frac{1}{2}d.$ The various persons through whose hands has passed the silver that existed in the fourteenth century, have thus experienced a constant depreciation in the quantity of labor that their capital would command. An axe made fifty years since, of equal quality with the best of the present time—and which had remained unused—would not now exchange for half as much as it would have done on the day of its production.

§ 4. Diminution in the value of capital is attended by a diminution in the proportion of the product of labor given for its use by those who, unable to purchase, desire to hire it. Had the first axe been the exclusive property of one of our colonists, he would have demanded more than half of the wood that could be cut, in return for granting the loan of it. Although it had cost him a vast amount of labor, it would do but little work; and large as was the *proportion* of its product he was thus enabled to demand, the *quantity* that he would receive would still be very small. His neighbor, on the other hand, would find it far more to his advantage to give three-fourths of the product of his labor for the use of the axe, than to continue to depend on his hands alone; as with it he could fell more trees in a day than without it he could do in a month. The arrival of the ship having given them better axes at smaller cost, neither would now give for their use so large a proportion as he would before have done. The man who, fifty years since, desired the use of such an instrument for a year, would have given the labor of far more days, than he would now, when by that of a single day he might become the owner of one of greatly superior power. When A possessed the only house in the settlement, he could have demanded of B, for permission to use it for any given time, a much larger number of days' labor than B would be willing to give, when the possession of an axe enabled him to construct a similar one in a month. At the time that a week's labor would command only $7\frac{1}{2}d.$ of silver, the owner of a pound of that metal could demand a much larger proportion in return for its use, than can now be done, when the laborer obtains that quantity by the exertions of little more than a fortnight. Every improvement by which production is aided, is attended not only by a reduction in the labor value of previously existing machinery; but, also, by a diminution in the proportion of the product of labor that can be demanded in return for granting the use of it.

The more perfect the power of association, and the greater the motion of society, the greater must be the tendency towards the development of individuality, the more rapid the increase of production, the greater the facility of accumulation, the greater the tendency to decline in the value of all existing accumulations—and the smaller the *proportion* of the products of labor that can be claimed in return for their use. In order that association may increase, there must, as the reader has seen, be difference; and that results from diversity of employments. The greater that diversity, the more rapid must be the growth of the power of accumulation, the greater the tendency to diminution in the proportion of the capitalist and increase in that of the laborer, and the greater the tendency to decline in the *rate* of rent, profit, or interest. In all the purely agricultural countries of the world, *the rate* of these is high; and it tends to increase because of diminution in the power of accumulation, consequent upon exhaustion of the soil — being precisely the reverse of what is observed in all those countries in which diversity of employment is increasing and individuality is becoming more and more developed.

*Value is the measure of the resistance to be overcome in obtaining those commodities or things required for our purposes—of the power of nature over man.*— The great object of MAN, in this world, is to acquire dominion over NATURE — compelling her to do his work; and with every step in that direction labor becomes less severe—while increasing in its reward. With each, the accumulations of the past become less valuable — with constant decline in their power to command the services of the laborers of the present. With each, the power of association grows—with constant increase in the tendency to the development of the various faculties of the individual man, and equally constant increase in the power of further progress; and thus it is, that while combination of action enables man to overcome the resistance of nature, each successive triumph is attended by increased facility for further combinations, to be followed by new and greater triumphs.

§ 5. The reader who desires now to verify for himself the correctness of the views thus far presented to him, may readily do so without leaving the room in which he sits. Let him commence by looking around him, and seeing *what* are the things to which he attaches the idea of value. Doing this, he finds that among them is not included the air that he is constantly inhaling, and without which he could not live. Reading by day, he finds that he attaches no value to the light; nor, if it is summer time, does he value the heat. If it is by night that he reads, he attaches value to the gas that affords him light; and if it is winter, to the coal or wood by whose combustion he is warmed. Inquiring next, *why* it is that he attaches that idea to one and not to the other, he finds that it is because the first is gratuitously supplied by nature, in abundant quantity, and at the place and time at which it is needed; whereas, to obtain the last, there is required a certain amount of human labor. Coal is supplied by nature in unlimited quantity, and as gratuitously as the air, but some effort is needed to place it at the spot at which it is to be consumed. The materials of which candles are made are as abundantly supplied—but to change them in form and place so as to make them fit to supply the wants of man, requires a certain quantity of labor; and it is because of the necessity for overcoming the obstacle impeding the gratification of our desires, that we value the coal and the candle, while attaching no value whatever to the light of day, or to the heat of summer.

Asking himself, next, *how much* is the value he attaches to the chair on which he sits, the table at which he writes, the book he reads, or the pen with which he writes; he finds that it is limited by the cost of reproduction—and that the greater the time which has elapsed since they were made, the greater has been the decline in their value below the cost of production. The pen, just now produced, can be replaced only by the expenditure of the same amount of labor that has been required for its production; and its value is unchanged. The chair and the table, now perhaps ten years old, have fallen much below their original value; because, in that time machinery has been invented by which steam has been applied in various processes connected with the manufacture of such commodities; which, therefore, have declined in value as compared with labor, while labor has risen as compared with them. The book he reads is, perhaps, still older, and since it was printed there have been many improvements in the manufacture—tending greatly to diminish the quantity of human effort required for its reproduction. The chemist has furnished bleaching powders by help of which the color of the paper has been improved. The railroad, by diminishing friction, has lessened the cost of transporting rags and paper. The power of steam has superseded the labor of the human arm, and has enabled the papermaker to turn out from within the same walls as many reams, as before he could manufacture quires. Steam, again, aids in converting metal into types; and the steam-press, that yields thousands of sheets per hour, has superseded the hand-press that yielded only hundreds. With every such increase in the mastery over nature acquired by man, there has been a decline in the value of existing books as measured by labor, and an increase in the value of labor as compared with books—as the reader may readily satisfy himself by looking around his library and comparing the value he now attaches to standard works that are constantly being reproduced, with that in which he had held them ten or twenty years before. A copy of the Bible, of Milton, or of Shakspeare, can now be obtained for the labor of a single day of a skilled workman, better in quality than could, half a century since, have been obtained in return for that of a week; the necessary consequence of which has been a decline in the value of all existing copies of such works, whether in private libraries or in the hands of booksellers—the cost of reproduction being the limit beyond which value cannot extend.*

Again, of the books in his possession all those that were bound forty years since, are in leather; whereas of the recent ones nearly all are probably in cloth. In the earlier period, cotton cloth required for its production a large amount of human labor, and

* Why, it may be asked, is it that a copy of the *Valdarfer* Boccacio sells for thousands of guineas, being probably a thousand times more than the price it had at first commanded? In answer, the real value of the book is to be found in the pleasure or instruction to be derived from its perusal; and that is now obtainable at a tenth of the cost of labor required in the early days of the printing art. All such values as that above referred to, are as purely imaginary, and as dependent upon fashion, as were some of those of Holland in the days of the tulipomania. Value is limited by the cost of reproduction; and where a commodity cannot be reproduced, as in the case of the Boccacio, or in those of pictures by Guido, or sculptures by Phidias, its value has no limit but in the fancy of those who desire to possess it, and have the ability to pay for it.

its value was great — so much so that twelve or fifteen yards were all that the laborer could purchase by the efforts of a week. Since then, however, various natural forces have been brought to aid the efforts of the clothmaker — steam having superseded the fingers that before had spun the wool, and the arms that before had woven the cloth; while the chemist has done the same by the light of the sun, and has enabled the bleacher to accomplish in an hour what before had required the labor of a week; and the consequence of this increased power over nature has been, that a yard of cloth that half a century since would have been a sufficient compensation for the labor of half a day, may now be had in return for that of an hour. The trader who may have retained on his shelves a piece of cloth made half a century since, must have found it steadily declining in value, with the reduction of the cost at which it could be reproduced. Let him continue to retain it, and, as new powers are impressed into the service of man, he may witness its further fall, until he will estimate it as being only the equivalent of a fiftieth part of the labor for which it would originally have paid. The utility of cotton has greatly increased, but the value of cotton cloth has as greatly diminished; and all because nature, who works gratuitously, has from year to year been more and more made to do what previously was performed by human labor — requiring a constant supply of food and clothing to keep the machine in order for doing the work.

§ 6. "Labor," says Adam Smith, "was the first price, the original purchase-money paid for all things;" and it constitutes in his opinion "the ultimate and real standard" by which their values can be "estimated and compared."* Comparing, then, the price paid with the commodity obtained, labor would be, according to this authority, the standard of value for things of every description; whether the cultivated land itself, or the commodities obtained in return for the labor given to its cultivation. In another place, however, he tells his readers that the price paid for the use of land "is not at all proportioned to what the landlord may have laid out upon the improvement of the land, or to what he can afford to take, but to what the former can afford to give," and "is naturally a monopoly price." We have here a

* Wealth of Nations, book 1, chap. v.

cause of value in land additional to the labor expended upon it, or for its benefit; and thus does he establish for it a law entirely different from that propounded as the cause of value in "all things."

Mr. McCulloch informs his readers that "labor is the only source of wealth;" and that "neither water, leaves, skins, nor any of the spontaneous productions of nature, has any *value*, except what it owes to the labor required for its appropriation." "Natural powers may, however," as he continues, "be appropriated or engrossed by one or more individuals, to the exclusion of others, and those by whom they are so engrossed may exact a price for their services; but does that," he inquires, "show that these services cost these engrossers anything? If A has a waterfall on his estate he may probably get a rent for it. It is plain, however, that the work performed by the waterfall is as completely gratuitous as that which is performed by the wind that acts on the blades of a windmill. The only difference between them consists in this: that all individuals having it in their power to avail themselves of the services of the wind, no one can intercept the bounty of nature, and exact a price for that which she freely bestows; whereas A, by appropriating the waterfall, and, consequently, acquiring a command over it, has it in his power to prevent its being used, or to sell its services."*

We have here the same contradiction already exhibited as existing in the Wealth of Nations. Labor is, we are assured, the only source of wealth—the only cause of value; and yet, the chief item among the values of the world is found in the hands of those persons who, according to our author, "intercept the bounty of nature, and exact a price for that which she freely bestows"—and that price they are enabled to demand because of having been enabled to "acquire a command" over certain natural forces, and to prevent them from being used by any who are unwilling to pay their owner "for their services." There are thus, according to both of these authorities, two causes of value—labor and monopoly—the first standing alone as regards all "the spontaneous productions of nature;" and the two being combined in reference to land, the great source of all production.

In like manner, Mr. Ricardo assures his readers that the price paid for the use of land is to be divided into two portions: first,

* Principles of Political Economy, part 1, chap. i.

that which may be demanded in return for the labor which has been "employed in ameliorating the quality of the land, and in erecting such buildings as are necessary to secure and preserve the produce;" and, second, "that which is paid to the landlord for the use of original and indestructible powers of the soil"—which latter is so much *additional* to what could be demanded in return for the use of any other of the various instruments of production.

Mr. J. B. Say informs us that—

"The earth is not the only material agent with productive power, but it is the only one, or nearly so, that can be appropriated. The water of rivers and of the sea, which supplies us with fish, gives motion to our mills, and supports our vessels, has productive powers. The wind gives us force, and the sun heat, but happily no man can say, 'The wind and the sun belong to me, and I will be paid for their services.'"*

Mr. Senior, on the contrary, insists that air and sunshine, the waters of the river and the sea, "the land and all its attributes," are equally susceptible of appropriation.† In order, in his view, that a commodity may have value in the eyes of men, it is required that it shall be useful, susceptible of appropriation, and of course transferable, and limited in supply—all of which qualities are, as he supposes, possessed by land, the owners of which are therefore enabled to charge monopoly prices for its use.

Mr. Mill says, that the rent of land is a "price paid for a natural agency;" that no such price is paid in manufactures; that "the reason why the use of land bears a price is simply the limitation of its quantity;" and that "if air, heat, electricity, chemical agencies, and the other powers of nature employed by manufacturers were sparingly supplied, and could, like land, be engrossed and appropriated, a rent would be exacted for them also." Here again we have a monopoly value *additional* to the price that could be demanded by the owner, as compensation for the labor bestowed upon, or for the benefit of, the land.

The reader has seen that of those portions of the earth which man converts into bows and arrows, canoes, ships, houses, books, cloth, or steam-engines, the value is determined by the cost of reproduction—that that, in all advancing communities, is less

* Econ. Pol., liv. 2, chap. ix.

† Outlines of Polit. Econ., p. 131.

than the cost of production—and that the decline in the former below the latter is always most rapid when population and the consequent power of association increase most rapidly. When, however, we look to those portions of it which he uses for the purposes of cultivation, we find, according to all these writers, a law directly the opposite of all this—the value of land being equal to the cost of producing it in its existing form, *plus* the value of a monopoly power increasing with the growth of numbers, and most rapidly when the growth of population and of the power of association is most rapid.

To admit the correctness of this view, would be to admit that while the clay through which the farmer guided his plough was subjected to one set of laws, it became the subject of other and directly opposite ones, so soon as it had passed through the potter's hands, and had been converted into china or earthenware—that there was no such thing as universality in the laws that govern matter—and, consequently, that the great Architect of the universe has given us a system abounding in discords; and in the working of which we could look for no approach to harmony. Whether or not this really is so, is to be determined by an examination of the facts of the case, as exhibited in the value of land compared with the labor that would now be required for its reproduction in its existing form. Should that result in proving the former to be greater than the latter, then the doctrine of all these writers must be admitted to be correct; but, should it prove that land will nowhere exchange for as much labor as would be required for such reproduction, it will then have to be admitted that value is, in all and every case, but a measure of the amount of physical and mental effort required to overcome the obstacles standing in the way of the accomplishment of our desires—that the price charged for the use of land is, like that charged for the use of all other commodities and things, but compensation for the accumulations resulting from the labors of the past—that that price tends everywhere to diminish in its proportion to the product obtained by help of the machine—and, that there is but one system of laws for the government of all matter, let the form in which it exists be what it may.

Twelve years since, the annual value of the land and of the mines of Great Britain, including therein the share of the Church, was estimated by Sir Robert Peel at £47,800,000—which, at twenty-five years' purchase, would give a principal sum of nearly twelve hundred millions of pounds. Estimating the wages of laborers, miners, mechanics, and those by whom their labors are directed, at £50 pounds per annum each, the land would, then, represent the labors of twenty-four millions of men for a single year; or of one million for twenty-four years.

Let us now suppose the island reduced to the state in which it was found by Cæsar; covered with impenetrable woods, (the timber of which is of no value because of its superabundance,) and abounding in marshes and swamps, heaths and sandy wastes; and then estimate the quantity of labor that would be required to place it in its present position, with its lands cleared, levelled, enclosed, and drained; with its turnpikes and railroads, its churches, school-houses, colleges, court-houses, market-houses, furnaces, and forges; its coal, iron, and copper mines, and the thousands and tens of thousands of other improvements required for bringing into activity those powers for the use of which rent is paid; and it will be found that it would require the labor of millions of men for centuries, even although provided with all the machinery of modern times—the best axe and the best plough, the steam-engine, the railway, and its locomotive.

The same thing may now be exhibited on a smaller scale. A part of South Lancashire, the forest and chase of Rossendale, embracing an area of twenty-four square miles, contained eighty souls at the beginning of the sixteenth century; and the rental, in the time of James I., little more than two centuries since, amounted to £122 13*s*. 8*d*. It has now a population of eighty-one thousand; and the annual rental is £50,000, equivalent, at twenty-five years' purchase, to £1,250,000. Without having seen this land, there can be no hesitation in saying, that if it were now given to Baron Rothschild in the state in which it existed in the days of James, with a bounty equal to its value—on condition of doing with the timber the same that had been done with that which then stood upon the ground—he binding himself to give to the property the same advantages as those for which rent is now paid; his private fortune would be expended in addition to the bounty long before the work had been half completed. The amount received as rent is interest upon the value of labor expended, *minus* the differerence between the productive power of Rossendale and that of the newer soils which can now be brought into activity by the application of the same labor that has been there given to the work.

The cash value of farms in the State of New York was returned by the marshal, under the last census, at $554,000,000; and adding thereto the value of roads, buildings, and other works of improvement, we shall obtain a sum probably double in amount—or the equivalent of the labor of a million of men working three hundred days in the year, for four years—and receiving a dollar a day for their labor. Were the land restored to the condition in which it stood in the days of Hendrick Hudson, and presented in free gift to an association of the greatest capitalists of Europe, with a bonus in money equal to its present value, their private fortunes and the bonus would be found to be exhausted before the existing improvements had been, even to the extent of one-fifth, executed.

The farming land of Pennsylvania was returned, under the census, at $403,000,000, cash value. Doubling this, to obtain the value of real estate and its improvements, we obtain $806,000,000—or the equivalent of the labors of six hundred and seventy thousand men for four years; being not one-tenth of what would be required to reproduce the State in its present condition, were it restored to that in which it stood at the date of the arrival of the Swedes who commenced the work of settlement.

William Penn followed them, profiting by what they had already done. When he obtained the grant of all that land which now constitutes Pennsylvania, and westward as far as the Pacific Ocean, it was supposed he had a princely estate. He invested his capital in the transport of settlers, and devoted his time and attention to the new colony; but, after many years of turmoil and vexation, found himself so much embarrassed in his affairs, that in the year 1708 he mortgaged the whole for £6600 sterling, to pay the debts incurred in settling the province. He had received the grant in payment of a debt amounting, with interest, to £29,200, and his expenditure, interest included, was £52,373; while the whole amount received in twenty years was only £19,460—leaving him *minus*, altogether, £62,113. Some years later, the government made an agreement with him to purchase the whole at £12,000, but a fit of apoplexy prevented the completion of the agreement. At his death, he left his Irish estates to his favorite child, as the most valuable part of his property — the American portion being worth far less than the cost of production. The Duke of York obtained a similar grant of New Jersey, but, many years afterwards, it was offered for sale at about £5000—being much less than had been expended upon it.

The owners of unoccupied lands in the United States have found, to their cost, that the "natural agent" had no value. Led away in the same manner with William Penn, the Duke of York, the grantees of Swan River Settlement, and many others, they supposed that land must become very valuable; and many men of great acuteness were induced to invest large sums therein. Robert Morris, the able financier of the Revolution, was the one who pushed this speculation to the greatest extent, taking up immense quantities at very low prices — often as low as ten cents an acre; but experience has shown his error. His property, although much of it was excellent, has never paid the charges upon it; and such has been the result of every operation of the kind. Numerous persons, owners of thousands and tens of thousands of acres, who have been paying county and road taxes, and have been thus impoverishing themselves; would now gladly receive the amount of their expenses and interest—losing altogether the original cost. Their difficulty has not resulted from any absence of fertility, but from the fact that—the cost of reproduction being a steadily diminishing one — better farms are obtainable in return to a smaller amount of labor.

The Holland Land Company purchased large quantities at exceedingly low prices, and their property was well managed; but the proprietors sunk a vast amount of capital. No portion of the United States has improved more rapidly than that part of the State of New York in which it was chiefly situated; none has derived greater advantage from the construction of the Erie Canal; and yet the whole of the original purchase-money was sunk. Had they given away the land, and employed otherwise the same amount of capital that was expended on it, the result would have been thrice more advantageous.

It would be easy to multiply cases in proof of the position, that property in land obeys the same law with that of all other descriptions; and that this applies to towns and cities as well as land. With all their advantages of situation, London and Liverpool, Paris and Bordeaux, New York and New Orleans, would exchange for but a small portion of the labor that would be required to reproduce them, were their sites again reduced to the state in which they were found by the people by whom they were first commenced. Throughout the Union, there is not a county, township, town, or city, that would sell for cost; or one whose rents are equal to the interest upon the labor and capital expended on their improvement.

Every one is familiar with the fact that farms sell for little more than the value of the improvements. When we come to inquire what "improvements" are included in this estimate, we find that the heaviest are omitted — nothing being put down for clearing and draining the land, for the roads that have been made, or for the court-house and the prison that have been built with the taxes annually paid; for the church and the school-house that have been built by subscription; for the canal that passes through a piece of fine meadow-land, the contribution of the owner to the great work; or for a thousand other conveniences and advantages that give value to the property, and produce the disposition to pay rent for its use. Were all these things estimated, it would be found that the selling price is—cost, *minus* a very large difference.

The United States Government has recently made a purchase of many millions of acres, for which it has contracted to pay to the Indian proprietors what appears a very low price; and yet the whole value of that land is due to the fact that our own people have been making roads leading to and from it, digging canals, and building vessels of all kinds, by means of which its products may cheaply go to market. Half a century since, the land of Missouri was equally valueless; and that of Indiana and Illinois, Michigan and Wisconsin, was little better. Sixty years since, such was the case as regarded Kentucky and Ohio; and seventy years since, it was so with Western Pennsylvania and New York. A century since, the eastern portions of those States were in the same situation; and the total value of the land of New England, at that date, was probably not as great as is now that of the little piece upon which stands the city of Boston. By slow degrees, the lands nearest the ocean have been acquiring value, until farm-land sells in some places at two or three hundred dollars an acre; and with every step in this direction, those more distant have gradually risen from nothing to ten, twenty, and fifty cents — then, to the government price of a dollar and twenty-five cents—and then, to ten, fifteen, and twenty dollars; but, rapid as has been the rise, the price that could now be obtained for all the real estate north of Mason and Dixon's line, and of the Ohio, would not pay for one-fifth of the labor that would be required to reproduce it in its present form, were it again reduced to a state of nature.

With every step in the progress of man towards obtaining dominion over nature — towards enabling himself to reduce to his service the forces by which he is everywhere surrounded — there is a diminution in the cost of reproducing the commodities and things required for his use; with constant decline in their value as compared with labor, and increase in the value of labor as compared with them. That this is so, as regards axes, spades, ploughs, and steam-engines, wheat, rye, cotton and other cloth, the reader has had abundant evidence; and that it is so, as regards land, is proved by the fact that it may be everywhere purchased at less than the cost of production.

§ 7. With the decline in the value of axes and spades, there is everywhere a diminution in the *proportion* of the product charged for their use; and that diminution is always most rapid when the improvement in their quality is greatest. Such, too, is the case with land, the rent of which steadily declines in the proportion it bears to the product of labor; and most rapidly where the march of improvement is most rapid. In the days of the Plantagenets, the land-owner of England took all, and gave what he pleased to his serf. Since then, as labor has become more productive, there has been a steady decline in the proportion claimed by the owner of land, until it has fallen to an average of one-fifth —leaving four-fifths to the man who works it, as compensation for his labor. The movement here, is, as we see, precisely the same that has been observed in regard to the hire of axes, the freight of ships, and the interest of money; and furnishes additional proof of the universality of the laws which govern matter — whatever the form under which it exists.

The error of all the economists to whom reference has been made, and indeed of all writers on social science, consists in this: that, instead of studying what it is that men have always done, and what they now do, in regard to land, they study in their closets what they ought to do, and what they imagine they themselves would do, under similar circumstances. When, for instance, Adam Smith wrote the passage in which he assumed that "the most fertile and best situated lands" having been first occupied, men could thereafter obtain less profit from the cultivation of those remaining, that were inferior in soil and situation — giving that as a reason for the diminution in the proportion of the capitalist that always attends advance in wealth and population; he totally overlooked the facts presented by the history of his own country; all of which show that men have, everywhere throughout its limits, commenced with the poorer soils of the hills, and have worked to, and not from, the richer ones of the river bottoms.

It was natural that he, and his successors in England and in France, should think, that when men had the choice between rich and poor soils, they would, of course, take the former, as capable of yielding the largest returns to any given quantity of labor. Had they, however, reflected that the early settlers of their respective countries had been obliged to work with their hands alone, and had therefore had little power to compel nature to labor for them—whereas nature herself, as exhibited in the rich bottom-lands, was all-powerful and capable of manifesting a most determined resistance to their efforts — it could scarcely have failed to become obvious to them that it was upon the poor and thin soils of the hills that the work of cultivation must of necessity have been commenced; and reference to history would have enabled them to satisfy themselves that such had been the universal fact.

To this assumption is due that error which has everywhere been made in reference to the cause of value in land; as will be obvious to the reader, when he sees that similar errors must have arisen in reference to all other commodities and things, if subjected to the same course of reasoning. Let us, for instance, suppose it to have been assumed, that nature had everywhere furnished ready-made axes, and that all the effort required of man had been that of making his selection between the first, second, third, tenth, or twentieth quality — and then examine the result.

Under such circumstances, it might be fairly assumed that the first settlers would take the best — those that would cut the largest quantity of timber in the shortest time — and that, when they had all been taken up, their successors would be forced to take the second quality; and so on in succession, until, with the growth of numbers, some persons would find themselves reduced to work with those of the tenth or twentieth class. What now would be the value of those of the first quality? Obviously, the cost of appropriation, *plus* the difference between the natural powers of axe No. 1 and axe No. 10, or 20; and the more rapid the increase of population, the greater would be the demand for additional supplies—the greater the necessity for resorting to those of inferior power—the more rapid the decline in the average return to labor — and the more rapid the growth of value in the axes first appropriated. The resistance presented by nature being a constantly growing one, the accumulations of the past would be attaining a constantly increasing power over the labors of the present.

Directly the reverse of all this we know to be the fact. Man commences the work of cutting timber with a sharpened shell, and thence he passes to a flint; next, he obtains copper, after which comes iron, and then steel; and with every step in this direction, there is an increased return to labor; with constant diminution in the value of all existing axes, as the cost of reproduction steadily declines. The resistance here offered by nature to the gratification of man's desires is constantly diminishing, and the laborers of the present are obtaining constantly increased power over the accumulations of the past.—In the first of these cases, the value of axes must have been composed of the labor of appropriation, *plus* that of the natural agent that had been appropriated. In the second, it is the same labor of appropriation, *minus* that which is economized by the substitution of the gratuitous forces always existing in nature, and more and more compelled to labor in the service of man.

Experience having shown a perfect similarity in the course of action in regard to the land and all the machinery into which parts of it are at times converted, whether axes or steam-engines, houses or ships — the isolated man having commenced with poor machinery of production, and the associated one having been enabled to command the services of that of a higher order — the same results should always follow, as like causes produce like effects. That they do follow, is shown in the fact, that the value of land obeys the same law as that of axes—declining in its power to command the services of the laborers, and enabling the laborer to command its services in return for a constantly decreasing proportion of the increased product of land and labor, claimed by the landlord as rent. Such being the case, it must be obvious that the latter possesses no more power to charge for the labor of the natural agent, employed in the production of wheat, than does the owner of the axe to charge for those of the natural agents employed in cutting timber; and that all that the one receives, is compensation for a portion of the labor that has been employed in reducing the land to cultivation, and otherwise improving it; while the other receives in like manner compensation for his services in mining and smelting the ore, and making the axe. It is population, and the consequent power of association, that enable men to obtain food from the rich soils, and to pass from the axe of stone to that of steel; and it is depopulation, with its consequent diminution in the power of combination, that drives them back to the poor soils in quest of food, and forces them to depend upon the axe of stone where before they had one of steel. With the first, there is a constant increase in the power of man over nature, with decline of values as compared with labor. With the second, there is as constant increase in the power of nature over man, with decline in the value of labor, as compared with machinery of every kind.

§ 8. It may, however, be said: Here are two fields upon which has been bestowed an equal quantity of labor, the one of which will command twice the rent, and will sell for twice the price, of the other; and it may be asked—If value results exclusively from labor, how does it happen that the owner of the one is so much richer than he who owns the other?

In reply to this question, it is easy to show that similar facts exist in relation to those other commodities and things whose value is, by all, admitted to result exclusively from labor. The glass-blower puts into his furnace a large quantity of sand, and kelp or other alkali, and takes from it glass; but the qualities of the latter are very various, although produced from the same mass of raw materials. Some of it passes in the market as No. 1, and some as Nos. 2, 3, 4, and 5; while a part may be of so inferior a quality as to be almost worthless; and yet the labor employed on all the parts has been exactly equal. All of it has the same limit of value — the cost of reproduction. The resistance offered by nature to the production of that of the first quality being great, it is equal in value to a large amount of labor; whereas the resistance to the production of that of the lowest quality being small, it exchanges against but a small amount of human effort. The value of all is due to the necessity for overcoming that resistance, and not, in any manner, to the natural properties known to exist in the glass itself.

A farmer raises a hundred horses, and upon each expends a similar quantity of food and labor. Arrived at maturity, they present to view a great variety of qualities, some having great speed and but little bottom, while others have bottom and but little speed. Some are good in harness, while others are worth little but under the saddle. Some are heavy, and others are light. Some have great power of traction, while others have little; and some are high, while others are low. Their values are likewise different—a single one, perhaps, commanding as large a price as could be obtained for a dozen others. Nevertheless, all those values are but measures of the resistance to be overcome in producing horses possessed of certain qualities; and all are but the rewards of labor and skill applied to this particular department of production. From year to year acquiring greater knowledge, the farmer learns that by care in the selection of his stock for breeding, he may diminish the resistance at first experienced; and with each succeeding one is enabled to obtain a larger proportion of animals of the highest quality — with steady increase in the return to his physical and intellectual efforts; and as steady decline in the value of all the stock remaining from previous years.

"Jenny Lind could get a thousand dollars for singing a single evening: she has doubtless sung at the opera, where young females who sang in the chorus received less than a single dollar. Suppose, however, that some enterprising Barnum should determine that he would train up a new Jenny Lind, or at least a tolerable rival for her, for his own profit. He would at once see it necessary to multiply his chances of success, by making the experiment with a large number of persons — some hundreds or thousands. He would be at enormous charges for years for their musical education; and if at last he produced one prodigy of song, who could earn by her vocal powers the revenue of Jenny Lind, he would also have on his hands a number of inferior songstresses, who might draw crowded houses but for the superior attraction of his *prima donna;* and scores of chorus-singers, whose earnings would not repay the outlay for their board, clothing, and education; to say nothing of the scores who died, lost their voices, or came to utter failure before earning any thing."*

Why is Jenny Lind so highly valued? Because of the obstacles to be overcome before an equal voice can be reproduced. So, too, is it with the fine horse, with the fine specimens of glass, and with the land that yields large returns to labor.—To what extent are they valued? To that of the cost of reproduction, and no more; and that tends to decline with every step in the growth of population and wealth. The same laws thus apply to all matter, whatsoever the form in which it exists.

In certain states of society, the horse preferred will be the one

* Smith's Manual of Polit. Econ., p. 131. "This illustration," says Mr. Smith, "is borrowed — substituting Jenny Lind for Rubini — from an able article by M. Quijano, in the *Journal des Economistes*, for May and June, 1852, in which the imaginary capitalist, who has succeeded in raising a Rubini, answers a remonstrance against the extravagant price put upon his singing, by pointing to the fact that the average compensation of the 2043 performers of all kinds in the twenty-five theatres, opera-houses, and circuses of Paris is but $328 per annum, and would be less, but for the fact that the government grants in aid of the theatres amount to about one-third of the aggregate salaries of their performers.

"Quijano makes use of this illustration incidentally, the main purpose of his article being to show that the enormous value of the *Clos Vougeot* — an estate producing a famous wine — is to be accounted for in the same way, and that it does not disprove the doctrine that land derives all its value from labor. How many fortunes have been wasted in vain endeavors to find the proper spot, and make a vineyard which will produce such wine! Suppose the fact be communicated to a vine-grower, that somewhere within a district ten thousand square miles in extent, a few acres existed which by proper cultivation would equal Clos Vougeot in the quality of its wines, and the offer to be made, either to communicate the secret of their precise location for a sum equal to the present market value of that vineyard, or to sell the same number of acres, to be selected by himself, at the average value of the entire tract—which offer would it be wise for him to accept? In accepting the first, what is it that he pays for, except the labor saved in making a multitude of unprofitable experiments?

fit for the purposes of war; whereas, in others, it will be that best fitted for those of peace. At some periods, the warrior will have the preference; while in others, the qualities of the statesman or the merchant will be most valued, and the warrior will be neglected. So is it with land, the present value of which represents but a portion — and generally a very small one — of its cost.

Labor is frequently wasted upon it, because its qualities are not of the particular description required at the moment. The settler who begins by draining swamps, throws away his labor, and dies of fever. The land is rich, but its time has not come. The man who bores into granite, searching for coal, throws away his labor. The land will be valuable when granite quarries are required, but its time has not come. The man who attempts to raise marl while surrounded by rich meadow-land, yet uncleared, loses his time. The land is rich, but its time has not come. All soils have qualities tending to render them useful to man, and all are destined ultimately to become utilized; but, it being the decree of nature that the best — those fitted to yield the largest return to labor—shall be obtained for his use only at the cost of long-continued and combined exertion; their attainment is the reward held out to him as the inducement to steady industry, prudence, and economy, and to a constant observance of that great law of Christianity which requires every man to respect in others those rights of person and property that he desires others to respect in himself. Where these exist, he is seen passing steadily and regularly from poor soils to those which are more productive, with constant increase of population, wealth, prosperity, and happiness, and steady decline of value in all the lands first cultivated; except where the constant application of labor has tended to render them more productive. The last historian of the world, prior to its dissolution, will have to say of the soils, as Byron said of the skies of Italy:—

> "Parting day
> Dies like the dolphin, whom each pang imbues
> With a new color as it gasps away,
> *The last still loveliest,* till — 'tis gone — and all is gray."

The value of land is a consequence of the improvement which labor has effected upon it, and it constitutes an important item of wealth. Wealth tends to augment with population, and the power of accumulation increases with constantly accelerating pace as new soils are brought into cultivation — each yielding in succession a larger return to labor. Rent tends, therefore, to increase in amount, and to diminish in its proportion, with the growth of wealth and population. The former is greatest in England, the wealthiest country of Europe. Diminishing as we pass thence to the poorer countries of France, Germany, Italy, and Spain, it at length disappears totally among the Rocky Mountains and the islands of the Pacific, where land is valueless.

§ 9. Robinson Crusoe was surrounded by objects capable of being rendered useful to him either as food or clothing, or as machinery by help of which he might procure the various commodities required for the satisfaction of his wants; but in his then condition he was unable to command their aid. The bird on the wing, and the squirrel that jumped from tree to tree, were as fully competent to satisfy his appetite for food as those he had caught in his trap; but they had for him no UTILITY. The water abounded in fish, but he had no hook with which to take them. It would float a canoe, but—having no knife, or axe, with which to fell a tree or hollow it out—its supporting power was to him as useless as if it had not existed. It was capable of producing steam that could be made to do the work of thousands of laborers, but he possessed none of the machinery by help of which he might command its services. The air abounded in electricity, susceptible of being rendered useful; but its uses were to him unknown. He being weak and nature being strong, the resistance offered by her, to the gratification of his desires, was too great to be overcome by his unassisted powers.

With time, however, we find him calling to his aid the various qualities of wood — its elasticity, hardness, and weight; next, obtaining a cutting instrument by which other forces are made to contribute to his purposes; again, hollowing out a tree and reducing to his service the supporting power of water; and thus gradually *utilizing* the various forces existing in nature and awaiting demand for their services.

The capability of being rendered useful to man belongs to every atom of matter of which the earth is composed—existing as much in the coal that lies thousands of feet below the surface, as in that which now burns in the grate; and as much in the ore while remaining in the mine, as in that which has been converted into stoves, grates, or railroad bars. To render them useful requires in most cases a considerable amount of physical and intellectual effort; and it is because of the necessity for that effort that man is led to attach the idea of value to the commodities and things that have been so obtained.

Being in some cases supplied to him in abundance, in the precise form, and at the precise place at which they are required — as is the case with the air we breathe — they are then wholly without value. In others, they are furnished by nature in the form in which they are used, as in the case of water and electricity; but even these require change of place, and have, therefore, a value in our estimation equal to the effort required for overcoming the resistance to their attainment. In a third — and the most numerous class of cases — they require to be changed in place and in form; and have then a much higher value, because of the increased resistance to be overcome.

That man may be enabled to effect these changes, he must first utilize those faculties by which he is distinguished from the brute. In the isolated man they are latent, association being needed for stimulating them into the motion required for the production of force. Had Bacon, Newton, Leibnitz, or Des Cartes, been placed alone upon an island, their capacity for being useful to their fellow-men would have been just the same that we see it to have been; but their faculties would have lain dormant, and without utility. As it was—being enabled to associate with others like and unlike themselves—their various idiosyncrasies were stimulated to activity, and individuality became more and more developed—with constant increase in the knowledge accumulated, and in the power of further accumulation.

That "knowledge is power," we are every day assured; and if we desire evidence of the fact, we need only to observe, on the one hand, how great are the poverty and weakness of various communities of the earth, occupying lands abounding in all the qualities required for enabling their owners to become rich and strong—which yet remain unimproved for want of that power of combination so indispensable to the development of the intellectual faculties; and, on the other, how great are the wealth and strength of others, whose lands appear to be deficient in almost all the qualities required for the production of either wealth or strength. Few countries offer to their inhabitants a poorer soil for cultivation than is found in our Eastern States — and they have little coal, while altogether deficient as regards most of the metallic products of the earth; and yet New England occupies a high position among the communities of the world, because among her people the habit of association is found existing to an extraordinary extent—with corresponding activity of their faculties. Turning our eyes to Brazil, we find a picture directly the reverse—nature there furnishing a soil rich for all the purposes of cultivation, and abounding in the most valuable minerals and metals — all of which remain almost altogether useless, for want of that activity of mind which results necessarily from the association of man with his fellow-men.

The capacity for obtaining command over the various powers of nature, is a force existing in man—latent, while he is compelled to live and work alone, but more and more stimulated into activity as he is more and more enabled to work in combination with his fellow-men.

The capability of being useful to man exists, as has already been said, in all matter; but, in order that it may have utility, man must have the power required for overcoming the resisting force of nature — and that he cannot have in a state of isolation. Place him in the midst of a large community where employment is infinitely diversified, and his faculties become developed. With individuality comes the power of association, always accompanied with that rapid motion of the intellect whence results power over nature; and every step in that direction is but the preparation for a new and greater one. A century since, he was surrounded everywhere by electricity, capable of being rendered useful to him; but he was totally deficient in the knowledge required for compelling it to do his work. Franklin made one step in identifying lightning with what had before been known as electricity; and since then, Arago, Ampère, Biot, Henry, Morse, and many others, have been engaged in the effort to obtain the knowledge of its qualities required for controlling its movements and utilizing its powers. That having been acquired, instead of looking upon the aurora, and upon the lightning, as mere objects of stupid wonder, we now regard them but as the manifestation of the existence of a great force that can be made to carry our messages, plate our knives and forks, and propel our ships.

The utility of things is *the measure of man's power over nature* — and this grows with the power of combination among men. Their value, on the other hand, is *the measure of nature's power over man*—and this declines with the growth of the power of combination. The two thus move in opposite directions, and are always found existing in the inverse ratio of each other.

The waste of food resulting from the various processes to which corn is subjected, with a view to improvement in the appearance of the bread made from it, is estimated at one-fourth of the whole quantity — and this, upon the twenty millions of quarters required for Great Britain, is equal to five millions. Were all this economized, the utility of corn would be greatly increased — but the corresponding increase in the facility with which food could be obtained, would be attended with large decline of value; and so is it, as we see, with all other commodities and things. As improved steam-engines enable us to obtain constantly increasing power from the same quantity of coal, the utility of coal increases—but its value declines, because of the increased facility of obtaining iron for the construction of new engines, by help of which to obtain more coal. As the old road becomes more useful from its more constant use by a growing population, its value declines; and this it does, because of the growing facility of obtaining new and better roads. The man who has to descend a hill to the distant spring pays largely in labor for a supply of water for his family; but when he has sunk a well, he obtains a supply quadrupled in quantity in return to a twentieth part of the muscular effort. The utility having increased, the exchangeable value has greatly diminished. Next, he places a pump in the well, and here we find a similar effect produced. Again, with the growth of population and wealth, we find him associating with his neighbors to give utility to great rivers, by directing them through streets and houses; and now he is supplied so cheaply that the smallest coin in circulation pays for more than his predecessors could obtain at the cost of a whole day's labor—as a consequence of which his family consumes more in a day than had before, of necessity, sufficed for a month; and has its benefits almost free of charge.

With every increase in the facility of obtaining food from the earth, by reason of passing from the poorer to the better soils, man obtains a constantly increasing power to utilize still richer ones — and the more rapid that increase, the more rapid is the decline in the value of the soils first cultivated. Such, too, is the case with the precious metals, whose value declines as their utility increases. The vast mass of gold and silver hoarded in France is useless to the community; and to the fact that it is hoarded is due the high value in which the precious metals are there held. Were it all set free, money would become more abundant, and interest would tend to fall, while labor would rise. Looking around, we see everywhere, that it is in the countries in which those metals render the smallest service to man, that they are the most valued — and that, here, their value in labor and land declines as we pass towards that community in which they render the largest service — New England; and especially in the manufacturing States of Rhode Island and Massachusetts. Such being the case, we can readily see why it is that they tend everywhere *from* those countries in which interest is high, and *to* those in which it is low. In the latter, their labor value is steadily diminishing; and this diminution is necessarily accompanied by a constant increase of ability to apply them to the various purposes for which they are fitted; sometimes to gilding books — and at others converting them into knives, forks, spoons, or otherwise changing their forms, so as to fit them for serving the purposes, or gratifying the tastes, of their owners. It is where, and when, interest tends downward, that their use for all such purposes most rapidly extends — thus proving that, with increased utility, value diminishes; and where, and when, interest tends upward, that their use most rapidly declines — furnishing further proof that utility and value are always in the inverse ratio of each other.

The utility of matter increases with the growth of the power of association and combination among men; and every step in that direction is accompanied by a decline in the value of commodities required for their use, and an increase in the facility with which wealth may be accumulated.

# CHAPTER VII.

## OF WEALTH.

§ 1. Robinson Crusoe had made a bow, and had thus acquired wealth. In what, however, did that wealth consist? In the possession of the instrument? Assuredly not; but in the *power* that it gave him over the natural properties of the wood and the cord — enabling him to substitute the elasticity of the one, and the tenacity of the other, for the muscular contraction by help of which, alone, he had thus far been enabled to obtain supplies of food. Having made a canoe, he found his wealth increased, because by help of his new machine he could command the services of water—and, as nature always works gratuitously, all the addition he was now enabled to make to his supplies, was obtained wholly free of cost. Having erected a pole in his canoe, and placed upon it a skin by way of sail, he was enabled to command the services of the wind, and thus still further to increase his power to move from place to place; and so did his wealth steadily increase.

Let us suppose, however, that instead of having been led by observation of the properties of wood to make a bow, he had found one, and had been so deficient in knowledge as to be unable to use it; would his wealth in this case have been increased? Certainly not. The bow would have been as useless as the trees with which the land was covered. Or, suppose he had found a canoe, and had been as ignorant of the properties of water, or of wood, as we may well suppose to have been the case with the wild men of Germany and of India; would he not have remained as poor as he before had been? That such would have been the case, cannot be doubted. If so, then wealth cannot consist in the mere possession of an instrument, unconnected with the knowledge how to use it. Were a thousand bows given to a man who had been blind from birth, he would be no richer than before

— and were we to transfer to the savages of the Rocky Mountains, all property in the mills and furnaces of the Union, they would find therein no addition to their wealth — for their liability to perish of hunger, or of cold, would remain unchanged; although they had thus become the owners of machinery capable of producing all the implements required for enabling them to obtain food and clothing in abundance, were they but possessed of knowledge Books and newspapers would not be wealth to the man who could not read, but food would be — and he might gladly give a whole library for as much grain as would support him for a single year.

For thousands of years, the people of England were in possession of almost boundless supplies of that fuel, a bushel of which is capable of raising one hundred thousand pounds a foot in a minute, and thus doing as much work as could be done by hundreds of men; and yet that fuel was not wealth, because of the want of knowledge how to utilize its powers. The force was there, latent; but it was not until the days of Watt, that man was enabled to compel it to labor in his service. So it has been with the anthracite coal-mines of Pennsylvania. That fuel was purer and better than any other — and capable, therefore, of doing a greater amount of work; but, *for that reason*, it required a higher degree of knowledge for the development of its latent powers. The greater the power to be useful — the greater the amount of utility latent in a commodity, or thing — the greater is always the amount of resistance to be overcome, in subjecting it to the control of man. That once done, the power thus acquired, centres in THE MAN, whose value steadily rises, as the utility of the raw material by which he is surrounded, becomes more and more developed.

The first poor cultivator commences, as we have seen, his operations on the hill-side. Below him are lands that have, for ages, received the washings of those above, as well as the leaves of trees, and the fallen trees themselves, all of which have, from time immemorial, decayed and become incorporated with the earth — thus forming soils fitted to yield the largest returns to labor; yet for that reason are they inaccessible. Their character exhibits itself in the large trees with which they are covered, and in their capacity for retaining the water required for aiding the process of decomposition; but the poor settler has no power either to clear them of their timber, or to drain them of the superfluous moisture. He begins on the hill-side; but with the increase of his family, and the improvement of his machinery of cultivation, we find him descending the hill, and obtaining not only more food for himself, but also the means of feeding the horse, or the ox, required to assist him in his labors. Aided by the manure yielded to him by the better lands, we see his successors next retracing his steps, improving the hill-side, and compelling it to yield a return twice greater than had been at first obtained. With each step down the hill, they obtain still larger reward for labor; and from each they return, with increased power, to the cultivation of the original poor soil. They have now horses and oxen; and while, by their aid, they extract from the new soils the manure that had for ages accumulated, they have also carts and wagons to carry it up the hill; and with every additional step, their rewards become increased, while their labors are lessened. They go back to the sand and raise the marl, with which they cover the surface; or return to the clay and sink into the limestone, by aid of which they double their products. They are all the time making a machine which feeds them while making it, and which increases in its powers the more there is taken from it. At first, it was worthless; but now—having fed and clothed them for years — it has become so greatly useful, that those who might desire to use it would pay largely for the permission so to do.

The earth is a great machine given to man to be fashioned to his purpose. The more he fashions it, the better it feeds him, because each step is but preparatory to a new one more productive than the last—requiring less labor and yielding larger return. The labor of clearing is great; yet the return is small, the earth being covered with stumps, and filled with roots. With each year the latter decay, and the ground becomes enriched; while the labor of ploughing is diminished. At length, the stumps having disappeared, the return is doubled, while the labor is less by one-half than at first. To forward this process, the owner has done nothing but crop the ground—nature having done the rest. The aid she thus grants him, yields far more food than had been at first obtained in return to the labor of clearing the land. This, however, is not all. The surplus thus yielded has given him the means of improving the poorer lands—furnishing manure with which to enrich them—and thus has he trebled, or quadrupled, his original return without further effort; that which he saves in working the new soils, sufficing to carry the manure to the older ones. He is thus obtaining a daily increased power over the various treasures of the earth.

With every operation connected with the subjection of the earth to the control of man, the result is the same — the first step being, invariably, the most costly one, and the least productive.* The drain commences necessarily near the stream, where the labor is heaviest; yet it frees from water but little land. Further distant, the same quantity of labor, profiting by what has been already done, frees thrice the extent; and now the most perfect system of thorough drainage may be established with less effort than had been at first required for one of the most imperfect kind. To bring the lime into connection with the clay, upon fifty acres, is lighter labor than had been the clearing of a single one; yet the process doubles the return for every acre of the fifty. The man who requires a little fuel for his own use, expends much labor in opening the neighboring vein of coal. To enlarge this, so as to double the product, is a work of comparatively small effort; as is the next enlargement, by which he is enabled to use a wagon, giving him a return fifty times greater than had been obtained while still dependent upon his own unassisted powers. To sink a shaft to the first vein below the surface, and erect a steam-engine, are expensive operations — but then to sink to a second, and tunnel to a third, are trifles in comparison with the first; yet each is equally productive. The first line of railroad runs by houses and towns occupied by a few hundred thousand persons Little branches are next made, costing altogether far less labor than the first, but bringing into connection with it probably thrice the amount of population. The trade increasing, a second track, a third, or a fourth, may be required. The original one facilitating

* The French proverb — *Ce n'est que le premier pas qui coute* — is true in regard to all the relations of life; but in none is it more emphatically so than in reference to the occupation of land. Such being the case, it will readily be seen how destructive of the best interests of man must be a system which, looking to the constant exhaustion of the soil, produces a perpetually increasing necessity for commencing the work of cultivation on new lands, to be in their turn exhausted.

the passage of the materials and the removal of the obstructions, three new ones may now be made for less than had been expended upon the first.

All labor thus given to fashioning the great machine is but the prelude to its further application, with increased returns and rise of wages; and hence it is that portions of the machine, as it exists, invariably exchange, when brought to market, for far less labor than they have cost. The man who cultivated the thin soils was happy to obtain a hundred bushels for his year's work—but with the progress of himself and his neighbors down the hill, into the more fertile soils, wages have risen, and two hundred bushels may be now required. His farm will yield a thousand bushels — but it requires the labor of four men, who must have two hundred bushels each; and the surplus is but two hundred bushels. At twenty years' purchase, this gives a capital of four thousand bushels, or the equivalent of twenty years' wages; whereas it may have cost — in the labor of himself, his sons, and his assistants—the equivalent of a hundred years of labor, or perhaps far more. During all this time, however, it has fed and clothed them all; and the farm has been produced by insensible contributions made from year to year, unthought of and unfelt.

It is now worth twenty years' wages, because its owner has for years taken from it a thousand bushels annually; but when it had lain for centuries, accumulating power to serve the purposes of man, it was worth nothing. Such is the case with the earth everywhere. The more there is taken from it the more there is found to exist. When the coal-mines of England were untouched, they were valueless. Now their value is almost countless; yet the land contains abundant supplies for thousands of years. Iron ore, a century since, being held in low esteem, leases were granted at almost nominal rents. Now, notwithstanding the great quantities that have been removed, such leases are deemed equivalent to the possession of large fortunes; although the amount of ore elsewhere known to exist, is probably a hundred times increased.

The rich lands above described—the coal, the lime, and the ore—were, a century since as much as they are now, possessed of the power to contribute to the comfort and enjoyment of man; yet they were not wealth, because he himself was deficient in the knowledge required for enabling him to compel them to labor in his service. Their utility was latent, waiting the action of the human mind for its development.

In the man of that day we find, however, a state of things precisely similar. His powers were then as great as are those of the men of the present day; but they, too, were latent. His brain was ready to serve him, had he made the demand for its services; but that he could not do. It, too, would have labored gratuitously; not only so, but by lessening the demand upon his muscular powers, it would largely have diminished the quantity of food required for repairing the waste consequent upon exertion. The time required for the supply of his necessities would thus have been reduced, with corresponding increase in the quantity at his command for further study of the powers of nature — and for preparation of the machinery needed for subjecting them to his service.

Wealth consists *in the power to command the always gratuitous services of nature* — whether rendered by the brain of man, or by the matter by which he is surrounded, and upon which it is required to operate. The greater the *power* of association — the greater the diversity of the demands upon the human intellect — the greater, as we have seen, must be the development of the peculiar faculties — or individuality — of each member of the society; and the greater the *capacity* for association. With the latter comes increase of power over nature and over himself; and the more perfect his capacity for self-government, the more rapid must be the motion of society — the greater the tendency towards further progress — and the more rapid the growth of wealth.

The supply of power waiting the demands of man is, as has been said, unlimited. To the world at large, it is what the accumulations in the robbers' cave were to Ali Baba, who needed but the magic word to make the doors fly open, and thus to become master of their wealth. To enable man to do the same, and thus to do, in his case, all that the genii, in the other, had power to do, he has only to qualify himself for crying "open sesame," by combining his efforts with those of his fellow-men.

§ 2. The greater the tendency towards combination of action among men, the greater is the rapidity with which knowledge is diffused, power is gained, and wealth accumulated. That there may be combination, there must be difference—and that the latter may exist, there must be diversity of employment. Where that is found, man is seen to be obtaining constantly increasing power over nature and over himself—thus acquiring freedom in the direct ratio of the development of his latent powers.

In the early periods of society, when men cultivate the poor soils, there can be little association, and, consequently, little combination of action. Having neither horse nor cart, the solitary settler is dependent, mainly, upon his hands and arms for power to harvest his little crop. Carrying a hide to his place of exchange, distant many miles, he seeks to obtain for it leather, shoes, or cloth.—Population increasing, roads are made, and richer soils are cultivated. The store and the mill coming nearer to him, he obtains shoes and flour with the use of less machinery of exchange; and having now more leisure for the preparation of his machine, the returns to labor are increased. More people now obtaining food from the same surface, new places of exchange appear. The wool being, on the spot, converted into cloth, he exchanges directly with the clothier. The saw-mill being at hand, he exchanges with the miller. The tanner gives him leather for his hides, and the paper-maker exchanges paper for his rags. His *power to command* the use of the machinery of exchange is thus a constantly augmenting one; whereas his *necessity* for its use is a constantly decreasing one—there being, with each successive year, a greater tendency towards having the consumer and the producer take their places by each other's side. With each, he finds increase of power to devote his time and mind to the process of fashioning the great instrument to which he is indebted for food and wool; and thus it is that increase of the consuming population is essential to the progress of production.

The loss from the use of machinery of exchange, is in the ratio of the bulk of the article to be exchanged. Food stands first; fuel next; stone for building, third; iron, fourth; cotton, fifth; and so on—diminishing until we come to laces and nutmegs. The raw material being that in the formation of which the earth has most co-operated, and by the production of which the land is most improved—the nearer the place of exchange or conversion can be brought to the place of production, the less must be the loss in the process, and the greater the power of accumulating capital to aid in the production of further wealth. That this must necessarily be so, will be obvious to all who reflect that, in physical science, it is a law, that whatever tends to diminish the quantity of machinery required, tends to the diminution of friction, and to the increase of power.

The man who raises food on his own land, is building up the machine for doing so to more advantage in the following year His neighbor, to whom it is *given*, on condition of sitting still, loses a year's work on his machine, and all he has gained has been the pleasure of idling away his time. If he has employed himself and his horses and wagon in bringing it home, the same number of days that would have been required for raising it, he has misemployed his time, for the farm is unimproved. He has wasted labor and manure. As nobody, however, gives, it is obvious that the man who has a farm, and obtains his food elsewhere, must pay for raising it, and also for transporting it; that although he may have obtained as good wages in some other pursuit, his farm, instead of being improved by a year's cultivation, is deteriorated by a year's neglect; and that he is a poorer man than he would have been had he raised his own food.

The article of next greatest bulk is fuel. While warming his house, he is clearing his land. He would lose by sitting idle, if his neighbor brought his fuel to him, and still more if he had to spend the same time in hauling it; because he would be wearing out his wagon, and losing the manure. Were he to hire himself and his wagon to another, and for the same quantity of fuel he could have cut on his own property, he would be a loser, for his farm would be uncleared.

In taking the stone from his own fields to build his house, he gains doubly, for as his house is built, his land is being cleared. If he remains idle, and lets his neighbor bring him stone, he loses—for his fields remain unfit for cultivation. If he performs as much work for a neighbor, receiving the same apparent wages, he is a loser, by the fact that he has yet to remove the stones—and, until they shall be removed, he cannot cultivate his land.

With every improvement in the machinery of exchange, there is a diminution in the proportion which that machinery bears to the mass of commodities susceptible of being exchanged—because of the extraordinary increase of product consequent upon the increased labor that may be given to building up the great machine. It is a matter of daily observation, that the demand for horses and men increases as railroads drive them from the turnpikes — and the reason is, that the farmer's means of improving his land increase more rapidly than men and horses for the work. The man who has, thus far, sent to market his half-fed cattle, accompanied by horses and men to drive them—and wagons and horses loaded with hay, or turnips, with which to feed them on the road, and to fatten them when at market — now fattens them on the ground, and sends them by railroad ready for the slaughter-house; and thus is his demand for machinery of exchange greatly diminished. He keeps his men, his horses and wagons, and the refuse of his hay and oats, at home; the former employed in ditching and draining, while the latter fertilizes the soil he has thus far cultivated. His production doubling, he accumulates rapidly, while the people around him have more to eat, more to spend in clothing, and can accumulate more themselves. He wants laborers in the field, and these require clothes and dwellings. The shoemaker and the carpenter, finding that there is a demand for their labor, now join the community — eating the food on the ground on which it is produced; and thus is the machinery of exchange improved. The quantity of flour consumed on the spot inducing the miller to come and eat his share, while preparing that of others, the labor of exchanging is again diminished, leaving more to be given to the land. The lime being now turned up, *tons* of turnips are obtained from the same surface that before gave *bushels* of rye. The quantity to be consumed increasing faster than the population, more mouths are needed on the spot; and next the woollen-mill comes. The wool no longer requiring wagons and horses, they are now turned to transporting coal; enabling the farmer to clear his woodland, and to reduce to cultivation the fine soil that has, for centuries, produced nothing but timber. Production again increasing, the new wealth now takes the form of a cotton-mill; and with every step in that direction the farmer finds new demands on the great machine he has constructed, attended with constant increase of power to build it up higher and stronger, and to sink its foundations deeper. He now supplies beef and mutton, wheat, butter, eggs, poultry, cheese, and every other of the comforts and luxuries of life, for which the climate is suited; and all of these from the same land which, when his predecessors commenced the work of cultivation on the light soil of the hills, had given scarcely the rye required for the support of life.

We have here the establishment of a local attraction tending to neutralize the attraction of the capital, or great commercial city; and where such local centres most exist, there, invariably, is found the greatest tendency to the development of individuality, and the combination of action — and the most rapid progress in knowledge, wealth, and power. The more nearly the social system approximates, in its arrangements, to that we see to have been established for the maintenance of order throughout the great system of which our planet forms a part, the greater will be the motion, and the more perfect the harmony—and the more will man be enabled to control and direct the various forces provided for his use; and the more rapidly will he pass from being a creature of necessity towards attaining his true position, that of a being of power.

With every step in this direction, there is, as has been shown, a decline in the value of all existing accumulations; because, on the one side, of the steady diminution in the resistance offered by nature to the gratification of man's desires; and, on the other, of the steady increase in the power of man to overcome the resistance which yet remains. That this must necessarily be the case, will be obvious to all who reflect that if coal, iron, cloth, or any other commodity, could be supplied as freely as is now the atmospheric air, the former could have no more value in our eyes than we are now accustomed to attach to the latter. Existing accumulations are the result of past labors. Whatever tends to increase the power of the present man, tends to give him increased control over the accumulations of the past, and to diminish the *proportion* of the product of labor that can be demanded by the owner of the latter for their use. All, therefore, who desire to diminish the control of capital over labor, and thus increase the freedom of man, should desire to promote the growth of wealth.

Wealth grows with the growth of the power of association and the development of individuality. Individuality is developed as employments become diversified; and hence it is that man has always become more free as the farmer and the artisan have tended more to take their places by each other's side.

3. We are accustomed to measure the wealth of individuals, or of communities, by the *value* of the property they hold; whereas wealth grows, as we see, with the decline of values, which are only a measure of the resistance to be overcome before similar property, or commodities, can be reproduced. This view might, therefore, seem to be in opposition to the general idea of wealth, but, when examined, the difference will be seen to be only apparent. The *positive* wealth of an individual is to be measured by the power he exercises; but his *relative* wealth, by the amount of effort that would be required to be given by others before they could acquire similar power. A man, owning a house that affords him shelter, and a farm giving him food and clothing, has positive wealth, although neither of them has any value in the estimation of other parties. If asked to fix a price at which he would part with them, he would estimate the amount of effort that would be required of others before they could acquire similar power — and that would be the measure of his wealth as compared with another who had neither house nor farm. His positive wealth consists in the extent of his power over nature. His relative wealth is the measure of his power, as compared with that exercised by his fellow-men.

At this moment, however, an improvement takes place in the mode of making bricks and clearing lands, and forthwith there is a diminution of his *comparative*, but without alteration in his *positive* wealth—the house still continuing to shelter him, and the farm to feed him, as before. The decline in the former is a consequence of increase in the wealth and power of the whole community of which he is a member — and that decline becomes more rapid as improvements multiply; because with each successive one, there is a diminution in the obstacles offered by nature to the production of houses and farms, and an increase in the number produced, with steady improvement in the condition of the community. The positive wealth of the individual remains unchanged, and yet his relative wealth is steadily diminishing; and this is equally true, whether considered with reference to intellectual or material accumulations. The man who can read, has wealth; and the more ignorant those around him, the greater is its value. Place him among others who can both read and write, and he becomes poorer than before, by comparison, although his positive wealth remains undiminished.

The wealth of a community is in the ratio of its power to command the services of nature; and the greater that power, the less will be the value of commodities, and the greater the quantity that may be obtained in return for any given amount of labor. With every step in this direction, there will be a diminution in the *proportion* borne by the time required for producing the necessaries of life, to that which may be given to the preparation of machinery required for obtaining further control over nature; or to the purposes of education, recreation, or enjoyment. The progress of man is, therefore, in the ratio of the decline in the value of commodities, and of the increase in his own.

§ 4. The tendency of modern political economy having been towards excluding from consideration all phenomena not directly connected with the production and consumption of *material* wealth, there had arisen a necessity for giving to the new science a title that should be more in harmony with this limitation in its field of action; and hence it is, that we have had various propositions looking to the adoption of Chrematistics, Catallactics, or other words which should expressly exclude the idea that the mind and morals of man were within the range of the economist. These names have never, it is true, been adopted; but the mere suggestion of them by distinguished economists, is evidence of the thoroughly material character of the system; and that such is its character has recently been shown, in a paper of great ability, by one of the most distinguished French economists, who tells his readers that—

"The greater part of the books on political economy, even to the last and best among them, have been written under the impression that there was no real wealth, nor were there any values susceptible of being regarded as wealth, but those which took a material form. Smith," as he continues, "sees no wealth except that which consists of material things.* Say commences by

* Adam Smith was less liable to this charge than any other of the writers here referred to. No one can read his book without being satisfied that he throughout looked to moral and intellectual improvement as being within the sphere of political economy. That such was the case is clearly shown by the extract given in a note on one of the next succeeding pages.

classing under the head of wealth *lands, metals, corn and other grain, clothing*, &c., without adding to this enumeration any description of values not realized in a material form. Whenever, according to Malthus, the question of wealth arises, *our attention is called almost exclusively to material objects.* The only labors, according to Rossi, with which the science of wealth has to do, are those *which contend with matter* for the purposes of adapting it to the supply of our wants. Sismondi does not recognise as wealth those products to which industry has not given *a material form.* Wealth, according to M. Droz, consists of all *those material things* which serve to satisfy our wants. The true idea, adds he, is that we must find it in *those material things that are useful to man.* Finally," says M. Dunoyer, "the author of these pages cannot forget, that he has but recently had to maintain a long discussion with several economists, his colleagues of the Academy of Moral Sciences, without having succeeded in persuading them that there existed any other wealth than that to which they have so improperly applied the term material."*

Modern political economy, having made for itself a being which it denominated man, and from the composition of which it excluded all those parts of the ordinary man that were common to him and the angel — retaining carefully all those common to him and the beast of the forest—found itself forced, necessarily, to the exclusion from its definition of wealth, of every thing pertaining to the feelings, affections, or intellect. In its view, man is an animal that *will* procreate, and *can be made* to work, but, in order that it may do so, it *must* be fed; and it is as a necessary consequence of this, that not only those named above, but numerous other distinguished economists, have found themselves driven to the necessity of treating as unproductive, all employments of time or mind that do not take a material form. Magistrates and men of letters, teachers, men of science, artists, and others — the Humboldts and the Thierrys, the Savignys and the Kents, the Aragos and the Davys, the Canovas and the Davids—are regarded by this school as unproductive, except so far as they produce *things;* and this leads, says, most justly, M. Dunoyer, to the inconsistency that—

"In the midst of this concert for declaring unproductive those pursuits which act directly upon mankind, these economists are

* *Journal des Economistes*, February, 1853.

unanimous in finding them productive when considered in their consequences — that is to say, in the utilities, the faculties, the values, which they succeed in producing in men. It is thus that Adam Smith, after having said in certain parts of his work that men of letters, men of science, and other laborers of the same description, are workmen whose labors produce nothing; says elsewhere, expressly, that *the useful knowledge acquired by the members of a society* (knowledge that they could not have acquired except by aid of these unproductive laborers) *is a product fixed and realized, so to say, in the persons who possess it, and forms an essential part of the wealth of the society, a part of its fixed capital.* It is thus that J. B. Say, who says of the same class of laborers that their products are not susceptible of being accumulated, and that they add nothing to the social wealth, formally declares, on another occasion, *that the learning of the public functionary, the skill of the workman,* (evidently creations of the very men whose products are not susceptible of being preserved,) *form an accumulated capital.* It is thus that M. Sismondi, who at one moment describes, as unproductive, the labors of teachers and others — at another declares, as positively, that *men of letters and artists* (incontestably the work of those teachers) *constitute a part of the national wealth.* It is thus that M. Droz, who says, on one occasion, that *it would be absurd to consider virtue as properly included under the term wealth,* closes his book by saying that it would be to commit a great error if we should regard as a non-producer *the magistracy which secures the triumph of justice, the learned man who diffuses knowledge,* &c."*

§ 5. By the definition of wealth above given, such inconsistencies are avoided, and the word is brought back to its original signification of general happiness, prosperity, and power — not the power of man over his fellow-man, but over himself, his faculties, and the numerous and wonderful forces provided for his use. Such, to no inconsiderable extent, was the idea of Adam Smith, as will be seen in the passage given below — in which he shows how greatly happiness, wealth, and progress, would be promoted by the adoption of a policy in accordance with those "natural inclinations of man" which lead him to combine with his fellow-

* Ibid. p. 166.

men for the development of the various faculties of all the members of society — facilitating the extension of commerce, and emancipating him from the exactions of the trader and the soldier.*

Dr. Smith was no advocate of centralization. On the contrary, he fully believed in a policy tending to the creation of local cen-

* "That order of things which necessity imposes, in general, though not in every particular country, is in every particular country promoted by the natural inclinations of man. If human institutions had never thwarted those natural inclinations, the towns could nowhere have increased beyond what the improvement and cultivation of the territory in which they were situated could support; till such time, at least, as the whole of that territory was completely cultivated and improved. Upon equal, or nearly equal, profits most men will choose to employ their capitals — rather in the improvement and cultivation of land, than either in manufactures or in foreign trade. The man who employs his capital in land has it more under his view and command, and his fortune is much less liable to accidents, than that of the trader, who is obliged frequently to commit it, not only to the winds and the waves, but to the more uncertain elements of human folly and injustice, by giving great credits, in distant countries, to men with whose character and situation he can seldom be thoroughly acquainted. The capital of the landlord, on the contrary, which is fixed in the improvement of his land, seems to be as well secured as the nature of human affairs can admit of. *The beauty of the country, besides the pleasures of a country life, the tranquillity of mind which it promises, and, wherever the injustice of human laws does not disturb it, the independency which it really affords, have charms that, more or less, attract everybody;* and as to cultivate the ground was the original destination of man, so, in every stage of his existence, he seems to retain a predilection for this primitive employment.

"Without the assistance of some artificers, indeed, the cultivation of land cannot be carried on but with great inconveniency and continual interruption. Smiths, carpenters, wheelwrights and ploughwrights, masons and bricklayers, tanners, shoemakers, and tailors, are people whose service the farmer has frequent occasion for. Such artificers, too, stand occasionally in need of the assistance of one another; and as their residence is not, like that of the farmer, necessarily tied down to a precise spot, they naturally settle in the neighborhood of one another, and thus form a small town or village. The butcher, the brewer, and the baker soon join them, together with many other artificers and retailers, necessary or useful for supplying their occasional wants, and who contribute still further to augment the town. The inhabitants of the town, and those of the country are mutually the servants of one another. The town is a continual fair or market, to which the inhabitants of the country resort in order to exchange their rude for manufactured produce. It is this commerce which supplies the inhabitants of the town both with the materials of their work and the means of their subsistence. The quantity of the finished work which they sell to the inhabitants of the country necessarily regulates the quantity of the materials and provisions which they buy. Neither their employment nor subsistence, therefore, can augment, but in proportion to the augmentation of the demand from the country for finished work; and this demand can augment only in proportion to the extension of improvement and cultivation. Had human institutions, therefore, never disturbed the natural course of things, the progressive wealth and increase of the towns would, in every political society, be consequential and in proportion to the improvement and cultivation of the territory or country." — *Wealth of Nations*, book 3, chap. i.

tres of action; and he did not believe in that one which looked to prevent association, by compelling all the farmers of the world to resort to a single and distant market when they desired to convert their food and wool into cloth. Such, however, was the policy of his country; and therefore did it become necessary for Mr. Malthus to prove that the pauperism which was the necessary consequence of centralization, had its origin in a great natural law, which forbade that the quantity of food should keep pace with the demands of an increasing population. Next came Mr. Ricardo, to whom the world is indebted for the idea that cultivation had always commenced on the rich soils of the earth — and that the men who were then flying from England to the colonies, were going from the cultivation of poor soils to that of rich ones; when directly the reverse had ever been the case. His doctrine, and that of all his followers, is therefore that of dispersion, centralization, and large cities; whereas that of Dr. Smith looked to association, to local self-government, and to countries abounding in villages and towns, in which should be performed the exchanges of the surrounding country.

The whole tendency of modern political economists has been in a direction opposite to that indicated as the true one, by the author of the Wealth of Nations; and therefore it has been, that their science has become limited to the single consideration, how it is that material wealth may be increased—leaving altogether out of view the consideration of the morality, or the happiness, of the communities they desired to teach. Hence it is that it has gradually taken so repulsive a form, and that one among its most eminent teachers has found himself called upon to say to his readers, that the political economist is required to look to the growth of wealth alone, and to limit himself to the discussion of the measures by help of which he thinks it may be promoted — allowing "neither sympathy with indigence, nor disgust at profusion or at avarice—neither reverence for existing institutions, nor detestation of existing abuses—neither love of popularity, nor of paradox, nor of system, to deter him from stating what he believes to be the facts, or from drawing from those facts what appear to him to be the legitimate conclusions."*

Happily, true science is required to make no such calls upon

* Senior: Outlines of Political Economy, p. 130.

its teachers. The more it is studied, the more must the "indigence" they see around them excite their "sympathy," and the more free must they become in its expression — because the more fully must they become satisfied that the existence of such a state of things is a consequence of human, and not of divine, laws; the greater must be the "disgust" excited by both "profusion and avarice," as tending to the production of "indigence"; the greater must be their "reverence" for all institutions tending to promote the growth of that habit of association by help of which, alone, man acquires the power over nature in which consists his wealth; the greater the "detestation of existing abuses" tending to perpetuate the existing poverty and wretchedness; and the stronger their determination honestly to labor for their extirpation.

Wealth grows with the growth of the power of man to satisfy that first and greatest want of his nature — the desire for association with his fellow-men. The more rapid its growth, the greater is the tendency towards the disappearance of "indigence," on the one hand, and "profusion and avarice," on the other — towards the termination of existing "abuses," tending to limit the exercise of the power of association, to restrain the development of individuality, and to impair the feeling of strict responsibility towards God and man — and towards having society assume that form which is most calculated for facilitating the progress of the latter towards the high position for which he was originally intended; and therefore the form most calculated to inspire respect and "reverence."

# CHAPTER VIII.

## OF THE FORMATION OF SOCIETY.

§ 1. Crusoe was obliged to work alone. In time, however, being joined by Friday, society commenced; but in what did this society consist? In the existence of another person on his island? Certainly not. Had Friday come so near as to be enabled to see him every day, but had refrained from talking with him, or exchanging services with him—hunting and fishing alone, and consuming alone the produce of his labors — there would still have been no society. This he did not do, but, on the contrary, talked with him, exchanged services with him, cooked the fish when Crusoe had caught it, and in a thousand ways combined his efforts with those of his fellow-prisoner on the island—and thus produced society, or, in other words, association; which is but the act of exchanging ideas and services, and is properly expressed by the single word commerce. Every act of association being an act of commerce, the terms society and commerce are but different modes of expressing the same idea.

That commerce may exist there must be difference, whether in the organic or inorganic world. Had Crusoe and Friday been limited to the exercise of any one, and the same, faculty, there could have been no more association between them than there could now be between two particles of oxygen, or of hydrogen. Bring those two elements together, and combination will, at once, take place; and so is it with man. Had Crusoe had the use of his eyes alone, and Friday been possessed of hands, while deprived of sight, combination between them would immediately have taken place. Society consists in combinations resulting from the existence of differences—of various individualities among the persons of whom it is composed; and the more perfect the *proportion* borne by the various elements, each to the other, the greater must be the tendency to combination, as has been already shown. Among purely agricultural communities association scarcely exists; whereas, it is found in a high degree where the farmer, the lawyer, the merchant, the carpenter, the blacksmith, the mason, the miller, the spinner, the weaver, the builder, the smelter of ore, the refiner of iron, and the maker of engines, are seen constituting portions of the community.

So is it in the inorganic world—the power of combination growing with the increase of differences, but always in harmony with the law of *definite proportions*, to which chemistry is indebted for a precision that without it could never have been attained. Place a thousand atoms of oxygen in a receiver, and they will remain motionless; but introduce a single atom of carbon, and excite their affinities for each other, and at once motion will be produced—a certain portion of the former combining with the latter, and producing carbonic acid. The remainder of the oxygen will continue motionless. If, however, successive atoms of hydrogen, nitrogen, and carbon be introduced, new combinations will be formed, until at length motion will have been produced throughout the whole; but in each successive case of combination the proportions will be as definitely fixed as they had been in the first; and so is it throughout the inorganic world.

Such being the case in regard to all other matter,* it must be so in regard to those combinations in which man is concerned, indicated by the term Society — the tendency to motion being in the direct ratio of the harmony of the proportions of the several parts of which it is composed. So, in fact, it is — association increasing with the increase of differences, and diminishing with any diminution therein, until motion at length ceases to exist; as has been the case in all those countries that have declined in wealth and population.

Combination in the inorganic world takes place in accordance with fixed and immutable laws. There, however, the bodies that combine have always, and in all places, the same power of combi-

* Speaking of the law of definite proportions, M. Comte says:—"The failure of the theory with regard to organic bodies, indicates that the cause of this immense exception cannot be investigated; and such an inquiry belongs as much to physiology as to chemistry."—*Positive Philosophy*, vol. i. p. 14. Knowing, as we do, how recent are both these sciences, it is no matter of surprise that a part of their relations to each other remains yet to be discovered.

nation — the atom of oxygen of the days of the Pharaohs having been precisely the same in composition as that of those of Lavoisier and Davy. With man the case is different. Capable of progress, his faculties become developed, each in succession, as his mind is stimulated into action by the habit of association with his fellow-man. With him, therefore, the power of combination is a growing one, and should increase from day to day, and from year to year, as differences increase in number; and as society more and more obtains those *proportions* which are required — as in the case of the oxygen and the carbon — for taking up each faculty of the individual men of whom it is composed; and this we shall see to be the case.

§ 2. In the inorganic world every act of combination is an act of motion, the various particles exchanging with each other their respective properties. So is it in the social one—every act of association being an act of motion; ideas being given out and taken in; services being rendered and accepted, and commodities or things being exchanged. All force results from motion, and it is where there is the greatest movement in society, that man is seen exerting the greatest power for the subjugation of the various natural forces by which he is every where surrounded. What then are the laws of motion? If it is true, that there is but one system of laws for the government of all matter, then those which govern the movements of the various inorganic bodies should be the same with those by which is regulated the motion of society; and that such is the case can readily be shown.

A body moved by a single force proceeds always in the same direction until stopped by some counteracting one. The latter, as we know, is found in gravitation, and so long as the force exercised by man is so counteracted, all his motions must be liable to constant intermission, as we see them everywhere to have been. In the early period of society he obtains power to grind his grain by means of raising and then dropping a stone — or he moves through the water by help of an oar — or he knocks an animal in the head by means of a club—all of these operations being the result of the application of a single force; and all of them consequently intermitted motions—requiring a constant repetition of the same force that had been required in the first passage from a state of rest to one of motion. There is thus a constant waste of power, and the motion produced is small.

That such is the case he feels, and therefore is it that we see him constantly endeavoring to obtain continuous motion — and this he does, by imitating as far as possible the mechanism he sees to govern the movements of the heavenly bodies. Desiring to move a body, and its form permitting him so to do, he causes it to revolve on its own axis, and thus brings gravitation to aid him in his efforts, where before it had resisted him — as when he rolls a ball, a hogshead, or a bale of cotton. There being, however, numerous bodies whose forms forbid that they should be rolled, he is next seen constructing an instrument that will revolve upon its own axis, as does the earth; and between two such machines he places the bodies he desires to move—thus obtaining far more continuous action. Finding himself yet, however, greatly limited by friction, he lays down an iron rail, and is thus enabled to obtain continuous action with high velocity; and the momentum increases in the direct ratio of the velocity — a body falling at the rate of a thousand feet in a minute, giving a force precisely ten times greater than would be given by it if falling at the rate of a hundred feet in the same space of time.

Examining now the progress of man towards obtaining power over nature, we find it to be in the direct ratio of the substitution of continued for intermitted motion. From the sharpened shell used by Robinson Crusoe, he passes, as we have seen, to the knife, the saw, the cross-cut saw, and finally to the circular one, that can be driven at the highest velocity; and, this done, he obtains from the application of the same amount of muscular power results thousands of times greater than at first.

In the process of drainage, the farmer is only seeking to establish continuity of motion. Knowing that when water is stagnant, it is destructive of vegetable life — and seeing himself surrounded by great bodies of the richest land, waiting only for the production of motion in the water with which it has been saturated — he digs canals and lays pipes, and cuts away the trees to admit the sun; and having thus enabled motion to take place, he obtains crops thrice increased in quantity.

Again, he substitutes the circular motion of the reaping-hook for the more angular one of the hand — thence passing to the scythe—and finally, to the constant motion of the reaping machine, by help of which he cuts more grain in an hour, than with his hands he could pull up in a week. The printer in like manner passes from the wooden block and hammer, to the more continuous action of the screw; and thence, by various stages, through the reciprocating motion of the hand-press, to the wonderful instrument now in use, by help of which we obtain in a single day, a greater return than was obtained by Caxton in a year. The manufacturer, in his turn, so arranges his mill, that his wool and his cotton enter at one door, and go out at an opposite one, becoming at each remove, more and more changed in form, until the raw material that entered at the one, goes out at the other, ready for use. In every pursuit of life, man thus seeks to obtain continuous motion; and his progress toward wealth and power is every where seen to be in the direct ratio of the accomplishment of that object.

Looking throughout the world, we find nature every where applying force by aid of continued motion. To develop electricity, a circuit must be formed, and this circuit is what we find around us everywhere, whether studying the motion of the winds, the formation of the dew, the circulation of the blood through the arteries which carry it from the heart, or through the veins by which it is returned to the place whence it came. The more rapid the motion, too, the more is it continuous, and the greater is the force exerted. The Rhine, taking its rise among the snowy peaks of the Alps, passes rapidly towards the ocean, and as it carries off the water that has been dissolved, new condensations are being formed at a higher elevation—thus furnishing, for the use of man, a motion that is constant during the heats of summer, and the colds of winter. The Ohio and the Mississippi—having their heads among the comparatively slight elevations bordering, on the east and north, the great valley of the west—have a more sluggish motion; and, as a consequence, those streams are almost useless for nearly half the year. Look where we may, throughout nature, we see that power exists in the ratio of the continuity of motion; and that similar continuity is what man is everywhere endeavouring to obtain.

In the movements of the isolated settler, however, there can be no continuity. Dependent for supplies upon his powers of *appro-*

*priation*, and compelled to wander over extensive surfaces, he finds himself not unfrequently in danger of perishing for want of food. Even when successful, he is compelled to intermit his search, and provide for effecting the *change of place* required for bringing his food, his miserable habitation, and himself together. There arrived, he is forced to be, in turn, cook and tailor, mason and carpenter. Deprived of artificial light, his nights are wholly useless, while his power productively to apply his days, is dependent altogether upon the chances of the weather.

Discovering, however, at length, that he has a neighbor, exchanges arise between them; but, occupying different parts of the island, they find themselves compelled to approach each other precisely as do the stones with which they pound their grain; and when they separate, the same force is again required to bring them once more together. Further, when they meet, difficulties exist in settling the terms of trade, by reason of the irregularity in the supply of the various commodities with which they desire to part. The fisherman has had good luck, and has taken many fish; but chance has enabled the hunter to obtain a supply of fish, and now he wants only fruit, which the fisherman has not.—Difference being, as we already know, indispensable to association, the want of difference would here oppose a bar to association difficult to be surmounted; and that difficulty is seen to exist in every community in which there are found no differences. The farmer has rarely occasion to exchange with his brother farmer — the planter has never need to exchange with his brother planter, nor does the shoemaker require to exchange with another shoemaker; and to the absence of diversity of employments it is due, that in the infancy of society there are so many obstacles standing in the way of commerce, as to render the trader, who aids in their removal, a most important member of the community.

In time, however, wealth and population grow, and with that growth there is an increase of motion in the community — the husband now exchanging services with the wife, the parents with the children, and the children with each other—one providing fish, a second meat, and a third grain; while a fourth converts the wool into cloth, and a fifth the skins into shoes. Motion now becomes more continuous, and with this increase of movement there is a steady increase in the power of man over nature, attended by diminution of her resistance to his further efforts. Everywhere around, are seen other families, each revolving on its own axis, while the community of which they form a part, is steadily revolving around a common centre; and thus, by degrees, we see established a system corresponding with that which maintains in order the wonderful system of the universe. At every step we witness an increased rapidity of motion, with increase of force on the part of man—exhibited in the fact that, great as are his numbers, he obtains steadily increasing supplies of corn from a surface that gave to the original settler the most scanty supplies of the poorest food.

With each step gained, we find a tendency to greater velocity at the next one; and as to man has been granted the capacity for further progress, such must necessarily be the case. To the first little community, the construction of a simple footpath was a matter requiring great exertion; but now, with the growth of population and wealth, it is seen obtaining in succession turnpike roads, plank roads, railroads and locomotive engines; and with less trouble than had been at first required to make the path by which the products of the chase had been conveyed on human shoulders. Here we have the accelerated motion that is witnessed in a body when falling towards the earth. In the first second, it may fall but a single foot; but at the end of ten seconds it is found to have fallen 100—at the end of the second ten, 400—of the third, 900—fourth, 1600—fifth, 2500—and so on until at the end of a thousand seconds it has fallen a million of feet. Had it been stopped at the end of each foot and required to take a new departure, it would have fallen through a distance of but a thousand feet; but by reason of the constantly increasing momentum resulting from continuous motion, it has fallen through a thousand times that distance. Such, too, must be the case with society. In the outset, there is little motion and little power of progress; but as its members are more and more enabled to associate, the power of further advance is found to grow with constantly increasing rapidity. The improvements of the last ten years have been greater than those of the preceding thirty, and they had been greater than those of the century that had preceded it; and in that century man had obtained more power over nature than had been acquired in the long period that had elapsed since the days of Alfred, or of Charlemagne.

In order, however, that there may be continuous motion in society, there must exist security of person and of property; but when men are poor, and widely scattered, neither of these can readily be obtained. There existing then no law but that of force, the strong man is seen to have been everywhere disposed to trample upon, and plunder, those who were weak — sometimes seizing on land, and compelling them to work it for his profit; at others, placing himself across the road, and forbidding all intercourse except upon terms to be settled by himself; again, by requiring each laborer to pay rent, tax, or *taille;* or, lastly, by dispossessing them of houses, farms, and implements — and, perhaps, selling husbands and wives, parents and children, into slavery, as further addition to the spoils of "glorious war." In all these cases, there is, as the reader will observe, a retardation of motion, at the cost of those who live by labor, for the benefit of those who live by appropriation of the produce of the labor of others.

The value of all commodities is the measure of the resistance to be overcome before they can be obtained. As that resistance diminishes, there is a decline in their value, and an increase in that of man. Whatever tends to promote increase in the motion of society, tends to diminish the value of the former, and to increase that of the latter. Whatever, on the contrary, tends to retard the movements of society, and prevent the growth of the power of association, or commerce, tends equally to prevent decline of values; to retard the growth of wealth; to arrest the development of individuality; and to diminish the value of man.

§ 3. In the picture thus far presented of the movements of early colonists, they have been represented as heads of the only two families on an island, each enjoying perfect security of person and property—both enabled to appropriate to their own uses and purposes the whole produce of their labor — and both, therefore, enabled to pass steadily onward towards increased wealth, prosperity, and happiness. Such, however, has not been the course of things in any of the countries of the world. In all there have existed causes of disturbance, tending greatly to arrest the progress of man; but in accordance with the law of the composition of forces, it has been deemed right to show what *would* have been the course of events, had no such causes existed. That done, we may now examine into those disturbances, with a view to ascertain how each and every of them has tended to produce the course of action recorded in our historical books.

Let us, with that view, add to the number of occupants of the island a third, remarkable for his strength of arm — able, if he will, to dictate laws to his fellow-colonists — and willing to live by their labor instead of his own. Placing himself midway between them, he says to A, the occupant of one side of the island and possessor of a canoe, "Bring your fish to me. It will give you less trouble than you would find in carrying them across the island, and I will arrange the terms of the exchange between you and B." To the latter, he says, "Bring me your birds, rabbits, and squirrels, and I will negotiate the terms on which you shall have fish."

To this they might object, that they were perfectly competent to manage their own exchanges, and that they would thus save the expense of employing an agent; and, were they united, they might oppose to the gratification of his wishes an effectual resistance. Any such effort at association being likely, however, to defeat him in his desire to live at their expense, it becomes essential that he should, as far as possible, prevent any thing like combination of action between them. He, therefore, stirs up strife; and discord produces weakness and poverty, where association would have been productive of wealth and strength. The more widely they are held apart, the larger is the *proportion* of the product of their labor that he himself appropriates; and thus, while they become from day to day more dependent upon his will, he increases steadily in wealth and power.

Their families, however, increasing, it occurs to some of the more intelligent among them that their situation might be improved by the adoption of measures tending to enable them to combine their efforts and work together. Although A has only a bow and arrows, there exists no reason why his son might not have a canoe; and the ocean around him abounds in fish. Although B has only a canoe, it would be easy for his son to obtain a bow and arrows; and, thenceforth, father and son could exchange fish for meat, without the necessity for crossing the island, at great cost for transportation, and subject to the demands of the trader who has thus placed himself across the road. Such an increase in the power of association, and in the continuity of motion, does not, however, suit the purposes of the latter, to whom traffic affords the means of living in luxury at the cost of his poor dependants; nor will he permit it to be done. Being rich, he can afford to pay for the help required for maintaining his authority; and among the children of his neighbors there are some who would prefer to live by the labor of others rather than by their own. Poor and dissolute, they are ready to sell their services to an employer who will enable them to eat, drink, and make merry, in return for aiding him in his efforts at the prevention of any intercourse except through himself; and the hired ruffian now makes his appearance on the stage.

Larger revenues are now required, and that they may be obtained, it is needed that there be new efforts at the prevention of association at home, or exchange abroad — without the payment of contributions to the trader's treasury. With every step in that direction we find a diminution in the ability to construct machinery by help of which to obtain power over nature, or give utility to the various substances provided for the use of man—an increase in the value of all commodities required for his use, consequent upon the increase in the obstacles to be surmounted before they can be obtained — a decline in the value of man — and a diminution in his progress towards wealth, happiness, and power. How far the view thus presented is in accordance with the facts of history, we may now examine.

In the absence of wealth, or of the power to command the services of nature that marks the origin of society, man is compelled to depend upon his own unassisted efforts for obtaining a supply of the necessaries of life. His intellectual faculties being then scarcely at all developed, he is obliged to rely almost entirely upon his physical powers; and these being necessarily widely different in different persons, there is, at this period, the greatest inequality of condition. The child and the woman are then the slaves of parents and of husbands; while those who, from disease or age, are incapacitated from labor, become, in turn, slaves to their children, and are generally abandoned to perish for want of food.

In the hunter state, when man merely appropriates the spontaneous gifts of nature, brute force constitutes his only wealth. Compelled to constant and severe exercise in search of food, while deficient in the clothing required for the maintenance of animal heat, the waste is great, and large supplies of food are consequently required; as is shown by the fact, that the hunters and trappers of the West are allowed no less than eight pounds of meat per day.

The necessities of man are thus very great, while his powers are very small. Eight hundred acres of land, equal to one and a quarter square miles, are required, as we are told, for furnishing to man in the hunter state the same quantity of food that could be obtained from half an acre under cultivation. Famines being therefore frequent, men are forced to have, at times, recourse to the most nauseous food; and hence it is, that on one hand we find the eaters of earth, and on another the eaters of men — both belonging to that stage of society in which man is least abundant, and may exercise at will his right of selecting among the poor and the rich soils, that then so much abound. Being, however, but nature's slave, she presents to his occupation of rich soils, obstacles so entirely insuperable as to force him, as we have seen, to commence everywhere on the poorer ones — those whose natural qualities least fit them to yield a return to labor. Food has, therefore, great value, because obtained at the cost of infinite effort.

Game becoming, from year to year, more scarce, famines become more frequent; and this involves a necessity for change of place. That, in its turn, produces a necessity for dispossessing the fortunate owners of places in which food can more readily be obtained; and thus it is, that deficiency of power over nature compels man everywhere to become the robber of his fellow-man. The land in which he was born having for him but small attractive power—his stay in it having been little else than a constant succession of sufferings for want of food—he is always ready to shift his quarter in search of plunder; as we see to be the case with the Camanches, and other savage tribes of the West. So has it everywhere been. The history of the world, throughout, shows us the people of the higher and poorer lands—those of the region of the Himalayas, the early Germans, the Swiss, and the Highlanders—plundering those whose peaceful habits had enabled them to accumulate wealth, and to cultivate the more productive soils.

In the early period, there being little property of any kind, we see the strong men everywhere to have appropriated to themselves large bodies of land; while men, women, and children have been converted into property, reduced to slavery, and forced to work for masters who perform the part of traders—standing between those who produced and those who desired to consume; and taking the whole results of the labor of the first, while giving to the last only what was absolutely necessary for the support of life. The whole business of the great proprietor consisting in the prevention of any combination of effort between his slaves, the more perfectly that object is attained, the larger is always the *proportion* of the products retained by him, and the smaller that divided among those who had labored for their production, and those who required them for consumption.

Trade thus commences with the traffic in bones, muscles, and blood—the trade in man. The warrior buys his commodities in the cheapest market, stealing upon them in the dead of night, burning their villages, murdering the males, and making prisoners of the women and children. His glory is measured by the number of his murders, and his wealth grows with the amount of booty he has been enabled to secure. Retaining for his own uses and purposes as many of his prisoners as are required, the remainder are sold to other traders, who, having bought in the cheapest market, transport their property elsewhere, in search of the dearest one, in which to sell at the largest profit.

At this period of society, men are always found either among the highlands of the interior, or on small and rocky islands, like those of the Ionian and Ægean seas, on which the formation of a soil for cultivation is a process that is very slow indeed. There being no roads, communication by land is very difficult, and the little that exists, is maintained by means of boats or ships, for the preparation and management of which these island people are early fitted; and here it is, therefore, that trade, to any considerable extent, is first developed. The facilities for trade being, however, accompanied by equal facility for robbing and murdering the people on the coast, and preventing any commerce that shall not contribute to the trader's profit, piracy and trade grow naturally up together. In time, however, population increasing, it is found more profitable to establish themselves at places through which exchanges must necessarily be made—there to levy contributions on the exchangers; and thus it is that we see great cities to have risen on the sites of Tyre, Sidon, Corinth, Palmyra, Venice, Genoa, and others whose growth was due exclusively to trade.

§ 4. Every act of association being, as has been said, an act of commerce, the maintenance of commerce it is that constitutes society. Man, therefore, seeks commerce, association, or combination, with his fellow-men. It is the first necessity, and without it he is not the being to which we attach the idea of man. The warrior opposes obstacles to commerce by preventing all intercourse except that which passes through himself. The great landed proprietor and owner of slaves is the middle-man — the trader — who regulates all the exchanges made by the people owned by him, with other persons, the property of his neighbors. The trader in merchandise opposes obstacles to all commerce carried on without his aid — desiring everywhere to have a monopoly, in order that the producer of food may obtain but little cloth, and that the maker of cloth may be forced to content himself with little food—his principle being to buy at the lowest price, and sell at the highest.

The words commerce and trade are commonly regarded as convertible terms, yet are the ideas they express so widely different as to render it essential that their difference be clearly understood. *All* men are prompted to associate and combine *with* each other—to exchange ideas and services *with* each other—and thus to maintain COMMERCE. *Some* men seek to perform exchanges *for* other men, and thus to maintain TRADE.

Commerce is *the object* everywhere desired, and everywhere sought to be accomplished. Traffic is *the instrument* used by commerce for its accomplishment — and the greater the necessity for the instrument, the less is the power of those who require to use it. The nearer the consumer and the producer — and the more perfect the power of association — the less is the necessity for the trader's services, but the greater are the powers of those who produce and consume, and desire to maintain commerce. The more distant they are, the greater is the need of the trader's services, and the greater is his power—but the poorer and weaker become the producers and the consumers, and the smaller is the commerce.

The value of all commodities being the measure of the obstacles standing in the way of their attainment, it follows necessarily that the former will increase with every increase of the latter, and that every step in that direction will be attended by a decline in the value of man. The necessity for using the services of the trader constituting an obstacle standing in the way of commerce, and tending to enhance the value of things, while depressing that of man, to whatever extent it can be diminished, to the same extent must it tend to diminish the value of the first, and increase that of the last. That diminution comes with the growth of wealth and population, with the development of individuality, and with the increase in the power of association; and commerce grows always in the direct ratio of its increase of power over the *instrument* known as trade, precisely as we see it to do in reference to roads, wagons, ships, and other instruments. The men who buy and sell, who traffic and transport, desire to prevent association, and thus to preclude the maintenance of commerce; and the more perfectly their object is accomplished, the larger is the *proportion* of the commodities passing through their hands, retained by them; and the smaller the proportion to be divided between the producers and the consumers.

In illustration of this we may take the post-office, an admirable machine for maintaining commerce in words and ideas, but totally useless to persons who live near together. Separate the latter, and the machine becomes a necessity, with great diminution in the power to maintain commerce. Bring them together again, and the necessity disappears, with great increase of commerce — conversation being accompanied by a rapidity in the motion of ideas that enables half an hour to accomplish more than might have been done with a correspondence of a year. The letter-writers are the people who maintain commerce, while the letter-carriers are the traders, used by them for its maintenance. In the early periods of society the obstacles to this commerce having been very great, its amount was, consequently, very small indeed. The trade in letters has been a monopoly of governments that have dictated the terms upon which commerce could be maintained — but, with the progress of population and of wealth, the people of various countries have been enabled to diminish the power of the trader; and, as a necessary consequence, commerce has largely grown. Even now, however, the intercourse between this country and Europe is heavily taxed by means of obstacles thrown in the way by Great Britain, which permits no letter to pass over its limited territory, but at a cost nearly equal to that required for transporting it across the thousands of miles of ocean that lie between the continents.

Ships are not commerce, nor are wagons, sailors, letter-carriers, brokers, or commission merchants. The necessity for using them constitutes an obstacle standing in the way of commerce, and adding largely to the value of commodities requiring their aid in passing from the consumer to the producer. The trader desires to increase that value, buying cheaply and selling dearly —thus increasing the power of the *instrument* used by commerce. The real parties to the exchange desire the reverse of this, thus diminishing the power of the *instrument*, and increasing that of those who use it. The greater the power of the trader, the smaller must be commerce; whereas the more perfect the power of the principals, the greater must it be.

That the necessity for employing the trader and transporter is felt, by all who have exchanges to make, to be an obstacle, is proved by the fact that every measure tending to the diversification of employment, or to the improvement of communications — and consequently to the reduction of their power — is universally hailed as leading to improvement in the condition of all other portions of society. The laborer rejoices when demand for his services is brought to his door by the erection of a mill or a furnace, or the construction of a road. The farmer rejoices in the opening of a market close at hand, giving him consumers for his food. His land rejoices in the home consumption of its products, for its owner is thereby enabled to return to it their refuse in the form of manure. The planter rejoices in the erection of a mill in his neighborhood, giving him a market for his cotton and his food. The parent rejoices when a market for their labor enables his sons and his daughters readily to supply themselves with the food and clothing they require. Every one rejoices in the growth of a home market for labor and its products, for commerce is then increasing surely and rapidly; and every one mourns the diminution of the home market, for it is one whose deficiencies cannot elsewhere be supplied. Labor and its products are then wasted — the power of consumption diminishes with diminution of the power of production — commerce becomes languid — labor and land diminish in value — and laborer and land-owner become daily poorer than before.

Every step in the former direction is attended with increase in the continuity of motion among the people who produce and consume—with increase in the power of association and combination — and increase of freedom. Every one tending to increase the power of the trader, or any other of the instruments used by commerce, is attended, on the contrary, with a deterioration in the condition of man, and a decline of freedom; and that this must necessarily be so, will be obvious to all who reflect, that the growth of wealth and freedom is everywhere seen to be a consequence of man's increased power over the machinery required for the accomplishment of his purposes. As axes and steam-engines are improved in quality, the men who use them acquire a constantly increased control over the constantly augmenting products of their labor, attended with a constant increase in the ability to become themselves owners of such machines. As the machinery required to be used in the performance of exehanges, is improved in quality, the producer and the consumer acquire a constantly increased control over the products of their labor, with steady tendency to come nearer together, and to emancipate themselves altogether from the trader's power.

Trade tending necessarily towards centralization, every step in that direction, whether in the moral or material world, is an approach to slavery and death. Commerce, on the contrary, tending towards the establishment of local centres and local action, — every movement in that direction is an approach to freedom. Whatever tends to increase the power of the one, tends to destruction of individuality and decrease in the power of association — but whatever tends to increase the power of the other, tends to development of mind and to increase in the desire of association, and in the power to enjoy the vast advantages that everywhere result from it.

The movements of trade being, like those of war, greatly dependent on the will of individuals, are necessarily very spasmodic. Collected together in great cities, traders find it easy to combine their operations when it is desired to depress the prices of the commodities they seek to obtain, or to raise those of the things they already possess; and thus do they obtain power to tax both the consumers and the producers. Commerce, on the contrary, tends to produce steadiness and regularity, and thus to diminish the power of the trader.—Regularity of motion is essential to its continuity, as is well known to all persons familiar with the movements of machinery. A steam-engine that was spasmodic in its action could not turn out good cloth or flour, nor could the machine itself long continue to exist. Slight as are the changes produced by a little excess of steam at one moment, or a corresponding deficiency at another, it was deemed necessary to invent *a governor*, whose action should tend to the production of perfect steadiness of motion; and the result was thus obtained.

Without steadiness, there can be no durability of machinery; and that quality is as essential to society as it can be to the steam-engine or the watch. With the growth of commerce, it increases, and therefore is it, that in all communities in which the power of association is growing, because of increased diversification of employments, and increased development of individuality, we witness a constant increase of strength and power. Steadiness diminishes with the increased necessity for trade; and therefore is it that in all communities in which employments have become less diversified, there has been a constant decline of both strength and power. "Strength," says Carlyle, "does not manifest itself in spasms, but in the stout bearing of burdens"—and in this it is, as there will be occasion to show, that trading communities have always failed.

War and trade regard man as the instrument to be used, whereas commerce regards trade as the instrument to be used by man; and therefore it is, that man declines when the power of the warrior and trader grows, and rises as that power declines.

Wealth increases, as the value of commodities — or the cost at which they may be reproduced — declines. Values tend to decline with every diminution of the power of the trader—and therefore it is that we see wealth to increase so rapidly when the consumer and producer are brought into close connection with each other. Were it otherwise, it would be in opposition to a well-known physical law, from the study of which we learn, that with every diminution in the machinery required for producing a given effect, there is a diminution of friction and consequent increase of power. The friction of commerce results from the necessity for the services of the trader, his ships, and his wagons. As that necessity diminishes — as men are more and more enabled to associate — there is diminution of friction, with constant tendency towards continuous motion among the various portions of society, with rapid increase of individuality and of the power of further progress.

Commerce, then, is the object sought to be accomplished. Trade is the instrument. The more that man becomes master of the instrument, the greater is the tendency towards the accomplishment of the object. The more the instrument becomes master of him, the less is that tendency, and the smaller must be the amount of commerce. These things premised, we may now proceed to examine the process by means of which society is formed.

§ 5. In science, as the reader has already seen, it is the most abstract and general that is first developed, leaving the concrete and special to follow slowly in the rear; and so it is with the pursuits of man. To rob and murder our fellow-men — to seek glory at the cost of the destruction of towns and cities — requires no scientific knowledge; whereas agriculture is a pursuit calling at every moment for the aid of science. So, again, is it with trading, which makes but small demand upon the intellectual faculties. To the postman it is unimportant whether the letter he delivers carries with it news of war or peace, births or deaths. To the dealer in cotton or sugar, it matters little whether his commodities grow on the hills or in the valleys, on trees, or on shrubs. To the dealer in slaves, it is immaterial whether the chattel be male or female, parent or child; all that he requires to know being, whether, having bought it cheaply, he can sell it dearly. Trade is to commerce what mathematics are to science. Both are *instruments* to be used for the accomplishment of an object.

The abstract mathematics deal simply with number and form, whereas chemistry looks to the decomposition, and physiolog to the recomposition, of the material of bodies. Trade deals with bodies to be moved or exchanged, having no reference to the qualities by which one body is distinguished from another; whereas, commerce looks to the decomposition and recomposition of the various forces of society resulting from the power to associate, and the exercise of the habit of association. Trade, abstract and general, is, like war, early developed, whereas agriculture and commerce require, for their development, a great advance in population, wealth, and power. The savage of the Rocky Mountains, or of the islands of the South Pacific, is as keen a trader as the one who has served his apprenticeship in New York or London; and the first desire of the Russian serf is to become a dealer in the produce of the labor of other hands.

In the early periods of society, robbery and murder were deified under the names of Odin, and of Mars. Alexander and Cæsar, Tamerlane and Nadir Shah, Drake and Cavendish, Wallenstein and Napoleon, were great, because of the number of murders they had committed, and of towns and cities they had ruined. The "merchant-princes" of Venice, and of Genoa, were great, because of the large fortunes they had realized from buying and selling slaves and other merchandise—doing nothing themselves but stand between the people who produced and those who consumed—thus adding largely to the value of the commodities passing through their hands, at the cost of all who found themselves forced to contribute to the growth of their enormous fortunes.

In this condition of society, the only qualities that command respect among men are brute force and craft—the one properly represented by Ajax, while the other is personified in the wise Ulysses. The morals of war and of trade are the same. The warrior rejoices in deceiving his antagonist, all being fair in war; while the trader acquires the respect of his friends by help of a large fortune, acquired, perhaps, by supplying the poor negroes of Africa with guns that exploded at the first attempt to fire them—or cloth that fell to pieces on the first attempt to wash it. In both, the end is seen to sanctify the means — the only test of right being found in success or failure. Pre-eminence of soldiers and traders may, therefore, be regarded as an evidence of barbarism.

The object of the warrior-chief being that of preventing the existence of any motion in society except that which centres in himself, he monopolizes land, and destroys the power of voluntary association among the men he uses as his instruments. The soldier, obeying the word of command, is so far from holding himself responsible to God, or man, for the observance of the rights of person or of property, that he glories in the extent of his robberies, and in the number of his murders. The man of the Rocky Mountains adorns his person with the scalps of his butchered enemies, while the more civilized murderer contents himself with adding a ribbon to the decoration of his coat; but both are savages alike. The trader — equally with the soldier seeking to prevent any movement except that which centres in himself — also uses irresponsible machines. The sailor is among the most brutalized of human beings, bound, like the soldier, to obey orders, at the risk of having his back seamed by the application of the whip. The human machines used by war and trade are the only ones, except the negro slave, who are now flogged.

The soldier desires labor to be cheap, that recruits may readily be obtained. The great land-owner desires it may be cheap, that he may be enabled to appropriate to himself a large proportion of the proceeds of his land; and the trader desires it to be cheap, that he may be enabled to dictate the terms upon which he will buy, as well as those upon which he will sell.

The object of all being thus identical—that of obtaining power over their fellow-men—it is no matter of surprise that we find the trader and the soldier so uniformly helping, and being helped by, each other. The bankers of Rome were as ready to furnish material aid to Cæsar, Pompey, and Augustus, as are now those of London, Paris, Amsterdam, and Vienna, to grant it to the Emperors of France, Austria, and Russia — and as indifferent as they in relation to the end for whose attainment it was destined to be used. War and trade thus travel together, as is shown by the history of the world; the only difference between wars made for purposes of conquest, and those for the maintenance of monopolies of trade, being, that the virulence of the latter is much greater than is that of the former. The conqueror—seeking political power—is *sometimes* moved by a desire to improve the condition of his fellow-men; but the trader, in pursuit of power, is animated by no other idea than that of buying in the cheapest market and selling in the dearest—cheapening merchandise in the one, even at the cost of starving the producers, and increasing his price in the other, even at the cost of starving the consumers. Both profit by whatever tends to diminution in the power of voluntary association, and consequent decline of commerce. The soldier forbids the holding of meetings among his subjects. The slave-owner interdicts his people from assembling together, except at such times, and in such places, as meet his approbation. The shipmaster rejoices when the men of England separate from each other, and transport themselves by hundreds of thousands to Canada and Australia, because it enhances freights; and the trader rejoices because the more widely men are scattered, the more they need the service of the middle-man, and the richer and more powerful does he become at their expense.

§ 6. Closely connected with the movements of the trader, and next in the order of development, come the labors given to effecting *changes of place*. In the early periods, these are almost altogether limited to changing the places of men who are held as slaves, as we see now to be the case in many parts of Africa; and to some extent in our Southern States. By degrees, however, the camel-driver, the wagoner, and the sailor, appear upon the scene—a highly important portion of society, because of the great quantity of muscular effort required for moving a little merchandise. Here, again, we see that the earliest in development is that which makes least demand for knowledge. To the wagoner, it is indifferent what it is he carries, whether cotton, rum, or prayer-books; and to the sailor, it is immaterial whether he carries gunpowder to the African, or clothing to the people of the Sandwich Islands—provided he is satisfied with the price paid for the work of transportation. With the growth of wealth and population, and consequent increase in the power of association, the necessity for transportation declines, while the facilities for effecting changes of place as steadily increase. The turnpike road, and the railroad, replace in quick succession the Indian path, as the ship and the steamer replace the canoe; and with every step in this direction, there is a diminution in the *proportion* of society required to be so employed, accompanied by an increase in the proportion of the muscular and mental powers that may be given to the work of increasing the quantity of things susceptible of being carried.

§ 7. Next in the order of development come *mechanical and chemical changes of matter in form*, more concrete and special, and requiring a much higher degree of knowledge.

A branch torn from a tree sufficed Cain for the murder of his brother Abel; but he would have required to understand the nature of the material to be used for making a knife, before he could have converted it into a bow, or the trunk from which it had been torn, into a canoe. The skin may be torn from a deer and used for a garment; but it requires some knowledge to enable the poor savage of the West to convert it into a moccasin. The stone may be used as a weapon of offence, but it requires some acquaintance with the properties of matter to discover that it contains iron, and still further knowledge to be enabled to convert iron into swords and spades.

With that knowledge comes man's power over matter — or, in other words, his wealth; and with every increase of power, he is more and more enabled to live in connection with his fellow-men — associating with them for the establishment, or maintenance, of their rights of person and of property. Motion becomes more continuous, with steady increase of its rapidity; and with every such increase society tends to take upon itself a more natural and consistent form — the *proportion* of those who live by appropriation steadily declining, with corresponding increase in the *proportion* of those who live by the exertion of their physical and intellectual faculties. Right tends, therefore, to triumph over might, with diminution in the *proportion* of the labors of the community required for self-defence, and corresponding increase in the *proportion* that may be given to the work of obtaining power over the forces of nature; and with every step in this direction the feeling of the responsibility which attends the exercise of power tends steadily to increase.

§ 8. Following the above in order of development, come the labors given to effecting *vital changes in the forms of matter*, and attended with an augmentation of the quantity of things suscepti-ble of being converted, transported, sold, or bought.

The labors of the miller make no change in the quantity of food to be eaten, nor do those of the spinner increase the quantity of cotton to be worn; but to those of the farmer we are indebted for an increase in the quantity of corn and of wool.

The exercise of that power is limited to the earth alone. Man fashions and exchanges, but he cannot, with all his science, fashion the elements by which he is surrounded, into a grain of corn, or a lock of wool. A part of his labor being given to the fashioning of the great machine itself, produces changes that are permanent: the drain, once cut, remaining a drain; and the limestone, once reduced to lime, not again becoming lime-stone. Passing into the food of man and animals, it ever after takes its part in the same round with the clay with which it has been combined. The iron rusting, gradually passes into the soil, to take its part with the clay and the lime. That portion of man's labor gives him wages while preparing the machine for greater future production; but that which he expends in fashion-ing and exchanging the products of the machine produces tempo-rary results, and gives him wages alone. Whatever tends to diminish the *proportion* of labor required for fashioning and ex-changing, tends to augment the *proportion* that may be given to increasing the quantity of things that may be changed again in form, and to developing the powers of the earth; and thus, while increasing the present return to labor, preparing for further increase.

The first poor cultivator obtains for his year's wages a hun-dred bushels, the pounding of which between stones requires much labor; and yet is most imperfectly done. Had he a mill in the neighborhood, he would have better flour; and he would have almost his whole time to bestow upon his land. He pulls up his grain. Had he a scythe, he would have more time for the preparation of the machine of production. He loses his axe, and it requires many days of travel to enable him to obtain an-other. His machine loses the time and the manure, both of which would have been saved had the axe-maker been at hand.

The real advantage derived from the mill and the scythe, and from the proximity of the axe-maker, consists simply in economizing time, and enabling him to devote his labor more continuously to the improvement of the great machine of production; and such is the case with all the machinery of preparation and exchange. The plough enabling him to do as much in one day as with a spade he could do in many, the time thus gained may be applied to drainage. The steam-engine draining as much as without it would require thousands of days of labor, he has now more leisure to marl, or lime, his land. The more he can extract from his machine the greater is its value—everything he takes being, by the very act of taking it, changed in form to fit it for further production. The machine, therefore, improves by use, whereas spades, and ploughs, and steam-engines, and all other instruments used by man, are but the various forms into which he fashions parts of the great original machine, to disappear in the act of being used; as much so as food, though not quite so rapidly. The earth is the great labor savings' bank, and the value to man of all other things, is in the direct ratio of their tendency to aid him in increasing his deposits in that only bank whose dividends are constantly increasing, while its capital is perpetually augmenting. That it may continue for ever so to do, all that it asks is, that motion may be maintained by returning to it the refuse of its produce — the manure; and that such may be the case, it is required that the consumer and the producer take their places by each other. That done, every change that is effected becomes permanent, and tends to facilitate other and greater changes. The whole business of the farmer consisting in making and improving soils, the earth rewards him for his kindness by giving him more and more food the more attention he bestows upon her.

The great pursuit of man is agriculture. It is the science that requires the greatest amount and variety of knowledge, and therefore is it that it is everywhere latest in development. It is only now, indeed, that it is becoming a science; and it is doing so by aid of geological, chemical, and physiological knowledge, the most of which is, itself, but the result of the labors of the present day. It is later, too, because most exposed to interference from soldiers, traders, and others engaged in the work of appropriation. The warrior feels himself safe within the walls of his castle; the trader, the shoemaker, the tailor, the maker of swords and battle-axes, shut themselves up within the town; and that town is itself always placed on the highest land of the neighborhood, with a view to the security of its occupants — as may be seen in the early ones of Greece and India, Italy and France. The agricultural laborer, on the contrary, being forced to labor without the city walls, his property is ravaged on every occasion of difference between the trading community of which he forms a part, and those to which he is a neighbor. On every such occasion, motion is intermitted, and he is forced to seek protection for himself and his family within the city walls—a proceeding involving daily intermission of effort by reason of the distance between the scene of his daily labor and his place of refuge. The more the power of man over nature, the greater is the power of association for the general security, and the greater the tendency towards the maintenance of peace—and then it is that wealth tends to increase with daily augmenting force.

§ 9. Last in the order of development comes *commerce*. Every act of association being an act of commerce, the latter tends, necessarily, to increase as, with the growth of power over nature, men are enabled to obtain larger supplies of food from constantly diminishing surfaces. While cultivating the poor soils alone, and forced to remain distant from each other, the power to maintain commerce scarcely exists, as we see to be now the case in Russia, Portugal, Brazil, and Mexico; but then it is that the power of the soldier, the trader, and of others who live by appropriation, is the greatest. With the progress of population and wealth, men find themselves enabled to cultivate the rich soils of the earth; and now they have more leisure for the improvement of their minds, and for the construction of machinery required for obtaining increase of power. This, in turn, enables them to improve their modes of cultivation, while diversity of employment brings with it the power of association and the development of individuality, with greater feeling of responsibility, and greater power of progress; and thus it is that each helps, while being helped by, the others. The greater the commerce, the less is the necessity for the trader's services — the less is the *proportion* required to pay for those services, the larger the *proportion* that may be given to developing the powers of the land, and the more rapid is the further growth of commerce.

§ 10. The machine of society, like that of the human frame, is composed of portions acting independently, yet all in perfect harmony, each with every other. The stomach acts while the eyes are closed in sleep; and the ear is open, though the nerves are unexcited. Each of these changes in its constituent parts from day to day—the machine remaining still the same; and the more rapid the assimilation of the food required for the accomplishment of those changes, the more healthful is the action of the whole; and the greater is the tendency to stability and durability of the machine itself. So is it, too, with society — its tendency towards steadiness and durability being in the direct ratio of the rapidity of motion among its various parts, and the activity of commerce.

The more natural the form, the greater, as we everywhere see, is the tendency to continuity of existence. Discharge a load of earth, and it will at once take upon itself nearly the form of a pyramid; and so will the pile continue to do, as long as matter shall continue to be added — the base widening steadily as the apex rises in height. The Himalaya, and the Andes, have endured for ever, because they have the natural form, that of a cone or pyramid — the most beautiful of all the forms of which matter is susceptible. How durable it is, is shown by the Egyptian pyramids — remaining, as they do, after the lapse of thousands of years, almost as perfect as they were in the days of the sovereigns by whose orders they were built. Turning next to the societary machine, we see that everywhere, as wealth and numbers increase, its members are engaged in sinking its foundations deeper — bringing to light the marl and the lime, the coal and the ore with which the earth so much abounds; that, as the foundations deepen, the height increases, with diminution of the proportion of the apex; and that every movement in this direction is attended with increase in the local attraction required for producing the same double motion seen existing throughout the universe; and to which are due the perfect harmony and wonderful durability of the system.

Looking to the vegetable world, we see, everywhere, that the tendency to durability is in the ratio of the depth and spread of the root, as compared with the length of the stem. The tree, growing in a forest, and surrounded by others like itself—"cabined, cribbed, confined"—obeys but the single centralizing influence, and runs up rapidly in quest of light and air; of which it would be deprived were it to permit others to overtop it. Making, however, but very little root, its want of stability is soon exhibited when, by reason of the clearing of the trees around it, it becomes exposed to the action of the winds. Those, on the contrary, which have grown in situations in which light and air have been abundant, have roots proportioned to their height and breadth, and stand for centuries—as has been the case with so many of the oaks of England.

The greater the number of people that can live together, the greater must be the power of association—the more uniform, regular, and rapid must be the motion—the more perfect must be the development of the faculties—and the greater the tendency to sink deeply the foundations of society, by means of the development of the wondrous treasures of the earth. The greater the tendency towards utilizing the various forces presenting themselves in the form of water-powers, masses of coal, iron, lead, copper, zinc, and other metals, the greater, necessarily, is the tendency to the formation of local centres—neutralizing the attraction towards the political or commercial capital; with steady tendency to decline of centralization, and constant diminution in the *proportion* borne by the soldiers, the politicians, the traders, and all others of the class that lives by appropriation, to the mass of which society is composed; and with a constant tendency to have society itself assume that form which everywhere is seen to combine beauty, strength, and durability—that of a cone or pyramid.

§ 11. A tree conforming in its structural provisions to the conditions above described—as may be seen in the diagram here given—and its ramifications, both of roots and branches, serving to illustrate the natural history of societary commerce—advantage may be derived from presenting somewhat in detail the illustrative facts in the correspondence. Let, then, the stem be commerce, in our meaning of the term, and the roots its subjects. In the earliest, or hunter, state, the business of man is simple appro-

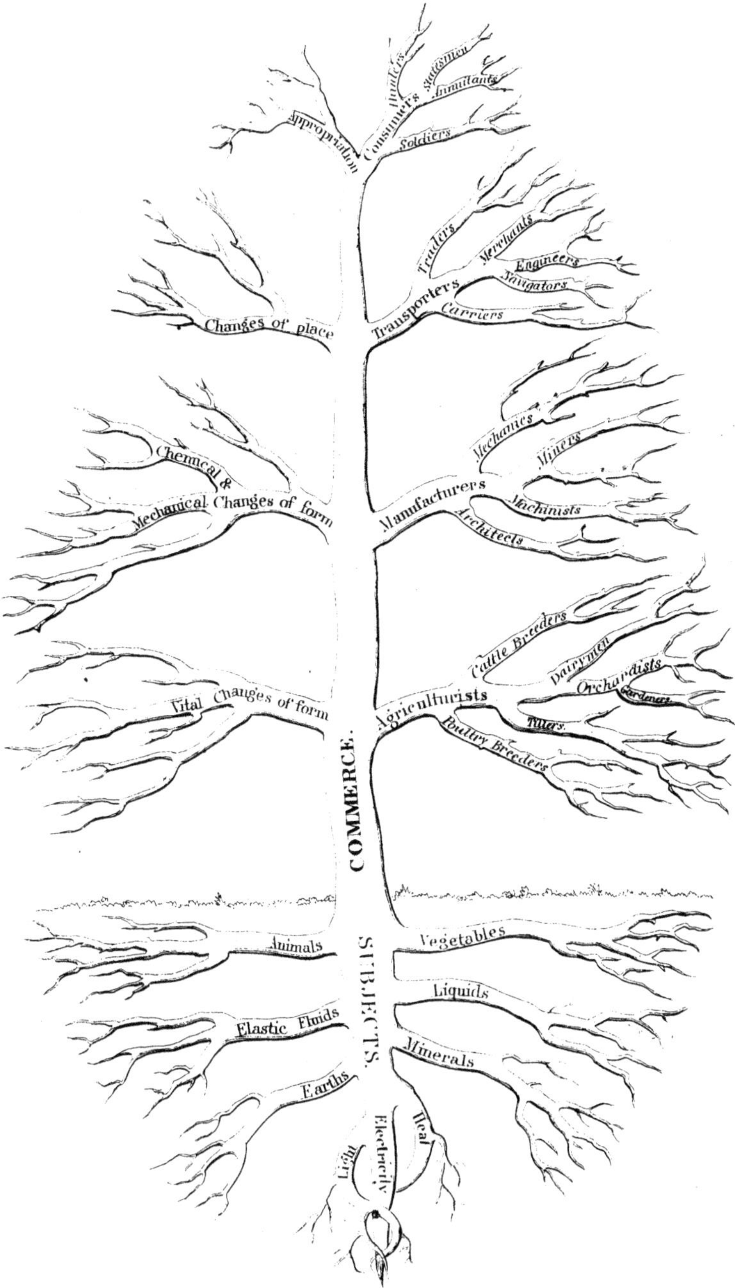

Appropriation
Consumers
Hunters
Statesmen
Annuitants
Soldiers
Changes of place
Transporters
Traders
Merchants
Engineers
Navigators
Carriers
Chemical &
Mechanical Changes of form
Manufacturers
Mechanics
Miners
Machinists
Architects
Vital Changes of form
Agriculturists
Cattle Breeders
Dairymen
Orchardists
Gardeners
Tillers
Poultry Breeders
COMMERCE.
SUBJECTS.
Animals
Vegetables
Liquids
Elastic Fluids
Minerals
Earths
Light
Electricity
Heat

priation — the wild animals and their products, and the vegetables and the fruits, produced without his care, and grown without his culture, being his prey. In this stage there is neither trade, manufactures, nor agriculture; and the young plant, in parallel circumstances, shows but the earliest branches and the slightly produced topmost roots. Having no terms precisely descriptive of the slighter stages of societary growth—the savage, the pastoral, and patriarchal states through which we arrive at that to which trade and transportation give their peculiar character—the diagram, as the reader will perceive, is necessarily deficient in the branches required for their methodic illustration.

In the second era, property being held by title somewhat more permanent than mere occupation and manual possession — trade arises, and is founded on its conventional recognition. Change of place being then effected by the rudest methods of transportation, the waters and the air — root branches — are the natural forces then used for the accomplishment of that object—the canoe and the sail-boat utilizing the rivers and the winds. The sailor and the merchant, and the land-carrier with his camel, or his ox, or his horse—and perhaps his wagon—constitute now the important portions of the societary system.

Next, in order, come manufactures, corresponding with the roots that are third in order, for among the earliest subjects that mark this epoch the minerals and earths are essential both as materials and implements. Long before this, however, the savage has been accustomed to effect changes in the forms of matter—his bow having been made of wood, and its string of the sinews of the deer — and his canoe having been of bark and provided with a skin in place of sail; but it is to a somewhat advanced stage of human progress we are required to look for the pursuits of men connected with the conversion of ores into implements, or of cotton and wool into cloth. The precious metals, gold, silver, and copper—being, like the wild fruits and animals, found ready, or nearly so, for use —are early employed for service and for ornament; but iron, the great civilizer, and mineral coal, the great agent for its conversion, are among the latest of human triumphs over the mighty forces of nature.

To the branch, manufactures, therefore, the metals and earths—root branches—very exactly correspond in necessary relation, and in the date of their development. This is the stage of scientific progress; and here, accordingly, we meet phenomena directly in accordance with those observed in reference to the occupation of the earth, and to which the reader's attention has before been called. The cultivator of the rich soils is enabled to return, with augmented force, to poorer ones that had been early occupied; and now it is that — developing their latent powers — he places them first upon the list, when before they had stood last; as is seen, to so great an extent, to be the case in England and in France.* In like manner, the science of the later period — returning upon the rude commerce of the earlier one — searches out the hidden elements of the vegetable and animal kingdoms, and the chemical and mechanical properties of the liquid and elastic fluids, and places them under the control of man — thus adding largely to his force, while in a corresponding degree diminishing the resistance offered to his further efforts. The water, at first used only as a beverage — or because of its capacity for supporting a boat or a ship — now yields steam; and the air, at first valued only as required for breathing purposes — or as a wind force in sailing — is now resolved into its gases, and made to furnish light and heat; while in a thousand other ways aiding the efforts, or contributing to the enjoyments, of man. The animal and vegetable worlds that, in the earlier ages, had yielded to the savage only food and medicine, now contribute acids, alkalies, oils, gums, resins, drugs, dyes, perfumes, hair, silk, wool, cotton, and leather — furnishing, under the touch of manufacturing skill and science, clothing, tenements, conveniences, comforts, and luxuries of life, in a thousand forms of beauty and of use.

Next, and last, comes agriculture — necessarily embracing the discoveries and agencies of all the earlier stages of advance in knowledge and in power. Beginning rudely in the savage state, it grows a little in the age of trade; but for its greatest growth

* In his recent work, (*Des Systèmes de Culture,*) Mons. Passy tells his readers that in those countries in which agriculture has improved, "the soils that, in past times, were regarded as too poor to merit continued and regular cultivation, are now regarded as the best," and after describing the course of things in this respect in Belgium and in France, says that "in England it is an established fact that in various counties the lands denominated good are farmed at twenty-two to twenty-five shillings an acre, while those formerly regarded as poor let for thirty to thirty-five shillings." Similar changes are now, as he also shows, taking place in France.

it waits the age of manufactures—that of scientific development—in which man is seen already to have obtained, to a great extent, control and direction of the natural forces provided for his use. Appropriating the ready-formed elements of nature, it commands the aid of trade and transportation, while pressing into its service all the chemical and mechanical forces furnished by the age of manufactures — thus covering all the progress of every antecedent stage. It demands not only the physiology of vegetable and animal life, and the chemistry of the organic and inorganic world, but also the conveniences and appliances of the transporting age, as exhibited in roads, ships, and bridges; and all the chemical and mechanical powers of the manufacturing one—finding its subjects, implements, and agencies in the material, and in the forces, of every branch of human commerce before developed.

The secondary branches of the tree mark the successive production of the agencies of the several classes; and thus it is, that, in the topmost branch, the hunter is followed by the soldier, the statesman, and the annuitant — all non-producers, growing in their order from the same stem, and with the growth of civilization; but diminishing in their proportions as society becomes more and more developed. In the infant state, this top branch—whether in the natural or social world—constituted the whole tree.

The next branch—transportation—sprouts into carriers by land and water, and traders in merchandise;* and, finally, when science and civilization have been well matured, into engineers; but the *proportion* to the mass of which society is composed, declines as the powers of man become more and more developed, and as society takes more and more its natural form.

The third — consisting of chemical and mechanical changes of form, swelling out, as the reader sees, into mechanics, architects, miners, machinists, and numerous other varieties — greatly overbalances the classes that live by appropriation, trade, and transportation.

Lastly, we have the agriculturists, branching, successively, into cattle-breeders, poultry-breeders, dairymen, gardeners, orchardists, and tillers, to fulfil the grand underlying function of producers for all other laborers in the work of social commerce.

* Trade in men, held as slaves, commences in the earliest period — that of mere brute force.

The reader must carry with him, in the theory of the parallels here attempted, the recollection that our *figure* is capable of no more than contemporaneous presentment of the social distribution of the various functions. The topmost branches are, in point of fact, the last produced by its growth; and the earliest are resolved, by change of form and increase of substance, into the lowest boughs of the perfected tree; but the identity of the boughs is, in fact, as much lost in the limbs of the tree, as in the successive functionaries of the social state — the hunters of a race growing, through their descendants, into transporters, manufacturers, and scientific cultivators of the soil, successively, and by the process of civilizing development. The native Briton — having passed, by the process of generation and regeneration, successively, into every form of man — now appears in the aristocracy of England; but his correspondent, in Australia, is still a hunter and a savage. The appropriators of his class, changing with the change of times, appear now in the form of soldiers, politicians, and annuitants. The primitive non-producer preyed upon nature; and his correspondents, each in own his way, now prey upon society and upon its industry — living at the expense of commerce. The rudest savage was, in his day, the topmost branch of the shrub — living upon plunder; and not producing by his labor. The soldier of our own day is, like him, a privileged spoliator; while the politician lives by tribute, and the state annuitant derives his whole support from contributions levied upon all the classes who contribute to the growth of commerce.

In relative position, therefore, the top branch is still in place; and throughout all changes in the general system, it always has occupied, and always must occupy, a position corresponding to the relation borne by the appropriators of the race to the social toilers.

The class of transporters, too, in the scale of supremacy, is found to be occupying its true position. The ship-owner and the dealer in merchandise follow the politician in power and rank, as the carrier follows the hunter — both classes, in their turn, dominating over society, until skilled industry, and close combination among men, develope a people into self-government, and thus abridge the powers of the classes who occupy themselves with trade and government.

Agriculturists are the last to be developed into their due efficiency; but here we encounter a difficulty resulting from defect of language — there being no words properly expressive of the essential difference between the savage, barbarous, and patriarchal, and the civilized and scientific, culture of the earth. The two differ so widely, that they should not be called by the same general name; and we but allude now to the differences between the infant, the youthful, and the mature husbandry, to account for the fact that unenlightened tillage is overshadowed by the other branches of human commerce, until the great function of production of every kind required for serving the world's highest uses is developed into the perfection to which it is destined, and which it is bound, ultimately, to attain. That done, and the cone standing geometrically and socially adjusted upon the basis of science —the harmonies of distribution will be complete.

The tap-root deepens, and the branches grow, as the tree rises in the air. The imponderable elements — light, heat, and electricity — are last among the elements subjected to the control of man, and made to contribute to the purposes of life. Fire and water, in their natural forms and activities, are early known; but it is in an advanced stage of progress, only, that their mechanical and chemical forces are brought under man's direction. Light was somewhat understood in the age of painting, but it is only now that it has been made subservient to the arts in photographic portraiture; electricity is used in the transmission of news, and in the treatment of diseases; but, as a motor power, or mechanical force — as a substitute for human labor — we are yet but on the threshold of discovery. Agriculture waits upon these, and upon the development of meteorology, for the command of its own proper sphere of service in the life of THE MAN.

In the horse and the man, that arrangement of the parts which gives the greatest strength being the one of the highest beauty, such should likewise be the case with those aggregations of men which constitute societies.

With every step in the direction that has above been indicated, the community acquires more perfect individuality — more complete power of self-government; and the more entire that power, the greater is its disposition to combine its efforts with those of other communities of the world — and its power to associate with them on terms of strict equality. As it is with individual men, so it is with communities. The more perfect the individuality of the man, the greater is his disposition for association, and the more perfect his power to combine his efforts with those of other men; and here we have further evidence of the universality of the laws which govern matter in all its forms, from the rock to the sand and the clay into which it becomes decomposed; and thence upward through trees and animals, until we reach communities of men.

§ 12. In accordance with a great mathematical law, it being required that when several forces unite to produce any given result, each be studied separately, and treated as if no other one existed, such precisely has been the course above adopted. We know that man tends to increase in numbers, and in his power over nature, and that each successive step in his road towards knowledge and power is but preparation for a new and greater one —enabling him to obtain increased supplies of food and clothing, more books and newspapers, and better shelter, with diminished muscular effort. It is seen, however, that despite this tendency, there are various communities in which numbers and wealth are steadily decreasing; while, among those which are advancing, there are no two whose rate of progress is the same. In some parts of the earth, places that once were occupied by vast communities of men are now entirely abandoned; while, in others, the miserable remnant exists in poverty, wretchedness, and slavery, although cultivating the same lands that formerly supplied food to numerous millions of wealthy and prosperous men — and hence it has been hastily concluded that it is the natural tendency of communities to pass through various forms of existence, ending in physical and moral death; but such is certainly not the fact. There is no natural reason why any society should fail to become more prosperous from year to year; and where such has not been the case, it has been a consequence of disturbing causes, each of which requires to be studied separately, with a view to understand how far it has tended to produce the existing state of things; but preliminary thereto it is needful that we understand what would be the course of things did no such causes exist. The physician, though not required to treat the man who is in the enjoyment of perfect health, invariably commences his studies by ascertaining what is the natural action of the system — having done which, he feels himself qualified to examine into the disturbing causes by which health and life are constantly destroyed. Physiology is the necessary preliminary to pathology; and this is as true of social as it is of physical science.

Having now completed the study of the Physiology of society, exhibiting its progress towards a natural and stable form, our next succeeding chapters will be devoted to its Pathology, with a view to ascertaining what have been the causes of the decline and fall of various communities that have perished; and why it is the rate of progress in those now existing is so widely different.

§ 13. The theory of Mr. Ricardo, in regard to the occupation of the earth, leads to results directly the reverse of those above described. Commencing the work of cultivation on the richer soils—always those of the valleys—it follows, that as men become more numerous, they must disperse themselves — climbing the hills, or seeking elsewhere valleys whose rich soils remain as yet unappropriated. Dispersion, bringing with it an increased necessity for the services of the soldier, the sailor, and the trader, is accompanied by constant increase in the power of those who have appropriated land to demand payment for its use; and thus is there produced a constant increase in the proportions, and in the importance, of the classes that live by virtue of the exercise of the power of appropriation. Centralization, therefore, grows, and its growth is in the direct ratio of the diminution of the power of man to indulge his natural desire for combination with his fellow-men — and for that development of his faculties which fits him for association and enables him to acquire enlarged control over the wonderful forces of nature. The many, in that case, become from year to year more and more the slaves of nature and of their fellow-men—doing, this, too in virtue of what, if we are to believe Mr. Ricardo and his successors, is a great law, instituted by the Creator for the government of mankind.

Were this so, society would assume a form directly the reverse of the one here given — that of an inverted pyramid — every increase in numbers and wealth being marked by an increasing irregularity and instability, with corresponding decline in the condition of man. "Order" being, however, "Heaven's first law," it is difficult to comprehend how such an one as that announced by Mr. Ricardo could follow in its train—and the mere fact that it would be productive of such disorder, would seem to be a sufficient reason for doubting its truth, if not, even, for causing it to be instantly rejected. So, too, with that of Mr. Malthus, which leads inevitably to the subjection of the many to the will of the few—to centralization and slavery. No such law can, or could, exist. The Creator established none in virtue of which matter was required to take upon itself its highest form, that of man, in a ratio more rapid than that in which it tended to take the lower ones, those of potatoes and turnips, herrings and oysters, required for the sustenance of man. The great Architect of the universe was no blunderer, such as modern political economy would make him. All wise, he was not required to institute different sets of laws for the government of the same matter. All just, he was incapable of instituting any that could be adduced in justification of tyranny and oppression. All merciful, he could make none that would afford a warrant for want of mercy among men towards their fellow-men, such as is now daily exhibited in politico-economical books of high authority.*

Speaking of the Ricardo theory, a recent and eminent writer assures his readers that that "general law of agricultural industry is the most important proposition in political economy;" and that, "were the law different, nearly all the phenomena of the production and consumption of wealth would be other than they are." Other, rather, than they have been described by political economists as being, but not "other than they are." The law *is* different, and produces totally different results. The suppositious one leads to the glorification of trade—that pursuit of man which tends least to the development of the human intellect, and most to the hardening of the heart towards the sufferings of his

* Labor is, as we are told by English economists, "a commoditity," and if men will, by marrying, indulge that natural desire which prompts them to seek association with their kind, and will bring up children "to an overstocked and expiring trade," it is for them to take the consequences, and "*if we stand between the error and its consequences, we stand between the evil and its cure*—if we intercept the penalty, (where it does not amount to positive death,) we perpetuate the sin." (Edinburgh Review, Oct. 1849. The italics are those of the reviewer.) It would be difficult to find elsewhere stronger evidence of the tendency of an unsound political economy to crush out all Christian feeling, than is contained in the above extract.

fellow-men; while the real one finds its highest point in the development of that commerce of man with his fellow-man which tends most to his advancement as a moral and intellectual being — and most to the establishment of the feeling of responsibility to his Creator for the use he makes of the faculties with which he has been endowed, and of the wealth he is permitted to obtain. The one is unchristian in all its parts, while the other in its every line is in strict accordance with the great law of Christianity, teaching that we should do to others as we would that they should do unto us — and with the feeling that prompts the prayer —

> "That mercy I to others show,
> That mercy show to me."

# CHAPTER IX.

## OF APPROPRIATION.

§ 1. In the early period of society, men being poor and widely scattered, there exists a necessity for being always prepared for self-defence. Such was the case with the early settlers of these United States; and so is it now with those engaged in occupying the Oregon, Washington, and other territories of the West. That necessity disappearing, however, with the growth of population, and consequent increase in the power of association, they are enabled more continuously to prosecute their labors — freed from fear of seeing their fields ravaged, their houses and implements destroyed, and their wives and children butchered before their eyes; and now it is that production rapidly increases, with growing tendency to the development of individuality, and to physical, moral, and social progress.

In that period, too, the services of the trader are among the necessities of life. Having but little to exchange, the scattered settlers hail the arrival of the travelling peddler, who receives from them their surplus products, in exchange for shoes or blankets, kettles, saws, or gloves. Here, however, we mark a course of operation similar to that observed in regard to preparation for self-defence — the necessity for the services of the soldier and the trader diminishing as the makers of shoes and blankets, kettles and gloves, come to take their places in the settlement; and every step in the progress of that diminution is seen to be attended with increase in the continuity of effort—in the development of individual faculties—and in the strength of the community of which the individuals are a part.

Diminishing wants being attended by diminution in the effort required for their satisfaction, each successive step in the direction that has above been indicated, is attended by diminution in the *proportion* of the labors of the community required to be given to the work of self-defence, and to that of trade or transportation; and the smaller the proportion thus required to be given, the larger, necessarily, must be that which may be given to the work of cultivation — with constant increase in the power of combination, and in the growth of commerce. The two necessities above described constituting the essential obstacles to the gratification of the first and greatest desire of man, the more completely they can be removed, the more perfect will be his security of person and of property — the more productive will become his labor — the less must be the value of all the commodities required for his consumption — and the greater must be his power of accumulating wealth; and that such is felt to be the case is obvious from the pleasant feeling among the members of a community whenever, from any cause, they are diminished, or removed; and the power of association for peaceful purposes is increased.

That feeling does not, however, extend to those who profit by the exercise of power over their fellow-men, either as warriors, politicians, or traders. The soldier—seeking plunder, in quest of which he is always willing to risk his life — has, perhaps, appropriated large bodies of land, requiring slaves for their cultivation; or there are others ready to purchase the captives he may make. The trader, too, profiting by the irregularity of motion in time of war, buys men or merchandise when, and where, they are cheap; and sells them when, and where, they are dear. All seek to centralize in their own hands the control of those by whom they are surrounded—the soldier monopolizing the power to collect taxes; the great landholder monopolizing the commodities yielded by the labor of his slaves; and the trader desiring everywhere to monopolize the collection and distribution of those commodities — that he may be enabled to dictate the prices at which he will buy, and those at which he will sell. All are middlemen, standing in the way of association, and preventing any continuous motion between those who produce and those who need to consume, and desire to maintain commerce among themselves.

The progress of a community towards wealth and power being in the direct ratio of the combination of action among the people of whom it is composed, it follows that the advance towards both must be in the ratio in which they are enabled to dispense with the services of the politician, the soldier, the owner of slaves, and the trader — of that class which lives by virtue of the simple act of appropriation. Every movement, however, in that direction, looking necessarily to a diminution in the power of the latter, they are all — soldier, trader, and politician — found, uniformly, banded together for the subjection of the people; as was seen in Athens and in Rome, and as may now be seen in all the countries of Europe and America. The history of the world is but a record of the efforts of the few to tax the many, and of those of the many to escape taxation; and the tendency of society to assume a natural and stable form is in the precise ratio of the success of this latter class — a success, however, slowly and tediously accomplished, because of the power of those who live by appropriation to come together in towns and cities, while they who contribute to their revenues are scattered throughout the country.

§ 2. The close connection between war and trade is seen in every page of history. The Ishmaelites, whose hand was against every man, while every man's hand was against them, were extensive dealers in slaves and other merchandise. The Phœnicians, Carians, and Sidonians—being freebooters at one time, or traders at another, as might best suit their purposes—were always ready for any measures tending to increase their monopoly at home by adding to the number of their slaves; or their monopolies abroad by preventing others from interfering in the trade which they, themselves, carried on between distant men. The pages of Homer exhibit to us Menelaus boasting of his piracies, and of the plunder he had acquired; and the sage Ulysses as feeling his honor untouched by the inquiry, as to whether he came in the character of trader, or of pirate.—Turning next to a somewhat corresponding period in the history of modern Europe, we find the Norwegian sea-kings and their subjects alternately engaged in "gathering property," as robbery by sea and land was naively termed; or in carrying the produce of one kingdom to another—both pursuits being held in equally high esteem. Later, the same connection becomes obvious in the histories of Hawkins, Drake, and Cavendish; in that of the slave-trade, from its commencement to its close;* in that

* "There is no nation in Europe which has plunged so deeply into this guilt as Britain. *We* stopped the natural progress of civilization in Africa.

of the Buccaneers and the West India colonies; in the French and English wars on this continent—in the West Indies—and in India; in the closing of the Scheldt; in the wars of Spain and England; in the paper blockades of the wars of the French Revolution; in the occupation of Gibraltar as a smuggling depot;* in the late wars of India, and more particularly in the last with Burmah, commenced on account of a trader's claim of a few hundred pounds;† in the opium war of China; in the manner in which Indian wars are gotten up in this country; in our own recent war-

*We* cut her off from the opportunity of improvement. *We* kept her down in a state of darkness, bondage, ignorance, and bloodshed. We have there subverted the whole order of nature; we have aggravated every natural barbarity, and furnished to every man motives for committing, under the name of trade, acts of perpetual hostility and perfidy against his neighbor. Thus had the perversion of British commerce carried misery instead of happiness to one whole quarter of the globe. False to the very principles of trade, unmindful of our duty, what almost irreparable mischief had we done to that continent! We had obtained as yet only so much knowledge of its productions as to show that there was a capacity for trade which we checked." —*W. Pitt.*

* "Gibraltar was all that England did get out of that war, and as this robbery went a great way to ensure her discomfiture, and to establish Philip the Fifth upon the throne, we may consider Gibraltar as the cause of the first of those ruinous wars which, made without due authority, and carried on by anticipations of revenue, have introduced among us those social diseases which have counterbalanced and perverted the mechanical advancement of modern times.—Gibraltar was confirmed to us at the treaty of Utrecht, but without any jurisdiction attached to it, and upon the condition that no smuggling should be carried on thence into Spain. These conditions we daily violate. We exercise jurisdiction by cannon-shot in the Spanish waters, (for the bay is all Spanish.) Under our batteries, the smuggler runs for protection; he ships his bales at our quays; he is either the agent of our merchants, or is insured by them; and the flag-post at the top of the rock is used to signal to him the movements of the Spanish cruisers."—URQUHART: *Pillars of Hercules*, vol. i. p. 43.

† Two British subjects belonging to the barque Monarch had a dispute at Rangoon, which resulted in the captain of the ship being mulcted in the sum of £101. Two others, likewise British subjects, belonging to the ship Champion, had also a dispute at the same place, which resulted in one of them being required to pay £70; and out of these transactions grew, in a few weeks, the Burmese war, in which many thousands of lives were sacrificed, while towns and cities were plundered; and which, itself, resulted in the annexation to the British Empire of a territory larger than England. Those who desire to understand how war and trade feed each other, can obtain the desired information by reading Mr. Cobden's pamphlet, entitled "How Wars are got up in India:" London, 1853. It will there be seen that, as elsewhere in the East, the fable of the wolf and the lamb was fully acted out; war having been forced on the Burmese, who evinced throughout the strongest desire to do entire justice. The crime, however, brings with it its punishment, Burmah being a heavy charge on the Indian treasury, as are "Scinde, Sattarah, and the Punjaub, annexed," says Mr. Cobden, "at the cost of so many crimes."

like demonstration against Japan, with a view to compel that country to accept of the blessings that were to follow in the wake of trade; in the proceedings of France at the Sandwich Islands, and among those of the Marquesas group; and last, though not least, in the maintenance of war against private property on the ocean, as exhibited in the recent capture, in the Baltic and Black seas, of so many defenceless ships, owned by men who had no concern in the war, except that which arose out of the fact that they had found themselves compelled to pay taxes for its maintenance.

War and trade, seeking always a monopoly of power, and requiring fleets and armies, tend invariably towards centralization. The support of soldiers and sailors, generals and admirals, produces a necessity for taxation, the proceeds of which must seek a central point before they can be again distributed — and the distribution brings together, necessarily, hosts of men — waiters on Providence — anxious to secure their share; as is seen to have been the case in Athens and in Rome; and as is now so obvious in Paris and London, New York and Washington. The city, growing, becomes, from year to year, more and more a place in which trade in merchandise, or trade in principles, may advantageously be carried on; and the larger the city, the more rapidly increasing is the tendency towards augmented centralization — every increase of taxation tending to diminish the power of healthful association throughout the tax-paying districts, and to increase the unhealthy movement in the tax-receiving capital.

With every such increase of central attraction, society tends to take upon itself a form directly the reverse of the natural one — assuming more and more that of an inverted pyramid; and hence it is that in every community which has depended upon its powers of appropriation, in place of those of production — in every one that has diminished the rapidity of motion among its own people, while engaged in the effort to diminish that existing among those of its neighbors — there has been seen to arrive a period of splendor and apparent strength, but real weakness, followed by decline, even when not by death. While enriching the few, centralization impoverishes the many; and while enabling the former to build palaces and temples—to open parks, maintain armies, and almost to re-create cities—it drives the latter to seek refuge in the meanest hovels, and thus creates a population always ready to sell their services to the highest bidder, at any sacrifice of conscience. With every step in this direction, the societary machine becomes less stable and secure—and with each it tends more and more to topple over, until at length it falls, burying in its ruins those who had hoped most to profit by the state of things they had labored to produce. So has it been, even in our own day, in the cases of Napoleon and Louis Philippe; who were, however, but types of their class—that class which profits by the exercise of power over their fellow-men, and seeks distinction in the characters of warriors, politicians, or traders.

The more perfect the power of association—the higher the organization of society, and the more complete the development of individuality among its members—the more do all such men tend to occupy their natural place, that of *instruments to be used by society;* and the more does society itself tend to take its natural form, with hourly increase in the power of resistance to any invasion of its rights, and in the capacity for durability. Whatever tends to diminish the power of association, and to prevent the development of individuality, produces the reverse effect of *making society the instruments of these men*—centralization, slavery, and death travelling always hand in hand together, whether in the moral or material world.*

* The entire identity of the views of the trader and the slave-owner is exhibited in the following passages from recent journals:

"An *inexhaustible supply of cheap labor has so long been a condition of our social system,* whether in town or country, whether for work or for pleasure, that it remains to be seen whether a great enhancement of labor would not disturb our industrial, and even our political, arrangements to a serious extent. *Two men have been after one master so long, that we are not prepared for the day when two masters will be after one man;* for it is not certain either that the masters can carry on their business, or that the men will comport themselves properly under the new *regime.* Commercial enterprise and social development require an actually increasing population, and also that the increase shall be in *the most serviceable*—that is, the laborious—part of the population, *for otherwise it will not be sufficiently at the command of capital* and skill."—*London Times.*

"*Cheapness of labor* is essential to the material progress of every people. But this can only obtain with the abundance of supply. Now, slave labor is, and ought to be, the *cheapest kind of labor.* It will only become otherwise when foreign and hostile influences are made to bear against it. The abolition of the slave-trade, by cutting off the supply, tends to this result. Slaves were never before so high in the South. * * * Slavery is, and so long as the South preserves her existence must continue to be, *the basis of all property values in the South.* * * * Increase the supply of labor, and thus cheapen the cost of slaves, and the South will escape im-

To the fact that the policy of Athens, of Rome, and of other communities of ancient and modern times, tended directly to the production of this latter state of things, it is due that there has been, in many of them, seen to arise a state of things giving colour to the idea that societies, like trees and men, have their various stages of growth and of decline — ending, naturally and necessarily, in death. How far this is so, the reader will perhaps be prepared to decide after a brief examination of the course of action pursued by some of the leading communities of the world.

§ 3. In the early period of Grecian history, we find the people of Attica divided into several small and independent communities — but becoming at length united under Theseus; when ATHENS became the capital of the kingdom. The communities of Bœotia in like manner associated themselves with Thebes; and the several little states of Phocis united in following their example. The tendency to combination thus exhibited in the various states was early shown in relation to the affairs of Greece at large — in the

minent peril. *The number of slave-owners would multiply, the direct interest in its preservation would be more universally diffused*, and that great necessity of the South — *union in defence of slavery* — more readily accomplished. If it were possible, every man in her limits should be a slave-owner."—*Charleston Mercury.*

"The great works of this country depend upon cheap labor."—*Lon. Times.*

"Slavery is the corner-stone of our institutions."—*McDuffie.*

"*The whole question has become one of a cheap and abundant supply of labor.* * * * The operation of the repeal of the corn laws was, first, to equalize, or approximate, the wages here and on the continent; and, secondly, not, indeed, to lower them here at once, but to make it possible to lower them, if at any future time the relation between demand and supply in the labor-market should render such reduction just and necessary. * * * For half a century back, the western shores of our island have been flooded with crowds of half-clad, half-fed, half-civilized Celts, reducing the standard of living and comfort among our people by their example, swelling the registers of crimes, to the great damage of the national character and reputation;" but, as the writer continues, "the abundant supply of cheap labor which they furnished had no doubt the effect of enabling our manufacturing industry to increase at a rate, and to reach a height, which, without them, would have been unattainable; *and so far they have been of service.*"—*North British Review*, Nov. 1852.

"As long as the larger proportion of women are incompetent or unwilling to earn anything except by plain sewing, it is as idle to abuse the order of Davises for the misery of his operatives, as it would be to abuse Providence for bringing them into the world with appetites. *It would be better for all of them, in the long run, to reduce wages to the famine point, so as to force all who had sufficient strength into other employments.* This at least would diminish competition, and give the remaining ones a better chance."—*New York Evening Post.*

institution of the Amphictyonic league, the Olympic and other games.

During a long period, the history of Athens appears almost a blank, because of its peaceful and quiet progress. With its immediate neighbors it had occasional disputes, but, the tendency towards union being great, peace was "the habitual and regular condition of their mutual intercourse." Peace brought with it so steady a growth of population and of wealth, that, long prior to the days of Solon, the men engaged in trade and in the mechanic arts constituted an affluent and intelligent body; while everywhere throughout the state, labor and skill were being given to the development of the hidden treasures of the earth. The power to associate and the habit of association grew steadily, with constant increase of that individuality to which Athens stands indebted for her prominent position in the history of man.

Under the legislation of Solon, the whole body of the citizens exercised the right of voting in the popular assemblies — but all were not equally eligible for filling the offices of state. On the other hand, all were not equally liable to taxation for the maintenance of government — the heaviest contributions being required of the first class, eligible to the highest offices; and their amount diminishing in passing downward, until they finally disappeared on reaching the fourth, which was exempt from taxation, as it was excluded from the magistracy; and here we find the most equal apportionment of rights and duties exhibited in the history of the world. Elsewhere, the few have monopolized the offices, while taxing the many for their support; whereas, here, the few who enjoyed the offices paid the taxes, and the many who were excluded from the former, found themselves wholly relieved from the payment of the latter.

The century succeeding the organization thus effected, exhibits Attica, in the general enjoyment of peace, gradually increasing in both wealth and population. Towards its close, we find the state to have been divided into a hundred townships, each having its local assembly, and its magistracy for the regulation of its own local affairs; and thus was constituted a system more perfectly in accordance with the great physical laws to which reference has heretofore been made, than any the world had seen, prior to the settlement of the provinces now constituting the United

States. The beneficial effect of peace was, at this time, still further exhibited in the fact, that the constituency was enlarged, by the enfranchisement of numerous slaves, and by the admission of many aliens to the rights of citizenship.

With the Persian invasion, terminating in the battle of Marathon, and with the subsequent occupation of Attica by the troops of Xerxes, there came, however, a total change. Fields had been wasted, houses, cattle, and machinery of cultivation had been destroyed, and population had largely diminished; and henceforth we find the Athenians passing from the condition of a peaceful democracy, in which every man was engaged in combining his efforts with his fellow-citizens at home, to that of a warlike aristocracy, engaged in preventing the existence of association abroad — and using their power of disturbance as a means of enriching themselves. Having accumulated fortunes by means of extortion and robbery, Themistocles and Cimon were enabled to secure the services of thousands of poor dependants who exhibited themselves in the streets, gladly following in the train of the men whom war had rendered now their masters. Poverty produced a thirst for plunder, the hope of which rendered it easy to fill the army and to man the ships; and next the army and the fleet were employed in reducing to subjection states and cities that had been regarded, hitherto, as equals and allies. One by one they fell, and the plunder thus acquired stimulated the desire for fresh supplies, with constantly increasing power to gratify the appetite. Athens had now become mistress of the seas, and no state, as we are told by Xenophon, could be permitted to have commerce with distant people, unless profoundly submissive to her commands. "Upon her will depends," as he continues, "the exportation of the surplus produce of all nations;" and to enable her to exercise that will wholly unrestrained, we find her next persuading, or compelling, the allies to compound for personal service by money payments, by help of which nearly the whole Athenian people were maintained in the service of the state.

War having now become the trade of Athens, her armies are everywhere seen — in Egypt and in the Peloponnesus, at Megara and at Œgina — and to enable her to support these armies, she seizes upon the public treasury, which is transferred to the great central city. Next, we find an increase in the tribute required of the allies, who are required to pay taxes upon all goods imported, and all exported; the collection of which is farmed by men who find in every stoppage of the societary motion the means of adding to their fortunes. Further, Athens declares herself the court of final resort in all criminal cases, and in nearly all civil ones; and now, the city being thronged with applicants for justice, its people are converted into judges, all ready to sell their awards to the highest bidder. The states themselves now find it necessary to employ agents within the city, and to distribute bribes, by help of which to purchase protection against the demands of the sovereign state.

With every step in this direction, the few become enriched, while the many become more and more impoverished. Temples are erected, and the splendor of the city increases from day to day. Theatres are built, in which the Athenians may gratuitously indulge their tastes; but the right thus to live by the labor of others being now regarded as a privilege whose enjoyment should be limited to the few, inquiry is made into the claim for citizenship—resulting in the rejection of no less than five thousand persons, all of whom are sold as slaves. With every increase of splendor we find an increase of indigence, and an increased necessity for exporting a portion of the people to take possession of distant lands—there to exercise upon the earlier settlers the same power the rich have learned to exercise at home. The people — their time being now fully occupied in the management of public affairs — next require that they should be paid out of the public purse; and so great has become the general poverty that an obolus — a piece of three cents' value — as compensation for the day's service in the courts, has become an object of desire.

Tyranny and rapacity — everywhere exhibited, and producing everywhere a decline of commerce between man and man, and between state and state — next give rise to the Peloponnesian war, closing with the passage of Attica under the dominion of the Thirty Tyrants. Private property is now to a vast extent confiscated to the public use; and to secure the services of the poor in the spoliation of the rich, the wages of attendance at public meetings are trebled in amount. Taxation grows, and with its growth the inducements to honest exertion as steadily decline. Population becomes, to use the modern phrase, superabundant; and as man diminishes in value, we mark a growing thirst for plunder, and an increased facility in obtaining troops by help of whom it may be secured. Licentiousness and dissipation become universal, and towns and cities are everywhere plundered by mercenaries, always ready to sell their services to the highest bidder. Military command is courted as the only road to fortune, and the fortunes thus acquired are expended in bribing the people to secure their votes.—New oppressions next produce the Social War, carried on—as had been that of the Peloponnesus—by exterminating the males, selling the women and children as slaves, and confiscating all their property; and thus on and on may we trace the people of Attica, exhausting themselves in the effort to impede the movement of others—until, at length, they find themselves mere instruments in the hands of Philip of Macedon, from whom they pass, successively, to Alexander and his lieutenants.

The object of the Athenians, from the date of the Persian wars, is everywhere seen to have been that of obtaining a monopoly of power, and a monopoly of trade as a means of securing the enjoyment of power. The more the city and its port could be rendered the emporium, the greater would be its ability to control the action of those dependent upon it as a place in which their exchanges might be made. Not only, therefore, were those with whom they were at war driven from the ocean, but neutral vessels were constantly seized and detained in defiance of law; and it was with great difficulty that ships, or goods, so detained, were ever extricated from their captors' hands. In reading the history of the proceedings of the "Mistress of the Seas" of that day, and of her prize courts, it is difficult to avoid being struck with the resemblance between them and those of recent days, when the seas were swept of neutrals by help of "the Rule of '56," paper blockades, and "Orders in Council." With every step in that direction, there became developed a greater tendency towards embargoes, and prohibitions of intercourse; to one of which latter was, in no slight degree, due the Peloponnesian war. All these measures tended to diminish the movement of society abroad; but equally to produce a diminution in the power of voluntary association at home;

and that diminution went on increasing from year to year, until the once proud republic — having first passed through the hands of Macedonian kings and Roman proconsuls—is seen to be represented by troops of slaves; while Atticus remains almost sole owner, and sole improver, in the land that, in earlier and happier days, had given food and raiment, prosperity and happiness, to hundreds of thousands of industrious freemen.

§ 4. Commencing, necessarily, the work of cultivation on the poorest soils, SPARTA never went beyond them; and for the reason that her institutions were based upon the idea of preventing all voluntary association, and discouraging commerce, in all and every form. Man was there regarded in no other light than that of a machine, or instrument, forming a component part of an imaginary being called The State; to the gratification of whose pride, rancor, or revenge, all his feelings and affections required to be sacrificed. Failing to marry, he was liable to be punished; but when married, the intercourse between himself and his wife was rendered difficult, in hopes thereby to stimulate the sexual appetite, and thus promote the growth of population. Children being the property of the State, the parents could exercise no control whatever over their education, whether physical, moral, or intellectual. The *home* had no existence, for not only were parents deprived of the society of their children, but they might not even eat in private. Her people could neither buy nor sell; nor might they in any manner whatever avail themselves of the services of those most useful metals, gold and silver. They might not study the sciences, nor might they indulge their tastes for music; while from all descriptions of theatrical amusement they were entirely debarred. The tendency of the system being thus adverse to the development of the individual faculties, wealth could not grow, nor could they, themselves, advance beyond the earliest and rudest pursuits — those looking to the appropriation of the property of others; and therefore it was that, while always engaged in war, they proved themselves ever ready to sell themselves to the highest bidder. Poor and rapacious, perfidious and tyrannical, the history of Sparta is but a long record of growing inequality and constantly retarded motion of society — until at length we find her soil passing under the control of a few proprietors, surrounded by hosts of slaves; preparatory to her passage out of existence — leaving, as her sole bequest to posterity, the record of her avarice and her crimes.

§ 5. The history of CARTHAGE is little more than a record of wars made for the purpose of monopolizing trade, and of which Corsica and Sardinia, Sicily and Spain, were the most important theatres. Colonies were to be secured, that they might be deprived of all intercourse with the world, except through the medium of Carthaginian ships and merchants; and the contributions of the colonists furnished to the central treasury means for the extension of the system under which they suffered. Elsewhere, where colonies could not be established, all the movements of the trader were shrouded in the strictest secresy — monopoly being the object; and means the most unscrupulous being everywhere resorted to, for securing that it should be maintained. Tolerating no rivals, they guarded, as state secrets, everything connected with the caravan trade — while ever ready to license pirates who desired to seize their neighbors' ships. Monopolies filled the treasury, the disposal of whose revenues gave power to an aristocracy with whom trade was the first and most important object; and to secure themselves in the exercise of power, they subsidized barbarians of all the countries from the southern Sahara to the northern Gaul. The splendor of the city greatly increased; but, as usual in all such cases — the real weakness existing in the ratio of the show of apparent strength — the day of trial proved that the foundation of the social edifice had been laid upon "gold dust and sand," and not upon a rock; and Carthage passed from existence, leaving behind nothing but the further proof afforded by its history, of the truth of the proposition, that "those who live by the sword must die by the sword."

§ 6. In the days of Numa and of Servius, the people of ROME cultivated the fertile soils, and the Campagna was filled with cities, having each an independent existence—and constituting, each, a local centre towards which gravitated the people of the surrounding country. Under their successors, the Tarquins, we find a change, and from that time forward, until we reach the downfall of the empire, the energies of Rome are seen to have been unceasingly devoted to the prevention of all peaceful association among her neighbors—towards appropriation of their property—and towards the centralization of all power within her walls. The city grew in splendor, but with that growth there came a corresponding decline in the condition of her people, until, at length, we find them reduced to pauperism, and dependent upon daily distributions of bread—the contribution of distant provinces taxed for their support; and thus is the history of Rome but a repetition, upon a grander scale, of that of Athens. Palaces rise within and without the city, but with every step in this direction we see a diminution in the power of voluntary association among its people. The land that formerly gave support to thousands of small proprietors is next abandoned, or, when cultivated at all, is tilled by slaves; and the more enslaved the people of the country, the greater becomes the necessity for public distributions in the city — towards which flock all who seek to live by means of plunder. *Panem et circenses* — free bread and free exhibitions of gladiatorial and other brutal fights — constitute now the sole bill of rights of the degraded populace. From age to age the city grows, with corresponding decline in the motion of society constituting commerce. Depopulation and poverty spread from Italy to Sicily and Greece—to hither and further Gaul—to Asia and to Africa; until, at length, decayed at the heart, the empire passes away, having existed for almost a thousand years, a model of rapacity, dishonesty, and fraud; and having, in the whole period, produced scarcely a dozen men whose names have descended to posterity with an untarnished fame.

Traders, gladiators, and buffoons were regarded by the Romans as belonging to the self-same class, and yet the Roman history is but a record of traders' operations on the largest scale. For centuries following the expulsion of the Tarquins, and the establishment of aristocratic power, we witness a perpetual war between plebeian debtors — impoverished by means of the constant wresting of the law to the purposes of the rich and noble — and their patrician creditors, proprietors of private dungeons, in which they incarcerated the men whose only crime consisted in an inability to pay their debts. Later, we find the city filled with knights, accustomed to place themselves as middlemen between those who had taxes to pay and revenue to receive, purchasing the right of taxation at the cheapest price, and selling it at the dearest one — paying to the receiver the smallest sum, and collecting from the poor tax-payer the largest one. Scipio traded his conscience for plunder of the treasury, and when requested to produce his accounts, adjourned the meeting to the temple, there to return thanks to the gods for the victories by help of which he had been enriched.* Verres, in Sicily, and Fonteius, in Gaul, were but traders. Brutus lent money at four per cent. per month, and Cæsar would probably have paid at a higher rate than even this for the millions he had borrowed, had he succeeded in placing himself on an imperial throne. All dealt in slaves, the products of whose labors they monopolized, while treating in the harshest manner the unfortunate people subjected to their power.

§ 7. Turning now to VENICE, we witness a perpetual succession of wars for trade, with constant tendency to the centralization of power in the hands of the few whom the chances of birth, or fortune, had placed in the direction of the state. Originally democratic, we find its government becoming with each succeeding age more aristocratic, until at length we reach the closing of the grand council against all who had not already places there.† That, in its turn, was followed by the establishment of the celebrated Council of Ten, whose spies penetrated into every house; whose tortures might reach every individual, however elevated; and whose existence was totally incompatible with any approach towards freedom of commerce. Following up her history, we find her always seeking trade by means of warlike interferences with the movements of others—obtaining colonies to be adminis-

* In relation to this period, M. Guizot says, (History of Civilization, p. 14:) "Take Rome, for example, in the splendid days of the republic, at the close of the second Punic war; the moment of her greatest virtues, when she was rapidly advancing to the empire of the world — *when her social condition was evidently improving.*" This was, nevertheless, the period in which land was everywhere becoming consolidated — when the free citizens were disappearing — when slaves were most rapidly increasing in number — when gladiatorial games were introduced — when the people were most rapidly becoming demoralized — and when the great men of Rome were building the largest palaces within and without the city—all of these things being evidences of a decline of "social condition."

† 1286.

tered for the sole benefit of her trading aristocracy — taxing her distant subjects to such an extent as to produce a constant succession of attempts at revolution, requiring great fleets and armies for their suppression; and thus, in every manner, building up the class that lived by means of appropriation of the property of others — while preventing movement in any direction looking to the development of individuality, or to the promotion of the habit of association. Her whole history is one of perpetually increasing monopoly of trade and centralization of power—the consequences of which are seen in the facts, that she struck no roots into the earth; and that when the day of trial came, she fell, as had done Athens, Carthage, and Rome; and almost without a blow.

The histories of GENOA and PISA are, like that of Venice, but those of a constant succession of wars for securing a monopoly of trade and of power; and the power thus acquired proved to be as fleeting as had been that of Athens and of Carthage.

§ 8. The early history of HOLLAND exhibits a people among whom the habit of association, and the development of individuality, grew with great rapidity; but her later one is distinguished among those of modern Europe for the manifestations it presents of a desire to monopolize trade — for the resistance it provoked in both France and England — for the wars into which she was led by the thirst for trade — for the exhaustion consequent upon those wars — and for the proof it furnishes that where trade ceases to be the instrument of society, and comes to be regarded as the object for the promotion of which society is to be used — there can be little progress, either physical or intellectual. The land that once gave to the world such men as Erasmus, Spinoza, John de Witt, and William of Orange, now exercises not the smallest influence in reference to either literature or science, and but little even in regard to trade.

§ 9. In the history of PORTUGAL we have striking evidence of the weakness of communities dependent entirely upon trade for the prosperity they may, for the time, enjoy. The close of the fifteenth century witnessed the passage of the Cape of Good Hope, and the establishment of Portuguese power throughout

India, where war was everywhere fomented for the promotion of trade. Lisbon, growing by help of the monopolies that had been, as it was thought, secured, speedily rose to occupy the chief place among European cities; but here, as everywhere else, the strength of the community declined as the capital grew in size and splendor—and before the lapse of another century, Portugal itself became a province of Spain.

§ 10. Turning next to SPAIN, we find that, as the result of a long succession of wars among the various claimants of power, anarchy had, in the period immediately anterior to the union of the several kingdoms, in 1474, attained its highest point. The castles of nobles were converted into dens of robbers, from which they sallied forth to plunder travellers, whose spoil was afterwards sold publicly in the cities, while they themselves were sold to slavery among the Moors. Communications on the highway were everywhere suspended, while within the cities rival nobles carried on private wars—attacking churches, and burning dwellings to the number, at times, of thousands. Instead of five royal mints, there were now no less than a hundred and fifty private ones; and the coin became so much debased, that the common articles of life were three, four, and even sixfold, enhanced in price.

There being no security for person or for property, the husbandman—stripped of his harvest and driven from his field—abandoned himself to idleness, or resorted to plunder as the only means of preserving life. Famines were, therefore, frequent, and were succeeded by widespread pestilences; and thus were the people reduced to the most squalid poverty, as their many masters were enabled to acquire property and power. With the union of Castile and Aragon under Ferdinand and Isabella, however, we find a change of condition in both the sovereigns and the people—castles being everywhere destroyed, and the country being cleared of the swarms of banditti by which it had been overrun.

Security of person and of property being thus established, and the attention of the sovereigns being now given to the resuscitation of commerce, internal restrictions were removed, and foreigners were invited to visit the ports of Spain. Roads and bridges, moles, quays, and lighthouses, were constructed, and harbors were deepened and extended, with a view to accommodate the great "increase of trade." The power of coinage was limited to the royal mints, and arrangements were made for establishing throughout the kingdom a uniform system of weights and measures. Numerous oppressive tolls and monopolies were abolished, and the *alcavala*, a tax upon exchanges, which previously had been arbitrary, was now fixed at ten per cent.

The habit of association now growing rapidly, with great development of individuality, the mercantile marine, at the close of the century, amounted to a thousand vessels; and the woollen and silk fabrics of Toledo gave employment to ten thousand workmen. Segovia manufactured fine cloths, while Granada and Valencia produced silks and velvets; and Valladolid became remarkable for its curiously wrought plate and fine cutlery, while the manufactures of Barcelona rivalled those of Venice. The fair of Medina del Campo became the great mart for the exchanges of the peninsula; and the quays of Seville began to be thronged with merchants from the remotest parts of Europe. The impulse thus given being speedily felt in the arrangements for intellectual improvement, ancient seminaries were remodelled, and new ones were created—all swarming with disciples, and giving employment to more printing-presses than exist in Spain at the present day.

Union at home gave, however, power to sovereigns who desired, most unhappily, to use it for the destruction of the habit of association abroad—and for centralizing in their own hands the direction of the modes of action and of thought of all their subjects. Millions of the most industrious people of the kingdom—among whom individuality was developed to an extent then unknown in any other part of Europe—were expelled for differences of belief; and thus was the incipient motion of society to a great extent arrested. That, in its turn, tended greatly to facilitate the recruitment of armies to be employed in the work of plundering Italy and the Netherlands, Mexico and Peru; and the greater the tendency to dispersion, the more rapid proved to be the reduction in the compensation of honest labor. The more numerous the armies, the greater was the growth of splendor, and of weakness; and the result is seen in the fact that, for a hundred and fifty years, Madrid has been the focus of intrigues having reference to the question whether France or England should have the direction of its government — and the kingdom has been impoverished by repeated wars for the determination of the succession to its throne. In the effort to destroy all power of self-government abroad, Spain had lost all individuality at home.* Mistress of the Indies, she was too weak to preserve command over her own Gibraltar; and she has now for more than a century been forced to see it held for the sole and exclusive purpose of enabling foreigners to set at naught her laws. In every page of her history we find confirmation of the lesson that had before been taught by Athens and Sparta, Carthage and Rome—that if we desire to command respect for our own rights, we can do so only on condition of respecting those of others.†

§ 11. For more than a thousand years, the sovereigns, nobles, and gentlemen of FRANCE have been engaged in the effort to destroy the power of association in, and among, the various nations of

* That the folly of oppression is equal to its wickedness, is proved by every page in the history of Spain, but in none more clearly than in those which record the proceedings of the Duke of Alva in the Netherlands, thus described in Mr. Motley's recent work:

"During the daily decimation of the people's lives, he thought a daily decimation of their industry possible. His persecutions swept the land of those industrious classes which had made it the rich and prosperous commonwealth it had been so lately; while, at the same time, he found a 'Peruvian mine,' as he pretended, in the imposition of a tenth penny upon every one of its commercial transactions. He thought that a people, crippled as this had been by the operations of a Blood Council, could pay ten per cent., not annually, but daily, not upon its income, but upon its capital; not once only, but every time the value constituting capital changed hands. He boasted that he should require no funds from Spain, but that, on the contrary, he should make annual remittances to the royal treasury at home, from the proceeds of his imposts and confiscations; yet, notwithstanding these resources, and notwithstanding twenty-five millions of gold, in five years, sent by Philip from Madrid, the exchequer of the provinces was barren and bankrupt, when his successor arrived. Requesens found neither a penny in the public treasury, nor the means of raising one." — *Rise of the Dutch Republic*, vol. ii. p. 103.

† "The Spaniard alone in Europe has retained the faculty of looking at a nation's acts as those of a man, and appreciating it thereby. He does not ask what it says or intends, or what food it eats, or how many servants it has. He looks at its *dealings* with himself. The Spaniard knows that his two neighbors, for one hundred and forty years, have been seeking to rob and overreach him; plotting, one day, the partition of his property — the next, the supplanting of his heir; constantly engaged in intrigues amongst his servants, and the one or the other insisting on ruining his steward. He sees that, during all that time, they have gained nothing; but while injuring him, have themselves squandered incalculable fortunes and innumerable lives — what can he feel towards them but hatred and disgust?"—URQUHART: *Pillars of Hercules*, vol. i. p. 48

the world; as is shown in the histories of the Netherlands and Germany, Spain and Italy, India and Egypt, Northern and Southern America. The study of that nation, more uninterruptedly than that of almost any other recorded in history, has been to increase the machinery of trade and to destroy the power to maintain commerce. Swords have abounded, while spades were rare; and ships of war have been numerous, while roads were bad, and canals had no existence. Camps have everywhere grown as towns and villages decayed, and gentlemen have become more numerous as ploughmen disappeared. The soil they cultivated has, however, borne

> "Dead Sea fruits, that tempt the eye,
> But turn to ashes on the lips"—

the crop that has been harvested having been, invariably, weakness, disgrace, and almost ruin.

The history of that country is a record of a series of interferences with the rights of other communities, rarely intermitted except when it has itself been rendered powerless for injury abroad by the existence of disturbances at home. Pepin and Charlemagne, having sought glory in Italy and Germany, bequeathed to their successors a kingdom so exhausted as to be entirely incapable of defence against a few Norman pirates, and a kingly power wholly unable to sustain itself against the robber chiefs by whom its sovereigns were surrounded. As a consequence, the social system became resolved into its original elements; and it is to the anarchy which then existed that historians have given the pompous title of "The Feudal System," where system there was none.

Population and wealth grew very slowly, but with their growth may be observed a gradual approach towards the re-establishment of a central power—a sun to the system, around which might peacefully revolve the various parts of French society; but accompanied, as we see to have been the case in Spain, by a strong desire to use the power thus acquired for the prevention of motion in societies abroad. Louis IX. squandered the resources of his kingdom in carrying war into the East; and his successors employed themselves in disturbing the repose of their neighbors of the West—invading their territories, plundering their towns and cities, and murdering the inhabitants. The constant pursuit of glory being, however, attended by increasing weakness at home, but little time elapsed before English armies were seen repeating on the soil of France the scenes of plunder and devastation that she, herself, had enacted abroad — occupying her capital, and dictating laws to her people. The reign of anarchy having again returned, all power of voluntary association disappeared.

Again, under Louis XI., we meet with some approach towards the reorganization of society — followed, however, by repeated invasions of the neighboring countries; and now, again, the effect of unceasing war is seen in the almost perfect chaos of which it was the cause, as exhibited in the closing reigns of the House of Valois, when, the kingly power having almost disappeared, foreign armies fearlessly invaded France, incapable of resistance.

Once again, and for the fourth time, society became, in some degree, reorganized under the Bourbon Henry IV., and his descendants. With the resuscitation of power, returned, however, the desire for its exercise to the injury of the communities around. Centralization grew with the growth of armies, and the exhaustion of the people increased with the increase of splendor in the throne; but now, again, we see splendor and weakness travelling together — the closing years of the reign of Louis XIV. having been embittered by the necessity for begging a peace that was refused except on terms to be dictated by Marlborough and Prince Eugene.*

* "Vauban and Boisguilbert have described in the most pathetic terms the melancholy reduction of the productive power of France in these deplorable times. 'Nothing,' as they said, 'remained to the people but their eyes with which to shed tears;' and we cannot hesitate to believe in the reality of their misfortunes, confirmed as they are by such unexceptionable witnesses. Such was the state of things at the death of Louis. Down to his last moment, the government had been kept alive only by means of the most wretched expedients. To obtain some little money from the new *employés*, the ministry had been compelled to create numerous ridiculous offices; and while England and Holland could borrow at three or four per cent., the farmers of the revenue charged the king of France ten, twenty, and even fifty, per cent. The enormous taxation had exhausted the country, deprived as it had been of laborers by reason of the demands for the war; commerce had almost ceased to exist; and manufactures, decimated by the proscription of the Protestants, seemed condemned to lose all the conquests for which they had been indebted to the genius of Colbert."—BLANQUI: *Histoire d'Economie Politique*, vol. ii. 65.

The wars of Louis XV. and XVI. next paved the way for the Revolution, in the course of which all kingly authority disappeared—the great-grandson of the founder of Versailles being seen, in the *Place de la Revolution*, paying forfeit with his head for all the previous splendor of the throne. Order again, and for the fifth time, re-established, we find the whole effort of the country once more given to the destruction of all power of association among the various communities of Europe. Again were Spain and Italy, the Netherlands and Germany, desolated by invading armies; and again did France exhibit the effect of constant interference with the movement of others in utter weakness at home—her capital having twice been occupied by foreign armies—and her throne having twice been filled by direction of foreign sovereigns.*

* "From 1803 to 1815, twelve campaigns cost us nearly a million of men, who died in the field of battle, or in the prisons, or on the roads, or in the hospitals, and six thousand millions of francs. * * * * *

"Two invasions destroyed or consumed, on the soil of old France, fifteen hundred millions of raw products, or of manufactures, of houses, of workshops, of machines, and of animals, indispensable to agriculture, to manufactures, or to commerce. As the price of peace, in the name of the alliance, our country has seen herself compelled to pay fifteen hundred additional millions, that she might not too soon regain her well-being, her splendor, and her power. Behold, in twelve years, nine thousand millions of francs" (seventeen hundred millions of dollars) "taken from the productive industry of France and lost for ever. We found ourselves thus dispossessed of all our conquests, and with two hundred thousand strangers encamped on our territory, where they lived, at the expense of our glory and of our fortune, until the end of the year 1818."—*Dupin.*

As a consequence of this enormous waste of wealth and population, commerce scarcely existed between the several parts of the kingdom, as is seen by the following statements, made a few years later by an eminent French engineer:—"I have frequently traversed, in different departments, twenty square leagues, without meeting with a canal, a road, a factory, or even an inhabited estate. The country seemed a place of exile abandoned to the miserable, whose interests and whose wants are equally misunderstood, and whose distress is constantly increasing, because of the low prices of their products, and the cost of transportation."—*Cordier.*

The following view of the condition of a large portion of the people of France, in the present day, is from the pen of M. Blanqui, successor of M. J. B. Say in his professorship; and was written after a careful examination of the various provinces of the kingdom.

"Whatever diversity exists in the soil occupied by the people, in their customs, aptitudes, dispositions, the salient, characteristic fact of their situation is wretchedness—a general insufficiency of the means of satisfying even the first necessities of life. One is surprised how small is the consumption of these myriads of human beings. They constitute, however, the majority of the tax-payers; and the slightest difference in their favor, of income, would not merely benefit them, but vastly advance all fortunes and the prosperity of the state. Those alone who have seen it can believe the degree

Order once again restored, we find the armies and fleets of France for twenty years engaged in the destruction of life and property in Northern Africa; and to the glory thus acquired it was that Louis Philippe looked for the means of fortifying himself, and establishing in his family the succession to the throne. He proved, however, to have been all this time building an inverted pyramid—centralizing power in Paris, and destroying it throughout the provinces; and when the day of trial came for him, he, too, fell without a blow. Again, we see the present emperor employed in the work of centralization — diminishing the power of association at home, while laboring to do the same abroad — enlarging the armies and the fleets on the one hand, while on the other denying to his people the right freely to discuss his measures. The end remains to be seen, but glory having always, hitherto, been followed by exhaustion, we might, perhaps, assume that the future weakness of France would be in the precise ratio of her present splendor.

In no country of modern times have the intimacy of war and trade, and the close connection between all the classes who live by appropriation, been more fully exhibited than in the one whose history has above been given. Its sovereigns have been, uniformly, traders—buying the precious metals at low prices, and selling them at high ones, until the pound of silver degenerated to the *franc;* selling offices to their subjects with a view to divide with them the taxation of their people; and selling to that people the privilege of applying their labor in such manner as might enable them to pay the taxes. Farmers-general — traders on the grandest scale—scourged the nation, that they might accumulate enormous fortunes; and warriors sold their services and their consciences — receiving in return shares in the confiscations of their neighbors' properties, and thus constituting themselves centres of the exchanges of a population only one remove from serfage.

in which the clothing, furniture, and food of the rural population are slender and sorry. There are entire cantons in which particular articles of clothing are transmitted from father to son —in which the domestic utensils are simply wooden spoons, and the furniture a bench and a crazy table. You may count by thousands men who have never known bed-sheets; others, who have never worn shoes; and, by millions, those who drink only water, who never eat meat, or very rarely — nor even white bread." — *Quoted by* SMITH: *Manual of Political Economy*, p. 97

§ 12. The history of ENGLAND, from the date of the Revolution of 1688, is one of almost unceasing wars for the extension of trade; but, as the system proposed to be established differed essentially from all that had preceded it, the consideration of those wars, and of their effects, will find a place more properly in another chapter.

In our own country, all the warlike disposition is found in the Southern States, in which the owner of slaves acts as the trader — regulating all the exchanges between the people who labor to produce cotton and tobacco, and those who need to consume cloth. Here, as everywhere else, the predominance of the warlike and trading spirit is attended by growing weakness, consequent upon the daily increasing necessity for dispersion, and constant diminution of the power of association. Here, however, as in the case of England, there exist reasons why the consideration of the policy of the Union may properly be referred to a future chapter.

§ 13. That the power of voluntary association — or the ability to maintain commerce — exists in the direct ratio of the development of individuality, is a fact whose truth will not be questioned by those who have observed the movements of the people of whom society is composed. It is as true, however, of nations as it is of persons — individuality among them, too, growing with the growth of peace and commerce, and declining with the growth of warlike habits, and of the necessity for dependence on the trader's services. Every step in the one direction is followed with increase in that mastery over nature which constitutes wealth; whereas every one in the opposite direction is followed by a decline of power — and therefore is it that we witness the abandonment of the rich soils in all those countries in which war or trade obtains the mastery over commerce; as in Ireland, Italy, India, Turkey, Virginia, and Carolina.

The less the power of local association, the greater is the tendency towards centralization, and towards the creation of great cities, as was seen in the growth of Athens and of Rome, both of which were most magnificent when on the eve of ruin; and as may now be seen in London, Paris, and Calcutta. With the growth of centralization, we witness a constantly increasing inequality in the condition of the various portions of society—the few accumulating fortunes most rapidly as the chances of war and trade tend to deprive the poorer classes of bread. Thus it was that the vast fortunes of Crassus and Lucullus were accumulated at the time when the people of Rome were compelled to look to the treasury for support; that of *Jaques Cœur* when France was becoming almost depopulated; that of the millionaire Venetian, who defeated Carlo Zeno in his candidature for the dogate, during the war of the Chiozza, in which Venice was saved by the latter from entire ruin;* and that of the Medici, in the period of the greatest distress in Florence. Weakness of the community, however, grows in the ratio of the magnificence of private fortunes, and splendor of the capital; and with growing weakness, we observe, invariably, a tendency to the employment of mercenaries — men who, for the sake of pay or plunder, are willing to fight in any cause, as was the case with Athens, Carthage, Rome, and Spain — and is now with Britain.

War and trade, being the pursuits of man requiring the smallest amount of knowledge, take precedence of all others in their development. The necessity for carrying arms in self-defence, and for dependence on the services of the trader, tending, in the progress of society, to decline, that decline should everywhere be accompanied by diminution in the *proportion* borne by soldiers and traders to the mass of which the community is composed. This being so, society tends more and more to assume that form in which strength and beauty are most combined; but being otherwise—the *proportions* of trade and war tending to increase, and commerce tending to decline — it takes a form directly the reverse, that of an inverted pyramid. Stability, of course, diminishes; and, if the movement in that direction be long continued, it ends in ruin, as we see to have been the case with Athens and Carthage, with Venice and Genoa, and with Portugal and Turkey; or it is productive of an endless series of revolutions, as in France.

* "Zeno alone survived this disastrous war; and the public voice designated him as the successor of Contarini in the dogate. His name was in the mouths of all, people and army. The choice lay between him and Michael Morosini, who had tripled his fortune by speculation during the war. The latter was elected, and was proclaimed doge June 10, 1382."—DARU: *Histoire de Venise.*

§ 14. Resistance to gravitation, whether in the vegetable, or animal, world, is in the direct ratio of organization. So, too, as the reader has seen, is it with man. The higher his organization, the greater is his prospect of life. So, again, is it with societies — the chance of life increasing as, with the development of the various faculties of their members, they become more highly organized. The policy of the various communities above referred to having looked to the maintenance of the power of the soldier and the trader, and to the prevention of that development, their resistance to gravitation necessarily declined, until, at length, as with Athens, Carthage, and Rome, death closed their uneasy lives.

Every increase in the *proportion* of society engaged in war and trade tends towards centralization and slavery — it being a necessary result of declining individuality, and diminished power of voluntary association. Every diminution of that proportion tends towards decentralization, life, and freedom—it being a consequence of higher development of individuality, increased power of association, and more perfect organization of society.

The strength of a community grows in the ratio of the growth of the power of association, and the perfection of its organization. The more numerous the *differences* among the members, the more perfect must be the organization, and the greater, therefore, the strength.

Differences result from association, or commerce — and commerce grows with the development of individuality and the production of differences; and the less the necessity for the services of the soldier and the trader, the more rapid becomes the growth of commerce.

The power of association grows in the ratio of the observance by communities of that great law of Christianity which teaches respect for the rights of our fellow-men — and as strength grows with the growth of association, it follows, naturally, that the nation which would increase in strength, and in the durability of its institutions, should carry into the management of its public affairs the same system of morals recognised as binding on its individual members.

Desiring now to find the causes of the decline and ultimate ruin of various communities of the world, we must seek them through an examination of the policy they have, of choice, or of necessity, pursued — whether the one tending to increase in the *proportion* of the classes of society above referred to; or that tending to its diminution; and in all cases we shall find that while the former has led to ruin and death, the latter has brought increase of wealth, prosperity, happiness, and life.

§ 15. The Ricardo-Malthusian doctrine having been invented to account, by means of laws instituted by the Creator, for the existence of social disease — and thus to relieve from all responsibility the class that lives by appropriation and directs the affairs of nations — it is no matter of surprise that modern political economy looks upon the men whose occupations are war and trade in a light different from that in which they have here been represented. Mr. McCulloch tells us that the wagoner is as much a producer as the farmer, and that absenteeism — requiring the employment of middlemen, or traders, between the owner of the land and those who cultivate it—is a benefit, and not an evil. M. Chevalier limits the sphere of political economy to transactions in which merchandise is bought or sold;* and M. Bastiat informs us that it is one of the errors of modern socialism to class among the parasitic races the *intermediaires*, or middlemen, between the producer and the consumer. The broker and the merchant being, as he tells us, creators of value, it is, as he thinks, perfectly correct to class them with agriculturists and manufacturers; each and all being equally middlemen — performing services for which they expect to be remunerated.

It is quite true that the middleman is "a creator of values," but for that reason it is, that men so universally rejoice in being enabled to dispense with his services. Value being the measure of nature's power over man, and the value of man increasing with the decline in that of the commodities required for his use, it follows, necessarily, that to whatever extent the trader adds to the value of the commodities he sells, he must diminish the value of man. Of the price charged to the people of England for the commodities they consume, a very large proportion goes to the

* "I have defined political economy in saying that it is a science which has for its object the application of the existing and recognised principles of public law to a certain species of facts — that species which gives rise to the transactions ordinarily expressed by the terms buying and selling" — *Journal des Economistes*, February, 1853.

middlemen, who are thus enriched at the cost of both consumer and producer. So is it, too, in Turkey, where the profits of trade are enormously large. So, again, in India — in Mexico — in our Western States—and in the islands of the Pacific; and indeed in all those countries in which men are unable to combine their efforts with those of their fellow-men. The trader is a *necessity*, and *not a power* — and so is it with all the classes of society to which reference has here been made. With every increase in population and wealth, men become more and more enabled to come together and arrange their affairs for themselves—with constant diminution in their need for employing middlemen, whether in the capacity of brokers, traders, policemen, soldiers, or magistrates; and the more they can dispense with the services of such persons, the stronger must they themselves become, and the greater must be the tendency of society to take upon itself a form uniting strength and durability — and one most accordant with our ideas of beauty.

Of the classes here referred to, all desire that men shall be cheap, while the men themselves desire that labor shall be dear. The politician knows that when men are cheap, they are more readily managed than when they are dear. The sovereign finds it more easy to obtain soldiers when wages are low than when they are high. The great landholder desires that men may be cheap, and therefore easily obtained.* The trader desires that labor may be cheap when he buys his goods; and that goods may be high, and labor, of course, low, when he sells them. All these persons regard man as the instrument to be used by trade. All of them are necessary in the early stages of society, but the necessity for their services should diminish — and men should as much

* "The Chinese slave-trade is very busy in Peru, whither they are conveyed from China by English and American vessels. They are enticed from their homes, smuggled on shipboard, and treated like brutes. One American ship, which sailed from China with six hundred and five, lost two hundred and one on the passage.

"There has been for many months a project on foot for the introduction of six thousand from China into Cuba, as plantation laborers, to supply the place of negroes, the importation of whom from Africa is to be prohibited, if possible. The English capitalists having the matter in charge were delayed in their arrangements by the urgent want of vessels for the Crimea, which rendered it difficult to effect suitable charters in London. They have finally transferred the scene of their labors to this city, and a vessel is now fitting out at this port for China, under a contract for twelve hundred and fifty emigrants."—*New York Journal of Commerce.*

rejoice at every such diminution as at the substitution of the steamship for the sailing one — the pump for the hand — or the great waterworks for the pump. The less the machinery required for the maintenance of commerce among men, the greater must that commerce be.

The great difficulty in all these cases is that resulting from the fact of the same word being constantly used to express totally different ideas. The man who makes a thousand pairs of shoes for a thousand people, each of whom comes to him to be fitted, maintains a commerce altogether unimpeded by any necessity for paying porters, or commission merchants. His neighbor, making the same number, finds it necessary to employ a porter to carry them to the trader, and then to pay the trader for finding persons to buy and pay for them. We have here three distinct operations, each requiring to be paid for: first, that of the trader who simply arranges the terms of exchange, appropriating a part of the proceeds as compensation for his services; second, that of the porter, who effects *changes of place;* and, third, that of the shoemaker, who effects *changes of form* — the reward of the last being dependent entirely upon the quantity that remains to him, after the others have been paid. All of these operations, it is the habit to include under the general head of commerce; whereas the real parties to the commerce are only the man who makes the shoes and those who wear them. The others are useful, in so far as they are necessary; but whatever tends to diminish the need for their services is as much a gain to man, as is improvement in machinery of any other description whatsoever. His value rises with every diminution of the obstacles to commerce, and the greatest of all these obstacles, is the necessity for employing the trader and transporter in the work of effecting changes of place.*

* According to Mr. McCulloch (*Principles*, Part I., Ch. 3) wealth increases most rapidly when the rate of profit is the highest. Who, however, is it, that receives these profits? It is the *intermediaire*, or middleman — the representative of those obstacles to commerce which cause increase of values. The more the number, and the greater the extent, of the difficulties to be overcome by commodities, on the road from the producer to the consumer, the greater is always the rate of profit, the higher are values, and the lower is the condition of man; and yet, according to this authority, it is then, and there, that wealth must most rapidly accumulate!

# CHAPTER X.

## OF CHANGES OF MATTER IN PLACE.

§ 1. THE first poor colonist, unable to raise the logs by help of which to construct himself a house, is compelled to depend for shelter upon projecting rocks; or to bury himself in cavities of the earth—affording little protection against the summer's heat, or the winter's cold. Unable to command the services of nature, he is obliged to wander over extensive tracts of land in quest of food, whose transportation to his home, even when obtained, not unfrequently exceeds his own unassisted powers; and thence it is, that the spoils of the chase lie wasting on the ground, while he and his wife are suffering from want of proper nourishment. In time, however, his sons grow up, and now, combining their exertions, they make for themselves instruments, by help of which to command the natural forces to such extent, as to enable them to cut and transport logs, and to build for themselves something like a house. Again, they are seen constructing other instruments, by aid of which they obtain increased supplies of food, and from diminished surfaces, with constant decline in the *proportion* of their labor required for effecting changes in the place of matter, and increase in the *proportion* that may be given to changing its form, with a view to fitting it for furnishing nourishment, or for aiding in the work of production.

The life of man is a contest with nature. His prime necessity, and his first desire, is that of association with his fellow-men—and the obstacle to the gratification of that desire is found in the necessity for effecting changes of place. Poor and weak, the early settler, unable to obtain an axe, a spade, or a plough, is forced to cultivate the poorest soils—yielding so little food, that he must, of necessity, remain apart from other men. As numbers increase, wealth grows, and with the growth of wealth and numbers, he is enabled to cultivate the richer soils—yielding increased supplies of food, and diminishing his need for going abroad, and separating himself from his fellow-men. From a mere creature of necessity, he passes into a being of power, from year to year more enabled to obtain machinery by help of which to maintain commerce with distant men, while becoming from year to year more individualized, and less dependent on that commerce for his command of the conveniences, comforts, and luxuries of life. The powers of nature become embodied in THE MAN, whose value grows as that of all commodities declines; and with that growth he finds a daily diminution in her resistance to his further efforts.

§ 2. Looking now to the solitary settler of the West, even where provided with both axe and spade, we see him with difficulty obtaining the commonest log hut. A neighbor, however, arrives, bringing with him a horse and cart; and now a second house may be built with less than half the labor that had been given to the first. Others coming, more houses are required; and now, by the combined efforts of the settlement, a third is completed in a day, whereas the first had required months, and the second weeks, of severe exertion. These new neighbors having brought with them ploughs and hoes, better soils are cultivated; with large increase in the return to labor, and in the power to preserve the surplus for the winter's use.

The Indian path that they at first had used, now becomes a road, and exchanges with distant settlements begin—the preludes to the establishment of the store, destined to become the nucleus of the future town. Population and wealth again increasing, and better soils being cultivated, the town begins to grow, and with each successive addition to its numbers, the farmer finds a consumer for his products, and a producer ready to supply his wants—the shoemaker seeking to have leather and corn in exchange for shoes, and the carpenter shoes and corn in exchange for his labor. The blacksmith requires fuel and food, and the farmer needs shoes for his horses; and thus from day to day commerce increases, with corresponding decline in the necessity for transportation. More time being now given to production, the reward of labor rises, with constant increase of commerce. The road becoming a turnpike, and the town becoming a city, the market near at hand grows steadily, while the railroad facilitates exchanges with distant towns and cities.

The tendency to union, and to combination of exertion, thus grows with the growth of wealth. In a state of extreme poverty it cannot be developed. The insignificant tribe of savages that roams over millions of acres of the most fertile land, looks with jealous eyes on every intruder—knowing that each new mouth requiring to be fed, increases the difficulty of obtaining food; whereas, the farmer rejoices in the approach of the blacksmith and the shoemaker, because they come to eat in his neighborhood the corn which hitherto he has carried to the distant market, there to be exchanged for shoes for his horses and himself. With each new consumer of his products that arrives, he is enabled more and more to concentrate his action and his thoughts upon his home; and his power to consume the commodities brought from other lands increases with the diminution of the necessity for seeking at a distance a market for the products of his farm. Give to the poor tribe spades, and the knowledge how to use them, and the power of combination will arise. The supply of food becoming more abundant, they hail the arrival of the stranger who brings them knives and clothing to be exchanged for skins and corn; wealth grows, and with it grows the habit of association.

The little tribe is, however, compelled to occupy the higher and poorer lands — the lower and richer ones consisting of dense forests and dreary swamps, among which nature reigns supreme—setting at defiance all the efforts of poor and scattered men. On the opposite slope of the valley, but a few miles distant, may be found another little tribe, but — the river bottom being yet uncleared, and bridges as yet unthought of—there is no intercourse between them. Population and wealth, however, continuing to increase—and food being obtained in return to less exertion—the power of association as steadily augments, with constantly increasing appreciation of the advantages to be derived from further combination. Roads being now made in the direction of the river bank, the supply of food increases rapidly, because of the increased facility for cultivating the richer soils; and still more rapid is the growth in numbers and in wealth.

The river bank at length being reached, the new wealth now takes the form of a bridge, by help of which the little communities are enabled more readily to combine their efforts for the common good. One requires carts, or wagons, while the other has corn seeking to be converted into flour; one has hides to spare, while the other has an excess of shoes, or cloth. One has a windmill; while the other rejoices in the possession of a saw-mill. — Exchanges increase; employments become from day to day more diversified; and the towns increase in numbers and in strength, by reason of the increased amount of commerce. Roads being now made in the direction of other settlements, the forests and swamps by which they have thus far been separated, gradually disappear — yielding to cultivation the richest soils, with increased returns to labor, enabling the laborer to obtain from year to year better food, clothing, and shelter, and with less expenditure of muscular force. The danger of famine now disappears; life is prolonged, and numbers increase; with corresponding increase in the facility of combination for every useful purpose—the distinguishing characteristic of civilization.

With further growth of population and of wealth, the desires of man, and his ability to gratify them, steadily advance. The nation that has now been formed has an excess of wool, but is deficient in sugar; whereas, in a neighboring one may be found excess of sugar, while the supply of wool is insufficient. The two are, however, separated from each other by broad forests, deep swamps, and rapid rivers — obstacles to intercourse the removal of which is required to await the further progress of population and of wealth. Both of these now further grow, and next the forests and swamps disappear — giving place to rich farms, through which broad roads are made, with great bridges, and enabling the merchant readily to transport wool to exchange with his now rich neighbors for their surplus sugar. Nations next combining their exertions, wealth grows with still increased rapidity — facilitating the drainage of marshes, and thus bringing into activity the richest soils; while coal-mines cheaply furnish fuel for converting limestone into lime, and iron ore into spades and axes—or into rails for the new roads required for sending to market the vast products of the fertile soils now cultivated; and for bringing back the large supplies of sugar, tea, coffee, and other products of distant lands, with which intercourse is now maintained. At each step, population and wealth, happiness and prosperity, make a new bound; and men realize with difficulty the fact that the country which now affords to tens of millions all the necessaries, comforts, conveniences, and luxuries of life, is the same that — when the superabundant land had been occupied by tens of thousands only — gave to that limited number scanty supplies of the poorest food — so scanty, that famines were frequent, and followed in their wake by pestilence, which, at brief intervals, swept from the earth the population of the little and scattered settlements of the hills.

We have here a constantly accelerating motion of society and an increase of commerce, resulting from a steady diminution in the proportion of the labor of the community required for effecting changes of place, consequent upon a steady increase in the power of combination, and in the development of individuality resulting from diversity of employment. As the village grows and becomes more self-sufficing, it acquires the ability to improve its communications with neighboring villages; and all are next enabled to aid in effecting improvements in the roads to the more distant town. As employment becomes more diversified in the town, it is enabled to combine its efforts with its neighbor towns, to effect improvements in the transport to and from the more distant city; and as the cities grow, they, in like manner, are enabled to unite in facilitating intercourse with distant nations. The power to maintain commerce grows thus, with every diminution in the necessity for trade and transportation.

§ 3. The necessity for effecting changes of place is an obstacle interposed by nature to the gratification of the wishes of man; and it was required that it should exist, in order that his faculties might be stimulated to exertion for its removal. Those faculties exist in all men, but they remain latent when not stimulated into action by a feeling of the advantage that must result from increased power to maintain intercourse with their fellow-men. The greater the facility of intercourse, the more are its benefits appreciated, and the greater becomes the consciousness of power to effect further improvement — looking to entire removal of the obstacle standing in the way of direct intercourse between men and their fellow-men — or, commerce. In the early stages of society, it is so great as to be almost insuperable; and hence it is that we even now see that while the value of commodities at the place of consumption is, in many cases, so great as to cause them to be almost beyond the reach of any but the wealthy, their value at the place of production is so small as to keep their producer in a state of poverty, and retain him in the position of slave, not only to nature, but also to his fellow-man. The sugar producer of Brazil cannot obtain clothing with which to conceal his nakedness; while the cloth producer of England is equally unable to obtain the sugar required for the sustenance of his family and himself. That such should be the case, results from no defect in the arrangements of Providence — nature yielding abundantly in return to the efforts of both, and doing her part towards enabling them to be well clothed and fed; but it does result from error in the arrangements of men. The man of England, and of Brazil, would have full supplies of food — would be well clothed—and would become more free, could the one obtain all the cloth given for his sugar, and the other all the sugar given for his cloth; and it is because so large a portion is absorbed in the passage from one to the other, that the condition of both is so near akin to slavery.

But thirty years since, the price of a bushel of wheat in Ohio was less than a third of that at which it would sell in Philadelphia or New York—all the difference being absorbed in the passage from the producer to the consumer. The first then obtained little cloth in exchange for his food, and the latter little food in exchange for his cloth.—But recently, corn abounded in Castile, for which no market could be found; while Andalusia, part of the same kingdom, looked to America for supplies of food.—At the present day, food is wasted in one part of India, while hundreds of thousands perish of famine in another. So is it everywhere, in default of that diversity of employment which makes a market for its products on, or near, the land. "In Russia, a propitious season and an abundant crop," says a recent traveller, "do not guaranty a profitable season to the farmer. The prices," dependent as they are upon the chances and changes of distant lands, "may," as he continues, "suddenly have fallen so low, that no physical combination of circumstances can benefit him. * * * He is thus the victim of circumstances"— over which he can exercise no control whatsoever. "Totally unable to affect the price of grain himself, it depends on the demand for foreign countries, the facilities of communication, and his position with regard to them — with many other causes incidental to an immense, but thinly-peopled, country, affected in its extremities by very different temperatures, liable during the same year to famine and plenty occurring in distant quarters, between which it is matter of pure hazard if there exist any means of communication."* The picture here presented is that of all purely agricultural countries — their crops being almost altogether absorbed in the cost of transportation, because of the exceeding distance of the consumer from the producer. Hence it is, that slavery, or serfage, prevails in those communities in which employments are not diversified.

Sixty years since, the *utility* of the produce of Ohio was very small indeed — so small, that it required, as then was said, all that an acre could be made to yield, "to pay for a pair of breeches." Thirty years since, its utility had much increased, but yet was very trivial — the major part of it being required for feeding the men and horses who carried it to market; whereas, the *value* of all commodities needed by the farmer was so great, that it required fifteen tons of wheat to pay for a single ton of iron. The people of that State had then but little power over nature; but, as they have increased in numbers, power has been obtained, and they are now in the enjoyment of wealth—because of the removal of some of the obstacles standing in the way of commerce.

To this it is due, that while the utility of their own products has largely increased, by reason of the diminished proportion required to feed the men and animals engaged in transportation; the value of the iron has so greatly diminished, that six or eight tons may now be obtained in return for the same wheat that would then have been given in exchange for one. As a consequence of this, a single year enables the farmer to add more, in quantity and quality, to his machinery of cultivation, than before he could do in twenty—substituting the continuous motion of the horse-rake and of the reaping and threshing machines, for the constantly intermitted one of the hand-rake, the reaping-hook, the scythe, and the flail — and enabling him to apply himself with in-

* OLIPHANT: Russian Shores of the Black Sea, p. 134.

creased rapidity to the removal of the yet remaining obstacles consequent upon the necessity for effecting changes of place. The better the roads, the greater is the demand for machinery; and the greater the latter, the greater is the tendency to have the miller, the blacksmith, the carpenter, the spinner, the weaver, the miner, and the iron-founder come to take their places near the farmer; with great increase in the motion of society, in the attraction of home, and in the power of combination with people abroad.

Man's power over nature tends, thus, steadily to grow, and every stage of his progress towards power is accompanied, naturally and necessarily, with diminished resistance to his further efforts. There is, therefore, a constant tendency towards acceleration of motion; and the momentum of a body is, as the reader knows, as its weight, multiplied by its velocity. The Indian trails of the Six Nations must have cost a greater amount of effort than was subsequently required for laying out, clearing, and making the State road; and that, in its turn, was a work of more serious labor than was, but a few years later, the construction of the railroad. The turnpike road from Baltimore to Cumberland, a distance of a hundred and eighty miles, was, but forty years since, so great a work, that the Federal treasury was required to bear the cost of its construction; but railroads now increase with such rapidity, that the people of the Ohio Valley already have the choice among many such, when they desire to visit the Atlantic cities. The Santa Maria, Columbus's great ship, had a capacity of but ninety tons; and yet the construction of such a vessel was then a far more serious matter than is now that of a steamer which would accomplish the same voyage in fewer weeks than she required of months. Here, as everywhere, the first step requires the most effort, and yields the smallest return. With every additional one, the value of man rises, and that of commodities falls; and with each we see an increase in the wealth at his command, giving him increased facilities for further accumulation.

Thus far, however, we have made but a single step in that direction. The power to become useful to man is a force latent in all the matter by which he is surrounded; but the development of that force is everywhere retarded by the difficulty attendant upon effecting changes of place. The savage is compelled to leave upon the ground, for the consumption of birds of prey, a most valuable portion of the spoils yielded by the chase; whereas the man who lives in society with his fellow-man, is enabled to utilize not only the flesh, but the skin, the bones, and even the yet undi gested contents of the stomach. The isolated man fells the tall tree, that he may obtain the cabbage which constitutes its head—leaving the trunk to become the prey of worms; but the associated man utilizes not only the trunk, but the limbs, the bark, and even the leaves. The few and scattered people who cultivate the poor soils of a new settlement, carry their food and their wool to a distant market—losing the manure, and thus adding the exhaustion of the soil, and consequent stoppage of motion in their land, to the cost of transportation; whereas the associated man saves all that cost, and makes his land richer with every crop. The isolated man wanders over extensive tracts rich with coal and metallic ores, and continues poor; but the associated man utilizes such deposits, and improves his machinery for the production of food—and the more he does so, the greater is the power of further association and further increase of combination. Look to it where we may, we see that as men are enabled to come together, they obtain power to command the services of nature—improving their roads as they diminish their dependence on the machinery of transportation—and transporting tons with less effort than had been required for the removal of pounds; although with each successive year they find themselves more and more enabled to compress their raw materials into cloth and iron, and thus diminish the weight of the commodities requiring to be transported.

§ 4. The first and heaviest tax to be paid by land and labor is that of transportation; and it is the only one to which the claims of the state itself are forced to yield precedence. It increases in geometrical proportion, as the distance from market increases arithmetically; and therefore it is, that agreeably to tables recently published, corn that would produce at market $24.75 per ton, is worth nothing at a distance of only a hundred and sixty miles, when the communication is by means of the ordinary wagon road—the cost of transportation being equal to the selling price. By railroad, under ordinary circumstances, that cost is but $2.40—leaving to the farmer $22.35, as the amount of tax saved to him by the construction of the road; and if we now take the product of an acre of land as averaging a ton, the saving is equal to interest, at six per cent., on $370 an acre. Assuming the product of an acre of wheat to be twenty bushels, the saving is equal to the interest on $200; but, if we take the more bulky products — hay, potatoes, and turnips — it will be found to amount to thrice that sum. Hence it is that an acre of land near London sells for thousands of dollars, while one of exactly equal quality may be purchased in Iowa, or Wisconsin, for little more than a single dollar. The owner of the first enjoys the vast advantage of the endless motion of its products — taking from it several crops in the year, and returning to it, at once, a quantity of manure equal to all he had abstracted; and thus improving his land from year to year. He is *making* a machine; whereas, his western competitor, forced to lose the manure, is *destroying* one. Having no transportation to pay, the former can raise those things of which the earth yields largely — as potatoes, carrots, or turnips — or those whose delicate character forbids that they should be carried to distant markets; and thus does he obtain a large reward for that continuous application of his faculties, and of his land, which results from the power of combination with his fellow-men.

In the case of the latter, all is widely different. Having heavy transportation to pay, he cannot raise potatoes, turnips, or hay, because of them the earth yields by tons; as a consequence of which, they would be almost, even when not wholly, absorbed on the road to market. He may raise wheat, of which the earth yields by bushels; or cotton, of which it yields by pounds; but if he raises even Indian corn, he must manufacture it into pork before the cost of transportation can be so far diminished as to enable him to obtain a proper reward for labor. Rotation of crops being, therefore, a thing unknown to him, there can be no continuity of motion in either himself or his land. His corn occupies the latter but a part of the year, while the necessity for renovating the soil, by means of fallows, causes a large portion of his farm to remain altogether idle, although the cost of maintaining roads and fences is precisely the same as if it were all fully employed.

His time, too, being required only for certain portions of the year, much of it is altogether lost — as is that of his wagon and horses—the consumption of which latter is just as great as if they were always at work. He, and they, are in the condition of steam-engines, constantly fed with fuel, while the engineer as regularly wastes the steam that is produced — a proceeding involving heavy loss of capital. Further stoppages in the motion of himself and his land, resulting from changes in the weather, are consequent upon this limitation in the variety of things that may be cultivated. His crop, perhaps, requires rain that does not come, and his corn, or cotton, perishes of drought. Once grown, it requires light and heat, but in their place come clouds and rain; and it and he are nearly ruined. The farmer near London, or Paris, is in the condition of an underwriter who has a thousand risks, some of which are maturing every day; whereas, the distant one is in that of a man who has risked his whole fortune on a single ship. Having made the voyage, she arrives at the entrance of her destined port, when, striking on a rock, she is lost, and her owner is ruined. Precisely such is the condition of the farmer who — having his all at risk on his single crop — sees it destroyed by blight, or mildew, almost at the moment when he had expected to make his harvest. With isolated men, all pursuits are extra-hazardous; but as they are enabled to approach each other, and combine their efforts, the risks diminish, until they almost altogether disappear. Combination of action thus makes of society a general insurance office, by help of which each and all of its members are enabled to secure themselves against almost every imaginable risk.

Great, however, as are these differences, they sink almost into insignificance, compared with that which exists in reference to the maintenance of the powers of the land. The farmer distant from market is always selling the soil, which constitutes his capital; whereas, the one near London not only returns to his land the refuse of its products, but adds thereto the manure resulting from the consumption of the vast amount of wheat brought from Russia and America — of cotton brought from Carolina and India — of sugar, coffee, rice, and other commodities, yielded by the tropics — of lumber and of wool, the products of Canada and Australia — not only maintaining the motion of his land, but increasing it from year to year.

§ 5. Of all the things required for the purposes of man, the one that least bears transportation, and is, yet, of all the most important, is manure. The soil can continue to produce on the condition, only, of restoring to it the elements of which its crop had been composed. That being complied with, the supply of food increases, and men are enabled to come nearer together and combine their efforts — developing their individual faculties, and thus increasing their wealth; and yet this condition of improvement, essential as it is, has been overlooked by all economists. The subject being one of much importance, and having been treated at considerable length in a work to which reference has heretofore been made, it is deemed expedient to submit for the consideration of the reader the following passage:—

"Every crop is made from matter furnished by its predecessors; and whatever is lacking in the manure will surely, sooner or later, disappear in the product. Exhaustion and renovation must reciprocate in equal measure. If any element, however minute in quantity, is constantly withdrawn and removed from the soil, the product of which it is a constituent must finally cease to reappear. If animals are fed upon the land, their excrements restore a large portion of the inorganic matter, of which the plants on which they feed have robbed the soil. But the richest pasture will, after a time, show signs of exhaustion, if the young cattle that grow upon it are sent to distant markets Let the cattle remain, and their manure be faithfully restored: if they are cows, a considerable quantity of phosphate of lime is contained in their milk; and if this is sent away in its original form, or in the shape of butter and cheese, the soil must cease to furnish pasture which will make milk. The grass-lands of Cheshire, in England, famous for its dairy husbandry, were thus impoverished. They were restored by the application of ground bones — human bones, in a great measure, imported from the battle-fields of the continent — which contain essentially the same substances as the milk. The importance of what might seem an insignificant loss to the land, is shown by the fact stated by Professor Johnston, that lands which paid but five shillings an acre of rent, have been, by restoring the bone phosphates, of which they had been ignorantly robbed, made to yield a rent of forty shillings, besides a good profit to the dairyman. Different crops take away the inorganic substances of the soil in different proportions; the grains, for instance, take chiefly phosphates; potatoes and turnips, mostly potash and soda; but all crops, natural or artificial, deprive the land of some essential ingredient, and, in whatever shape the ingredient is finally removed, in animal or human muscle and bones, in cloth made from the cotton, the wool, or the flax, boots or hats made from the skin or the fur of the animals, no matter how many transformations the elements may have undergone, the vegetative power of the earth from which they were withdrawn has been diminished to an equivalent extent. Nature is an easy creditor, and presents no bill of damages for exhausted fertility. We are, therefore, little accustomed to take account of what is due to the earth. An idea, however, of the great pecuniary magnitude of the debt may be gained from the fact, that the manure annually applied to the soil of Great Britain, at its market prices, was estimated in 1850* at £103,369,139, a sum much exceeding the entire value of its foreign trade. In Belgium, which sustains a population of 336 to the square mile— one to every arable acre in the kingdom — which, according to Mr. McCulloch, 'produces commonly more than double the quantity of corn required for the consumption of its inhabitants;' and where immense numbers of cattle are stall-fed for the sake of their manure, the liquid excrements of a single cow sell for ten dollars a year. The people of Belgium are able, by making their own population, animal and human, the most dense of any country in the world, to raise beef, mutton, pork, butter, and grain, cheaply enough to admit of their exportation to England, to feed people who believe in over-population.

"The necessity of taking into account the comparative exhaustion resulting from the growth and removal of different crops, as well as their comparative cheapness of transportation, modifies considerably the inferences which would otherwise be made in regard to their value. A work in which all the circumstances which can affect the economy of different modes of cultivation, are subjected to rigorous mathematical calculation† — the necessary

* Macqueen's Statistics, p. 12.

† DE THUNEN: "Recherches sur l'Influence que le Prix des Grains, la Richesse du Sol, et les Impots, exercent sur la Culture," p. 178. The work is only known to the writer in the French translation, made from the original German, under the auspices of the National and Central Agricultural Society of France.

elements being derived from exact accounts, kept by its author during fifteen years of superintendence of an agricultural school and model farm in Germany — supplies us with this illustration. Three bushels of potatoes, it is said, have been ascertained to possess the same amount of nutritive power as one bushel of rye — the standard with which all crops are compared by this writer. It is also stated that ground, equal in extent and of equal quality, will produce nine bushels of potatoes where it would yield but one of rye, while one bushel of the latter demands as much labor as $5\frac{7}{10}$ of the former. A given quantity of nutriment could therefore be obtained upon one-third the area of land, and with half the amount of labour, by the cultivation of potatoes, which would be required to produce it in the shape of rye. But in order to keep the soil in heart, so that it will continue to yield either rye or potatoes, a certain portion of the farm must be devoted to pasturage, that manure may be made. Taking into account the requirements in this respect of the two crops in question, it is found that the same area which suffices for the production of 39 measures of nutritive matter in rye, instead of producing three times that number in potatoes, yields but 64. The actual value of the two crops, instead of bearing the proportion of 100 to 300, has that of 100 to 164.

"The above calculation proceeds upon the assumption, that the farm must manufacture and save its own manure. Every town, however, every hamlet where artisans are congregated, is a place whence the refuse of crops, after subserving human nutrition, may be removed with great advantage to the health of the inhabitants, and no detriment to the productiveness of their industry. The sewer-water of large towns contains its refuse in a state of dilution, highly favorable to the growth of plants and the increase of fertility. 'From every town of a thousand inhabitants,' says Professor Johnston, 'is carried annually into the sea, manure equal to 270 tons of guano, worth, at the then current price of guano in England, $13,000, and capable of raising an increased produce of not less than 1000 quarters of grain.' It is alleged by competent engineers, that liquid manure can be distributed at a much less cost than that of carting an equal fertilizing value in a solid form. The drainage-water from a large portion of the city of Edinburgh has been conducted into a small brook, and made to overflow some three hundred acres of flat land, which is thus rendered so productive as to be sometimes mown seven times in a season. A portion of it, held under a long lease at £5 per acre, is sub-let at £30, and some of the richest meadows at even higher rates. Advantages of this character are the result of combination upon a large scale. The centres of population, however, supply manures which may be made immediately available by the individual farmer, with no other assistance than that of his own carts and horses. Whether it is more profitable to manufacture manure upon the farm, by devoting to that object portions of the land which might otherwise grow crops for sale, or to procure the manure from town, depends upon the price which must be paid for it, and the distance to which it has to be carried. The German agriculturist, to whom we before referred, has deduced the relation between the prices the farmer can afford to pay for fertilizing material at the town—for the purpose of growing potatoes with the same economy as if it were made from other crops upon the farm — and the distance it is to be transported. The result at which he arrives is, that a quantity of manure which would be worth $5.40, for the purpose of applying to land in the immediate suburbs of the town, or where the expense of cartage is so trifling that it may be disregarded, is worth $4.20, if the farm be one German mile (4·60 English miles) distant—$3.10, if the distance be two German miles — $1.90, at three miles — 83 cents at four; and that at the distance of 4¾ German, or about 22 English, miles, he can pay nothing for it, though he may still carry it away as cheaply as to give up the growing of potatoes upon that portion of his land which must otherwise be devoted to the growth of crops for restoring the fertility which the tubercles exhaust.

"It follows, from considerations which in the preceding paragraphs it has been sought to elucidate, in scant proportion to their importance, that the vicinity of the producer to the place where conversion and exchange are effected — in other words, to the consumers— is an indispensable condition of his being able to raise those crops which the earth yields most abundantly. The same space which, sown with wheat, gives what has been termed muscular matter — that is, muscle-sustaining power — to the amount of two hundred pounds, if planted with cabbages gives fifteen hundred pounds; in turnips, a thousand pounds; in beans, four hundred. It is, however, as we have seen, but a limited circle around the centres of population in which the agriculturist has the capacity to determine freely to what object he will consecrate his land and his labor. In proportion to his distance from the consumer, two causes act in concert to contract his power. The first is the cost of transporting the crop to market, which compels him to select those whose bulk is small compared to their value, because they require much land and much labor for their production. The second is the difficulty of bringing back, over the increasing distance, the refuse of the crop; in default of which the crop itself runs out. Whatever may be the quality of soil cultivated, these conclusions are equally valid. They hold good, without reference to the truth or falsehood of the theory of Ricardo, in regard to the occupation of the earth; while they are fatal to that of Malthus, as showing that density of population is essential to the plenitude of subsistence."*

The sum of all the taxes thus far described is immense, and yet they constitute but a portion of those to which our Western farmers are subjected. The man who *must* go to any market, *must pay the cost of getting there, let it take what form it may;* and among the charges are those of marine and fire insurance, always estimated in fixing the price of his commodities. All the losses from the numerous fires in great commercial cities — such as have been witnessed in New York and Liverpool, Hamburg, Memel, and London—are payable out of the commodities furnished by the farmer; and are not, in any manner, payable by those who stand between him and his market. So far, indeed, to the contrary is it, that the latter profit largely by the losses that are incurred — among the most advantageous portions of their business being that of insurance against losses that never could occur were the markets for raw produce everywhere near at hand. The farmer near London has no insurance to pay — all his commodities finding a demand on the instant, and at the place of production.†

* SMITH: Manual of Political Economy, p. 203.

† Rev. Henry Ward Beecher, in a sermon which he delivered in New York, stated that over fifty American vessels have sailed from port, and since been given up as lost—never heard from—in the last twelve months. Within the same time, three large ocean steamers and three sailing packets, all loaded with passengers, have been wrecked and totally lost on the American coast. Besides these there is the "City of Glasgow," with another freight of human

Such are a portion—and a portion only—of the taxes imposed upon land and labor by the necessity for effecting changes of place, consequent upon dependence on a distant market. Having examined them, the reader can scarcely doubt that they account fully for the facts that in all purely agricultural countries land is valueless, and man continues in a state of slavery. Wherever mills and furnaces are built, and mines are opened, there arises a demand for potatoes and turnips, cabbages and hay, strawberries and raspberries — enabling the farmer to take from the land tons, where before he had taken bushels; and to restore to it, again all the elements of which it had been deprived. Being at market, and saving all the cost of transportation and commission, he is enabled to improve his machinery of cultivation. Clearing and draining his richest lands, while bringing into activity the lime, or other minerals and metals, abounding in his poorer ones, he has a succession of crops ripening at various periods of the year; the perfect success of some of which makes amends for partial failure of others — thus giving to his pursuit a certainty of remuneration that before had no existence. He now finds on his farm a continuous demand for his own labor, and for that of his horses; and this he does for the reason, that whenever he sends a load of food to market, his wagon returns laden with offal yielded at that market—enabling him to improve his land. Time becoming more valuable, he is constantly substituting machinery of continuous motion for that heretofore in use, by help of which intermitted motion had been obtained; and thus on and on he goes, with constantly accelerated force—enabling constantly increasing numbers to obtain larger supplies of food, with steady increase in the power of association, in the development of individuality, and in the power of further progress.

§ 6. Every step in the progress of association being attended by a diminution in the *proportion* of labor of a community re-

life—given up. Two hundred and one vessels have been reported lost within a single week. The losses paid by marine insurance companies, in New York alone, exceed twelve million dollars for the last year. From a return to the British House of Commons, it appears that from January, 1847, to December, 1850, there happened at sea upwards of twelve thousand casualties, varying in magnitude from the shipwreck at the dead of night, with all its horrors, to a clumsy collision in the Channel. The amount of the loss of life averages (per year) twelve hundred and fifty.

quired to be given the effectuation of changes of place — and by an increase in that which may be given to effecting changes of form by the processes of agriculture or manufactures, the farmer is enabled to subdue to cultivation still richer soils, and daily more and more to elaborate their products so as to fit them on the instant for consumption at home — or cheaply to seek consumers in distant lands; *the power* to maintain commerce with distant men increasing with every step towards individuality in the community, resulting from diminution in the *necessity* for seeking a distant market. The power of man for effecting changes of place increases, therefore, in a ratio greatly exceeding that of the growth of population, with steady increase in the utility of the commodities produced, in the wealth, strength, and force of the community, and in the prosperity and happiness of the people of whom it is composed.

That every act of association is an act of commerce, is a truth of such high importance that it cannot be too strongly impressed upon the reader's mind, and he may, therefore, forgive its repetition. The growth of commerce being in the direct ratio of increase in the power of association and combination, the motion of a community towards the goal of its desires — towards that point at which there is found the most perfect facility for combining the efforts of man with those of his fellow-men — must be in the direct ratio of its increase in numbers, and in the variety of their employments; and with every such increase the necessity for effecting changes of place tends more and more to pass away. The greater that variety, and the more perfect the commerce, the greater must be the development of individuality, the higher must become the feeling of responsibility, and the greater the capacity for further progress. The more rapid the motion of society, the greater must be its tendency to take upon itself that form which in the material world gives the greatest stability and the largest capacity for resistance to any attack from without — that form, consequently, which insures the greatest durability.

In order that commerce may increase, it is *indispensable* that man shall be enabled to pay the debt he contracts towards his great mother earth, when taking from the soil the elements which enter into the composition of the commodities required for his support. *It is the condition upon which alone progress can be made.* When it is complied with, she increases her loans from year to year — enabling more and more persons to obtain both food and clothing, with constant increase of power to combine their efforts. When that is not done, motion in the earth diminishes, and men are seen gradually increasing their distances from each other, with steady diminution in the power of association, and constant increase in the taxation resulting from the necessity for effecting changes of place. Such we see to have been the case in Greece and Italy, in Spain and Mexico; and such we now see it to be, not only in Virginia and the Carolinas, but even in the comparatively recently occupied States of Ohio, New York, and Georgia. Why this has been so in times that are past, and why it is so now, requires to be explained.

To the men who live by the work of appropriation, increase of commerce is not desirable—its growth being everywhere attended by diminution in the splendor and magnificence of those who desire to control the movements of society with a view to their own advantage. The politician profits by the separation of his fellow-men, and so is it with the lawyer, the trader, the great proprietor of badly-cultivated land, and all others of the classes whose means of support and illustration are derived from standing between those who produce commodities and those who require them for consumption. All these men profit, temporarily, by preventing continuity in the motion of society; and the greater their power so to do, the greater is the *proportion* of the product of labor that enures to them, and the smaller that which remains to be divided among the laborers.

The broker does not desire that his principals may come together, and arrange their affairs without his intervention. So far, indeed, is it to the contrary, that the more widely they are separated, the greater is his power to accumulate fortune at their expense — purchasing for himself, to their injury, when prices are low, and selling for himself, again at the cost of his principals, when prices are high. The owner of slaves lives by preventing association among his people—requiring them to bring to him all the commodities they produce, and to come to him for all they need to consume. The wagoner knows that the more numerous the obstacles between the producer and his market, the greater will be the demand for horses and wagons, and the larger will be the proportion of the commodities retained by him as compensation for his services. The ship-owner rejoices when men are forced to separate from each other, as in the case of the late Crimean war; or when poverty compels them to abandon their homes and fly to distant lands — because it produces a demand for ships. Equally does he rejoice when crops are large, and the quantity seeking transportation steadily accumulates — causing a rise of freights. The real and permanent interests of all classes of men are one and the same, but their apparent and temporary interests are different; and therefore it is that we see individuals and nations constantly engaged in pursuing the latter, to the entire exclusion of the former. Blinded by the idea of present profit and grandeur, the great men of Greece, and of Rome, overlooked the fact that they were steadily exhausting the powers of the community of which they formed a part; and, blindly following in their track, those of Venice and Genoa, France and Holland, Spain and Portugal, have pursued a course precisely similar, and attended always with the same results.

So has it been, invariably, with the trader, whose great desire has always been, to maintain at their highest point, and even to increase, the necessities of men for the use of the machinery of transportation, and to limit them to the use of that of which he himself was owner. The more completely those ends could be attained, the more perfect became the centralization of power — the more splendid became the places at which exchanges were required to be made — and the greater was his temporary prosperity; but the more rapid was his decline, and the more complete his ruin. The Phœnicians and Carthaginians, the Venetians and Genoese, the Spaniards and Portuguese, the Hanseatics and their rivals of Holland, showed themselves at all times unsparing in their efforts to compel their colonists to come to their ports, and to use their ships. While seeking thus a monopoly of power as a means of obtaining wealth, all their power was used for the purpose of maintaining at its highest point the burden imposed upon others by the necessity for effecting changes of place. This, again, gave them advantages for the purchase of raw produce, by causing its accumulation in their ports — subject, of course, as in the present day, to heavy charges and great risk; and equal advantages for its sale, when finished, and ready for consumption.

Thus did they enrich themselves for the moment, while greatly impoverishing all dependent upon their aid — precisely as we see now to be the case with individuals and companies trading with the poor aborigines of this western continent; with the people of Mexico; with the Finns and Lapps of Northern Europe, the natives of the Pacific, and of Africa.

Exhausting the people with whom they traded, they found a perpetually increasing difficulty in the maintenance of trade, because of constantly increasing famines and pestilences, such as now so frequently occur in Ireland, and in India. As population declined, so declined the power to maintain the roads and bridges by which to go to market — whether to sell the wretched produce of their lands, or to purchase the things required for consumption—a process now seen in operation in Jamaica and Ireland, in India, and in Mexico; in all of which the variety of the products of the land is constantly diminishing, with correspondent tendency to diminution in their quantity. In no country is this more emphatically the case than in Turkey, in regard to which a recent traveller says that "in each district the great bulk of the agricultural classes cultivate the same articles of produce, and pursue the same routine of culture; consequently, every man possesses a superfluity of the articles which his neighbor is desirous of selling"* — being precisely the state of things existing in Brazil and India, Virginia and Carolina. Under such circumstances — there being no power to maintain commerce — the poor cultivator finds himself subjected to the "tender mercies" of the trader, whose power over him grows with the decline of his ability to maintain intercourse with his fellow-men; and therefore it is, that he is there so much enslaved.—Such are the results which follow necessarily from rendering man an instrument to be used by trade; but, that the latter fails to profit by such injustice, is proved by the decline, and ultimate fall, of the communities whose prosperity has been due exclusively to trade.

§ 7. Freedom grows with the growth of the power of association and combination. The obstacle to association is that resulting from the distance between men and their fellow-men. That distance diminishes as men are enabled to obtain instruments by

* Blackwood's Magazine, November, 1854.

help of which to command the services of nature, and to develop the treasures of the earth. With every new development, they are enabled to command the aid of better machinery to be used in the work of transportation, while steadily diminishing the necessity for transportation — with constant increase in the power of combination, and in the growth of freedom.

Such, however, are not the doctrines of modern political economy — of the system which is based upon the idea of the "constantly increasing sterility of the soil," and which finds in tables of imports and exports, in an increased demand for ships, and in a growing necessity for the services of the trader, evidences of national prosperity and power. Now, as when, almost a century since, the idea was denounced by Adam Smith, "England's Treasure" is sought in the "foreign trade;" and "the inland, or home trade," which he regarded as "the most important of all" — as the one "in which an equal capital afforded the greatest returns, and created the greatest employment to the people of the country" — is considered as being "only subsidiary to the foreign trade."* To what extent it is, that we owe to the continued existence of this essential error, the invention of the idea of over-population, the reader will be prepared to judge after an examination of the working of the British colonial system.

* Wealth of Nations, book 4, chap. 1. Mr. McCulloch, in his Discourse introductory to the Wealth of Nations, denounces this as one of the important errors of its author — contending that the labor employed in carrying goods is as advantageous as that given to their production. Dr. Smith loved Commerce. His successors glorify Trade; and therefore is it that the latter are led, to use the words of M. Droz, to consider men as having been "made for products, and not products for men."

# CHAPTER XI.

## THE SAME SUBJECT CONTINUED.

§ 1. The states to whose policy reference has thus far been made, were content to limit themselves to restrictions upon the communities within their control, as regarded their connections with each other, and with other communities that were beyond it — without attempting in any manner to restrict them in regard to their internal arrangements. The early Grecian colonies were as free to maintain commerce at home, or abroad, as were the states by whose citizens they had been founded; and hence it is, that there was seen in the cities of Sicily, and of Magna Græcia, the same development of individuality that everywhere else distinguished the Grecian civilization. The people of Spain, Corsica, or Sardinia might, if they would, make such alterations in the forms of their various products as were required to fit them for immediate consumption; but, if they desired to send them to Egypt, or to Greece, they were then obliged to pass them through the port of Carthage. Spain and Portugal denied to the Indies the right of trading with Holland, or with England, except through the ports of Seville or of Lisbon; but they never interfered with the domestic employments of Mexico, or of Brazil—of the people of Goa, or Manilla. France sought to establish colonies in the Eastern and Western Indies, but the policy of Colbert was based upon the idea of developing agriculture, by means of manufactures, and of commerce. Far otherwise has it been, in the great colonial system of modern times, to which the attention of the reader will now be asked — a system differing as much from that of Greece, as did that of early Attica—which gave to colonists the enjoyment of all the rights exercised by the people of the parent state — from that later one, which annihilated all local institutions by making the populace of Athens judges in the last resort, in all cases affecting the lives and fortunes of those who had now, from the position of fellow-citizens, fallen into that of subjects.

In the colonial system of England it is, that we, for the first time, meet with *prohibitions of that association of man with his fellow-man which leads to the development of the individual faculties*—and with regulations having for their object the maintenance, and at its highest point, of the difficulties resulting from the necessity for effecting changes in the place of matter. Nearly two centuries have now elapsed since the merchants of London prayed their government to use its best efforts for "the discouragement of the woollen manufacture of Ireland;" in order thus to diminish the habit of combined action which was then rapidly obtaining in that country, and to prevent in future the consumption of Irish wool until it should first have passed through the looms of England. Instead of converting it into cloth at home, they were required to send it abroad in its rudest state, and receive it back again in a finished one—thereby establishing the supremacy of trade, at the expense of commerce. Already interdicted from all direct intercourse with foreigners, the same interdiction was now extended to commerce among themselves; and thus did the system go far ahead of all that previously had existed, in increasing the necessity for transportation, and augmenting the difficulty of association.

Trade becoming paramount, wars were waged for the purpose of obtaining colonies; or, according to Adam Smith, for "raising up colonies of customers;" for the accomplishment of which desire it was required that all attempts at local association among the colonists should be as effectually discouraged as they had already been in Ireland.

That they were so, is seen in the fact that the first attempt at manufacturing any species of cloth in the American provinces was followed by interference on the part of the British legislature. In 1710, the House of Commons declared, "that the erecting of manufactories in the colonies had a tendency to lessen their dependence on Great Britain." Shortly after, complaints being made to Parliament that the colonists were setting up manufactories for themselves, the House of Commons ordered the Board of Trade to report upon the subject, as, at great length, was done. In 1732, the exportation of hats from province to province was prohibited, and the number of hatters' apprentices was limited by law. In 1750, the erection of any mill, or other engine, for splitting or rolling iron, was prohibited; but pig iron was allowed to be imported into England duty free, that it might there be manufactured, and sent back again. At a later period, Lord Chatham declared, that he would not allow the colonists to make even a hobnail for themselves. Such was the system practised towards these colonies. That in relation to the world at large is found in the following list of acts of Parliament:—

By the act, 5 George III., [1765,] the exportation of artisans was prohibited under a heavy penalty. By that of 21 George III., [1781,] the exportation of utensils required for the manufacture of woollens or silk was likewise prohibited. By that of 22 George III., [1782,] the prohibition was extended to artificers in printing calicoes, cottons, muslins, or linens, or in making blocks and implements to be used in their manufacture. By that of 25 George III., [1785,] it was further extended to tools used in the iron and steel manufactures, and to the workmen employed therein. By that of 39 George III., [1799,] it was further extended so as to embrace colliers.*

These laws continued in full force until thirty years since, when, much machinery having been smuggled abroad, the prohibition as to the export of artisans was abolished; and all those relating to that of machinery were so far relaxed, that permission might be had for the exportation of all the more common articles—discretion having been given to the Board of Trade, which decides upon each application, "according to the merits of the case." But little difficulty is now, it is said, experienced by merchants, who generally know as to what machines "the indulgence will be extended, and from what it will be withheld," almost as certainly as if it had been settled by act of Parliament; yet it is deemed ad-

* "If any artificer has gone beyond the seas, and is exercising or teaching his trade in any foreign country, upon warning being given to him by any of his majesty's ministers, or consuls, abroad, or by one of his majesty's secretaries of state for the time being, if he does not, within six months after such warning, return into this realm, and from thenceforth abide and inhabit within the same, he is from thenceforth declared incapable of taking any legacy devised to him within this kingdom, or of being executor or administrator to any person, or of taking any lands by descent, devise, or purchase. He likewise forfeits to the king all his lands, goods, and chattels, is declared an alien in every respect, and is put out of the king's protection."—*Wealth of Nations*, book 4, chap. viii.

vantageous to have it left discretionary with the Board, that they may have "the power of regulating the matter, according to the changing interests of commerce."*

The whole legislation of Great Britain on this subject was thus directed to the one great object of preventing the people of her colonies, and those of independent nations, from obtaining machinery that might enable them to combine their exertions for the purpose of obtaining cloth or iron—and thus *compelling* them to bring to her their raw materials, that she might convert them into the commodities required for consumption, to be then, in part, returned to the producers—burdened with heavy charges for the work of transportation and conversion.

The wide extent of the British empire, and the extraordinary amount of influence that has been exercised by the British people, would, under any circumstances, have rendered its system—differing, as it does, from all others—worthy of special attention by the economist; but the necessity therefor is greatly increased by the fact, that it is to the country by which that policy was established, that the world has been indebted for the theory of over-population. That theory is correct, or it is not. Matter tends to take upon itself the form of man in a ratio more rapid than that in which it tends to take that of potatoes and turnips; or it tends to take upon itself that of potatoes and turnips in a ratio more rapid than that of man. That the former is the case, and that we should, therefore, discourage the growth of population, we are assured by all the English economists; and, in proof that such are the facts, we are pointed to the misery and destitution of both Britain and Ireland; but, before admitting the existence of error on the part of the Creator, it is proper that we examine the actions of his creatures, with a view to ascertain to what extent it is to them that this state of things is due. If the natural laws are really such as, by Messrs. Malthus and Ricardo, they are said to be, then, the more thorough the investigation of the working of the system under which this misery and destitution has arisen, the more completely will the accuracy of those gentlemen, and their reputation as social philosophers, be established; but, if they are wrong—if no such natural laws exist—then may careful examination enable us to detect the cause of the error into

* Porter: Progress of the Nation, p. 163.

which they fell. In making it, space will be required, and for the reason that TIME constitutes so important an element in the problem to be solved. "The child is," as we are told, "father to the man" — and, in like manner, the communities of the past are fathers to those of the present. The pauperism of England— to the study of which the idea of over-population was due — was the growth of time; and if we desire to understand the causes of its existence, we must examine the policy of that country for the half century that preceded Mr. Malthus, and the one which has since elapsed. The causes of the existing condition of Ireland date back hundreds of years; and if we seek to understand why Jamaica is being abandoned, we must study the course of operation there pursued in the last and present century.

§ 2. The one great need of man is that of combination with his fellow-men; and the one great obstacle to its accomplishment is, as the reader has already seen, the absence of those differences which result from diversity of employments, and fit him for association. The object that, by means of the laws above referred to, was sought to be obtained, was the prevention of the existence of those differences, and the perpetuation of a state of society in which the people of other lands should continue mere tillers of the earth—compelled to constant exhaustion of the soil, by reason of the necessity for sending abroad their commodities in the rudest forms, to be worked up abroad — and constant exhaustion of themselves, consequent upon the enormous transportation to which they thus were subjected. This, in its turn, involved dispersion — constantly increasing by reason of the perpetually increasing necessity for resorting to new and more distant soils; with constant increase in the *proportion* of the labor of the community required to be given to the works of trade and transportation, and diminution in the *proportion* that could be given to producing commodities to be transported or exchanged. It was, in effect, *the sacrifice of commerce at the shrine of trade*, and tended, *necessarily*, to the enslavement of man in all the communities in which it could be enforced.*

* That the objects of the system were precisely what is here described, is shown in the following passages from a work of authority in its day — Gee on Trade, published in 1750:—

The harmony of the system of which our planet forms a part is due to the existence of local gravitation, by help of which each and every of its members is enabled to preserve its perfect individuality, although exposed to attraction so mighty in extent as is that exerted by the sun. So long as those forces continue in equal balance, harmony will be preserved; but should the central force ever, even for a moment, predominate over the local ones, every planet would fall at once to ruin, and universal chaos would be the inevitable consequence. Such, too, should be the result of excess of centralization in the social world, and that it has been so, is shown by the experience of Athens and Rome, Carthage and Venice; and yet, the centralization sought to be effected by their

"Manufactures in American colonies should be discouraged, prohibited." * * * "We ought always to keep a watchful eye over our colonies, *to restrain them from setting up any of the manufactures which are carried on in Great Britain;* and any such attempts should be crushed in the beginning, for if they are suffered to grow up to maturity, it will be difficult to suppress them." * * * "Our colonies are much in the same state as Ireland was in when they began the woollen manufactory, *and as their numbers increase, will fall upon manufactures for clothing themselves, if due care be not taken to find employment* for them in raising such productions as may enable them to furnish themselves with all the necessaries from us." * * * "As they will have the providing rough materials to themselves, so shall we have the manufacturing of them. If encouragement be given for raising hemp, flax, &c., doubtless they will soon begin to manufacture, if not prevented. Therefore, to stop the progress of any such manufacture, it is proposed that no *weaver* have *liberty* to set up any looms, without first registering at an office kept for that purpose, and the name and place of abode of any journeyman that shall work for him." * * * "That all slitting-mills, and engines for drawing wire or weaving stockings, *be put down.*" * * * "*That all negroes shall be prohibited from weaving either linen or woollen, or spinning or combing of wool, or working at any manufacture of iron,* further than making it into pig or bar iron. That they also be *prohibited* from manufacturing *hats, stockings, or leather of any kind.* This limitation will not abridge the planters of any liberty they now enjoy—on the contrary, it will then turn their industry to promoting and raising those rough materials." * * * "If we examine into the circumstances of the inhabitants of our plantations, and our own, it will appear that *not one-fourth part of their product redounds to their own profit, for, out of all that comes here, they only carry back clothing and other accommodations for their families,* all of which is of the merchandise and manufacture of this kingdom." * * * "All these advantages we receive by the plantations, *besides the mortgages on the planters' estates and the high interest they pay us, which is very considerable;* and, therefore, very great care ought to be taken, in regulating all the affairs of the colonists, that the planters are not put under too many difficulties, but encouraged to go on cheerfully." * * * "New England and the northern colonies have not commodities and products enough to send us in return for purchasing their necessary clothing, but are under very great difficulties; and, therefore, any ordinary sort sell with them; and when they have *grown out of fashion with us, they are new-fashioned enough for them.*"

systems of policy was to the last degree unimportant when compared with that endeavored to be produced by the system above described. In their cases it was commerce with distant men, alone, that was to be impeded; but here it was the greatest of all commerce—commerce at home—the power of association, and all development of individuality, that were to be annihilated. For the accomplishment of that object no effort was omitted. Commodities in a crude state, subject to heavy charges for transportation, as in the case of paddy (or rough rice) and sugar, were admitted at low duties; whereas clean rice and refined sugar were charged with duties so heavy as to offer a large bounty in favor of their export from India or the West Indies in the crudest shape — and even then they could be sent to the world only through an English port, or an English ship.

Prohibitions of manufactures, on one hand, and bounties on the import of raw materials, on the other, were thus resorted to, with a view to prevent the colonists from making those changes in the forms of matter that were required for fitting the products of the earth for consumption among themselves. The one great object of the system was that of maintaining in its most bulky form the commodity requiring to be transported, while diminishing to the smallest size the machinery by which the work of transportation and conversion was to be effected — thereby enriching the trader and transporter at the cost of both consumer and producer. The more perfectly it could be carried out, the smaller would be the quantity of cloth obtainable by the man who produced sugar; the smaller would be the quantity of sugar obtainable by him to whose labor the cloth was due; the greater would be the tendency to have the appearance of population pressing on the limits of subsistence; and the greater would be the tendency to find in erroneous arrangements of the Creator an apology for a state of affairs whose existence was due solely to the contrivances of man.

§ 3. Society, association, and commerce are, as has been shown, but different forms of expression for the same idea — and that idea the first of all the needs of man. Without association there can be no society, and without society there can be no commerce. All of these words describe the motion among men resulting from exchange of services or ideas, the products of muscular or intellectual effort. The more perfect the form of society, the greater will always be the differences among its parts, the more continuous and regular will be their motion among each other, and the greater will be the force exerted. So is it with all the machinery contrived by man for the purpose of subduing to his service the wonderful forces of nature. The marvels accomplished by the steam-engine are great — so great, that they would be deemed wholly incredible by a man who had passed from the world half a century since; and yet, it is scarcely possible to fix a price that might not now be paid for the secret of a perfectly acting rotary engine, because by its help the rapidity of motion could be still so much increased. It is the continuous motion of society that is sought for by men when they prefer to arrange business face to face, by means of conversation, in preference to the constantly intermitting motion of correspondence. It is that motion which is sought by every inventor of a machine — every mill-owner—every man, in fact, that desires to increase his power over the natural forces furnished for the use of man. It is that motion which is described by Adam Smith in the following passages, given thus at length, because their illustrious author is so frequently quoted as authority for the system that looks to the building up of trade at the cost of commerce :—

"An inland country, naturally fertile and easily cultivated, produces a great surplus of provisions beyond what is necessary for maintaining the cultivators; and on account of the expense of land carriage, and inconveniency of river navigation, it may frequently be difficult to send this surplus abroad. Abundance, therefore, renders provisions cheap, and encourages a great number of workmen to settle in the neighborhood, who find that their industry can there procure them more of the necessaries and conveniences of life than in other places. They work up the materials of manufacture which the land produces, and exchange their finished work, or, what is the same thing, the price of it, for more materials and provisions. *They give a new value to the surplus part of the rude produce, by saving the expense of carrying it to the water-side or to some distant market;* and they furnish the cultivators with something in exchange for it, that is either useful or agreeable to them, upon easier terms than they could have obtained it before. The cultivators get a better price for their surplus produce, and can purchase cheaper other conveniences which they have occasion for. They are thus both encouraged and enabled to increase this surplus produce by a further improvement and better cultivation of the land; and as the fertility of the land has given birth to the manufacture, so the progress of the manufacture reacts upon the land, and increases still further its fertility. The manufacturers first supply the neighborhood, and afterwards, as their work improves and refines, more distant markets. *For, though neither the rude produce, nor even the coarse manufacture, could, without the greatest difficulty, support the expense of a considerable land carriage, the refined and improved manufacture easily may. In a small bulk it frequently contains the price of a great quantity of the raw produce. A piece of fine cloth, for example, which weighs only eighty pounds, contains in it the price, not only of eighty pounds of wool, but sometimes of several thousand weight of corn, the maintenance of the different working people, and of their immediate employers.* The corn which could with difficulty have been carried abroad in its own shape, is in this manner virtually exported in that of the complete manufacture, *and may easily be sent to the remotest corners of the world.* In this manner have grown up naturally, and, as it were, of their own accord, the manufactures of Leeds, Halifax, Sheffield, Birmingham, and Wolverhampton. Such manufactures are the offspring of agriculture."*

"The great commerce of every civilized society is that carried on between the inhabitants of the town and those of the country. It consists in the exchange of rude for manufactured produce, either immediately, or by the intervention of money, or of some sort of paper which represents money. The country supplies the town with the means of subsistence and the materials of manufacture. The town repays this supply, by sending back a part of the manufactured produce to the inhabitants of the country. The town, in which there neither is, nor can be, any reproduction of substances, may very properly be said to gain its whole wealth and subsistence from the country. We must not, however, upon this account, imagine that the gain of the town is the loss of the country. The gains of both are mutual and reciprocal, and the division of labor is in this, as in all other cases, advantageous to

* Wealth of Nations, book 3, chap. iii.

all the different persons employed in the various occupations into which it is subdivided. The inhabitants of the country purchase of the town a greater quantity of manufactured goods with the produce of a much smaller quantity of their own labor, than they must have employed had they attempted to prepare them themselves. The town affords a market for the surplus produce of the country, or what is over and above the maintenance of the cultivators; and it is there that the inhabitants of the country exchange it for something else which is in demand among them. The greater the number and revenue of the inhabitants of the town, the more extensive is the market which it affords to those of the country; and the more extensive that market, it is always the more advantageous to a great number. The corn which grows within a mile of the town sells there for the same price with that which comes from twenty miles distance. But the price of the latter must, generally, not only pay the expense of raising it and bringing it to market, but afford, too, the ordinary profits of agriculture to the farmer. The proprietors and cultivators of the country, therefore, which lies in the neighborhood of the town, over and above the ordinary profits of agriculture, gain, in the price of what they sell, the whole value of the carriage of the like produce that is brought from more distant parts; and they save, besides, the whole value of this carriage in the price of what they buy. Compare the cultivation of the lands in the neighborhood of any considerable town, with that of those which lie at some distance from it, and you will easily satisfy yourself how much the country is benefited by the commerce of the town."*

The motion here described is properly characterized as commerce. The plain good sense of Adam Smith enabled him clearly to comprehend the error of the system which found in exports and imports the only index to prosperity; and also, fully to understand the enormous waste of labor resulting from imposing upon communities a necessity for exporting wool, corn, cotton, and other products of the earth, in their rudest shape, to be returned again in the form of cloth. He was no believer in centralization of any kind. Least of all did he believe in that which looked to compelling all the farmers and planters to go to a single market, and to augmenting the necessity for de-

* Ibid.

pendence on wagons and ships — while increasing the profits of trade, and the *proportion* of every population required to be employed in the work of effecting changes of place. On the contrary, he had full and entire faith in the system of local centres by help of which, as he so clearly saw, commerce had been everywhere so much developed — and that was the system to whose advantage he desired to call the attention of his countrymen. From that hour to the present, however, the system he denounced has been pursued — all the efforts of his countrymen having been directed towards producing the effect of continuing at its highest point the tax of transportation; and here it is, perhaps, that we may find the cause of the idea of over-population.

§ 4. From the date of the conquest of the several WEST INDIA COLONIES, manufactures of every kind were strictly prohibited — the interdiction being carried so far that their inhabitants were not permitted even to refine their own sugar. There was, of course, no employment, even for women and children, but in the labors of the field. All were required to remain producers of raw commodities — maintaining no commerce among themselves, except through the intervention of a people thousands of miles distant, who used their power to such effect as not only to prohibit manufactures, but also to prevent diversification of employment in agriculture itself. In Jamaica, indigo had been tried, but of the price for which it sold in England so large a portion proved to be absorbed by ship-owners, commission-merchants, and the government, that its culture had been abandoned. Coffee was extensively introduced, and as it grows on higher and more salubrious lands, its cultivation would have been of great advantage to the community; but here, as in the case of indigo, so small a portion of its price was received by the producer, that its production was almost abandoned, and was saved only by an agreement to reduce the claims of government to a shilling a pound. The estimated produce being about seven hundred and fifty pounds of merchantable coffee, this amounted to about $180 per acre.* The ultimate effect of the system was that of terminating all commerce among the people — even that which previously had existed between those who raised coffee, on the one hand, and those

* Dallas's History of the Maroons, vol. i. page c

who had sugar to dispose of, on the other — all cultivation but that of the sugar-cane, the one most destructive of life and health, being entirely abandoned.

While commerce among themselves was thus prohibited, all intercourse with foreign nations was interdicted, except through the medium of British ships, ports, and merchants. The trade direct with Africa, however, was sanctioned, for it furnished slaves; and this traffic was continued on a most extensive scale — most of the demand for the Spanish colonies being supplied from the British islands. In 1775, however, the colonial legislature, desirous to prevent the excessive importation of negroes, imposed a duty of £2 per head; but this being petitioned against by the merchants of England, the home government directed its discontinuance.* At this period, the annual export of sugar is stated† to have been 980,346 hundredweights, the gross sales of which, duty free, averaged £1 14*s*. 8*d*. per hundred — making a total of £1,699,421; so large a portion of which, however, was absorbed by freight, commissions, insurance, &c., that the net proceeds of seven hundred and seventy-five sugar estates are stated to have been only £726,992, or less than £1000 each. If to the £973,000 thus deducted, be now added the share of the government, (12*s*. 3*d*. per hundredweight,) and the further charges before the sugar reached the consumer, it will be seen that the producer received but a fourth of the price at which it sold. The planter was, therefore, little more than a superintendent of slaves, who were worked for the benefit of the merchants and the government of Great Britain, and not for his own. Placed between the slave, whom he was obliged to support, on the one hand, and the mortgagee, the merchants and the government, whom he was also obliged to support, on the other, he could take for himself only what was left; and when the crop proved large, and prices fell, he was ruined. The consequences of this are seen in the fact, that in the twenty years following this period, there were sold by the sheriff no less than one hundred and seventy-seven estates; while ninety-two remained unsold in the hands of creditors, and fifty-five were wholly abandoned. Seeing these things, it is not difficult to understand the cause of the extraordinary waste of life exhibited in the British islands. The plan-

* Macpherson, vol. iii. p. 574. † Ibid. vol. iv. p. 255.

ter, unable to accumulate machinery by help of which to command the services of nature, was obliged to depend upon brute force alone; and it was easier for him to buy such force, ready made, on the coast of Africa, than to have it made on his own plantation. Hence it was, that a constant supply of negroes was required for keeping up the population — and hence it has been, that of all who had been imported, little more than one in three was represented on the day of emancipation.*

The planter himself, however, was nearly as much a slave as the negro he had purchased. Ever in debt, his property was generally in the hands of middlemen representing the parties to whom he was indebted — the factors in England, who accumulated fortunes at his expense, and whose agents in the islands enriched themselves at the cost of the nominal owner of the land, on one hand, and of the slaves by whom it was worked, on the other.† At the period above referred to, such persons, one hundred and ninety-three in number, held in charge no less than six hundred and six works—yielding eighty thousand hogsheads of sugar, and thirty-six hundred puncheons of rum, the value of which might be taken at £4,000,000, upon which they were entitled to six per cent. The more, however, the planter was distressed, the more the attorney fattened — and thus have we here a state of things precisely similar to that existing in Ireland, where absentees' estates were managed by middlemen having no interest in the land, or in the virtual slaves upon it; and anxious only to take from both all that could be taken — giving as little as possible back to either. In both, centralization, absenteeism, and slavery walked hand in hand together, as they had done in the days of the Scipios, the Catos, the Pompeys, and the Cæsars.

To what, however, was this absenteeism due? Why was it that in Jamaica, as well as in Ireland, the land-owners did not reside on their estates — attending personally to their management? Because the policy which forbade that even the sugar

* The total number imported into the British islands cannot have been less than 1,700,000; and yet the number at the date of emancipation was but 660,000. The number imported into the United States cannot have exceeded half a million; but they have grown to three and a half millions.

† The reader who desires fully to understand the waste and robbery of a British West Indian plantation, the slavery of its owner, and the causes of the exhaustion of those fertile islands, may do so by consulting the History of the Maroons, by R. C. Dallas, 2 vols. 8vo: London, 1803.

itself should be refined on the island—and thus limited the whole population, old and young, male and female, to the mere culture of sugar—effectually prevented the growth of any middle class to form the population of towns in which the planter might find the society required for inducing him to regard the island as his home. In the French islands, all was different. The French government never having interfered to prevent the growth of commerce among their colonists, towns had grown up, and men of all descriptions had come from France—intending to make of the islands *their home;* whereas, the English colonists looked only to realizing fortunes, and then returning to England to spend them. The one system looked to the development of individuality and the promotion of commerce; whereas, the other looked to the destruction of both.

Widely different were the systems, and as widely so have been the results—the French islands presenting everywhere evidence of their being occupied by men who feel themselves at home, and the English ones offering almost everywhere evidence of having been occupied by men bent on extracting from the land and the laborer all that could be obtained, and then abandoning the one and burying the other. In the one were to be found shops of every kind, at which clothing, books, jewellery, and other commodities, could be obtained; whereas, in the other—no such shops existing—those who had purchases to make, were obliged to import directly from England. In the one, there was combination of effort—commerce, society; whereas, in the other, there was only trade.*

Under such a system no towns could arise, and therefore could there be no schools. Hence it was, that the planter was forced to send his children to England to be educated; there to contract a love for European, and a dislike for colonial, life. At death, his property passed, as a matter of course, into the hands of agents—of men whose profits were to be augmented by increase of shipments, at whatever cost of life obtained. Such was the natural result of a policy which denied to the men, the women, and the children the privilege of giving themselves to any in-door pursuits—the mechanic not being needed where machinery could not be used, and the town being unable to grow where there could be neither artisans nor schools.

* COLERIDGE: Six Months in the West Indies, p. 131.

The export of rum generally brought the planter in debt—that is, more than the whole amount for which it sold was absorbed in the various charges upon it. The people of England paid a million of pounds sterling for a certain product of the laborers of Jamaica, not a shilling of which ever reached the planter to be applied to the amelioration of his estate, to the improvement of his cultivation, or to the advantage of the people by whom the work was performed.* The reader will thus see that Mr. Gee did not exaggerate, when he gave it as one of the recommendations of the colonial system, that the colonists left in England three-fourths of all their products — the difference being swallowed up by those who made or superintended the exchanges. Such was the result desired by those who compelled the planter to depend on a distant market in which to sell all he raised, and to purchase all he required to consume. The more he took from his land, the more it was exhausted, and the less he obtained for its products—large crops swelling greatly the amount of freights, storages, commissions, and profits, while as much depressing prices; as we see to be now the case with cotton. The more his land was being ruined, and his slaves were being destroyed, the less, consequently, was his power to purchase machinery by help of which to increase the powers of either. A slave himself to those by whom his labors were directed, it would be unfair to attribute to him the extraordinary waste of life resulting necessarily from the fact that a whole people was thus limited to the labor of the field, and deprived of all power for the maintenance of commerce.

With inexhaustible supplies of timber, the island possessed, even in 1850, not a single saw-mill — although affording an exten-

* The rum sold on its arrival at 3*s.* or 3*s.* 6*d.* a gallon, but the consumer paid for it probably 17*s.*, which were thus divided:—

| | | |
|---|---|---|
| Government, representing the British people at large....... | 11*s.* | 3*d.* |
| Ship-owners, wholesale and retail dealers, &c................ | 5 | 9 |
| Land-owner and laborer.............................................. | 0 | 0 |
| | 17*s.* | |

If we look to sugar, we find a result somewhat better, but of similar character. The English consumer gave for it 80*s.* worth of labor, and those shillings were nearly thus divided:—

| | |
|---|---|
| Government.......................................................... | 27*s.* |
| Ship-owner, merchant, mortgagee, &c. ............................ | 33 |
| Land-owner and laborer............................................ | 20 |
| | 80*s.* |

sive market for lumber from abroad. Yielding, in the greatest abundance, the finest fruits, there were yet no towns-people, with their ships, to carry them to the markets of this country; and for want of markets, they rotted under the trees. "The manufacturing resources of this island," says a recent traveller, "are inexhaustible;"* and so have they always been, but, deprived of the power of combination, its people have been compelled to waste power that, if properly employed, would have paid, a hundred times over, for all the commodities for which they were required look to the distant market. "For six or eight months in the year," as he further says, "nothing is done on the sugar or coffee plantations." "Agriculture, as at present conducted, does not occupy more than half their time"—nor has it ever done so; and it is in this waste of labor, consequent upon the absence of diversification of employment, that we are to find the cause of poverty and decline.

Population diminished, because there could be no improvement in the condition of the laborer, who, while thus limited in the employment of his time, was compelled to support not only himself and his master, but the agent, the commission-merchant, the ship-owner, the mortgagee, the retail trader, and the government; and this under a system that looked to taking every thing from the land and returning nothing to it. Of the amount paid in 1831 by the British people for the products of the 320,000 black laborers of this island, the home government took no less than £3,736,113 10*s.* 6*d.*,† or about $18,000,000, being almost $60 per head; and this for merely superintending the exchanges. Had no such claim been made on the product of the labor of these poor people, the consumer—having his sugar cheaper—would have absorbed twice the quantity, and would thus have enabled the sugar producers to become larger customers to himself.

The contribution of each negro, old and young, male and female, to the maintenance of the British government, amounted, in that year, to not less than £5, or $24—a large sum to be paid by a people limited entirely to agriculture, and destitute of the machinery necessary for making even that productive. If, now, to this heavy burden we add the commissions, freights,

* BIGELOW: Notes on Jamaica, p. 54.

† Martin's West Indies.

insurance, interest, and other charges, it will readily be seen that a system of taxation so grinding could end no otherwise than as it did—in ruin. That such was the tendency of things was seen in the steady diminution of production. In the three years ending with 1802, the average exports were, of

| | Sugar, hhds. | Rum, puncheons. | Coffee, lbs. |
|---|---|---|---|
| | 113,000 | 44,000 | 14,000,000 |
| Whereas, those of the three ending with 1829 were only.................... | 92,000 | 34,000 | 17,000,000 |

The system that looked to depriving the cultivator of the advantage of a market near at hand, in which to sell his products; and from which he could carry home the manure—thus maintaining the powers of his land—was here producing its natural results, in causing the slave to become from day to day more barbarized; and that such was the case was shown by the enormous excess of deaths over births. Evidence of exhaustion was, therefore, seen in every thing connected with the island. Labor and land were declining in value, and the security for the payment of the debt due in England was becoming less from year to year, as more and more the people of other countries were being driven to the work of cultivation, because of the impossibility of competing with England in manufactures. Sugar having declined to little more than a guinea a hundredweight, and rum to little more than two shillings a gallon,* nearly the whole crop was swallowed up in commissions and interest. Under such circumstances, waste of life was inevitable; and therefore it is, that we have seen the importation of hundreds of thousands of men who have perished—leaving behind them no traces of their existence. On whom, however, must rest the responsibility for a state of things so hideous as that which is here exhibited? Not, surely, upon the planter, for he exercised no volition whatsoever. He was not permitted to employ his surplus power in refining his own sugar, nor could he legally introduce a spindle or a loom into the island. He could neither mine coal nor smelt copper ore. Unable to repay his borrowings from the earth, the loans he could obtain from her diminished in quantity; and then, small as they were, they were absorbed by the exchangers and those who superintend the exchanges—exercising the duties of government. Being himself

* Tooke's History of Prices, vol. ii. p. 412.

a mere instrument in their hands for the destruction of negro morals, intellect, and life, it is upon them, and not upon him, must rest the responsibility for the fact that, of all the slaves imported into the island, not more than two-fifths were represented on the day of emancipation.

Nevertheless, he it was that was branded as the tyrant and the destroyer of morals and of life; and public opinion — the public opinion of the same people who had absorbed so large a portion of the product of negro labor—drove the government to the measure of releasing the slave from compulsory service, and appropriating a certain amount to the payment, first, of the mortgage debts due in England — leaving the owner, in most cases, without a shilling for carrying on the work of his plantation. The consequences are seen in the extensive abandonment of land, and in the decline of its value. Any quantity of it may be purchased, prepared for cultivation, and as rich as any in the island, for five dollars an acre; while other land, far richer, naturally, than any in New England, ranges from fifty cents to one dollar. With the decline in the value of land, the laborer tends towards barbarism, and the reason of this may be found in the fact, that the power of association has no existence — that there is no diversity of employment — and that after centuries of connection with a community that boasts of the perfection of its machinery, there is not even a tolerable axe to be found on the island.*

* "I could not learn that there were any estates on the island decently stocked with implements of husbandry. Even the modern axe is not in general use; for felling the larger class of trees, the negroes commonly use what they call an axe, which is shaped much like a wedge, except that it is a little wider at the edge than at the opposite end, at the very extremity of which a perfectly straight handle is inserted. A more awkward thing for chopping could not be well conceived — at least, so I thought until I saw the instrument in yet more general use about the houses in the country, for cutting firewood. It was, in shape, size, and appearance, more like the outer half of the blade of a scythe, stuck into a small wooden handle, than any thing else I can compare it to: with this long knife, for it is nothing else, I have seen negroes hacking at branches of palm for several minutes, to accomplish what a good wood-chopper, with an American axe, would finish at a single stroke. I am not now speaking of the poorer class of negro proprietors, whose poverty or ignorance might excuse this, but of the proprietors of large estates, which have cost their thousands of pounds."—*Bigelow's Notes on Jamaica*, p. 129.

"They have no new manufactories to resort to when they are in want of work; no unaccustomed departments of mechanical or agricultural labor are open to receive them, to stimulate their ingenuity and reward their industry. When they know how to ply the hoe, pick the coffee-berry, and tend the

That the artisan has always been the ally of the agriculturist in his contest with the trader and the government, is shown in every page of the world's history. The first desires to tax him by buying cheaply and selling dearly. The second taxes him for the *privilege* of maintaining commerce; and the more distant the place of exchange, the greater is the power of taxation. The artisan coming nearer to him, the raw materials are converted on the spot, subject to no tax for the maintenance of ship-owners, commission-merchants, or shopkeepers — and then commerce grows with great rapidity.

In a piece of cloth, says Adam Smith, weighing eighty pounds, there are not only more than eighty pounds of wool, but also "several thousand weight of corn, the maintenance of the working people;" and it is the wool and the corn that travel cheaply in the form of cloth. What, however, finally becomes of the corn? Although eaten, it is not destroyed. Going back upon the land, and paying the debt of him by whose labor it had been produced, the land itself becomes enriched, the larger become the crops, and the greater is the power of the farmer to make demand for the services of the artisan. The reward of human effort growing with the growth of value in land, all become rich and free together — and thus it is that the interests of all the members of a community are so closely connected with the adoption of a policy looking to increase in the amount of commerce, and in the value of land. The more perfect the power of combination among men, the greater will be the development of individual faculty, the less will be the power of the trader — and the greater will always be the freedom of man.

The colonial policy above described — looking to the production of results directly the reverse of this — forbade association,

sugar-mills, they have learned almost all the industry of the island can teach them. If, in the sixteen years during which the negroes have enjoyed their freedom, they have made less progress in civilization than their philanthropic champions have promised or anticipated, let the want I have suggested receive some consideration. It may be that even a white peasantry would degenerate under such influences. Reverse this, and when the negro has cropped his sugar or his coffee, create a demand for his labor in the mills and manufactories of which nature has invited the establishment on this island, and before another sixteen years would elapse the world would probably have some new facts to assist them in estimating the natural capabilities of the negro race, of more efficiency in the hands of the philanthropist than all the appeals which he has ever been able to address to the hearts or the consciences of men."—*Ibid.*, p. 156.

because it limited the whole people to a single pursuit. It forbade the immigration of artisans, the growth of towns, or the establishment of schools; and, consequently, forbade the growth of intellect among the laborers, or their owners. It forbade the growth of population, because it drove the women and children to the culture of sugar among the richest and most unhealthy soils of the island. It thus impoverished the land and its owners, exterminated the slave, and weakened the community — making it a mere instrument in the hands of the people who effected and superintended the exchanges — the class of persons that, in all ages, has thriven at the cost of the cultivators of the earth. By separating the consumer from the producer, they were enabled, as has been shown, to take to themselves three-fourths of the whole product, leaving but one-fourth to be divided between the land and labor that had produced it. They, of course, grew strong, while the land-holder and laborer grew weak; and the weaker the latter became, the less was the need for regarding their rights of person or of property.

In this state of things it was, that the master was required to accept a fixed sum of money as compensation for relinquishing his claim to demand of the slave the performance of the work to which he had been accustomed. Unfortunately, however, the system pursued had effectually prevented that improvement of feeling and taste required for producing in the latter a desire for any thing beyond what was indispensable to the maintenance of existence. Towns and shops not having grown, he had not been accustomed even to see the commodities by which his fellow-laborers in the French islands were tempted to exertion. Schools not having existed, even for the whites, he had acquired no wish for books for himself, or for instruction for his children. His wife had acquired no taste for dress — having always been limited to field labor. Suddenly emancipated from control, he gratified the only desire that had been permitted to grow up in him — the love of perfect idleness, to be indulged to whatsoever extent was consistent with obtaining the little food and clothing needed for the support of life.

Widely different would have been the state of affairs had they been permitted to make their exchanges at home — giving cotton and sugar for cloth and iron produced by the labor, and from the soil, of the island. The producer of sugar would then have had all the cloth given for it by the consumer, instead of obtaining a fourth of it—and then the land would have increased in value, the planter would have grown rich, and the laborer would have become free; and that, by virtue of a great natural law, which provides that the more rapid the augmentation of wealth, the greater must be the demand for labor, the greater must be the *quantity* of commodities produced by the laborer, the larger must be his *proportion* of the product, and the greater must be the tendency toward his becoming a free man, and himself a capitalist.

The more perfect the power of association and combination, the less is the need of man for machinery required for effecting changes of place, because his exchanges are chiefly made at home—but the greater is his power to obtain that machinery, because combination enables him to obtain command over the great natural forces given for his use. The less his power to maintain commerce, the greater is his dependence on machinery of transportation, and the less his power to obtain it; and that such was the case in the West Indies is shown by the fact, that in the capital of the rich island of Jamaica, Spanishtown, with a population of five thousand, there was not, five years since, to be found a single shop, nor a respectable hotel, nor even a dray-cart;* and in the whole island there was not a stage, nor any other mode of regular conveyance, by land or water, except on the little railroad, of fifteen miles, from Kingston to the capital.† As a necessary consequence of this state of things, so large a *proportion* of the labor of the community was required for performing the work of transportion within and without the limits of the island, that but a very small *proportion* of it could be given to any other purpose.‡

§ 5. The power to command the services of nature grows with the growth of the power of association—and that the latter may increase, it is essential that larger numbers should be enabled to

* Bigelow's Notes on Jamaica, p. 31. † Ibid. p. 69.

‡ Heavy duties on refined sugar still prevent the colonies from making any step towards improvement. But recently, the governor of Demerara, in a despatch to the British government, stated that by a very trifling additional outlay the planter could ship his whole crop "of a quality almost equal to refined sugar, though made, *bona fide*, by a single process from the raw materials;" but that he dared not do, because it would thereby be subjected to a duty so high as to be prohibitive.

obtain supplies of food from any given space. Modern political economy, however, teaches directly the reverse of this — that, as numbers increase, there arises a necessity for resorting to inferior soils, with constant decline in the power to command nature's services, and constantly increasing difficulty in obtaining food; and that hence arises the disease of over-population. That theory, as the reader has seen, had its origin in England, and was simply an attempt to explain unnatural phenomena, the work of man, by help of imaginary natural laws, attributed to man's Creator.

In a state of barbarism, population is always superabundant. As civilization grows, larger numbers obtain more and better food in return to diminished labor. That such is the fact is proved by the history of the world, in its every page; and yet, if we are to believe Messrs. Malthus, Ricardo, and their disciples, the disease that invariably accompanies the absence of the power of combination, is the one that rages most when the power of association most exists.

In order that the power of man shall increase, there must be development of his latent faculties; but in order that such development may take place, it is indispensable that employments be diversified, and men be enabled to associate. The more rapid the growth of the power over nature, the less is the necessity for effecting changes of place—the less is the *proportion* of the labor of society required for the work of transportation — the less is the power of the soldier, trader, or transporter — and the more completely is it proved that matter takes upon itself the form of food for man in a ratio more rapid than that in which it tends to take the form of man himself.

The system above described, and so much reprobated by Adam Smith, tended to the production of results entirely different. Looking, as it did, to the prevention of association, it increased the *proportion* of the labor of society required for the work of transportation; while by preventing the development of the latent faculties of man, it reduced the subject of its operations to the condition of a mere brute beast. Hence it is that the world has been called upon to witness the extermination of the vast body of people imported into the British West India islands, the pauperization of the people of England, and the invention of a system of political economy that ignores the distinctive qualities of man — retaining only those he has in common with the ox, the wolf, and the horse.

The destruction of life and happiness in both Jamaica and England resulted from the power of trade to control commerce, and to tax it for its purposes. The man of Jamaica producing largely of sugar, and the man of England producing largely of cloth, could they have made their exchanges directly, both would have been well fed and clothed; but, in the process of making their exchanges, so large a proportion was absorbed, that the one could obtain but little cloth, and the other but little sugar. Hence arose the idea of over-population.

That idea having had its origin among British economists, and being now the received theory among the British people, it is required for its refutation to examine the history of the various communities subject to the British system, with a view to ascertain if it is really a law of nature, or if it is only a natural consequence of a policy that looked to the separation of the artisan from the agriculturist, and to the creation of a single workshop for the world. Portugal, Turkey, Ireland, and India having been the countries most subjected to it, all of these will be now examined, with a view to ascertain how far the phenomena there observed correspond with those exhibited in Jamaica.

* How widely different were the foundations upon which the French and English colonial systems were based, may be seen in the facts — first, that Colbert granted to the colonists, the most entire liberty, as regarded the conversion of their rude products of every kind: second, that — regarding their dispersion as tending towards barbarism—he prohibited them from engaging in the collection of furs and skins: third, that he limited, as far as possible, the exportation, to the colonies, of fermented liquors: and fourth, that he interested himself, most warmly, in the prevention of that prostitution of female slaves, which so much abounded in the British islands, and so much disgraces the United States.—For further information respecting the French colonial system, see the recent work of M. Joubleau, *Études sur Colbert*, liv. iii., ch. iii.

# CHAPTER XII.

## THE SAME SUBJECT CONTINUED.

§ 1. THE splendor of PORTUGAL in the sixteenth century, resulting from the exercise throughout the East of her power of appropriation, had, as has ever been the case, been attended with growing weakness; and the close of that century found her, as the reader has seen, reduced to the condition of a Spanish province. Forty years later, she succeeded in re-establishing her independence, and at the close of the seventeenth century she was seen to be engaged in a vigorous effort for securing its continuance, by establishing among her people the habit of association and combination which was required for the development of their faculties and the extension of their commerce. From an early period she had been celebrated for her wool, but had long been deficient in the means of converting it into cloth. Now, however, with a view to carry into effect the idea so well expressed by Adam Smith, that to enable commerce to grow it is essential to compress "not only" the "eighty pounds of wool" but also the "several thousand pounds of corn, the maintenance of the working people," into "a piece of cloth," she had imported foreign artisans by help of whom the woollen manufacture had already so rapidly grown, as fully to meet the home demand for cloth; and thus, while promoting commerce, greatly lessening her dependence on the chances and changes of trade abroad.

The administration, however, passed into other hands, and in 1703 was signed the famous Methuen treaty, by which, in return for favors accorded to her wines, the idea of creating at home a market for food and wool, and thus promoting commerce, was entirely repudiated. At once, her markets were inundated, her manufactures were ruined — and the precious metals disappeared.*

* "But after the taking off of the prohibition, we brought away so much of their silver as to leave them very little for their necessary occasions; and then we began to bring away their gold."—*British Merchant*, vol. iii. p. 15.

Thus reconverted into a purely agricultural country, exhaustion of her soil followed as a necessary consequence; and exhaustion was followed by decline in the numbers of her people, so long continued that the population is now only three millions — the decrease, in the last century alone, having been nearly seven hundred thousand. With declining numbers and diminished power of combination, there has been an increase in the difficulty of effecting changes in the place of things or people; and in the country that even in the days of the Cæsars was supplied with roads, the mails are now carried on horseback, and at the rate of three miles an hour, between the capital and the provincial cities. There being no public conveyance of any kind throughout the country, except on the road between Lisbon and Oporto, travellers are compelled to hire mules to enable themselves to pass from place to place. "Not only," says a recent traveller, "are there no roads worthy of the name," but "the very streets and thoroughfares are converted into nurseries for manure;" and "the only mode of conveying heavy goods from one port to another is in bullock-carts, and for light goods on mules, or on the backs of *gallegos*"—the value of man being there so small that he is regarded as a mere beast of burden.

Isolation follows necessarily in the train of depopulation, and the human faculties diminish in their development—machinery then declining in quality, and nature acquiring power at the cost of man. "It is surprising," says another traveller, "how ignorant, or at least superficially acquainted, the Portuguese are with every kind of handicraft: a carpenter is awkward and clumsy, spoiling every work he attempts; and the way in which the doors and woodwork even of good houses are finished would have suited the rudest ages. Their carriages of all kinds, from the hidalgo's family coach to the peasant's market cart, their agricultural implements, locks and keys, &c., are ludicrously bad. They seem to disdain improvement, and are so infinitely below par, so strikingly inferior to the rest of Europe, as to form a sort of disgraceful wonder in the middle of the nineteenth century."

The *utility* of the earth, and of its products, consequently diminishes, with constant increase in the *value* of commodities required for the use of man, and decline in the value of man himself—being directly the reverse of what is observed in all those countries in which he is permitted the indulgence of that prime want of his nature which leads him to seek association and combination with his fellow-men.

The system has endured for a century and a half, during all which time the power to command the services of nature has declined, as is manifest from the constantly growing difficulty of obtaining the food, the clothing, and the shelter required for man's support. The *proportion* of the products of labor required for paying the expenses of transportation has steadily increased, as the quantity of things produced has decreased; and the result is now seen in the fact that with the decline of commerce at home, the power to maintain it abroad has so far diminished that Portugal has ceased to enter into the consideration even of those by whom, in 1703, her trade was so greatly coveted. Individuality of the community has disappeared with the disappearance of individuality in the people of whom it is composed; and, as we are told in a recent work of high reputation, "the finances are in the most deplorable condition, the treasury is dry, and all branches of the public service suffer. A carelessness and a mutual apathy reign not only throughout the government, but also throughout the nation. While improvement is sought everywhere else throughout Europe, Portugal remains stationary. The postal service of the country offers a curious example of this, nineteen to twenty-one days being still required for a letter to go and come between Lisbon and Braganza, a distance of 423½ kilometres, (or little over 300 miles.) All the resources of the state are exhausted, and it is probable that the receipts will not give one-third of the amount for which they figure in the budget."*

Such was the state of affairs a few years since, but the exhaustive effects of an exclusive agriculture are becoming from year to year more manifest. The domestic market for corn was exchanged for a foreign one for the grape, but now that itself has failed because of the unceasing withdrawal from the soil of all the elements of which grapes are composed. Whole classes in Portugal are now reduced to utter poverty, while in Madeira men perish by thousands for want of food — as happens everywhere in the absence of that diversification of employments which gives rise to commerce, and developes the latent faculties of man. The nation

* Annuaire de l'Economie Politique, 1849, p. 322.

that commences with the export of the raw products of the soil, must end with the export, or extermination, of men.

When population increases and men come together, even the poor land is made rich; and thus it is, that "the power of manure causes the poor lands of the department of the Seine to yield thrice as much as those of the Loire."* When population diminishes, and men are thereby forced to live at greater distances from each other, even the rich lands become impoverished; and of this no better evidence need be sought than that here furnished. In the one case, each day brings men nearer to that perfect freedom of thought, speech, and action essential to the growth of commerce. In the other, they become from day to day more barbarized and enslaved, and the women are more and more driven to the field, there to become the slaves of fathers, husbands, brothers, and sons, while the community becomes, from day to day, more and more the prey of those classes which "live, and move, and have their being," by virtue of the exercise of their powers of appropriation — the soldier and the trader. The strength of nations is in the inverse ratio of the *proportions* borne by them to the mass of which the community is composed. Those proportions grow with the decline of commerce. Commerce grows with every diminution in the necessity for effecting changes of place, and for depending on the services of men who live by carrying arms, sailing ships, or driving wagons. It declines with every increase therein. Were evidence of this desired, it would be found on comparing the past and present of the naturally rich country of Portugal, so long subjected to the policy of the country in which originated the theory of over-population.

§ 2. Of all the countries of Europe, there is none possessed of natural advantages to enable it to compare with those constituting the Turkish Empire in Europe and Asia. Wool and silk, corn, oil, and tobacco, might, with proper cultivation, be produced in almost unlimited quantity; while Thessaly and Macedonia, long celebrated for the production of cotton, abound in lands uncultivated, capable of yielding it in sufficient extent to clothe all Europe. Coal and iron ore abound, and in quality equal to any in the world; while in parts of the empire "the hills seem a mass

* De Jonnès's Statistique de la France, p. 129.

of carbonate of copper." Nature has done every thing for that country; and yet, of all the people of Europe, the Turkish rayah approaches in condition nearest to a slave; and of all the governments of Europe, that of Turkey is most compelled to submit to the dictation, not only of foreign nations, but also of foreign and domestic traders in money and other merchandise. Why it is so, we may now inquire.

Two centuries since, the trade with Turkey constituted the most important portion of that maintained by Western Europe; and Turkish merchants ranked among the wealthiest of those who frequented the markets of the West. A little later, its government united with those of France and England in a treaty by which it bound itself to charge no higher duty upon their imports than three per cent.; and as their vessels were, by the same treaty, exempted from all port-charges, the system thus established was, practically, one of the most absolute and entire freedom of trade.

For more than a century following, Turkey was still enabled to some extent to compete in manufactures with the nations of the West, and to preserve among her people the power and habit of association. "Ambelakaia," says M. de Beaujour, "supplied industrious Germany, not by the perfection of its jennies, but by the industry of its spindle and distaff. It taught Montpellier the art of dyeing, not from experimental chairs, but because dyeing was with it a domestic and culinary operation, subject to daily observation in every kitchen; and by the simplicity and honesty, not the science, of its system, it reads a lesson to commercial associations, and holds up an example — unparalleled in the commercial history of Europe — of a joint-stock and labor company ably and economically and successfully administered, in which the interests of industry and capital were long equally represented. Yet the system of administration with which all this is connected is common to the thousand hamlets of Thessaly that have not emerged from their insignificance; but Ambelakaia for twenty years was left alone."*

Revenue from the customs being at an end, whatever deficiency might by the treaty have been created, required, of course, to be supplied by means of direct taxation; and, accordingly, the govern-

* Tableau du Commerce de la Grèce, quoted by Urquhart, Resources of Turkey, p. 47.

ment has from that time to the present been wholly dependent upon poll taxes, house taxes, and land taxes — the latter collected first in the form of an assessment upon the land itself, and again in that of export duties.* Trade was freed from all let, or hindrance; but commerce at home was shackled by means of constant interferences.

Despite those interferences, the system of local centres, neutralizing the attractions of the great political and trading capitals, continued in existence, as we have seen, until the close of the last century; and, as a consequence, the country remained, as yet, both rich and strong. Even then, however, Great Britain had invented machinery for spinning cotton, and had — by prohibiting its export, as well as that of all the artisans by whose help it might elsewhere have been made—provided that all the cotton of the world should be brought to her looms, to be there converted into cloth. Turkey, having cotton to sell, had been accustomed to sell it in the form of cloth; and the power so to do had enabled her to maintain commerce at home and abroad. Now, however, that commerce was to cease—giving place to trade; and cease it did — Ambelakaia, and various other seats of manufactures, having been entirely abandoned within twenty years from the date of the description given above. Of 600 looms at Scutari in 1812, but 40 remained in 1821; and of the 2000 weaving establishments at Tournovo in 1812, but 200 remained in 1830. Since then, the manufacture has, it is believed, entirely disappeared.

For a time, cotton went abroad, to be returned in the form of yarn, thus making a voyage of thousands of miles in search of the little spindle; but this trade, even, has passed away, and as a consequence, there has been a great decline in wages, affecting every description of labor. "The profits, twenty years since," says Mr. Urquhart, writing in 1832, "had been reduced to one-half, and sometimes to one-third, by the introduction of English cottons, which, though they have reduced the home price, and ar-

* The reader who reflects that the price of the commodities exported is fixed in the general market of the world, and is not in any manner affected by the distribution of the proceeds between the people and the government, will readily see that such duties are in effect a land tax, with the additional disadvantage of involving constant interference with commerce. So far as foreigners were concerned, the system was, and is, one of perfect free trade and direct taxation.

rested the export of cotton-yarn from Turkey," had then "not yet supplanted the home manufacture in any visible degree"—the people having been compelled to go on "working merely for bread, and reducing their price, in a struggle of hopeless competition. The industry, however, of the women and children," as he continues, "is most remarkable; in every interval of labor, tending the cattle, and carrying water—the spindle and distaff, as in the days of Xerxes, being never out of their hands. The children are assiduously at work, from the moment their little fingers can turn the spindle. About Ambelakaia, the former focus of the cotton-yarn trade, the peasantry has suffered dreadfully from this, though formerly the women could earn as much in-doors as their husbands in the field, at present, their daily profit does not exceed twenty paras, if realized, for often they cannot dispose of the yarn when spun.*"

Women's wages were then but four cents a day — the "unremitting labor of a week" being required for earning a quarter dollar. Men, employed in gathering mulberry-leaves and attending silk-worms, could earn, when employed, five cents a day; but at Salonica, the shipping port of Thessaly, wages were as high as fifty cents a week. Commerce had ceased, and with the decline in the power of association, the value of man and the *utility* of the earth had almost disappeared; while the *value* of commodities had become so great as to cause men, women, and children to perish for want of food.

While manufactures existed, and while commerce could be maintained, agriculture flourished; and it did so because — the market for its products being near at hand — it was subject to little taxation consequent upon the necessity for effecting changes of place. Roads and bridges could then be kept in order; but, as manufactures declined, and as it became more and more necessary to carry the bulky products of the earth to the distant market, *the need of roads* increased, but *the power to maintain them* declined —always a result of the sacrifice of commerce at the shrine of trade. "The increased expense of transport," says a recent traveller, "enabled a few capitalists to monopolize the whole trade in all articles of export"— as a consequence of which "the ruin of the landed proprietors and agriculturists soon commenced," and "families were impoverished and villages disappeared;" while

* Resources of Turkey, p. 146.

"in many extensive districts the whole rural population abandoned the cultivation of their native soil to emigrate to the nearest commercial cities."* Thus it is that as the dependence on the distant market increases, the power to go to it declines; while as the dependence on it declines, the power to resort to it as steadily increases. In the one case, nature is constantly obtaining greater power over man; whereas, in the other, man is as constantly obtaining power over nature. In the one case, utility diminishes, and the value of commodities increases; whereas, in the other, utilities increase, and value declines. In the one, man becomes from day to day more enslaved; whereas, in the other, he becomes more free.

"No improvement," as we learn from the same authority, "can now be attempted, except in the vicinity of large towns, which afford a constant and immediate market for all kinds of agricultural produce;" or, in other words, those parts of the country in which commerce is still maintained. Nothing of the kind is to be hoped for in those districts from which "even the heaviest articles must be transported by pack-horses," with an expense for carriage "that has of late years been constantly increasing"—causing "the cultivation and export of several articles, peculiarly adapted to the soil and climate, to have diminished;" and yet those are the portions of the country that most require it. The *proportion* of the labor of the country given to the work of transportation is a constantly increasing one, and, as a necessary consequence, that given to production is a decreasing one, with constant decline in the power of the community, and of the individuals of whom it is composed.

Depopulation and poverty having, in every country of the world, been consequent upon increase in the power of the trader, and diminution of power to maintain commerce, it is no matter of surprise that all recent travellers should have exhibited the nation as passing steadily onward toward ruin, and the people toward a state of slavery the most complete—the inevitable result of a policy that excludes the mechanic and prevents the development of individuality among the people. Among the latest, is Mr. Mac Farlane,† at the date of whose visit, not only

* Blackwood's Magazine, December, 1854.
† Turkey and its Destiny. By C. Mac Farlane. London, 1850.

had the silk manufacture entirely disappeared, but even the filatures for preparing the raw silk were closed — weavers having become ploughmen, and women and children having been deprived of all employment. The silk cultivators had become entirely dependent on a foreign market in which there existed no demand for the products of their land and labor. Great Britain being then in the midst of one of her periodical crises, had deemed it necessary to reduce the prices of all agricultural products, with a view to stop their importation. On one occasion during Mr. Mac Farlane's travels, there came a report that silk had risen in England, producing a momentary stir and animation, that, as he says, "flattered his national vanity to think that an electric touch parting from London, the mighty heart of commerce, should thus be felt in a few days at a place like Biljek." Such is trading centralization! It renders the agriculturists of the world mere slaves, dependent for food and clothing upon the will of a few people, proprietors of a small amount of machinery, at "the mighty heart of commerce." At one moment, speculation being rife, commodities rise in price; and every effort is made to induce large shipments of raw produce. At the next, money is said to be scarce, and the shippers are ruined.

The ruins of once prosperous villages may everywhere be seen and the results of this diminution in the force of local attraction exhibit themselves in the universal decline of agriculture. The plough, the wine-press, and the oil-mill, now in use, are all equally barbarous in their construction. The once productive cotton-fields of Thessaly lie untilled, and even around Constantinople itself "there are no cultivated lands to speak of within twenty miles — in some directions within fifty miles. The commonest necessaries of life come from distant parts: the corn for daily bread from Odessa; the cattle and sheep from beyond Adrianople, or from Asia Minor; the rice, of which such a vast consumption is made, from the neighborhood of Philipopolis; the poultry chiefly from Bulgaria; the fruit and vegetables from Nicomedia and Mondania. Thus a constant drain of money is occasioned, without any visible return, except to the treasury or from the property of the Ulema."*

The silk that is made — being badly prepared, because of the

* Slade's Travels in Turkey, vol. ii. p. 143.

difficulty of obtaining good machinery — is now required to go to England in its rudest state, to be there prepared and sent to Persia — and thus does commerce with foreign nations decline with the diminution of the power to maintain commerce at home.

Not only is the foreigner free to introduce his wares, but he may, on payment of a trifling duty of two per cent., carry them throughout the empire until finally disposed of. Travelling by caravan, he is lodged without expense. He brings his goods to be exchanged for money, or what else he needs; and, the exchange effected, he disappears as suddenly as he came. As a necessary result of this entire freedom of *trade*, local *commerce* has no existence — the storekeeper, who paid rent and taxes, having found himself unable to contend with the travelling pedlar, who paid neither the one nor the other.* The poor cultivator, therefore, finds it impossible to exchange his products, small as they are, for the commodities he needs, except on the occasional arrival of a caravan, which has generally proved far more likely to absorb the little money in circulation, than any of the more bulky and less valuable products of the earth.

As usual in purely agricultural countries, the whole body of cultivators is hopelessly in debt, and the money-lender fleeces all. If he aids the peasant before harvest, he must have an enormous interest, and be paid in produce at a large discount from the market price. Weakness and poverty among the agricultural classes is found in all communities in which agriculture has not been permitted to strengthen itself by means of that natural alliance between

* "It is impossible to witness the arrival of the many-tongued caravan at its resting-place for the night, and see, unladen and piled up together, the bales from such distant places — to glance over their very wrappers, and the strange marks and characters which they bear — without being amazed at so eloquent a contradiction of our preconceived notions of indiscriminate despotism and universal insecurity of the East. But while we observe the avidity with which our goods are sought, the preference now transferred from Indian to Birmingham muslins, from Golconda to Glasgow chintzes, from Damascus to Sheffield steel, from Cashmere shawls to English broadcloth; and while, at the same time, the energies of their commercial spirit are brought thus substantially before us; it is indeed impossible not to regret that a gulf of separation should have so long divided the East and the West, and equally impossible not to indulge in the hope and anticipation of a vastly extended traffic with the East, and of all the blessings which follow fast and welling in the wake of commerce." — URQUHART: *Resources of Turkey*, p. 143.

Nevertheless, every part of Mr. Urquhart's work is a record of the decline of *commerce*, consequent upon the growing ascendency of trade and traders.

the plough and the loom, the hammer and the harrow, so much admired by Adam Smith; and it is to the resemblance to each other in this respect of Portugal, Jamaica, and Turkey, that we may find the causes of their resemblance in the fact that the value of man is steadily declining, and that he is, himself, becoming from day to day more and more a slave to nature and to his fellow-man. The government, as weak as the people, is so entirely dependent on the will of domestic and foreign traders, that they may be regarded as the real owners of the land, with power to tax its occupants at discretion; and to them, certainly, enure all the profits of cultivation.

As a consequence of this, real estate is almost wholly valueless. In the great valley of Buyukdere, once known as *the fair land*, and close in the vicinity of Constantinople, a property twelve miles in circumference had, but a short time previously to Mr. Mac Farlane's visit, been sold for less than five thousand dollars; while, elsewhere, another almost as large had been disposed of for a much less sum. Small, even, as are these prices, they cannot fail to become yet smaller, under a system that compels the poor cultivator to exhaust the soil in the effort to supply a distant market. In the neighborhood of Smyrna, land may readily be purchased at six cents an acre; but those who are content to go to a little distance from the city may have it altogether free of charge. Domestic commerce having scarcely an existence, it follows here, as everywhere, that the foreign one is entirely insignificant. But recently, the whole amount of exports was but thirty-three millions of dollars, or about two dollars a head; while the total exports from Great Britain to Turkey were but £2,221,000, or $11,000,000 — being but little more than fifty cents per head; and yet, much of even this small quantity went there only *en route* for foreign markets.

Throughout the world, commerce has grown, land has become divided and has increased in value, men have become free, and communities have become strong, in the direct ratio of the power of combination for obtaining command over the forces of nature. That power has everywhere grown with the growth of demand for the various faculties of men — resulting from variety in the modes of employment, and leading to the development of individuality among the people of whom the community has been composed. With the progress of that development, there has been witnessed an increased economy of human force, both mental and physical; and the force thus economized at one instant has constituted the capital to be used in the one that next succeeded. The greater that economy, the greater has been the power to obtain new machinery by help of which to obtain further dominion over nature — compelling water, wind, steam, and electricity to do the work that before had required the human arm. As progress has diminished, and as differences among men have become less numerous, individuality has declined, with constant increase in the waste of human force — each step in that direction being but the preparation for a new and greater one. As mills have stopped, and manufactures have declined, the people who had wrought in them have been forced to seek abroad the means of subsistence denied to them at home. As population has diminished, the power to maintain roads and bridges has declined; and, as the bridges have disappeared, the rich lands have been abandoned.— Malaria next decimating the scattered population that yet remains, we find, with every stage of the progress, a diminution of the quantity of things produced, accompanied by an increase in the obstacles lying between the producer and his market—requiring, for their removal, a constantly increasing *proportion*, and enabling the wagoner and the trader to grow rich at the expense of the poor men who yet desire to till the earth. Trade thus tends as certainly towards slavery as does commerce towards freedom.

In the real and permanent interests of nations there are no discords. Whatever tends to the injury of one tends equally to that of others, and the day may, perhaps, arrive, when such will be admitted to be the case; and when, too, it will be admitted that, among nations as among individuals, an enlightened self-interest dictates a constant observance of the golden rule lying at the foundation of Christianity—Do unto others as ye would that they should do unto you! But a century since, Turkey, Portugal, and the West India islands, were the most profitable of all of England's customers—those whose trade was most anxiously sought; yet where are they now—and what are they? The cause of wars, difficulties, and expenditures, of all kinds; poor in themselves, and neglected and despised by all others; and most especially so by England herself. Compelled to the pursuance of a policy that destroyed commerce among themselves, they have been becoming, from year to year, more and more mere instruments to be used by trade; until at length they have ceased at all to command respect among the communities of the earth. Such is the real cause of the decline and fall of the Turkish empire, whose strength would now be greater than it ever before had been had its policy looked to the development of the latent powers of its people and its land — and to the promotion of commerce.

As Portugal, Turkey, and Jamaica have become more entirely dependent on trade, there has been a decline in their power to consume the products of British labor and skill; and thus it has been that, in our own day, the fable of Æsop, of the goose and the golden egg, has been re-enacted. Hence it is that, while, on the one hand, we have had occasion to witness a decline in all the foreign countries in which commerce was being sacrificed to trade; we have seen, on the other, a wonderful growth of pauperism in England—giving rise to the doctrine of over-population, and leading to the belief that the necessities of trade require labor to be cheap that capital may be enabled to command its services; or, in other words, that to enable trade to thrive, man must be enslaved. Such is the moral of that modern political economy which ignores the existence of all the distinctive qualities of man, and confines itself to those material ones common to him, the ox, the horse, and all other animals. Real science — leading us in a direction totally opposed to this — enables us to find in every page of history confirmation of the truth of the proposition, that in the moral as in the physical world, centralization, slavery, and death travel always hand in hand with each other — and that this is equally true whether considered in relation to nations exercising power, or those over whom it is so exercised.

§ 3. At the date of the Revolution of 1688, the woollen manufacture was rapidly advancing in IRELAND,* but the government of William and Mary, in reply to the application of the London

* "Here is the Moneys gone, (and taken out of Trade in England,) and carried into Ireland; and our People too, with this Money, make Cloth, and serve it cheap in all places where we send our Cloth; and carry to Holland cheap Wool, and cheap Victuals, and pay the Money back again in Four years." — YARRANTON: *England's Improvement by Sea and Land,* London, 1677, p. 182,

merchants, pledged itself to "discountenance" that manufacture, with a view to compel the export of raw wool to England, whereas its export to foreign countries was prohibited; and thus to place the producers of wool entirely in the hands of the English makers of cloth. Woollen cloth, or yarn, was allowed to go from Ireland to England only through certain ports; but its export, as well as that of other manufactures, to the colonies, was entirely prohibited. Irish ships were next deprived of all participation in the benefits of the navigation laws, as well as excluded from the fisheries. Sugar could be imported only through England; and as no drawback was allowed on its exportation to Ireland, the latter was thus taxed for the support of the foreign government, while maintaining its own. All other colonial produce had to be carried first to England, after which it might be shipped to Ireland; and the voyage of importation was required to be made in English ships, manned by English seamen, and owned by English merchants — thus increasing to the utmost the tax of transportation, while denying to the Irish people any participation in the expenditure of the taxes thus collected.

While thus, as far as practicable, prohibiting them from all pursuits tending to the diversification of employments — and thus depriving them of the power of combination for the promotion of their interests—every inducement was held out to them to confine themselves to the production of commodities required by the English manufacturers; and wool, hemp, and flax were admitted into England free of duty. Men, women, and children were regarded as instruments to be used by trade; and here, as in Jamaica, they were to be deprived of all employment except in the labor of the field; and of all opportunity for intellectual improvement, such as elsewhere results from the combination of agriculture and the mechanic arts.

Pending the war of the American Revolution, however, freedom of commerce was claimed for Ireland, and under circumstances that produced compliance with the demand; as a consequence of which, changes were gradually made until at length, in 1783, her legislative independence came fully to be admitted. First among the measures then adopted, was the imposition of duties on various articles of foreign manufacture, with the avowed intention of enabling the Irish people to employ their own surplus labor in converting their corn and their wool into cloth; and thereby enabling them to carry into effect the system so much admired by Adam Smith. Thenceforward, commerce made rapid progress, and was attended with corresponding development of the intellectual faculties; as may be inferred from the fact, that small as was her population, there existed so great a demand for books as to have warranted the reproduction of all the principal English law reports of the day, very many of the earlier ones, as well as the principal novels, travels, and miscellaneous works. More books were published in Dublin by a single house, than now, probably, are required for the supply of the kingdom, notwithstanding the increase of population.

With 1801, however — centralization being established — there came a change. By the act of Union, the copyright laws were extended to Ireland, and at once the large, and rapidly growing, manufacture of books entirely disappeared. The patent laws being also extended to that country, it became, at once, clear that Irish manufactures, of every kind, must retrograde. England had the home market, the foreign market, and that of Ireland open to her; while the Irish manufacturers were forced to contend for existence, and under the most disadvantageous circumstances, on their own soil. The former could afford to purchase expensive machinery, and to adopt whatever improvements might be made; while the latter could not. As a natural consequence of this, Irish manufactures gradually disappeared as the act of Union took effect. By virtue of its provisions, the duties established by the Irish Parliament, for the purpose of protecting the farmers of Ireland in their efforts to bring the artisan into close proximity with themselves, were gradually to diminish, until free trade should fully be established; or, in other words, Manchester and Birmingham were to have a monopoly of supplying Ireland with cloth and iron. The duty on English woollens was to continue twenty years. The almost prohibitory duties on English calicoes and muslins were to continue until 1808; after which they were to be gradually diminished — finally ceasing in 1821. Those on cotton-yarn were to cease in 1810. The effect of this in diminishing the demand for Irish labor is shown in the fact, that the master woollen manufacturers of Dublin, who were in 1800 no less than 91 in number, had declined in 1840 to 12 — that the hands employed had fallen in number from 4918 to 602; and that the wool-combers and carpet manufacturers had almost entirely disappeared. Such, too, was the case in Cork, Kilkenny, Wicklow, and all other of the seats of manufacture. In the first of these, cotton-spinners, bleachers, and calico-printers abounded; while in the last, braid and worsted weavers, hosiers, linen and woollen weavers, counted by thousands; whereas, in 1834, the whole number of people so employed did not exceed five hundred.*

Deprived of all employment, except in the labor of agriculture, land became, of course, the great object of pursuit. "Land is life," had said, most truly and emphatically, Chief Justice Blackburn; and the people had now before them the choice between the occupation of land, *at any rent*, or *starvation*. The lord of the land was thus enabled to dictate his own terms; and therefore it has been, that we have heard of the payment of five, six, eight, and even as much as ten, pounds an acre. "Enormous rents, low wages, farms of an enormous extent, let by rapacious and indolent proprietors to monopolizing land-jobbers, to be re-let by intermediate oppressors, for five times their value, among the wretched starvers on potatoes and water," led to a constant succession of outrages, followed by Insurrection Acts, Arms Acts, and Coercion Acts; when the real remedy was to be found in the adoption of a system that would enable them to combine their efforts together, and thus maintain the commerce that was then being sacrificed at the shrine of trade.

That commerce may anywhere arise, or that it may anywhere

* "For nearly half a century Ireland has had perfectly free trade with the richest country in the world; and what" — says the author of a recent work of great ability—

"Has that free trade done for her? She has even now," he continues, "no employment for her teeming population except upon the land. She ought to have had, and might easily have had, other and various employments, and plenty of it. Are we to believe," says he, "the calumny, that the Irish are lazy and won't work? Is Irish human nature different from other human nature? Are not the most laborious of all laborers in London and New York, Irishmen? Are Irishmen inferior in understanding? We Englishmen, who have personally known Irishmen in the army, at the bar, and in the church, know that there is no better head than a disciplined Irish one. But, in all these cases, that master of industry, the stomach, has been well satisfied. Let an Englishman exchange his bread and beer, and beef and mutton, for no breakfast, for a lukewarm lumper at dinner, and no supper. With such a diet, how much better is he than an Irishman—a Celt, as he calls him? No, the truth is, that the misery of Ireland is not from the human nature that grows there — it is from England's perverse legislation, past and present."—*Sophisms of Free Trade*, by J. BARNARD BYLES, Esq.

be maintained, there must be differences among men, for farmers do not need to exchange potatoes with each other, however great may be their need for the services of the blacksmith, the carpenter, the miner, or the miller. Centralization was annihilating all the differences that had existed, and driving all the people to agriculture; and the results obtained were precisely those which might reasonably have been expected. The demand for human effort, whether of mind or of body, gradually ceasing, millions of people found themselves forced into the position of consumers of capital in the form of food, while totally unable to sell the labor thence produced. Go where the traveller might, he found hundreds and thousands anxious to work, but unemployed; while tens of thousands were wandering throughout Great Britain, seeking to sell their labor for the pittance by help of which they might pay their rent at home. Interdicted from all pursuits but one, they were compelled to waste more power than would have paid, a hundred times over, for all the British manufactures they now consumed; and thus it was that they became, as the London *Times* expresses it, "hewers of wood and drawers of water for the Saxon."*

English writers assure us that Ireland has been deficient in the capital required for manufactures; but such must always be the case with purely agricultural countries. Nothing is required, in any country, for making capital abundant, but the existence of that power of combination which enables each and every man to find a purchaser for his own labor, and to become a purchaser of that of others. The power to render either bodily or mental service is a result of capital consumed, and it constitutes the capital the laborer has to offer in exchange. When diversity of employments exists, the motion of society is rapid, and all that capital reappears in the form of new commodities; but when there is no pursuit but agriculture, the motion is slow, and most of it is

* "There are nations of slaves, but they have, by long custom, been made unconscious of the yoke of slavery. This is not the case with the Irish, who have a strong feeling of liberty within them, and are fully sensible of the weight of the yoke they have to bear. They are intelligent enough to know the injustice done them by the distorted laws of their country; and while they are themselves enduring the extreme of poverty, they have frequently before them, in the manner of life of their English landlords, a spectacle of the most refined luxury that human ingenuity ever invented."—KOHL: *Travels in Ireland.*

wasted. Millions of Irishmen were daily wasting capital; and therefore it was, that capital was deficient. No such deficiency was experienced in the period between 1783 and 1801, because commerce was then steadily growing — producing a demand for all the physical and intellectual force of the community. From and after that time, commerce gradually declined until it finally died away; and then was wasted, *in each and every year*, an amount of Irish capital *equal, if properly applied, to the creation of all the cotton and woollen machinery existing in England.* To this enforced waste of capital we must look, if we desire to find the cause of the decline and fall of the Irish nation.

As commerce declined, the power of the trader grew; and middlemen accumulated fortunes that they *could* not invest in machinery of any kind, and *would* not apply to the improvement of the land of Ireland — as a consequence of which, large quantities of capital were, from year to year, transferred to England. By an official document, it was shown, that in the thirteen years following the final triumph of trade over commerce, in 1821, the transfer of the British public securities from England to Ireland amounted to as many millions of pounds sterling; and thus it was that cheap labor and cheap capital were forced to contribute towards building up "the great works of Britain." Further, it was provided by law, that, whenever the poor people of a neighborhood contributed to a saving fund, the amount should not be applied in any manner calculated to furnish local employment; but should be transferred for investment in the British funds. The landlords fled to England, and their rents followed them. The middlemen sent their capital to England. The trader, or the laborer, that could accumulate a little capital saw it sent to England; and he was then compelled to follow it.

That centralization, slavery, depopulation, and death travel always together, is a fact whose proof is to be found in every page of history; but in none is the proof more thorough and complete than in that which records the story of Ireland, from the day when she ceased to have a Parliament, and became a mere appendage to the crown of England.

The form in which rents, profits, and savings, as well as taxes, went abroad, was that of raw products of the soil, to be consumed elsewhere — yielding nothing to be returned to the land, which became, of course, impoverished. The export of grain in the first three years following the passage of the act of Union, averaged about 300,000 quarters; but, as the domestic market gradually disappeared, it increased, until at the close of thirty years, it had attained an annual average of two and a half millions, or 22,500,000 of our bushels. The poor people were, in fact, selling their soil to pay for cotton and woollen goods that they should have manufactured themselves; for coal which abounded among themselves; for iron, all the materials of which existed at home in great profusion; and for a small quantity of tea, sugar, and other foreign commodities; while the amount required to pay rent to absentees, and interest to mortgagees, was estimated at more than thirty millions of dollars. Here was a drain that no nation could bear, however great its productive power; and its existence was due to the system which — by forbidding the application of labor, talent, or capital to any thing but agriculture — forbade advance in civilization. The inducements to remain at home steadily diminished. Those who could live without labor— finding that society had changed — fled to England, France, or Italy. Those who desired to work, and felt that they were qualified for something beyond mere manual labor, fled to England or America; and thus by degrees was the unfortunate country depleted of every thing that could render it a home in which to remain, while those who could not fly were "starving by millions,"* and happy when a full-grown man could find employment at sixpence a day, without clothing, lodging, or even food.

The existence of such a state of things was, said the advocates of the system which looks to converting all the world, outside of England, into one great farm, to be accounted for by the fact, that the population was too numerous for the land; and yet a third of the surface, including the richest lands in the kingdom, was lying unoccupied and waste. "Of single counties," said an English

* "Throughout the west and south of Ireland, the traveller is haunted by the face of the *popular starvation*. It is not the exception—it is *the condition* of the people. In this fairest and richest of countries, men are suffering and *starving by millions*. There are thousands of them, at this minute, stretched in the sunshine at their cabin doors, with *no work*, scarcely any food, no hope seemingly. Strong countrymen are lying in bed, '*for the hunger*' — because a man lying on his back does not need so much food as a person afoot. Many of them have torn up the unripe potatoes from their little gardens, and to exist now must look to winter, when they shall have to suffer starvation and cold too." — *Thackeray.*

writer, "Mayo, with a population of 389,000, and a rental of only £300,000, has an area of 1,364,000 acres, of which 800,000 are waste! No less than 470,000 acres, being very nearly equal to the whole extent of surface now under cultivation, are declared to be reclaimable. Galway, with a population of 423,000, and a valued rental of £433,000, has upwards of 700,000 acres of waste, 410,000 of which are reclaimable! Kerry, with a population of 293,000, has an area of 1,186,000 acres — 727,000 being waste, and 400,000 of them reclaimable! Even the Union of Glenties, Lord Monteagle's *ne plus ultra* of redundant population, has an area of 245,000 acres, of which 200,000 are waste, and for the most part reclaimable, to its population of 43,000. The Barony of Ennis, that abomination of desolation, has 230,000 acres of land to its 5000 paupers — a proportion which, as Mr. Carter, one of the principal proprietors, remarks in his circular advertisement for tenants, 'is at the rate of only one family to 230 acres; so that if but one head of a family were employed to every 230 acres, there need not be a single pauper in the entire district; a proof,' he adds, '*that nothing but employment is wanting to set this country to rights!*' In which opinion we fully coincide."

Nothing but employment — nothing but the power to maintain commerce—*was* needed; but commerce could not exist under the system which had, in a brief period, caused the annihilation of the cotton manufacture of India, notwithstanding the advantage of having the cotton on the spot, free from all cost for carriage. As in Jamaica, and as in India—the land having been gradually exhausted by the exportation of its products in their rudest state, —the country had been drained of capital; as a necessary consequence of which the labor, even of men, found no demand, while women and children starved, that the women and children of England might spin cotton, and weave cloth, that Ireland was too poor to purchase.

Bad, however, as is all we have thus far seen, a state of things far worse was near at hand. Poverty and wretchedness compelling the wretched people to fly in thousands and tens of thousands across the Channel — thus following the capital and the soil that had been transferred to Birmingham and Manchester — the streets and cellars of those towns, and of London, Liverpool, and

Glasgow, were filled with men, women, and children, unable to sell their labor, and perishing for want of food. Throughout the country, men were offering to perform the farm labor for food alone; and a cry arose among the people of England, that the laborers were likely to be swamped by these starving Irishmen; to provide against which it was needed that Irish landlords should be compelled to support their own poor, as they were forthwith required by act of Parliament to do — although for about half a century previously, England had rung with denunciations of poor laws, as being in entirely in contravention of all sound economical principles. The system, however — looking as it did to the destruction of the power of association, and to the consequent waste of labor — was, itself, in opposition to all such principles; and therefore was it, that the action of the legislature was required to be directly opposed to all that had been taught in the schools. The practice, under a sound system, may be consistent; but under an unsound one, it cannot be.

With the passage of the Irish poor law, there arose, of course, an increased desire to rid the country of people who, unable to sell their labor, could pay no rent; and from that time to the present, Ireland has presented the most shocking scenes, consequent upon the destruction of houses and the expulsion of their inhabitants — scenes far more worthy of the most uncivilized portions of Africa, than of an integral portion of the British Empire.*

Thus far, Irish agriculture had been protected in the English market, as some small compensation for the sacrifice of the domestic one; but now, even that boon, trivial as it was, was withdrawn. Like the people of Jamaica, those of Ireland had become poor, and their trade had ceased to be of value, although but seventy years before they had been the *best* customers of England. The system having exhausted all the countries in which commerce

* "In Galway Union, recent accounts declared the number of poor evicted, and their houses levelled, within the last two years, to equal the numbers in Kilrush—4000 families and 20,000 human beings are said to have been here also thrown upon the road, houseless and homeless. I can readily believe the statement, for to me some parts of the country appeared like an enormous graveyard — the numerous gables of the unroofed dwellings seemed to be gigantic tombstones. They were, indeed, records of decay and death far more melancholy than the grave can show. Looking on them, the doubt rose in my mind, Am I in a civilized country? Have we really a free constitution? Can such scenes be paralleled in Siberia or Caffraria?" — *Irish Journal.*

had been sacrificed to trade—India, Portugal, Turkey, the West Indies, and Ireland herself—it had become necessary to make an effort to obtain markets in those which had to a greater or less extent placed the consumer by the side of the producer, to wit: this country, France, Belgium, Germany, and Russia; and the mode of accomplishing this was that of offering them the same system by which Ireland had been exhausted. The farmers were everywhere invited to impoverish their soil by sending its products to England to be consumed; and the corn laws were repealed for the purpose of enabling them to enter into competition with the starving Irishman, who was thus at once deprived of the market of England, as, by the act of Union, he had been deprived of his own. The cup of wretchedness, before well-nigh full, was now filled. The price of food fell, and the laborer was ruined, for the whole product of his land would scarcely pay his rent. The landlord was ruined, for while unable to collect rents, he was heavily taxed for the support of his impoverished tenants. His land was encumbered with mortgages and settlements, created when food was high; but he could now no longer pay the interest thereon. In this state of things it was, that the British people resorted to the revolutionary measure of creating a special court for the sale of all encumbered property, and the distribution of its proceeds—thus furnishing the clearest evidence of the unsoundness of the system under which Ireland had been governed.

The impoverished landholder now experienced the same fate that had befallen his poor tenant; and from that date famine and pestilence, levellings and evictions, have been the order of the day. Their effect having everywhere been to drive the poor people from the land, its consequences are seen in the fact that the population numbered, in 1850, *one million six hundred and fifty-nine thousand less than it did in* 1840; while the starving population of the towns had largely increased. The county of Cork had diminished 222,000, while Dublin had grown in numbers 22,000. Galway had lost 125,000, while the city had gained 7422. Connaught had lost 414,000, while Limerick and Belfast had gained 30,000. The number of inhabited houses had fallen from 1,328,000 to 1,047,000, or more than twenty per cent. Announcing these startling facts, the London Times stated that "*for a whole generation man had been a drug in Ireland, and population a nuisance.*" The "inexhaustible Irish supply had," as it continued, "kept down the price of English labor," but this cheapness of labor had "contributed vastly to the improvement and power" of England, and largely to "the enjoyment of those who had money to spend." Now, however, a change appeared to be at hand, and it was to be feared that the prosperity of England, based as it had been on cheap Irish labor, might be interfered with, as famine and pestilence, evictions and emigration, were thinning out the Celts who had so long, as it is said, furnished that "stagnant weight of unemployed population," by help of which English capital had obtained so entire a control of the labor of England.

To the stagnation resulting from the absence of differences among the various portions of the community all these effects are due. The whole system tends to separate the consumer from the producer, and to augment to the highest degree the taxation incident to the necessity for effecting changes of place; and to this are due the exhaustion of Ireland, the ruin of its landholders, the starvation of its people, and the degradation of the country which has furnished to the continent its best soldiers, and, to the empire, not only its most industrious and intelligent laborers, but also its Burke, its Grattan, its Sheridan, and its Wellington. English journals, nevertheless, rejoice at the gradual disappearance of the native population, and find in "the abstraction of the Celtic race at the rate of a quarter of a million a year, a surer remedy for the inveterate Irish disease than any human wit could have imagined."

The "disease" here spoken of is a total absence of demand for labor, resulting from the unhappy determination of the people of England to destroy the power of association throughout the world. The sure remedy for it is found in famines, pestilences, and expatriation, the necessary results of that exhaustion of the land which follows the exportation of its products in their rudest state. A stronger confirmation of the destructive character of such a course of policy to the people of England themselves, than is contained in the following paragraph, could scarcely be imagined:—

"When the Celt has crossed the Atlantic, he begins for the first time in his life to consume the manufactures of this country, and indirectly to contribute to its customs. We may possibly live to see the day when the chief product of Ireland will be cattle, and English and Scotch the majority of her population. The nine or ten millions of Irish who by that time will have settled in the United States, cannot be less friendly to England, and will certainly be much better customers to her than they now are."*

When the Celt leaves Ireland, he leaves an almost purely agricultural country, and in such countries man is always little better than a slave. Coming here, he finds himself in a country in which to some little extent the farmer and the artisan have been enabled to come together; and here he becomes a freeman, and a customer of England.

That the nation that commences by exporting raw products must end by exporting men, is proved by the following figures, furnished by the last four censuses of Ireland:—

| | | | |
|---|---|---|---|
| 1821, population, | 6,801,827 | | |
| 1831, " | 7,767,491 | — Increase, | 965,574 |
| 1841, " | 8,175,124 | — Increase, | 407,723 |
| 1851, " | 6,515,794 | — Decrease, | 1,659,330 |

To what causes may this extraordinary course of events be attributed? Certainly not to any deficiency of land, for nearly one-third of the whole surface — including millions of acres of the richest soils of the kingdom — remains in a state of nature. Not to original inferiority of the soil in cultivation, for it has been confessedly among the richest in the empire. Not to a deficiency of mineral ores or fuel, for coal abounds, and iron ores of the richest kind, as well as those of other metals, exist in vast profusion. Not to any deficiency in the physical qualities of the Irishman—it being an established fact that he is capable of performing far more labor than the Englishman, the Frenchman, or the Belgian. Not to a deficiency of intellectual ability—Ireland having given to England her most distinguished soldiers and statesmen; and having throughout the world furnished evidence that the Irishman is capable of the highest intellectual improvement. Nevertheless, while possessed of every natural advantage, he is, at home, a slave to the severest taskmasters, and in a condition of poverty and distress such as is exhibited in no other portion of the civilized world. No choice being left him but between expatriation and starvation, we see him, everywhere, abandoning the

* London *Times*.

home of his fathers, to seek elsewhere that subsistence which Ireland—rich as she is in soil and in her minerals, in her navigable rivers, and in her facilities for communication with the world—can no longer afford him.

The value of land and labor being altogether dependent upon the power to maintain commerce—and that power having no existence in Ireland—the reader can now have little difficulty in understanding why both are there, as well as in Turkey, Portugal, and Jamaica, so nearly valueless. Neither can be *utilized*, because of the enormous extent to which they are subjected to that heaviest of all taxes—the one resulting from a necessity for dependence on ships, wagons, and all other of the machinery of trade and transportation. In his recent work on Ireland, Captain Head speaks of a property containing 10,000 acres, that had been purchased at five cents an acre; and in a paper read before the Statistical Section of the British Association, it was shown that the estates then purchased in Ireland, by English capital, embraced 403,065 acres; the purchase-money had been £1,095,000, or about £2 15*s.* ($13 20) per acre—being little more than is paid for farms, with very moderate improvements, in the new States of the Mississippi Valley.

The sugar of the laborer of Jamaica exchanges in Manchester for three shillings, of which he receives perhaps one; and he perishes because of the difficulty of obtaining clothing, or the machinery by help of which to make it. The Hindoo sells his cotton for a penny a pound, and buys it back, in the form of cloth, at eighteen or twenty pence. The Virginia negro raises tobacco that exchanges for six shillings' worth of commodities, of which he and his owner obtain threepence—all the difference being absorbed by the various persons who live by trade, and stand in the way of commerce. The Irishman raises chickens which sell in London for shillings, of which he receives pence; and thus sugar that has yielded the free negro of Jamaica a penny, commands in the west of Ireland a pair of chickens, or a dozen lobsters.* Having studied these facts, the reader will be at no loss

* The enormous loss incident to the wide separation of the consumer from the producer, is thus exhibited by Captain Head:—

"'Chickuns are about 5*d.* a couple—dooks, 10*d.* A couple of young gaise, 10*d.*; when auld, not less than 1*s.* or 14*d.*'

"'And turkeys?' I asked.

to understand the destructive effects on the value of land and labor resulting from the absence of markets, such as arise naturally where the plough and the loom are permitted, in accordance with the doctrines of Adam Smith, to take their places by each other's side. More than seventy years since, that great man denounced the system which looked to compelling the exports of raw produce, as one productive of infinite injustice; and, certainly, the histories of Jamaica and Virginia, Ireland and India, since his time, would afford him, were he now present, little reason for changing the opinions then expressed.

§ 4. It is usual to ascribe the state of things now existing in Ireland to the rapid growth of population—that in its turn being charged to the account of the potato, the excessive use of which, as Mr. McCulloch informs his readers, has lowered the standard of living, and tended to the multiplication of men, women, and children. "The peasantry of Ireland live," as he says, "in miserable mud cabins, without either a window or a chimney, or any thing that can be called furniture," and are distinguished from their fellow-laborers across the Channel by their "filth and misery;" and hence, in his opinion, it is that they work for low wages.* We have here effect substituted for cause. The absence of demand for labor causes wages to be so low, that the laborer can obtain nothing but mud cabins and potatoes. It is admitted everywhere throughout the continent of Europe, that the introduction of the potato has tended greatly to the improvement of the condition of the people; but then, there is no portion of the continent in which it constitutes an essential part of the national policy to deprive millions of people of all mode of employment except agriculture — thus placing those millions at such a distance from market, that the chief part of their labor and its products is lost in the effort to reach it; and that their land is exhausted because

"'I can't say; we haven't many of thim in the counthry, and I don't want to tell yere Arn'r a lie. Fish, little or nothing. A large turbot, of 30 pounds weight, for 3*s*. Lobsters, a dozen for 4*d*. Soles, 2*d*. or 3*d*. a-piece. T'other day I bought a turbot, of 15 pounds weight, for a gentleman, and I paid 18*d*. for ut.'" — *Walks and Talks in Ireland*, p. 178.

"'What do you pay for your tea and sugar here?' I inquired.

"'Very dare, sir,' he replied. 'We pay 5*s*. for tea, 5*d*. for brown sugar, and 8*d*. for white; that is, if we buy a single pound.'" — *Ibid*, p. 187.

* Treatise on Wages, p. 33.

of the impossibility of returning to the soil any of the elements of which its crops are composed. Trading centralization produces all these effects. It looks to the destruction of the value of labor and land, and to the enslavement of man. It tends to the division of the whole population into two classes, separated by an impassable gulf—the mere laborer and the land-owner. It tends to the destruction of the power of association for any purpose of improvement, whether by the making of roads or the founding of schools; and, of course, to the prevention of the growth of towns, as we see to have been the case with Jamaica, so barbarous in this respect when compared with Martinique or Cuba—islands whose governments have not looked to the perpetual divorce of the artisan and the agriculturist.

The decay of towns in Ireland, subsequent to the Union, led to absenteeism, and thus added to the exhaustion of the land—Irish wheat being now needed to pay not only for English cloth, but for English services; and the more the centralization resulting from absenteeism, the greater, necessarily, was the difficulty attendant upon the maintenance of the productive powers of the soil. Mr. McCulloch, however, assures his readers, that "it is not easy to imagine any grounds for pronouncing the expenditure of the rent at home more beneficial" to the country than if it had been expended abroad.* By another distinguished political economist we are told that—

"Many persons" are "perplexed by the consideration that all the commodities which are exported as remittances of the absentee's income are exports for which no return is obtained; that they are as much lost to this country as if they were a tribute paid to a foreign state, or even as if they were periodically thrown into the sea. This is unquestionably true; but it must be recollected that whatever is unproductively consumed, is, by the very terms of the proposition, destroyed, without producing any return."†

The view is, as the reader will see, based upon the idea of the total destruction of the commodities consumed. Were it even correct, it would still follow that there had been transferred from Ireland to England a demand for services of a thousand kinds, tending to cause a rise in the price of labor in the one and a fall

* Principles of Political Economy, p. 157.
† Senior: Outlines of Political Economy, p. 160.

in the other; but if it were altogether incorrect, it would then follow, necessarily, that the loss to the country *would* be as great as if the remittances were "a tribute paid to a foreign state, or even as if they were periodically thrown into the sea." That the latter is the case the reader may readily convince himself. Man consumes much, but he destroys nothing. In eating food, he is merely acting as a machine for preparing the elements of which it is composed, for future production; and the more he can take out of the land, the more he can return to it, and the more rapid will be the improvement in the productive power of the soil.

If the market is near, he takes hundreds of bushels of turnips, carrots, or potatoes, or tons of hay, from an acre of land — varying the character of his culture from year to year; and the more he borrows from the great bank the more he can repay to it, the more he can improve his mind and his cultivation, and the more readily he can command improved machinery, by aid of which to obtain still increased returns. If, however, the market is distant, he must raise only those things that will bear carriage, and thus is he limited in his cultivation; and the more he is limited the more rapidly does he exhaust his land, the less is his power to obtain roads, to have association with his fellow-men, to obtain books, to improve his mode of thought, to purchase machinery, or to make roads. Such is the case even when he is compelled to sell and buy in distant markets; but still worse is it when, as in the case of rents paid to an absentee, nothing is returned to the land. Production then diminishes without a corresponding diminution of the rent — the poor laborer being daily more and more thrown upon the mercy of the landlord, or his agent, and becoming more and more subjected to his will. The *proportion* of rent then rises, but its *quantity* declines. The value of commodities increases, but that of man diminishes—and with every step in this direction we witness a growing tendency to depopulation, such as has been exhibited in Turkey, Portugal, Jamaica, and especially in Ireland.

We are told of the principle of population, in virtue of which men increase faster than food; and, for evidence that such must always be the case, are pointed to the fact, that, when men are few in number, they always cultivate the rich soils, and then food is abundant; but, that, as population increases, they are forced to resort to the poor soils, when food becomes scarce. That the contrary of all this is true, is shown by the history of England, France, Italy, Greece, India, and most especially by the fact that Ireland possesses millions of acres of the most fertile soil remaining in a state of nature, and so likely to remain until she shall have markets for their produce — enabling their owners readily to exchange turnips, potatoes, cabbages, and hay, for cloth, machinery, and MANURE.

It is singular that modern political economy should so entirely have overlooked the fact that man is a mere borrower from the earth, and that when he does not pay his debts, she does as do all other creditors—expelling him from his holding. England makes of her soil a grand reservoir for the waste yielded by the sugar, coffee, wool, indigo, cotton, and other raw commodities of almost half the world — thus obtaining manure that has been valued at five hundred millions of dollars a year, or five times more than the value of the cotton crop produced by so many millions of people in this country; and yet so important is that commodity, that she imports in a single year more than two hundred thousand tons of guano, at a cost of almost two millions of pounds, or ten millions of dollars. Nevertheless, her writers teach other nations that the true mode of becoming rich is to exhaust the land by sending from it all its products in their rudest state; and then, when the Irishmen attempt to follow the soil that has been sent to England, the world is assured by Mr. McCulloch that—

"The unexampled misery of the Irish people is directly owing to the excessive augmentation of their numbers; and" that "nothing can be more perfectly futile than to expect any real or lasting amendment of their situation until an effectual check has been given to the progress of population. It is obvious too," he continues, "that the low and degraded condition into which the people of Ireland are now sunk is the condition to which every people must be reduced whose numbers continue, for any considerable period, to increase faster than the means of providing for their comfortable and decent subsistence."*

Such is the erroneous view to which men of high ability are led by the Malthusian doctrine, that man—the being of highest development — tends to increase more rapidly than potatoes, turnips,

* Principles of Political Economy, p. 383.

fish, and oysters, the things of lowest development, on which he feeds; and by the Ricardo doctrine, that it is upon the fertile soils that men begin the work of cultivation. All Ireland proves that the richest soils are yet undrained and uncultivated — that those in cultivation have been exhausted by reason of the necessity imposed upon their owners for sending away their produce, in its rudest state — and that the real cause of difficulty is to be found in the annihilation of the power to maintain commerce, and consequent destruction of the capital daily consumed in the maintenance of so many millions of human beings — compelled to waste their days in idleness, when they would so gladly be at work. "How," asks the Times, "are they to be fed and employed?" "That," as it continues, "is the question which still baffles an age that can transmit a message round the world in a moment of time, and point out the locality of a planet never yet seen. There is the question which founders both the bold and the wise."

It is, nevertheless, a question readily answered. Let them have commerce — let them be emancipated from the dominion of trade — and they will find at once a demand for their powers, whether mental or intellectual. All then meeting purchasers for what they have to part with, all will be able to become purchasers of the labor of others — their friends and neighbors, and the wives and children of those friends. What Ireland needs is, the motion of society — the power of combination — which results from differences in the modes of employment. Let her have that, and she will cease to export food, while her people perish of famine at home.* Give her that, and — her land ceasing to be impoverished by the extraction and exportation of its most valuable elements—her people will be both "fed and employed;" and then, the doctrine of over-population will cease to find support in the harrowing details of Irish history.

* The exports of food from Ireland in 1849, '50, '51 — years in which famine and pestilence combined to limit the growth of population — were as follows:—

| Year. | Wheat, qrs. | Flour, qrs. | Live stock, No. |
|---|---|---|---|
| 1849 | 844,000 | 1,176,000 | 520,000 |
| 1850 | 751,000 | 1,055,000 | 475,000 |
| 1851 | 850,000 | 823,000 | 472,000 |

# CHAPTER XIII.

## THE SAME SUBJECT CONTINUED.

§ 1. In no part of the world has there existed a greater tendency to voluntary association, the distinguishing mark of freedom, than in India. In none did the smaller communities to a greater extent exercise the power of self-government. Each village had its distinct organization, and under its simple and "almost patriarchal arrangements, the natives of Hindoostan seem to have lived from the earliest, down, comparatively speaking, to late times—if not free from the troubles and annoyances to which men in all conditions of society are more or less subject, still in the full enjoyment, by each individual, of his property, and of a very considerable share of personal liberty." * * * "Leave him in possession of the farm which his forefathers owned, and preserve entire the institutions to which he had from infancy been accustomed, and the simple Hindoo would give himself no concern whatever as to the intrigues and cabals which took place at the capital. Dynasties might displace one another; revolutions might recur; and the persons of his sovereigns might change every day; but so long as his own little society remained undisturbed, all other contingencies were to him subjects scarcely of speculation." * * * "Perhaps there are not to be found on the face of the earth a race of human beings whose attachment to their native place will bear a comparison with that of the Hindoos. There are no privations which the Hindoo will hesitate to bear, rather than voluntarily abandon the spot where he was born; and if continued oppression drive him forth, he will return to it again after long years of exile with fresh fondness."*

The Mohammedan conquest left these simple and beautiful institutions untouched. "Each Hindoo village," says Col. Briggs, in his work on the land tax, "had its distinct municipality, and

* Greig: History of British India, vol. i. p. 46.

over a certain number of villages, or district, was an hereditary chief and accountant, both possessing great local influence and authority, and certain territorial domains or estates. The Mohammedans early saw the policy of not disturbing an institution so complete, and they availed themselves of the local influence of these officers to reconcile their subjects to their rule."

Local action, and local combination, are everywhere conspicuous in the history of India. Having numerous rulers, some of whom, to a certain extent, acknowledged the superiority of the distant sovereign, the taxes required for the support of government were heavy, but—being locally expended—if the cultivator contributed too large a portion of his grain, it was at least consumed in a neighboring market, and nothing went from off the land. Manufactures, too, were widely spread, and thus was made a demand for the labor not required in agriculture. "On the coast of Coromandel," said Orme,* "and in the province of Bengal, when at some distance from a high road or principal town, it is difficult to find a village in which every man, woman, and child is not employed in making a piece of cloth. At present," he continues, "much the greatest part of whole provinces are employed in this single manufacture." Its progress, as he said, included "no less than a description of the lives of half the inhabitants of Hindostan."

While employment was thus locally subdivided, and neighbor was thus enabled to exchange with neighbor, the exchanges between the producers of food, or of salt, in one part of the country, and the producers of cotton and manufacturers of cloth in another, tended to the production of commerce with more distant men—whether within, or without, the limits of India itself. Bengal was celebrated for the finest muslins, the consumption of which at Delhi, and in Northern India generally, was large; while the Coromandel coast was equally celebrated for the best chintzes and calicoes—leaving to Western India the manufacture of strong and inferior goods of every kind. Under these circumstances, it is no matter of surprise that the country was rich, and that its people, though often over-taxed, and sometimes plundered by invading armies, were prosperous in a high degree.

* Historical Fragments, London, 1805, p. 409.

From the date of the battle of Plassey, by the event of which British power was established in India, centralization grew rapidly, and, as usual in such cases, the country became filled with adventurers, very many of whom were wholly without principle — men whose sole object was that of the accumulation of fortune by any means, however foul; as is well known to all familiar with the indignant denunciations of Burke.* England was thus enriched as India became impoverished, and as centralization became more and more established.

Step by step, the power of the Company was extended, and everywhere was adopted the Hindoo principle, that the sovereign — as proprietor of the soil, and sole landlord — was entitled to one-half of the gross produce of the land. Under the earlier Mohammedan sovereigns, this land tax, now designated as rent, had been limited to a thirteenth, and from that to a sixth; but in the reign of Akbar (sixteenth century) it was fixed at one-third—numerous other taxes being then abolished. With the decline and gradual dissolution of the empire, the local sovereigns had not only increased it, but had also revived the taxes that had been discontinued — while instituting others of a most oppressive kind all of which were continued by the Company—while allowing no reduction of the rent.† Further, the Company — having a monopoly of trade — could dictate the prices of all it had to sell, as well as of all that it needed to buy; and here was another

* "The country was laid waste with fire and sword, and that land distinguished above most others by the cheerful face of fraternal government and protected labor, the chosen seat of cultivation and plenty, is now almost throughout a dreary desert covered with rushes and briers, and jungles full of wild beasts." * * * "That universal, systematic breach of treaties, which had made the British faith proverbial in the East! These intended rebellions are one of the Company's standing resources. When money has been thought to be hoarded up anywhere, its owners are universally accused of rebellion, until they are acquitted of their money and their treasons at once! The money once taken, all accusation, trial, and punishment ends."—*Speech on Fox's East India Bill.*

† "Wherever the British power supplanted that of the Mohammedans in Bengal, we did not, it is true, adopt the sanguinary part of their creed; but from the impure fountain of their financial system did we, to our shame, claim the inheritance to a right to seize upon half the gross produce of the land as a tax; and wherever our arms have triumphed, we have invariably proclaimed this savage right: coupling it, at the same time, with the senseless doctrine of the proprietary right to these lands being also vested in the sovereign, in virtue of the right of conquest." — RICKARDS: *India*, vol. i. p. 275.

and most oppressive tax, imposed for the benefit of absentee landlords.*

With the farther extension of power, the demands on the Company's treasury increased without an increase of means with which to meet them — exhaustion being a natural consequence of absenteeism, or centralization; as has so well been proved in Ireland. The ability to pay taxes being in course of diminution, there was thus produced a necessity for resorting to the creation of a sort of landed aristocracy, that should be responsible to the government for their payment; for which purpose the private rights of the small proprietors were sacrificed in favor of the Zemindars, hitherto mere officers of the crown. Become, now, great landed proprietors, the latter were constituted masters of a host of poor tenants, holding their lands at will, and liable to torture and punishment of every kind, if they failed to pay a rent to whose amount the only limit was found in deficiency of power to compel its payment. The middleman system of Ireland, and of the West Indies, was thus transplanted to India.

At first, however, it worked unfavorably to the Zemindars themselves, the rents for which they had become bound being so entirely out of proportion to the ability of the poor tenants, that even torture could not compel their payment; and but a few years elapsed before they in turn were sold out, to make way for another set, "as keen and as hard-hearted as they themselves had been." That system having failed to answer the purpose, it was next determined to arrest the extension of the permanent settlement, and to settle with each little ryot, or cultivator, to the entire exclusion of the village authorities, by whom, under the native governments, the taxes had uniformly been so equitably

* "The misgovernment of the English was carried to a point such as seemed hardly compatible with the existence of society. They forced the natives to buy dear and sell cheap. They insulted with impunity the tribunals, the police, and the fiscal authorities of the country. Enormous fortunes were thus rapidly accumulated at Calcutta, while 30,000,000 of human beings were reduced to the extremity of wretchedness. They had been accustomed to live under tyranny, but never under tyranny like this. They found the little finger of the Company thicker than Surajah Dowlah's loins. Under their old masters, they had at least one resource: when the evil became insupportable, the people rose and pulled down the government. But the English government was not to be so shaken off. That government, oppressive as the most oppressive form of barbarian despotism, was strong with all the strength of civilization. It resembled the government of evil genii, rather than the government of human tyrants."—*Macaulay.*

distributed. The perfectly centralized ryotwar system was thus established, and how it has operated may be judged from the following sketch, presented by Mr. Fullerton, a member of the Council at Madras :—

"Imagine the revenue leviable through the agency of one hundred thousand revenue officers, collected or remitted at their discretion, according to the occupant's means of paying, whether from the produce of his land or his separate property; and in order to encourage every man to act as a spy on his neighbor, and report his means of paying, that he may eventually save himself from extra demand, imagine all the cultivators of a village liable at all times to a separate demand, in order to make up for the failure of one or more individuals of the parish. Imagine collectors to every county, acting under the orders of a board, on the avowed principle of destroying all competition for labor by a general equalization of assessment, seizing and sending back runaways to each other. And, lastly, imagine the collector the sole magistrate or justice of the peace of the county, through the medium and instrumentality of whom alone any criminal complaint of personal grievance suffered by the subject can reach the superior courts. Imagine, at the same time, every subordinate officer employed in the collection of the land revenue to be a police officer, vested with the power to fine, confine, put in the stocks, and flog any inhabitant within his range, on any charge, without oath of the accuser or sworn recorded evidence of the case."*

Under such a system, there could be no circulation — no commerce; and, without that, there could be neither force nor progress. Exert himself as he might, the poor cultivator found that the profits of his exertion were required for the benefit of the Company's treasury — an increase of rent at once being claimed whenever increase of products had been obtained. In some districts, the government's share is stated to have been no less than sixty or seventy per cent. of the whole; and yet, to this were further added, taxes upon all the machinery in use — requiring interferences of the most inquisitorial kind, and forbidding all improvement. In settling the taxes paid by looms, it was required that the weaver should report how many children he had, and what assistance they rendered him; and the more they

* Quoted in *Thompson's Lectures on India*, p. 61.

all exerted themselves, the higher became the amount of contribution.*

The oil-mill, the potter's kiln, the goldsmith's tools, the sawyer's saw, the blacksmith's anvil, the carpenter's tools, the cotton-beater's bow, the weaver's loom, and the fisherman's boat — all were taxed. No machinery of any description was allowed to escape; and to guard against the employment of untaxed labor, either in cultivation or manufactures, large allowances were made to informers, with a view to induce those who did not desire to work to become spies on those who did — *and this system is still in force.*†

§ 2. The tendency thus far has been, as we see, to sweep away the rights not only of kings and princes, but of all the native authorities, and to centralize in the hands of foreigners in Calcutta the power to determine for the cultivator, the artisan, or the laborer, what work he should do, and how much of its products he might retain — thus placing the latter in precisely the position of a mere slave to people who — having no interest in him but simply as a tax-payer — were represented by strangers in the country, whose authority was everywhere used by the native officers in their employ, to enable them to amass fortunes for themselves.

The poor manufacturer, as heavily taxed as the cultivator of the earth, found himself compelled to obtain advances from his employers, who, in their turn, claimed, as interest, a large proportion of the little profit that was made. The Company's agents, like the native merchants, advanced the funds necessary to produce the goods required for Europe; and the poor workmen are described as having been "in a state of dependence almost amounting to servitude, enabling the resident to obtain his labor at his own price."‡

Further taxes were collected, at local custom-houses, on all

* RICKARDS: *India*, vol. i. p. 500.

† "Fifty per cent. on the assessment is allowed as a reward to any informer of concealed cultivation, &c.; and it is stated that there are, 'in almost every village, dismissed accountants desirous of being re-employed, and unemployed servants who wish to bring themselves to notice,' whose services as informers can be relied on." — CAMPBELL: *Modern India*, London, 1852, p. 356.

‡ BAINES: *History of the Cotton Manufacture.*

exchanges between the several parts of the country; and to these were again added others imposed by means of monopolies of opium and tobacco; as well as of salt, one of the most important necessaries of life. The manufacture of coarse salt from the earth was strictly prohibited.* The salt lakes of the upper country furnish a supply so great that it is of little value on the spot;† but they being even yet in the possession of native princes, the monopoly could then, and can now, be maintained only by aid of strong bands of revenue officers, whose presence renders that which is almost worthless on one side of an imaginary line so valuable on the other, that it requires the produce of the sixth part of the year's labor to enable the poor Hindoo to purchase salt for his family. Along the sea-shore, it is abundantly furnished by nature—the solar heat causing its constant deposition; but the mere fact of its collection was constituted an offence punishable by fine and imprisonment; and the quantity collected by the Company's officers was limited to that required for meeting the demand at a monopoly price — all the remainder being regularly destroyed, lest the poor ryot should succeed in obtaining for himself, at cost, such a supply as was needed to render palatable the rice which constituted almost his only food. The system has since been rendered less oppressive, but the mere money tax, even now, is ten times greater than it was under enlightened Mohammedan sovereigns‡ — but, if we add to this that the poor ryot is forced to waste the labor that might be employed in collecting the salt his family requires to consume, it will be seen that the loss in this single case is enormous in amount.

Under the native princes, the produce of taxation was locally expended — producing a demand for commodities, or services, at home; but, under the centralized system that now exists, it is required to go abroad, to be employed in purchasing the services, or paying the dividends, of distant people; and thus is the real weight of taxation almost indefinitely increased by the destruction of the power of association and combination. Commerce is, thus, everywhere sacrificed to trade.§

* CAMPBELL: *Modern India*, p. 382. † Ibid. p. 381. ‡ Ibid. p. 105.

§ The difference between an absentee landlord expending at a distance all his rents, and a resident one distributing them again among his tenants in exchange for services, and the difference in the value of the products of the land resulting from proximity to market, are so well exhibited in the follow-

§ 3. Cotton abounded; and to so great an extent, half a century since, was the labor of men, women, and children applied to its conversion into cloth, that, even with their imperfect machinery, they not only supplied the home demand for the beautiful

ing passage from a recent work on India, that the reader cannot fail to profit by its perusal:—

"The great part of the wheat, grain, and other exportable land produce which the people consume, as far as we have yet come, is drawn from our Nerbudda districts, and those of Malwa which border upon them; and, *par consequent*, the price has been rapidly increasing as we recede from them in our advance northward. Were the soil of those Nerbudda districts, situated as they are at such a distance from any great market for their agricultural products, as bad as it is in the parts of Bundelcund that I came over, no net surplus revenue could possibly be drawn from them in the present state of arts and industry. The high prices paid here for land produce, arising from the necessity of drawing a great part of what is consumed from such distant lands, enables the rajahs of these Bundelcund states to draw the large revenue they do. These chiefs expend the whole of their revenue in the maintenance of public establishments of one kind or other; and as the essential articles of subsistence, *wheat* and *grain*, &c., which are produced in their own districts, or those immediately around them, are not sufficient for the supply of these establishments, they must draw them from distant territories. All this produce is brought on the backs of bullocks, because there is no road from the districts whence they obtain it over which a wheeled carriage can be drawn with safety; and, as this mode of transit is very expensive, the price of the produce, when it reaches the capitals, around which these local establishments are concentrated, becomes very high. They must pay a price equal to the collective cost of purchasing and bringing this substance from the most distant districts to which they are at any time obliged to have recourse for a supply, or they will not be supplied; and as there cannot be two prices for the same thing in the same market, the wheat and grain produced in the neighborhood of one of these Bundelcund capitals fetch as high a price there as that brought from the most remote districts on the banks of the Nerbudda river; while it costs comparatively nothing to bring it from the former lands to the markets. Such lands, in consequence, yield a rate of rent much greater compared with their natural powers of fertility than those of the remote districts whence produce is drawn for these markets or capitals; and as all the lands are the property of the rajahs, they draw all these rents as revenue.

"Were we to take this revenue, which the rajahs now enjoy, in tribute for the maintenance of public establishments concentrated at distant seats, all these local establishments would of course be at once disbanded; and all the effectual demand which they afford for the raw agricultural produce of distant districts would cease. The price of the produce would diminish in proportion; and with it the value of the lands of the districts around such capitals. Hence the folly of conquerors and paramount powers, from the days of the Greeks and Romans down to those of Lord Hastings and Sir John Malcolm, who were all bad political economists, in supposing that conquered and ceded territories could always be made to yield to a foreign state the same amount of gross revenue they had paid to their domestic government, whatever their situation with reference to the markets for their produce—whatever the state of the arts and their industry—and whatever the character and extent of the local establishments maintained out of it. The settlements of the land revenue in all the territories acquired in Central India tissues of Dacca and the coarse products of Western India, but exported to other parts of the world no less than 200,000,000 of pounds of cloth per annum. Exchanges with every part of the world were so greatly in their favor, that a rupee, which would now sell for but 1s. 10*d.*, or 44 cents, was then worth 2*s.* 8*d.*, or 64 cents. The Company had a monopoly of collecting taxes in India, but, in return therefor, it preserved to the people the control of their domestic market, by aid of which they were enabled

during the Mahratta war, which ended in 1817, were made upon the supposition that the lands would continue to pay the same rate of rent under the new, as they had paid under the old, government, uninfluenced by the diminution of all local establishments, civil and military, to one-tenth of what they had been; that, under the new order of things, all the waste lands must be brought into tillage; and be able to pay as high a rate of rent as before tillage; and, consequently, that the aggregate available net revenue must greatly and rapidly increase! Those who had the making of the settlements, and the governing of these new territories, did not consider that the diminution of every *establishment* was the removal of a *market*—of an effectual demand for land produce; and that when all the waste lands should be brought into tillage, the whole would deteriorate in fertility, from the want of fallows, under the prevailing system of agriculture, which afforded the lands no other means of renovation from over-cropping. The settlements of the land revenue which were made throughout our new acquisitions upon these fallacious assumptions, of course failed. During a series of quinquennial settlements, the assessment has been everywhere gradually reduced to about two-thirds of what it was when our rule began; and to less than one-half of what Sir John Malcolm, and all the other local authorities, and even the worthy Marquis of Hastings himself, under the influence of their opinions, expected it would be. The land revenues of the native princes of Central India, who reduced their public establishments, which the new order of things seemed to render useless, and thereby diminished their only markets for the raw produce of their lands, have been everywhere falling off in the same proportion; and scarcely one of them now draws two-thirds of the income he drew from the same lands in 1817.

"There are, in the valley of the Nerbudda, districts that yield a great deal more produce every year than either Orcha, Jansee, or Duteea; and yet, from the want of the same domestic markets, they do not yield one-fourth of the amount of land revenue. The lands are, however, rated equally high to the assessment, in proportion to their value to the farmers and cultivators. To enable them to yield a larger revenue to the government, they require to have larger establishments as markets for land produce. These establishments may be either public, and paid by government, or they may be private, as manufactories, by which the land produce of these districts would be consumed by people employed in investing the value of their labor in commodities suited to the demand of distant markets, and more valuable than land produce in proportion to their weight and bulk. These are the establishments which government should exert itself to introduce and foster, since the valley of the Nerbudda, in addition to a soil exceedingly fertile, has, in its whole line from its source to its embouchure, rich beds of coal reposing, for the use of future generations, under the sandstone of the Sathpore and Vindhya ranges; and beds no less rich of very fine iron. These advantages have not yet been justly appreciated; but they will be so by-and-by." — SLEEMAN: *Rambles in India*, vol. i. p. 296.

to convert their rice, their salt, and their cotton into cloth that could be cheaply carried to the most distant countries. Such protection was required, because, while England prohibited the export of even a single collier who might instruct the people of India in the mode of mining coal — of a steam-engine to pump water, or raise their coal, or a mechanic who could make one — of a worker in iron who might smelt the ore such vast bodies of which exist—of a spinning-jenny, or power-loom—or, of an artisan who could give instruction in the use of such machines; and thus systematically prevented them from acquiring control over the great forces of nature — she at the same time imposed very heavy duties on the produce of Indian looms received in England. The day was at hand, however, when that protection was to disappear. The Company did not, it was said, export sufficiently largely of the produce of British industry; and in 1813 the trade to India was thrown open — *but the restriction on the export of machinery and artisans was maintained in full force;* and thus were the poor and ignorant people of that country exposed to competition with a community possessed of machinery greatly more effective than their own; while not only by law deprived of the power to purchase machinery, but also of the power of competing in the British market with the produce of British looms. Further than this, every loom in India, and every machine calculated to aid the laborer, was subject to a tax increasing in amount with every increase in the industry of its owner, and generally absorbing all the profit resulting from its use.* Such were the circum-

* The following humble petition of the unfortunate natives exhibits in full force the character of the system:—

"CALCUTTA, *September* 1, 1831.

"To the Right Honorable the Lords of His Majesty's Privy Council for Trade, &c.

"The humble Petition of the undersigned Manufacturers and Dealers in Cotton and Silk Piece Goods, the fabrics of Bengal;

"SHOWETH—That of late years your Petitioners have found their business nearly superseded by the introduction of the fabrics of Great Britain into Bengal, the importation of which augments every year, to the great prejudice of the native manufacturers.

"That the fabrics of Great Britain are consumed in Bengal, without any duties being levied thereon to protect the native fabrics.

"That the fabrics of Bengal are charged with the following duties when they are used in Great Britain:

"On manufactured cottons, 10 per cent.

"On manufactured silks, 24 per cent.

"Your Petitioners most humbly implore your Lordships' consideration of

stances under which the poor Hindoo was called upon to meet unprotected, the "unlimited competition" of foreigners in his own market. Four years afterwards, the export of cottons from Bengal still amounted to £1,659,994; but ten years later, it had declined to £285,121; and at the end of twenty years we find a whole year to have passed by without the export of a single piece of cotton cloth from that country—and thus did commerce perish under the oppressive demands of trade.

When the export of cotton, woollen, steam, and all other machinery was prohibited, it was done with a view to compelling all the wool of the world to come to England to be spun and woven, thence to be returned to be worn by those who had raised it—thus depriving all other nations of the power to apply their labor except in taking from the earth cotton, sugar, indigo, and other commodities, for the supply of the great "workshop of the world." How effectually that object has been accomplished in India, will be seen from the following facts:—From the date of the opening of the trade, in 1813, the domestic manufacture, and the export of cloth, have gradually declined, until the latter has finally ceased; and the export of raw cotton to England has gradually risen until it had, six years since, attained a height of about sixty millions of pounds,* while the import of twist from England had risen to twenty-five millions of pounds, and of cloth, to two hundred and sixty millions of yards, weighing probably

these circumstances, and they feel confident that no disposition exists in England to shut the door against the industry of any part of the inhabitants of this great empire.

"They therefore pray to be admitted to the privilege of British subjects, and humbly entreat your Lordships to allow the cotton and silk fabrics of Bengal to be used in Great Britain 'free of duty,' or at the same rate which may be charged on British fabrics consumed in Bengal.

"Your Lordships must be aware of the immense advantages the British manufacturers derive from their skill in constructing and using machinery, which enables them to undersell the unscientific manufacturers of Bengal in their own country; and, although your Petitioners are not sanguine in expecting to derive any great advantage from having their prayer granted, their minds would feel gratified by such a manifestation of your Lordships' good-will toward them; and such an instance of justice to the natives of India would not fail to endear the British government to them.

"They therefore confidently trust that your Lordships' righteous consideration will be extended to them as British subjects, without exception of sect, country, or color.

"And your Petitioners, as in duty bound, will ever pray."

[Signed by 117 natives of high respectability.]

* Chapman: *Cotton and Commerce of India*, London, 1851.

fifty millions of pounds, which, added to the twist, make seventy-five millions—requiring for their production somewhat more than eighty millions of raw cotton. We see thus that every pound of the raw material sent to England is returned. The cultivator receives for it one penny, and pays for it, when returned in the form of cloth, from one to two shillings — the whole difference being absorbed in the payment of the numerous brokers, transporters, manufacturers, and operatives of all descriptions, that have thus been interposed between the producer and the consumer.

The power of consumption is consequently small; and the great domestic seats of manufacture, at which men, women, and children were accustomed to combine their labors, have disappeared. Dacca, one of the principal seats of the cotton manufacture, contained 90,000 houses, but its splendid buildings, factories, and churches are now a mass of ruins, and overgrown with jungle. The cotton of the district found itself compelled to go to England, that it might there be twisted and sent back again — thus performing a voyage of twenty thousand miles in search of the little spindle; because it was a part of the British policy not to permit the spindle, anywhere, to take its place by the side of the cultivator of cotton.

The change thus effected has been shown, in official documents, to have been attended with ruin and distress, to which "no parallel can be found in the annals of commerce." What were the means by which it was effected is shown in the fact that, at the time at which it was being accomplished, Sir Robert Peel stated that, in Lancashire, *children* were employed fifteen and seventeen hours per day, during the week; and on Sunday morning, from six until twelve, in cleaning the machinery. In Coventry, ninety-six hours in the week was the time usually required; and of those employed, many obtained but 2*s.* 9*d.* — 66 cents — as the wages of a week. The object to be accomplished was that of underworking the poor Hindoo, and driving him from the market of the world; after which he was to be driven from his own. The mode of accomplishment was that of cheapening labor — the laborer, according to modern doctrines, being only an instrument to be used by trade.

With the decline of Indian manufactures, the demand for the

services of women or children has ceased, and they are forced either to remain idle, or to seek employment in the field; and here we have one of the distinguishing marks of a retrocession towards slavery and barbarism. The men, too, who had been accustomed to fill up the intervals of other employments in pursuits connected with the cotton manufacture, were also driven to the field — all demand for labor, physical or intellectual, being at an end, except so far as it was required for raising indigo, sugar, cotton, or rice. This last they were not permitted even to clean, having been debarred therefrom by a duty twice greater than that which was paid on paddy, or rough rice, on its import into England. The cotton-grower, after paying to the government seventy-eight per cent.* of the product of his labor, found himself deprived of the power to trade directly with the man of the loom, and forced into "unlimited competition" with the better machinery and almost untaxed labor of our Southern States — thus being subjected to "the mysterious variations of foreign markets," in which the fever of speculation was followed by the chill of revulsion, and with a rapidity and frequency that set at naught all calculation. If American crops were small, his English customers would take his cotton; but if they were large, the Indian article became a mere drug in the market. To such an extent was this the case, that, on one occasion, as was stated in the House of Commons, a Mr. Turner, unable to find a purchaser, threw upon the dunghill cotton that had cost him £7000.

With every increase in the necessity for effecting changes of place, the motion of society—or commerce—diminishes; and the less that motion, the greater must be the quantity of labor and its products pressing on the market, to the advantage of those who live by appropriation, and to the destruction of the value of land and labor. The direct effects of the system above described having been that of destroying commerce and diminishing the demand for the laborer's services, they, in their turn, were followed by

* "Taking the last six of the thirteen years, the price of cotton was 2*d.* a pound, and if the produce of a beegah was 6*s.* 6*d.*, of this the government took sixty-eight per cent. of the gross produce; and, taking the two years 1841 and 1842, cotton was 1¾*d.* a pound, and the produce of a beegah was 5*s.* 8*d.* On this the assessment was actually equal to seventy-eight per cent. on the gross produce of the land." — *Speech of Mr. Bright in the House of Commons.*

diminution of his power to make demand for cloth, attended, necessarily, by increase in the quantity of cotton for which a foreign market was required. The more these effects were produced, the lower became the price of cotton; and thus was realized the effect of an almost total annihilation of the value of agricultural labor, as a consequence of measures adopted with a view to compel the whole people to look to agriculture alone for the means of supporting life. Further, while the price of cotton has thus been rendered wholly dependent upon the market of England, there, too, is fixed the price of cloth — the consequences of which are seen in the facts, that this whole people has become a mere instrument to be used by trade, and that in India, as in Ireland, Portugal, Turkey, and the West Indies, may, in most abundance, be found the data upon which to rest the doctrine of over-population.

§ 4. The poor ryot pays, as we see, twelve, fifteen, or twenty pence for the pound of cotton that had yielded him but a single penny; and all this difference is paid for the services of others, while he, himself, is unemployed. "A great part of the time of the laboring population in India is," says Mr. Chapman, "spent in idleness. I," as he continues, "don't say this to blame them in the smallest degree. Without the means of exporting heavy and crude surplus agricultural produce, and with scanty means, whether of capital, science, or manual skill, for elaborating on the spot articles fitted to induce a higher state of enjoyment and of industry in the mass of the people, they have really no inducement to exertion beyond that which is necessary to gratify their present and very limited wishes: those wishes are unnaturally low, inasmuch as they do not afford the needful stimulus to the exercise requisite to intellectual and moral improvement; and it is obvious that there is no remedy for this but extended intercourse. Meanwhile, probably the half of the human time and energy of India runs to mere waste. Surely, we need not wonder at the poverty of the country."*

"Half the human time and energy," as we are here told, "runs to waste," but the author of this passage might have gone much further, and yet been far within the truth. Where there is no commerce, and men are, consequently, forced to depend on the

* Chapman: *Cotton and Commerce of India*, p. 110.

distant trade, *nine-tenths* of the physical and mental efforts of a community "run to waste;" and therefore it is that not only does capital not accumulate, but the accumulations of past times are then in course of daily diminution. With the decline in the power to maintain commerce, there is a daily increase in the necessity for resorting to the distant market, but with every such increase the commodities requiring to be transported increase in bulk and decline in value; and therefore it is, that the trader and transporter are enabled to take for themselves a constantly increasing *proportion* of a diminished product — leaving a constantly diminishing one for the cultivator. Their cotton and their food travelled readily to all portions of the world in the form of cloth, and they then consumed liberally of clothing; but now, when their raw cotton, their rice, and their sugar, have to go abroad in their rudest shapes, the quantity of finished commodities they have the power to pay for is so small, that the price paid for their transportation scarcely enters into the compensation of the men, oxen, wagons, and ships, required for the work. Nearly the whole burden of the double voyage is therefore borne by the raw material; and, as in Turkey, Portugal, Ireland, and all other agricultural countries, the difficulty of making new roads, or of maintaining old ones, increases from year to year.

From important cotton districts, transportation is effected at the rate of seven miles per day, and requires more than a hundred days; and if the "herd of bullocks is overtaken by rain, the cotton, saturated by moisture, becomes heavy, and the black clayey soil, through which lies the whole line of road, sinks under the feet of a man above the ankle, and under that of a laden ox to the knees. In this predicament the cargo of cotton lies sometimes for weeks on the ground, and the merchant is ruined."*

"So miserably bad," says another writer, "are the existing means of communication with the interior, that many of the most valuable articles of produce are, *for want of carriage and a market, often allowed to perish on the farm*, while the cost of that which found its way to the port was enormously enhanced; but the quantity did not amount to above twenty per cent. of the whole of the produce, the remainder of the articles always being greatly deteriorated."

* London *Economist*.

Such being the modes of transportation, we can readily understand why it is that cotton yields its cultivator but a penny a pound — and why, too, it is, that the producer of the more bulky food is in a condition that is even worse, now that the consumer has disappeared from his side. When the crop is large, scarcely any price can be obtained for grain;* and when it is small, the people perish, by thousands and tens of thousands, of famine, because, in the existing state of the roads, there can be little or no exchange of the rude products of the earth.

§ 5. The state of things above described, results necessarily from the maintenance of a system which looks to the annihilation of commerce through the exclusion of the great middle class of mechanics and working-men; and which thus resolves a great nation into a mass of wretched cultivators on the one hand, and grasping money-lenders on the other. The chain of society is, here, totally destitute of the connecting links, as a consequence of which there is neither motion nor force. *Capital being wasted weekly to an amount greater than the annual value of the goods imported,* there can be no accumulation. "None," says Colonel Sleeman,† "have stock equal to half their rent." They are dependent, everywhere, on the produce of the year, and however small may be its amount, the taxes must be paid; and, of all that thus goes abroad, nothing is returned. The soil gets nothing,‡ and, as the condition upon which the earth makes her loans to man is daily, hourly, and universally violated, no surprise need be felt on reading, in Colonel Sleeman's interesting volumes, the numerous evidences he has furnished of the growing infertility of the land.

The works constructed in former times, for the purposes of irrigation, have been allowed to go to ruin,§ and the richest lands are being abandoned. Even in the valley of the Ganges, not a third of the cultivable lands is, says Mr. Chapman, under cultivation;‖ while elsewhere he tells his readers, that of the cultivable

* "In 1846 or 1847, the collector was obliged to grant remission of land tax, 'because the abundance of former years lay stagnating in the province, and the low prices of grain from that cause prevented the ryots from being able to pay their fixed land assessment.'"—Chapman: *Cotton and Commerce of India*, p. 97.

† *Rambles in India*, vol. i. p. 205.

‡ Ibid. p. 268.

§ Chapman: *Cotton and Commerce of India*, p. 97.

‖ Ibid. p. 22.

surface of all India, one-half is waste.* In the Madras presidency, not one-fifth of the land is cultivated;† and yet famines are of constant occurrence, and of a severity known in no other portion of the world, while labor and land abound for which no employment can be obtained. The site of the so recently great manufacturing city of Dacca, presented to the view of Bishop Heber but an "impenetrable jungle;" and it is as a necessary result of this, that East Indian journals are required to remind their readers of the millions of acres of rich lands that might be made to yield cotton—that now are lying waste. Look to what quarter we may of that magnificent country, we meet with evidence of declining individuality and diminished power of combination, accompanied by daily increasing centralization, of which the annexation of Oude affords the most striking of all the late examples‡—and centralization, slavery, and death travel always together, whether in the material or the moral world.

When population and wealth diminish, the rich soils are first abandoned, as is shown in the Campagna of Rome, in the valley of Mexico, and in the deltas of the Ganges and the Nile. Without combination of effort, they could never have been brought under cultivation, and their present abandonment is but the evidence of the disappearance of the power of association and combination. Driven back to the poor soils, and forced to send abroad the product, the wretched Hindoo becomes poorer from day to day, and the less he obtains, the more does he become a slave to the caprices of his landlord; and the more is he thrown upon the mercy of the money-lender, who lends *on good security* at three

* *Cotton and Commerce of India*, p. 25.

† "If a ryot sunk a well, his rent was raised; if he cut a small canal, it was nearly doubled. There was, therefore, no possibility of improvement. Moreover, the land being divided among cottiers whose only capital was their labor, two bad seasons reduced them to the verge of starvation. In such cases, the whole revenue was occasionally lost in remissions. Of course, nobody ever grew rich, and in all the presidency there are probably not ten farmers worth £1000. The area of cultivation is only one-fifth the area of the presidency, and shows no tendency to increase."—*London Times.*

‡ Hitherto, the proceeds of the taxation of the people of Oude have been, to a considerable extent, locally expended; and have aided in making a demand for labor and its products. Now, they are to be transferred to Calcutta, and are likely to add, as we are told, two millions of pounds to the Company's revenue. Taxation, when its proceeds are locally expended, is but a question of *distribution*. When not so expended, it is a question of *exhaustion*. Ten millions, in the one case, would not work as large an amount of ruin, as one in the other.

per cent. per month, but *from him* must have fifty or a hundred per cent. for a loan until harvest. That, under such circumstances, the wages of labor are very low, even where the wretched people are employed, is only what might naturally be expected. In some places, the laborer has two, and in others three, rupees, or less than a dollar and a half, per month. The officers employed on the great zemindary estates have from three to four rupees, and the police receive but forty-eight rupees ($23) per annum, out of which they supply themselves with food and clothing! Such are the rewards of labor in a country possessing every conceivable means of accumulating wealth; and they become less from year to year.*

§ 6. Throughout the world, and in all ages, the advance towards civilization having been in the ratio of the tendency towards local activity, and towards the development of individual faculty, and the system now under consideration looking to results directly the reverse of this, we might reasonably expect to find, at every step, an increasing tendency in the reverse direction. Growing civilization is marked by increased security of person and property, and that increase is found as we pass *from* the old possessions of the Company, and towards the newly-acquired ones.† Crime of every kind, gang robbery, perjury, and forgery, abound in Bengal and Madras, and the poverty of the cultivator

* "The Court of Directors inform us that 'there has been a diminution in the total receipts from land in the old provinces of Bengal since 1843–44;' and certainly no one can be surprised to hear it. In the Madras presidency the people are wretchedly poor, the land of little value, and cultivation kept up only by forced methods, the inhabitants being unwilling to cultivate it on any terms. In Bombay, 'the receipts have fallen off, and the country generally,' we are told, 'is not prosperous.' From a member in the council of that presidency we learn that India 'is verging to the lowest ebb of pauperism;' and that the payments to government are made by the inhabitants pawning or selling their personal ornaments, and even their cattle, furniture, and tools; that is, the capital of the country is encroached upon to pay the taxes. It was the same officer who told a parliamentary committee, five years since, that the condition of the cultivators in India was 'greatly depressed, and, he feared, declining.' The aristocracy among the natives are sinking out of sight, the race of native gentry has almost everywhere disappeared, and the peasantry are becoming reckless through ruin. Every few years a famine occurs; and government spends, in hopeless efforts to keep the people alive, the money which would have made roads to the granaries, to the ports, and to the surplus of happier provinces. Where food should have been passing, in exchange for other commodities, the way was strewn with the gaunt corpses of half millions of people starved tc death."—*London Daily News.*

† See *Campbell's Modern India*, chap. xi.

is so extreme, that the revenue is there the least, and is collected with the greatest difficulty; and there, too, it is that the power of association has been most effectually annihilated. Passing to the northwestern provinces, more recently acquired, person and property become comparatively secure, and the revenue increases; but when we reach the Punjab—until recently subject to the rule of Runjeet Singh and his successors—we find that, tyrants as he and they have been represented, the village communities, and the beautiful system of association, have remained untouched. Officers of all kinds are there more responsible for the performance of their duties than are their fellows in the older provinces, and property and person are more secure than in any other part of India. Gang robbery is rare, perjury is unfrequent, and, as Mr. Campbell assures his readers, a solemn oath is "astonishingly binding." "The longer we possess a province," he continues, "the more common and general does perjury become;" and the stronger, consequently, becomes the evidence of the fact that the feeling of responsibility towards God and man declines with the decline of individuality and the diminution of the power of association. That feeling grows, everywhere, with the growth of the power to maintain commerce, and it declines, everywhere, as man is made the mere instrument to be used by trade. The "hill tribes" of India are remarkable for their "strict veracity," "as little falsehood" being, says Colonel Sleeman, "spoken in the village communities," as in any other part of the world with equal area and population.*

In the newly-acquired provinces, the people read and write with facility, and they are men of physical and moral energy, good cultivators — and understanding well both their rights and their duties; whereas from the older ones education has disappeared, and, with it, all power to associate together for any useful purpose. In the new provinces, commerce is large, as is shown by the following facts, representing the population and post-office revenue of Bengal, the N. W. Provinces and the Punjab, placed in the order of their acquisition by the Company:—

| | Population. | Post-office revenue. |
|---|---|---|
| Bengal | 41,000,000 | 480,500 rupees. |
| N. W. Provinces | 24,000,000 | 978,000 " |
| Punjab | 8,000,000 | 178,000 " |

* *Rambles in India*, vol. ii. p. 109.

We have here presented the remarkable fact, that, in the country of the Sikhs, so long represented as a scene of grasping tyranny, eight millions pay as much postage as is paid by fifteen millions in Bengal, although in the latter we find Calcutta, the seat of all the operations of a great centralized government. That such should be the case is not extraordinary, for the power advantageously to employ labor diminishes with the approach to the centre of British power, and increases as we recede from it. Idleness and drunkenness go hand in hand with each other, and therefore it is that Mr. Campbell finds himself obliged to state that "intemperance increases where our rule and system has been long established;"* while Captain Westmacott tells his readers that "in places the longest under our rule, there is the largest amount of depravity and crime."

Calcutta grows, the city of palaces, but poverty and wretchedness grow as commerce is more and more sacrificed for the promotion of the interests of trade. Under the native rule, the people of each little district could exchange with each other — giving food for cotton, or cotton cloth, paying nobody for the privilege. Now, every man must send his cotton to Calcutta, thence to go to England with the rice and the indigo of his neighbors — *before he and they can exchange food for cloth, or cotton;* and the larger the quantity they send, the greater is the tendency to decline in price. Centralization grows daily, and every stage of its growth is marked by increased inability to pay the taxes, and increased necessity for seeking new markets in which to sell cloth and collect what are called rents — and the more wide the extension of the system, the greater is the difficulty of collecting revenue sufficient for keeping in motion the machine of government. This it was, that forced the representatives of British power and civilization into becoming traders in that pernicious drug, opium, by means of which the people of China are taxed, annually, to the extent of nearly twenty millions of dollars, and not less than half a million of lives. "The immolations of an Indian Juggernauth," says a recent writer, "dwindle into insignificance before it;" and yet for the maintenance of this trade it was that the towns and cities of China were sacked, and their people ruined, even where not exterminated. Trade and war have, however,

* *Modern India*, p. 394.

gone hand in hand with each other from the commencement of the world, and all their triumphs have been obtained at the expense of commerce.

§ 7. The gross land revenue obtained from a country with an area of 491,448 square miles, or above three hundred millions of acres, is 151,786,743 rupees, equal to fifteen millions of pounds sterling, or seventy-two millions of dollars.* What is the value of private rights of property, subject to the payment of this tax, or rent, may be judged from the following facts:—In 1848–49, there were sold for taxes, in that portion of the country subject to the permanent settlement, 1169 estates, at something less than four years' purchase of the tax. Further south, in the Madras government, where the ryotwar settlement is in full operation, the land "would be sold" for balances of rent, but "generally it is not," as we are told, "and for a very good reason, viz. that nobody will buy it." Private rights in land being there of no value whatsoever, "the collector of Salem," as Mr. Campbell informs us, "naïvely mentions 'various unauthorized modes of stimulating the tardy,' rarely resorted to by heads of villages, such as 'placing him in the sun, obliging him to stand on one leg, or to sit with his head confined between his knees.'"†

In the Northwest Provinces, "the settlement," as our author states, "has certainly been successful in giving a good market value to landed property;" that is, it sells at about "four years' purchase on the revenue."‡ Still further north, in the newly-acquired provinces, we find great industry, "every thing" being "turned to account;" the assessment—to which the Company succeeded on the deposition of the successors of Runjeet Singh—more easy; and land more valuable.§ The value of land, like that of labor, therefore increases as we pass *from* the old to the new set-

* *Campbell*, p. 377.

† Campbell: *Modern India*, p. 359. That torture of various kinds is one of the established modes of collecting revenue, is a fact admitted by the Company, and one to which the attention of the British Parliament has recently been called. It being one, however, whose existence grows out of the necessity of the case, no remedy can be applied. The poverty of the people grows daily, and with that growth the difficulty of collecting revenue increases—and whatever may be the disposition of the governors, they must, under such circumstances, claim a *constantly increasing proportion* of the *constantly decreasing products* of land and labor.

‡ Ibid. p. 332.

§ Ibid. p. 345.

tlements, being precisely the reverse of what would be the case if the system looked to the extension of commerce; and precisely what should be looked for in a country in which commerce was being sacrificed to trade.

With the data thus obtained, we may now ascertain, with perhaps some approach to accuracy, the value of all the private rights in the land of India. In no case does that subject to tax appear to be worth more than four years' purchase; while, in a very large portion of the country it appears to be worth absolutely nothing. There being, however, some tax-free lands, it is possible that the whole may be worth four years' purchase — giving two hundred and eighty-eight millions of dollars, or sixty millions of pounds sterling, as the value of all the rights in land acquired by the people of India in the thousands of years it has been under cultivation. The few people that have occupied the little and sandy State of New Jersey, with its area of 6900 square miles, have acquired rights in, and on, the land that are valued, subject to the claims of government, at one hundred and fifty millions of dollars; and those of the few that have occupied the little island on which stands the city of New York, would sell for almost twice as much as could be obtained for all the proprietary rights to land in India, with three huudred millions of acres and ninety-six millions of inhabitants!

§ 8. "Under the native princes," says Mr. Campbell, "India was a paying country." Under absentee rule, it has ceased to be so, and for the reason, that under that rule all power of combined action has been annihilated, by aid of the system that looks to compelling the whole people, men, women, and children, to work in the field—producing commodities to be exported in their rudest state. Every act of association being an act of commerce, whatever tends to destroy the former must destroy the latter. The internal commerce of India declines steadily, and the external one amounts to but fifty cents per head, and by no effort can it be increased to any extent. Cuba, exporting to the large amount of twenty-five dollars per head — or almost fifty times as much as India—takes of cotton goods from Britain four times as much per head; and this she does because it is a part of the policy of Spain to bring about combination of action, and to enable the planter and the artisan to work together; whereas the policy of the former looks to the destruction, everywhere, of the power of association, and thus, to the annihilation of the domestic commerce upon which, alone, the foreign one can be built. Centralization is adverse to commerce and to the freedom of man. Spain does not seek to establish centralization. Provided she receives a given amount of revenue, she is content to permit her subjects to employ themselves at raising sugar, or making cloth, and thus to advance in civilization; and by this course it is that she is enabled to obtain the aid she needs.

The people of Jamaica—having never been permitted to apply their spare labor even to the refining of it — are obliged to export their sugar in its crudest state; and the more they send, the lower is the price, and the larger the proportion taken by the government; but the poor negro is ruined. Spain, on the contrary, permits the Cubans to engage in whatsoever pursuits appear to them likely to afford a return to labor and capital; and, as a necessary consequence of this, towns and cities grow up, and capital is attracted to the land, which becomes from day to day more valuable. The power to resort to other modes of employment diminishes the necessity for exporting sugar, and when exported to Spain, the producer is enabled to take for himself nearly the whole price paid by the consumer, the government claiming only a duty of fifteen per cent.

"Vast heaps of humanity, festering in compulsory idleness, encumber the soil of India,"* because the Hindoo, like the negro of Jamaica, is shut out from the workshop. If he attempts to convert his cotton into yarn, his spindle is taxed to the extent of all of the profit it might yield him. If he attempts to make cloth, his loom is subjected to a heavy tax, from which that of his wealthy English competitor is exempt. His iron ore and his coal must remain in the ground, and if he dares even to collect the salt which crystallizes before his door, fine and imprisonment are the reward of all his labor. He must raise sugar to be transported to England, there to be exchanged, perhaps, for English salt. For the sugar, arrived in that country, the workman pays at the rate perhaps of forty shillings a hundred, of which the govern ment claims one-third, the ship-owner, the merchant, and others,

* CHAPMAN: *Cotton and Commerce of India.*

another third, and the remaining third is to be divided between the agents of the Company, anxious for revenue, and the poor ryot, anxious to obtain a little salt to eat with his rice, and as much of his neighbor's cotton, in the form of English cloth, as will suffice to cover his loins.

Iron, by aid of which the people might improve their processes of cultivation and manufacture, has little tendency toward India — the average export of it to that country in 1845 and '46 having been but 13,000 tons, value £160,000; or about twopence-worth for every five of the population. Efforts are now being made for the construction of railroads, but their object is that of carrying out the system of centralization, and thus still further destroying the power of association, because they look to the annihilation of what still remains of domestic manufacture—and thus *cheapening cotton.* With all the improvements in the transportation of that commodity, its poor cultivator obtains less for it than he did thirty years since; and the effect of further improvement can be only that of producing a still further reduction, and still further deterioration of the condition of the men who raise food and cotton. As yet, the power of association continues in the Punjab, but—it being proposed now to hold there great fairs for the sale of English manufactures — the day cannot be far distant when the condition of the new provinces will be similar to that of the old ones; as no effort is spared to carry out the system which looks to limiting the whole people to agriculture, and thus compelling exhaustion of their land. It is needed, says Mr. Chapman, the great advocate of railways in India, that the connection between "the Indian grower and English spinner" become more intimate, and "*the more the English is made to outweigh the native home demand, the more strongly will the native agriculturist feel that his personal success depends on securing and improving his British connection*" * — that is, the more that commerce can be annihilated, and the more the natives can be prevented from combining their efforts, the greater, as Mr. Chapman thinks, will be the prosperity of India. Centralization has impoverished, and to a considerable extent depopulated, that country; but its work is not yet done. It remains yet to reduce the people

* *Cotton and Commerce of India*, p. 86.

of the Punjab, of Affghanistan, and of Burmah, to the condition of the Bengalese.

That there is, throughout India, a steady decline in the power of association, in the development of individuality, in the feeling of responsibility, and in the capacity for progress, no one can doubt who will study carefully the books on that country. By several of the persons that have been quoted — Messrs. Thompson, Bright, and others — the responsibility for all this is charged upon the Company; but none that read the works of Messrs. Campbell and Sleeman can hesitate to believe that its direction is now animated by a serious desire to improve the condition of its poor subjects. Unfortunately, however, the Company is nearly in the condition of the landholders of Jamaica, and is itself tending towards ruin, because its subjects are limited to agriculture, and because they receive so small a portion of the value of their very small quantity of products. Now, as in the days of Joshua Gee, the largest portion remains in England, whose people eat cheap sugar while its producer perishes of famine in India. Cheap sugar and cheap cotton are obtained by the sacrifice of the interests of a great nation; and while the policy of England shall continue to look to limiting the whole population of India to the labors of the field, the soil must continue to grow poorer, the power of association must continue to decline, and the government must find itself more and more dependent on the power to poison the people of China; and therefore must it be that, however good the intentions of the gentlemen charged with the duties of government, they must find themselves more and more compelled to grind the poor ryot in the hope of obtaining revenue.

§ 9. An eminent English economist informs his readers that notwithstanding "the extreme cheapness of labor in India, and the excellence to which the natives had long attained," "the wonderful genius of our machinists, the admirable skill of our workmen, and our immense capital have far more than countervailed the apparently insuperable drawback of high wages, and have enabled our manufacturers to bear down all opposition, and to triumph over the cheaper labor, contiguous material, and traditional art of the Hindoos," as a consequence of which "the native manufacture has received a shock from which it is not likely it will ever recover."* "From Smyrna to Canton, from Madras to Samarcand," elsewhere says the same writer, "we are supplanting the native fabrics"—and, of course, everywhere annihilating that power of association which enables man to command the services of nature, and to pass from a state of slavery towards one of freedom.

Capital always grows as wages rise, and diminishes as wages fall. Wages always rise with the decline in the necessity for effecting changes of place, and always decline as it increases. The measures resorted to for the destruction of the manufactures of India looked to increasing that necessity on the part of the Hindoo producer of food and cotton, and thus inflicting upon him a taxation more severe than any other that could have been devised — and to diminishing it on the part of the British grower of food, and thus relieving him from the taxation to which he had before been subjected; and the effect is seen in the rise of wages and rapid accumulation of capital in the latter, as well as in the decline of wages and disappearance of capital in the former. When, therefore, Mr. McCulloch, in thus enumerating the causes of the change that has taken place, omits to add that further one of the exercise of power by the strong over the weak — of the power of the associated traders over the scattered people who desired to maintain commerce — he omits the most important of all the elements of the calculation. The Hindoo was as capable of applying the machinery of Arkwright as the Englishman, and, had the people of England and India been one, had their rights been held to be equal, that machinery would have made its way to the cotton-fields of India — enabling its people still more closely to associate, still more intimately to combine their operations, still more fully to develop their individual faculties, and still more extensively to maintain commerce at home and abroad. Under such circumstances, all India would now exhibit a scene of the highest prosperity, in place of which we meet with nothing but a constant succession of famines and pestilences, accompanied by decline of individuality and of freedom — and producing a necessity for a constant succession of wars for the acquisition of new territory in which to trade, and constantly increasing difficulty of

* McCulloch: *Commercial Dictionary*, article *Calcutta*.

obtaining the revenue by means of which the machinery of government is to be maintained.*

The history of the world is but a record of the efforts of the few who were strong, to restrain the growth of the power of association — to prevent the organization of society — to interfere with the maintenance of commerce — and to retard the acquisition of that power over nature which constitutes wealth; and thus to enslave the many who were weak. Its every page presents evidence of the fleeting character of all prosperity obtained by aid of measures in violation of that great and fundamental law of Christianity requiring us to respect the rights of our neighbor as we would have our own to be respected; but in none is found a more instructive lesson than in that which records the annihilation of commerce in India, and the growth in England of that pauperism which gave rise to the doctrine of over-population. Both waxed together, and together both must wane — the measures required for the relief of the Hindoo being precisely those required for the extirpation of pauperism among the Britons.

* "We are at war with the Burmese. Everybody knows it, and, what is more, everybody expects that we should be always at war with some power or other in the East. It was so at Rome. Everybody took it as a matter of course that there were one or two wars on the confines of the empire — with the Carthaginians, or the Mauritanians, or the Celtiberians, or the Helvetians, or the Syrians, or the Egyptians; and when at last it was found out, one wonderful year, that such was the terror of Rome, or the exhaustion of the whole human race, that there was no war actually raging, the temple of Janus was closed in state, games were celebrated, hymns were sung, and the emperor pronounced a present god. It has been so with all great empires." * * * "On the great fact of this disgraceful and now disastrous war there is no difference of statement. The cause of the Burmese war is not the claims of the two British captains, for they were promised settlement; not the conduct of the governor that gave rise to those claims, for he was promptly dismissed; not the absurd and fabulous grievances of the very scum of Rangoon raked together by the commodore after his arrival, for they were never formally urged; not any serious act or refusal whatever, but simply and solely that four officers of very miscellaneous and unequal rank, who had forced their way into the courtyard of the royal commissioner without previous arrangement, and at a very unusual time of the day, were kept a quarter of an hour in the sun. Explanations and apologies were offered innumerable, but none were received." — *London Times.*

# CHAPTER XIV.

## THE SAME SUBJECT CONTINUED.

§ 1. THE reader has now had placed before him a picture of the movements of four considerable nations, and of one assemblage of nations—comprising, in the whole, two hundred millions of people, or one-fifth of the total population of the globe. All of these have been subject to that system of policy which looks to the prevention of association, or combination; and to the maintenance at its highest point of that most oppressive of all taxes—the one resulting from the necessity for effecting changes in the place of matter, and requiring ships or wagons for its accomplishment. In all, he has seen the same results to have been obtained—an increase in the *proportion* of the labor of the community required to be given to the work of transportation—an increase in the *proportions* and in the power of the class that lives by means of simple appropriation—a diminution in the development of individual faculty—a diminution in the *proportion* of the labor of the community that could be given to increasing the quantity of things susceptible of being transported or exchanged—a decline of freedom, and a decay of commerce.—Others might be added, and the list might be so extended as to embrace every country in the world in which the *proportion* of its labor required to be given to the work of transportation is an increasing one; for *it is in the necessity for effecting changes of place that is found the great obstacle to human improvement, to the development of intellect, to the growth of freedom, and to the increase of commerce*—as was so clearly seen by Adam Smith when urging npon his countrymen the consideration of the advantage resulting from converting the bulky corn and wool into the compact cloth, that could so readily travel to the remotest corners of the world. Whenever the course of man is in the direction that thus was indicated, and wherever, consequently, he is gradually surmounting the obstacles standing in the way of commerce, the proportion borne by the trading and transporting classes to the rest of the community is, necessarily, a diminishing one; and then it is that he becomes from year to year more civilized. Whenever, on the contrary, the manufacturer disappears, and wherever there is thus produced an increased necessity for exporting commodities in an unfinished state, the tendency is directly the reverse of this — man then relapsing into barbarism, because of the diminished power of combination. This latter is the case in all the countries whose history has above been sketched; and it is so for the reason that the policy to which they have been subjected is one which looks to having but a single workshop for the world, to which are to be sent all the rude products of the earth, at greatest cost of transportation. In all of them, consequently, nature is daily obtaining greater power over man. In all, wealth diminishes, with constant decrease in the value of man, who becomes from year to year more and more the slave of his fellow-man.

It will, however, be said, that the people of India are indolent —that those of Turkey are Mohammedans and fatalists, and otherwise disqualified from entering into competition with those of the British isles — that the Portuguese and Irish peoples have a religious faith that is adverse to the development of mind — that the laborers of Jamaica are but little removed from barbarism — and that in facts like these may be found the causes of the growing weakness of the several communities whose situation is above described. The people of the Turkish Empire had, however, precisely the same modes of thought a century since that they have now, and they clung to them even more steadfastly than in modern times; and the commerce then maintained with them was accounted the most valuable portion of that of Western Europe. The enlightened Moors of the south of Spain held to a belief that was the same with that of the men who now are found on the shores of the Hellespont; but there was found therein, as we know, no obstacle to the advance of civilization. The Portuguese are no more Catholic than were their predecessors who made the Methuen treaty, and whose commerce was deemed of such high importance. They and the Irish people hold to the same faith with those of France, among whom agriculture and manufactures are now so rapidly advancing, and in whom individuality is becoming so much developed. The negroes imported into Jamaica were no more barbarian than were those received in Virginia and Carolina; and yet, while each of these latter is represented by seven of his descendants, the British islands present to view but two for every five that were received. The reasons above referred to not accounting for the state of things that has been described, we must look elsewhere for the causes of its existence.

Differing in religious faith, in color, in latitude, and in longitude, these communities are alike in the one respect, that they have been deprived of the power so to diversify the employments of their members as to develop their various individualities, and thus fit them for that association without which man can obtain no power to command the services of nature. Limited entirely to agriculture, they have been compelled to export their produce in its rudest state—a proceeding involving the exhaustion of the soil upon which they are dependent for support, with constant diminution in the return to human effort. Under such circumstances, commerce would necessarily decline, and the power of the trader and transporter would as necessarily increase; while the cultivator would become more and more a mere instrument to be used by those who lived by the exercise of their powers of appropriation. That he does so in all these countries is clear; and that such are the inevitable consequences of a policy which looks to the prevention of combination, and to diminution in the development of the latent powers of man, cannot admit of a moment's doubt. In attributing to it, then, the existing state of things, we obtain one great and uniform cause for one great and uniform effect — a policy tending to the production of barbarism, leading to famines and pestilences, ending in decay and death, and thus giving color to the theory of over-population.

§ 2. That man may acquire power over nature, it is *indispensable* that the market for his labor, and for his products, be near at hand. When it is distant, however perfect may be the means of transportation, the manure cannot be returned to the land, and unless its powers are maintained, he and it must become impoverished together, with constant diminution in the power of maintaining commerce. The facilities of transportation throughout Ireland were greatly increased in the half century that has just elapsed; but, with every stage of that improvement, famines and pestilences increased in number and in force, until, at length, the completion of an extensive system of railroads was signalized by one of such severity as entirely to have distanced all that had preceded it. With each such stage, the power of association declined—the soil was more rapidly impoverished—and now its laborers are everywhere flying from the homes of their youth; its property-holders are everywhere being dispossessed; and its men of intellect have almost entirely disappeared.

Railroads are now being made *for*, but not *by*, the people of India, but their effects must, inevitably, be the same with those observed in Ireland. The object for the attainment of which they are being made, is the further promotion of the export of the raw produce of the soil, and the further extension of the centralizing power of trade; to be followed by increased exhaustion of the land, declining power of association among its occupants, and more rapid decay of commerce. The little that yet remains of Indian manufactures must speedily disappear, and cotton must more and more be required to find its way from its producer in the heart of India, to his immediate neighbor—and even to his own wife and children—by the circuitous route of Calcutta or Bombay, and Manchester—a proceeding involving the use of bullocks, wagons, ships, and railroad cars, with constant increase in the *proportion* of the labor of the community required for effecting changes of place, and diminution in that which may be given to increasing the quantity susceptible of being converted or exchanged. The more railroads made in India, the smaller will be the demand for labor, and the less the price of cotton*—the greater will be the tendency of Indian men to abandon their wives and children, and fly to the sugar plantations of the Mauritius in search of food—the greater must be the decline in the power of combination—and the less the tendency to the development of individuality among the people.

Mexico has declined steadily from the time that her trade be-

* Mr. Chapman furnishes tables showing that while the reduction in the cost of transporting cotton from the place of production in India has been but *seven* pence per pound, the reduction in England has been *ten* pence—thus showing that the reward of land and labor in that country has fallen considerably with the substitution of trade for the commerce that before existed.—*Cotton and Commerce of India*, p. 77.

came more open to the world. Desiring to to find the cause of her decay and approaching dissolution, we must seek it in the fact, that her manufactures have almost altogether disappeared, that individuality has declined, and that trade has superseded commerce. Throughout Spanish America generally, the same phenomena have been presented—the labor required for transportation steadily augmenting, and that given to production diminishing; with constant decline in the power of the soil to yield return to labor, and decline in the power of man to subdue to cultivation the richer soils. Italy, Greece, Africa, Brazil, and the rich islands of the Indian Ocean, are similarly situated—having little commerce within themselves, and being compelled to depend almost exclusively on trade with distant countries. The distresses of the people of the Ionian islands are as constant in occurrence as are the famines of Madeira; and for the reason, that while compelled to depend exclusively on agriculture, there is, necessarily, an unceasing waste of capital.

The greater the power for good, the greater is that for evil. The most potent poisons are the most active remedies; and the men whose powers qualify them for conferring the greatest benefits on mankind, are precisely those who, when viciously disposed, are most injurious to society. Steam and gunpowder, properly directed, are of inestimable advantage to man; but when misdirected, their power for mischief is in the ratio of their capability of rendering service. So is it with the human body and its nourishment—the food that is capable of producing, in one state of the system, the greatest amount of force, being precisely that which, in another of its states, most tends to the destruction of force and the annihilation of life. So is it with roads and other improvements. To the highly organized community—the one in which diversity of employment most exists, and whose commerce is, therefore, great—every new road brings with it increase of power over nature, with increase of life; whereas to the one of low organization, each new one may but furnish another drain through which its life's blood may more readily be carried off—as we see to have been the case with Ireland. Trade has been "the curse of Polynesia;" and the greater that now becomes its power, the more rapid is the progress of deterioration among the people of the islands. Trade has been the curse of Northern and Western

Africa; and the Hottentots are disappearing from the earth as the facilities of intercourse with foreigners increase. Trade sweeps off the aborigines of the West, and it will do with the Japanese, when once it shall have been admitted, precisely what it has already done with the people of the Sandwich Islands and of India.

That such should be the case, results solely from the fact that communities have yet to learn and to appreciate the *advantage* that would accrue from carrying out, in their relations with other and weaker societies, the great law which prescribes to man that he shall do to others as he desires that they shall do towards him. In affairs of state, morality is unknown; and, as a necessary consequence, the great and permanent good is constantly sacrificed to the trivial and temporary profit — nations everywhere being governed in their conduct towards each other by motives precisely similar to those which so often prompt the individual to earn a place in the penitentiary by picking his neighbor's pocket, when by a different course of conduct he might readily place himself in a situation of permanent ease and comfort.*

Had the people of Africa been instructed in the ways of real civilization — had they been taught, in pursuance of the advice of Adam Smith, to combine their raw materials together, and thus fit them for distant transportation — they might now have roads, and might now be prepared to supply to Europe, to an almost unlimited extent, the productions of the tropics; while they, themselves, would be rapidly advancing in the development of their various faculties. Had the Irish people, and those of Turkey, and of Portugal, been permitted to acquire, and to extend, the arts of manufacture, they would now be adding largely to the stock of raw materials for the world, and the commerce with them would be of high importance. That it has become entirely valueless, is due to the fact that they have been compelled to have free intercourse with communities in a higher state of organization than themselves — potent for good or evil, and using their power as a means of securing advantage for themselves. Seeking always

* "When we pass from internal to international concerns, we seek in vain for a virtuous *nation*. Each community, as it in turn rises to power, disdains all law of right, and submits only to that law of force which it everywhere seeks to impose. Hence the history of the world is stained with every crime that makes man odious." — *Westminster Review*, January, 1851.

the present and temporary good, while careless in regard to the future and lasting injury, the latter have sought to strengthen themselves by weakening all around them — the doing of which intentionally would be a crime; but, as a result of want of knowledge of the true principles of social science, it has been "a blunder;" and would therefore, in the judgment of Talleyrand, be regarded as "even worse than a crime."

§ 3. An enlightened self-interest teaches all men that they profit by the improvement of their neighbors — and to such extent is this the case, that we see throughout a large portion of this country the rich gladly, and largely, contributing to the education of their poorer neighbors—and feeling themselves abundantly repaid therefor by the increased security thereby obtained for the enjoyment of their own rights of person and of property. Where there exists that feeling, the closer the connection between those who are strong of mind, or of body, and those who are weak in either, the better is it for all; but where the feeling is the reverse of this —where each man seeks to make of his fellow-man his prey — the less the intercourse, the better it must be for all. This last is the state of things existing in the early stages of society, when the soldier and the trader are the masters of those by whom they are surrounded; whereas, the former is that which tends to arise as the powers of the earth become more and more developed — as wealth increases — as men are more enabled to live in connection with each other—as commerce grows—and as society tends more and more to assume its highest form.

In the first of these conditions — society being in a state of low development — the resistance to gravitation is very small indeed. In the last — being that in which the various faculties of man are well developed — the attractive force is great. In the first, there is little power for good or evil. In the last, there is much for either, or for both; and whether its existence shall be a blessing, or a curse, to mankind at large, is as much dependent upon the manner in which its societary force is directed, as is the case with steam, at one time used for facilitating the acquisition of food and clothing, and at another devoted to the battering of city walls, and to the destruction of human life.

Between two communities differing in the manner above described, an enlightened self-interest would induce the stronger to protect and strengthen the weaker—to facilitate the division of employments and the development of individuality—to increase the power of association, with a view to enable its neighbor to obtain control over the forces of nature—and thus to aid the growth of freedom and of commerce. Such, however, is not, nor has ever been, the policy of nations; and the reason why it has not been so is, that they have, to so great an extent, been mere instruments in the hands of the class that lives by appropriation—the soldier, the slave-owner, the trader, and the politician. To this it is due that, even in the case of these United States, there has been so great a disposition to plunder and oppress their weaker neighbors—the Mexican Republic, and the poor remains of the native tribes. Even now, instead of rendering to the former the friendly counsel, or the aid, by help of which she might, perhaps, emerge from her present depressed condition, the American people, and their government, are waiting anxiously for the moment when it may become possible to make new treaties by means of which they may facilitate the resolution of Mexican society into its original elements, and thus enable themselves to acquire additional territory. Animated by the trading spirit, they seek to make good bargains, careless of their effect on the people with whom they are made. Hence it is that trade now grows as commerce declines—that cities increase in size as towns and villages become less populous—that property in land in the older States is becoming less and less divided—that political and trading centralization is rapidly superseding the local activity that once prevailed—that the slavery of man is now being viewed as but a consequence of great natural laws instituted by the Creator of all mankind—and that distrust has now so entirely replaced the confidence once felt by all the people of this continent, in the honor and honesty of the American government.

By no people of the world, however, has this course been so uniformly pursued, as by that of England—the only one whose policy has looked wholly to the advancement of the trader's interests; and the only one, too, that now recognises, as its cardinal principle, the trader's motto, "Buy in the cheapest market, and sell in the dearest one." By none has trade been so systematically pursued. By none has commerce been so much oppressed;

and by none has the power for oppression been so great. Prohibiting association where it did not as yet exist, and annihilating it where it did, the results are seen in the reduction to a dead level of mere tillers of the earth, of the people of all the communities subjected to its system; and in the decline and ruin of the communities themselves, as exhibited in the several cases above referred to. In all of them there is a yearly diminution of those differences of society required for the development of individual faculty, and for the perfection of organization. In all, society becomes from year to year more imperfect, and more obedient to the force of gravitation.* In all, there is a yearly increase of centralization; and centralization, slavery, and death go always hand in hand with one another. In all, the difficulty of obtaining food is a steadily increasing one; and in all, therefore, countenance is afforded to the idea that population tends to increase faster than the food required for man's support. Such, however, are but the consequences that, *in the existing state of national immorality*, must everywhere result from perfect freedom of intercourse between a strong and well-developed community on one side, and a weak and imperfect one on the other.†

* "The more imperfect a body, the more," says Goethe, "do the parts resemble the whole." In a purely agricultural community, all the parts are precisely similar, and the whole is but as one of the parts magnified.

† The author of the following passages, although differing greatly from the writer of this work in relation to highly important questions, has found himself forced, by an observation of facts occurring in our Southern States, into an agreement with the ideas above expressed:—

"Under the system of free trade, a fertile soil, with good rivers and roads as outlets, becomes the greatest evil with which a country can be afflicted. The richness of soil invites to agriculture, and the roads and rivers carry off the crops, to be exchanged for the manufactures of poorer regions, where are situated the centres of trade, of capital, and manufactures. In a few centuries, or less time, the consumption abroad of the crops impoverishes the soil where they are made. No cities or manufactories arise in the country with this fertile soil, because there is no occasion. No pursuits are carried on requiring intelligence or skill; the population is of necessity sparse, ignorant, and illiterate; universal absenteeism prevails; the rich go off for pleasure and education—the enterprising poor for employment. An intelligent friend suggests that, left to nature, the evil will cure itself. So it may when the country is ruined, if the people, like those of Georgia, are of high character, and betake themselves to other pursuits than mere agriculture, and totally repudiate free-trade doctrines. Our friends' objection only proves the truth of our theory. We are very sure that the wit of man can devise no means so effectual to impoverish a country as exclusive agriculture. The ravages of war, pestilence, and famine are soon effaced; centuries are required to restore an exhausted soil. The more rapidly money is made in such a country, enjoying free trade, the faster it is impoverished, for the draft on the soil is greater, and those who make good crops spend

§ 4. The steam-engine digests fuel, and power is produced. Man digests fuel in the form of food, by help of which he obtains power to labor with his body, or his mind, or with both together. Alike in the fact that both thus digest capital in one form, and reproduce it in another, they differ in the one important respect, that while the iron locomotive *can* exist without food, the other *cannot.* The railroad manager carefully avoids the consumption of fuel when he does not need the services of the engine, knowing that such a proceeding would be *waste of capital.* The manager of the human locomotive must burn the fuel even when there is no demand for power; and therefore is it that in countries in which the diversity of employments declines, and in which, consequently, commerce diminishes, the quantity of capital consumed so largely exceeds that which is reproduced, as to cause wealth to disappear, and man to return to his original position—that of the slave of nature. Muscular force and mental energy there go to waste, while the powers of the soil decline from year to year, because of the unceasing withdrawal of the constituent elements of food and clothing—a course of proceeding to which nature has affixed the penalties of poverty, famine, disease, and death.

It may, perhaps, be said that the people of all the countries we have named are uncivilized—that they dislike change, even when it is improvement—that they would continue to use their wretched substitutes for ploughs, hoes, and steam-engines, even were the latter offered to them; but this state of things results, necessarily, from the absence of power to maintain for themselves local centres of action, furnishing the attractive force required for resisting central attraction so great as that which exists in the British islands. Local attraction is as necessary for the maintenance of communities in the presence of each other, as is local gravitation in the planets in the presence of the sun. Under the centralizing influence of

them abroad—those who make small ones, at home. In the absence of free trade, this rich region must manufacture for itself, build cities, erect schools and colleges, and carry on all the pursuits and provide for all the common wants of civilized man. Thus the money made at home would be spent and invested at home; the crops would be consumed at home, and each town and village would furnish manure to fertilize the soil around it. We believe it is a common theory that, without this domestic consumption, no soil can be kept permanently rich. A dense population would arise, because it would be required; the rich would have no further occasion to leave home for pleasure, nor the poor for employment."—FITZHUGH: *Sociology for the South,* pp. 14–16.

Great Britain, the societies of India, of Ireland, of Portugal, and of Turkey have become so entirely decomposed, that they are now little better than masses of ruins; and as such must they continue unless there be a change of system. Such having been the case with old and established societies, how impossible must it have been to establish in Jamaica any system of counter-attraction, even had there existed none of the prohibitions of manufacture to which the reader's attention has above been called! *It is the first step in the way of improvement that is always the most difficult and the least productive* — but no such step is possible in presence of a system that prohibits association, and that is armed with power to give the prohibition full effect. There lies the difficulty, and not in the character of the people. Out of Ireland, Irishmen have, at all times, and everywhere, manifested the possession of all the qualities required for the production of one of the most distinguished nations of the world. The Portuguese of the present day have all the faculties of their predecessors, but they remain latent, waiting to be stimulated into activity; and that they will be, whenever the power of association and combination shall be obtained. The powers of the Hindoo are as great now as they were when Europe was indebted to India for all the fine commodities she used; and as regards his moral qualities, all unite in giving him the highest character.* The people of Turkey maintained a great commerce among themselves, two centuries since; and they could now do more, had they the same facilities therefor their predecessors then possessed. So, too, with those of Jamaica, to whom a nominal freedom has been given, but under circumstances that cause a constant destruction of capital, and as constant a diminution in the power to maintain commerce.

Commerce economizes the power resulting from the consumption of food and clothing, and therefore it is that capital so

* "I do not exactly know what is meant by civilizing the people of India. In the theory and practice of good government they may be deficient; but if a good system of agriculture—if unrivalled manufactures—if a capacity to produce what convenience or luxury demands — if the establishment of schools for reading and writing — if the general practice of kindness and hospitality—and, above all, if a scrupulous respect and delicacy towards the female sex, are among the points that denote a civilized people, then the Hindoos are not inferior in civilization to the people of Europe." — *Sir Thomas Munro.*

rapidly accumulates where the power of association and combination rapidly grows — with steady tendency to increase in the ability to repay the debt contracted to our great mother earth. Commerce declines with every increase in the necessity for the services of the trader; and does so because every step in that direction is attended with increase in the waste of that physical and mental power in which consists the most important portion of the real capital of a country — the representative of that which, in the form of food, is from day to day consumed. At twenty-five cents a head, the daily capital consumed in this country is nearly seven millions of dollars, and little short of fifty millions a week, or two thousand six hundred millions a year. The enforced loss here, of even a single hour per day, being equal to an annual one of more than two hundred millions, how enormous must be that of communities situated as are Ireland and India, where not even a tenth of the power of physical and mental effort is put to use! Add to this, the waste resulting from the constant exhaustion of the soil, and it will be seen that the injury to the former alone, from her limitation to the single pursuit of agriculture, is more than would be paid for, thrice over, by the free gift of the exports from England to all the world.

Annihilate in England herself those differences which at once qualify for, and lead to, association and combination, and her people would sink to the condition of the serfs of the days of the Plantagenets; and such, too, would be the case with those of all the other countries of Europe. Association is the condition of existence of MAN — of the being made in the likeness of his Creator. By means of it, and it alone, he obtains power to command the great forces of nature. When that is denied to him, he sinks to the condition of slave to her and to his fellow-man — and then it is, that population becomes superabundant.

§ 5. Every diminution of commerce, and increase in the necessity for the use of machinery of transportation, is attended with increase in the power of the few who live by trade, or by war, to tax the many for the accomplishment of their purposes; and with a diminution in the power of the latter to protect themselves from such taxation. The larger the surplus requiring to be transported, the greater become the facilities for combination for reduction of prices, and increase of freight and charges; and consequent increase of the trader's profits—with large increase in his *proportion* of the total products. The less the commerce, and the less the demand for labor, the greater is the facility with which armies may be recruited, to the profit of the man who lives by plundering his neighbor. In no country of the world has commerce more declined than it has done in India; and there it is that we witness a constant series of wars for the extension of trade*—the bill of costs for which is not presented to the people of England, for whose purposes they are made, but, as Mr. Cobden most truly says, "to the unhappy ryots of Hindostan;"† and when the new territories prove unprofitable, the poor laborer is further taxed for the maintenance of government in the possessions thus acquired.

The people, white and black, of Jamaica, had no interest in the wars of the French Revolution; and yet more than half of the price paid for their sugar by their English fellow-subjects was taken for the payment of its expenses. So, too, with Ireland, taxed to the uttermost for the maintenance of wars from which she had nothing to gain, and whose chief effect was that of converting into soldiers, at sixpence a day, hundreds of thousands of men, who, under a different system, would have become excellent artisans, or agriculturists. Every increase in the necessity for transportation being exhaustive, the supremacy of trade is seen everywhere to be attended by desire for war as a means of extending the fields in which to operate. Like Alexander, it sighs for worlds to conquer; and this it does, because of the unceasing failure of the conquests already made to realize the anticipations that had been formed.‡

* "Out of the nineteen years of the present charter, fifteen have been passed in war." — *London Daily News.*

† *How Wars are got up in India*, p. 56.

‡ "Trade is not absolutely powerful to support and extend itself, without it be pioneered and protected by other influences. If we had not been blinded by certain dominant economical dogmas, we might have learned that in other quarters of the globe." * * * "We have taken these instances at random; we might extend the list; but we have already sufficient to prove that *the sword may carve out the path for commerce*, that diplomacy may accomplish alliances and open territories, and that personal influence, such as that of an Ashburton or a Dunham, may bring large classes, or great continents, within the commercial league of free trade. It was boasted, not long since, that trade could act by itself; that it could excavate its own tunnels, purchase its own protection, and open its own ter-

That this must ever be the case, and that such discord is a necessary consequence of a system looking to exaggeration of the difficulties attendant upon the necessity for effecting changes of place, will be obvious to the reader on consideration of the following facts :— Ships are to be regarded but as floating bridges, and when we arrange them end to end, we are enabled to determine the extent of their capabilities for occupying the place of commerce, as they have been made to do, in all the operations of the hundreds of millions of whom the populations of Ireland, India, Turkey, and Portugal are composed. A foot in length, of a ship, being about the equivalent of ten tons, to bridge the Atlantic with ships, so as to make a road thirty feet in width, would require more than sixty millions of tons; but to make such a bridge connecting India, Australia, and America with England, would require some hundreds of millions; and as the total ocean tonnage of the world does not exceed five millions, it follows that all the shipping now in existence does not afford means of communication with the single market at which raw materials are to be converted into cloth and iron, equal to a road an inch in breadth. *It is, nevertheless, by means of such a narrow strait as this, thirty thousand miles in length, that the Hindoo who produces cotton maintains commerce with his next-door neighbor, who requires to consume cloth.* By means of such a strait as this, many thousand miles in length, the people of Portugal and Turkey maintain commerce among themselves, and with the world at large; and it is through such an one that the people of Jamaica at this moment make every exchange of service with each other — as a consequence of which there is no circulation of men or things, nor is there any value in their labor or in their land.

Being limited to the use of a passage so narrow as this, it follows, necessarily, that when nature is most bounteous — when she showers her benefits upon the heads of the people who raise rice, wheat, cotton, or wool — the markets become glutted with produce, to the ruin of the producers — but enabling the transporter to rejoice over his rapid accumulations. Further, the very fact

ritories; but *here we find that commerce waits upon the achievements of the sword, and the negotiations of diplomacy.*" — *Spectator*, September 4, 1854.

Views similar to these are contained in all the recent English journals — all of which find compensation for the extraordinary waste of life and treasure in the Crimea, in the probable future increase of trade.

that his profits are so large tends to render the glut yet more complete; and for the reason, that the larger his proportion of the cargo, the smaller is that of the producer, and the less the ability of the latter to make purchases in the great central market, and thus to help to make demand for the raw materials that he himself has furnished. Hence results the remarkable fact that it is precisely when cotton cloth is cheapest that the planter can least afford to purchase it—and that when refined sugar is cheapest the sugar-planter can least afford to consume it.

The greater the time required to elapse, and the greater the space required to be travelled over, between production and consumption, the greater must be the friction, the less the motion of society, and the less its force—but the greater will be the powers of the trader, transporter, and money-lender—the larger the proportion of the product that enures to them — and the greater the tendency towards the production of the disease of over-population, with its accompaniments, famine, disease, and death.

§ 6. The more rapid the circulation, the greater must be the economy of human power, and the greater the force of the community itself. The less the rapidity, the greater must be the waste of power, and the less the force. To have motion in society, there must be diversification in the demands for the various faculties of man. No such demand existing in any of the countries that have above been named, there is in all of them a constant waste of the capital produced in the form of mental or physical capacity for exertion, yielded in return to the capital consumed in the form of food.

In India, nine-tenths are wasted, while, of the trivial product of the remainder, a large portion is claimed by those who exercise the powers of government. The balance is subjected to the exhaustive process above described, by help of which the cotton that has yielded its producer but a penny returns to him at a cost of twelve, fifteen, or twenty pence. So is it in Ireland; and so, too, is it in Jamaica, Portugal, and Turkey — in all of which the men engaged in effecting those *mechanical and chemical changes in the forms of matter*—commonly designated by the term manufactures — become from year to year more widely separated from those engaged in the work of cultivation.

In all of them, consequently, there is a constantly increasing necessity for transportation. In all of them, the utility of the rude products of the earth steadily diminishes, and the power of the earth to yield them steadily declines, as the soil becomes exhausted. In all, there is an increase in the value of commodities required for the use of man, and a decline in the value of man himself. In all, the accumulations of the past acquire increased control over the labors of the present. In all, commerce diminishes as trade acquires increase of power. *With* all, the value of English trade declines — thus proving, to use the words of Colonel Sleeman, "the folly of conquerors and paramount powers, from the days of the Greeks and Romans down to those of Lord Hastings and Sir John Malcolm, who were all bad political economists, in supposing that conquered and ceded territories could always be made to yield to a foreign state the same amount of gross revenue they had paid to their domestic government, whatever their situation with reference to markets for their produce — whatever the state of their arts and industry — and whatever the character and extent of the local establishments maintained out of it."* With all the dependencies of England — even where nominally free — her course is an exhaustive one; and yet her people become daily more and more themselves dependent on those distant markets for the supplies required for the support of life. How far it is to this increased dependence that we owe the existence of the facts of English history upon which were founded the theory of over-population, will be examined in another chapter. Should they prove to have been due exclusively to the one great error of English policy, then will that examination furnish evidence that it is not only right, but profitable, for communities to carry into their relations with each other the strict observance of that great law which requires of man that he shall do by others as he desires that they shall do by him.

* See *anté*, p. 345.

# CHAPTER XV.

## OF MECHANICAL AND CHEMICAL CHANGES IN THE FORM OF MATTER.

§ 1. To transport the sticks of wood by means of which our colonist might, in some degree, shelter himself from the wind and the rain, required the exertion of brute force alone; but before he could succeed in converting any of them into a bow, it was requisite that he should make himself acquainted with those properties of matter known as elasticity and tenacity. For the effectuation of changes of form there was needed, therefore, a knowledge of the *qualities* of the things that were to be converted; whereas, for effecting changes of place, he needed only to know their *number*, *magnitude*, or *weight;* and, as a necessary consequence, the work of conversion, more concrete and special, followed, in the order of development, the more abstract one of transportation.

Few things are yielded by the earth in the precise form in which they are required for serving the purposes of man. He may eat apples, oranges, dates, or figs, as they come from the tree; but the potato requires to be cooked, the grain to be crushed, and the flour to be baked, before they can be made available for his nourishment. He may wrap the skin around his shoulders; but before he can convert the wool into a garment fitted to preserve him from the winter's cold, he must make himself familiar with the properties by which it is distinguished. The foliage may at times shield him from the sun, but to enable him to obtain proper shelter from the weather, he must learn to fell the tree and convert it into logs, or planks. To do these things requires knowledge, with every step in the acquisition of which, he obtains increased control over the natural forces provided for his use—while with each, is more and more developed the *utility* of the corn, the wool, and the timber, with constant decline in the *value* of the food, the clothing, and the shelter he requires—and as constant increase of wealth.

Of all the beautiful and wonderful provisions of nature, there is probably none more beautiful than that which may be here observed. The necessity for changing the form of animal and vegetable products before they can become fitted for man's consumption, constitutes an obstacle requiring to be surmounted; and one that does not exist in relation to birds, beasts, or fishes, to all of which food is furnished in the precise form in which it is required. So, too, with clothing, all of which is supplied to other animals by nature; whereas, man is obliged to change the form of the flax, the silk, and the wool, before they can be made to serve his purposes; and here it is that we find the great stimulus to activity of mind—leading to the development of individuality, and fitting him for association with his fellow-men. Had food and clothing been supplied to him in abundance, and in the form in which they were required, his faculties would everywhere have remained as inert and useless as are now those of the people of tropical countries, whole families of whom are supplied with the former by a single breadfruit-tree; while the latter is superseded by a constant summer's sun. Nature giving these unasked, there exists but little inducement for the exercise of those faculties by which man is distinguished from the brute, which remain, therefore, undeveloped; and, as a necessary consequence, the power and the habit of association are there found least developed. Man was placed here to obtain command over nature; and, to that end, he was endowed with faculties capable of action, but requiring to be stimulated into activity by the necessity for overcoming the forces by which he is surrounded—forces, whose powers of resistance are always in the direct ratio of their capability of aiding him in his further efforts, whenever they have been brought entirely under his control. The rich soils of the earth are capable of yielding large returns to labor, but—being destructive of life and health—he dare not attempt to occupy them. Therefore it is, that he is seen commencing his labors where the soil is poorest—and there it is, that he is earliest seen combining with his neighbors for the acquisition of further power; as in the rocky Attica; the almost ice-bound Norway and Iceland; the elevated Bohemia; the mountainous Savoy; and the granitic New England; in all of which we see the habit of association to have existed to an extent elsewhere unknown.

§ 2. Before, however, Crusoe could make a bow, he needed to have some species of cutting instrument; and that, as we know, he obtained in the form of a piece of flint, or other hard stone, whose edge he had sharpened by means of friction. Look where we may, among even the most savage tribes, we find them obtaining command of certain natural forces — and doing so by help of instruments the fabrication of which requires some acquaintance with the properties of matter. With knowledge comes power, and with the growth of power over nature they obtain a constantly increasing supply of food and clothing, in return for constantly diminishing muscular effort.

It is here, as everywhere, that the first step, while the most difficult, yields the smallest return. Beginning with the shell, man passes to the flint; thence to the knife of copper, bronze, iron, and steel; and finally to the circular saw — with every step acquiring power for making a next and greater one. The spindle and the loom must, in their day, have been very wonderful inventions—so much so, that they sufficed the world for ages. In time, however, came the spinning-jenny; and now the force of steam was substituted for that of the human hand, with vast increase of product. That, nevertheless, was but the first among the steps in that direction — steam having, since then, been made not only to weave the cloth, but to give to it every variety of color, and of figure. From year to year, we witness new improvements, any one of which exceeds in importance the whole of those for which we are indebted to the thousand years preceding the opening of the eighteenth century. The cloth now returned to the labors of half a dozen women is more in quantity than, a century since, could have been obtained in return to those of a hundred men. But fifty years since, every piece of bar-iron required, for its production, the constantly intermitted force of men working with hammers in their hands, and obliged, at every blow, to raise the instrument, with enormous waste of power. Arriving, however, at the knowledge that iron could be rolled, and by aid of steam, man acquired the command of a great natural force, by means of which his labors were rendered more continuous and effective, while greatly diminished in their demands upon his powers. Iron, becoming more easily acquired, facilitated the acquisition of increased supplies of coal and iron ore, and they in their turn did the same by machinery of every kind, from the little instruments employed in making pins and needles, to the great steam-engine that drains the mine, or drives the mill.

Power to direct the forces of nature constitutes wealth. The greater the wealth, the smaller is the *proportion* of the labors of man required for effecting chemical or mechanical changes in the forms of matter, and the larger is the *proportion* thereof that may be given to the accomplishment of those vital changes by means of which there is obtained an increase in the quantity of things susceptible of being converted. The mill, by help of which water, wind, or steam is made to do the work that before required the hand — converting the grain into flour — diminished the quantity of human effort required for effecting changes in the form of food, and greatly increased that which might be given to the work of adding to the quantity of grain requiring to be ground. So, too, the spinning-jenny, and the power-loom, by diminishing the labor required for effecting changes in the form of wool, set free a large amount of labor that might be given to augmenting the supply of wool. So, too, must it be, in all and every case in which the powers of nature are brought to aid the labors of man in the work of converting the things yielded by our great mother earth — the *proportion* of his labor that may be given to augmenting the quantity of raw materials, tending, with every such accession of power, steadily to increase.

The smaller the quantity of labor required for the work of conversion, the larger is that which may be given to the preparation of the great machine to which we are indebted for both food and wool; and the greater must be the ability to subject to cultivation the richer soils — thence obtaining the increased supplies of food required for enabling men to live in close connection with each other, combining their efforts for obtaining further triumphs. The more they can combine, the more rapid is the development of individuality, and the greater the power for further progress.

§ 3. The facility of conversion growing with the growth of the power of association, each step in the progress of society is attended with increased facilities for the maintenance of commerce. Wool and corn become converted into cloth; and iron ore, coal, cloth, and corn reappear in the form of bars of iron, which, in their turn, are combined with additional food, to reappear in the shape of knives; and thus are the products of the earth condensed in form. with constant diminution in the quantity of labor required for effecting changes in the place of matter — and here we have a further increase in the *proportion* of the labor of society that may be given to the augmentation of the supply of commodities required for the support and comfort of man. The steam-engines now in use in Great Britain, are estimated as being capable of doing the work of six hundred millions of men; and, as these are chiefly employed in the work of *condensing* corn and wool into cloth — corn, coal, and ore into iron—and iron into machinery—their effect should be found in a constantly increasing ability to devote both time and mind to the development of the powers of the great machine to which we are indebted for the food, the wool, the coal, and the ore.

The planing-machines of this country, driven by steam, have been stated as being no less than thirty thousand in number — each doing the work of sixty men; or, in the whole, that of eighteen hundred thousand men. Here is great economy of human effort, but to this must yet be added the economy of labor resulting from the transportation of finished, as compared with unfinished, products—the two combining to set free a vast amount of physical and mental effort, susceptible of being applied to increasing the quantity of lumber to be sawed or planed; of coal and ore to be converted into iron; or of wheat requiring to be ground; each and every of which operations tends to the development of the powers of the earth, and to fitting it for better serving the purposes of man.

§ 4. With every approach towards increased facility in the work of conversion near at home, there is witnessed a wonderful increase in the economy of human effort resulting from increased economy of the gifts of nature. The poor savage of the West spends days and nights roaming over the prairies in search of food, and is yet obliged to waste the larger portion of the products of the chase; while the early settler destroys the tree and sells its ashes to distant men who gladly pay for them, with all the enormous cost of transportation added to their original price. As wealth and population grow, the stem is made to yield planks for houses and mills; the bark to help in fitting skins for being converted into shoes; and the branches to furnish the pegs with which those shoes are made. The rags of a poor and scattered settlement are wasted, but as numbers increase, mills appear, and these rags become converted into paper. The little and lonely furnace of the West wastes half the power afforded by its fuel; but the great one of the East applies its heat to drive the engine, and its gas to heat the blast. In the hands of the chemist, clay becomes alumina, and promises soon to furnish a cheap and perfect substitute for the expensive silver. "The horse-shoe nails dropped in the streets during the daily traffic, reappear," says a recent writer, "in the shape of swords and guns. The clippings of the travelling tinker are," as he continues, "mixed with the parings of the horses' hoofs from the smithy, or the cast-off woollen garments of the poorest inhabitants of a sister isle, and soon afterward, in the form of dyes of the brightest hue, grace the dress of courtly dames. The main ingredient of the ink with which we write may have been part of the hoop of an old beer-barrel. The bones of dead animals yield the chief constituent of lucifer matches. The dregs of wine, carefully rejected by the port-wine drinker in decanting his favorite beverage, are taken by him in the form of seidlitz powders, to remove the effects of his debauch. The offal of the streets and the washing of coal-gas reappear carefully preserved in the lady's smelling-bottle, or are used to flavor blancmange for her friends."

The pound of flax, having passed through the hands of the lacemaker, exchanges for more than its weight in gold. The leaves of the fir and the pine, in Silesia, become blankets. The scraps of leather become glue, and the hair that is cut from the human head may be exchanged for gloves and ribbons—and thus it is that as men are more and more enabled to associate, and to combine their efforts, each and every particle of matter is *utilized,* with constant decline in the value of commodities required for their use, and constant increase in the value of man himself.

§ 5. Widely different is the course of things in countries whose scattered population is compelled to waste its labors on the poorer soils. In Carolina, where men yet cultivate land an acre of which yields but five bushels of wheat, whole forests of pines are frequently destroyed in the process of obtaining a few crops of turpentine — and then the refuse of the turpentine itself is wasted, because of its distance from any place at which it might be so changed in form as to fit it for serving the purposes of man.* The stalks of the cotton-plant, capable of producing flax of great strength and beautiful fibre, are burnt upon the plantation, because of the absence of that power which results from combination, and by help of which they might be rendered available for human purposes. The seeds of the same plant, capable of yielding oil, are, in like manner, wasted.† At home and abroad, "exceedingly few of the fibre-yielding plants have been taken up by manufacturers, and yet," says Mr. Ewbank,‡ "they abound everywhere — in reeds, sedges, and coarse grasses, and in the leaves of some of the commonest shrubs and trees. The banana and its relatives" would, as he says, yield, besides fruit, "from nine to twelve thousand pounds per acre of fibre of every fineness, from ropes to muslin." "Countless millions of tons of this, and kindred substances, spontaneously shoot up every year, and sink away into the ground, neglected by man;" while, at the same time, countless millions of tons of the most valuable dye-yielding woods are growing in their vicinity, waiting his coming to yield themselves to his service.

Every article here referred to, wheresoever found, is as capable of being useful to man as it would be were it in the neighborhood of Paris, or of London; but its utility is latent, and can be developed only by means of association and combination among men. Isolated, man finds himself unable to make the first and most difficult step, preparatory to the new and greater ones that would be sure to follow in its train. Population it is that makes the food come from the rich soils of the earth, and gives utility to all the matter of which that earth is composed; with constant decline

* "I saw this day, as I shall hereafter describe, three thousand barrels of an article worth a dollar and a half in New York, thrown away, a mere heap of useless offal, because it would cost more for transportation than it would be worth." — OLMSTEAD: *Seaboard Slave States*, p. 330.

† The present crop, of three and a half millions of bales, is capable, as we are told, of yielding ninety millions of gallons of oil.

‡ *The World a Workshop*, p. 89.

in the value of all the commodities required for the use of man, and constant increase in his own value. Depopulation, on the contrary—compelling resort to the poor soils—deprives of utility the matter by which man is everywhere surrounded, with constant decline in his own value, and in his power to obtain supplies of food, clothing, or other necessaries of life.

So, too, is it with intellect. Increase of numbers bringing into action all the various faculties of man, every individual finds his appropriate place, with steady increase of commerce. Depopulation, on the contrary — forcing all men back to the search for food — substitutes for intellect mere brute force, with constant decline of commerce. That commerce may exist, there must be difference; and the greater the diversity of employment, the more rapid must be the circulation, and the greater must be the commerce.

The *weight* of any given community tends to accelerated increase—every addition to its numbers being attended with corresponding increase in the development of the latent faculties of the men of whom it is composed. The *motion* of society tends likewise to increase at a constantly accelerated rate — every increase of individuality being attended with corresponding increase in the power of association and in the continuity of action. Momentum being the velocity multiplied by the weight, and both of these latter tending to constant acceleration in the rate of increase, we may now, without difficulty, understand why it is, that the force exerted by a community tends to grow at a rate so much more rapid than would be indicated by its increase in numbers. Taking ten for the present weight, and the same number for the velocity, the momentum would be a hundred. Doubling the numbers in a period of five-and-twenty years—and allowing the development of intellectual faculty to be in the same ratio, the weight, at the close of the term, would be quadrupled; and, allowing for increased facility of combination, resulting from increase of numbers and correspondent economy of labor, and of the products of the earth, we obtain the same quantity as representing the velocity; and the two, multiplied into each other, give now sixteen hundred, instead of the two hundred that would be obtained were the productive power of the individual to remain unchanged.

The tendency to the development of the resources of the earth, and of the powers of man, being in the direct ratio of the motion of society, and being always attended with that increase of local attraction which produces love of home; it follows, necessarily, that a community must grow in individuality, and in force, with the growth of the power of, and the desire for, association among the individuals of whom it is composed.

§ 6. The motion of society, and the power of man, tend to increase in a geometrical ratio, whenever men are permitted to proceed onward, and undisturbed, towards the establishment of power over nature, to be acquired by means of combination with their fellow-men. Look, however, where we may, we see his progress in that direction to have been, at times, impeded, and sometimes altogether arrested; while at others he has so far retrograded as to have been compelled to abandon the most fertile soils, after having incurred the great expenditure of physical and mental force required for their subjugation — as in hither Asia, Egypt, Greece, and Italy, of olden time; and in Ireland, India, Jamaica, Virginia, and Carolina, of the modern one — occurrences, into the causes of which we may now inquire.

The history of the world, in its every chapter, presents the strong man trampling on the weak one, and the latter seeking, by means of combination with his fellow-men, to set limits to the power of those by whom he was oppressed. The former, as we see, has everywhere appropriated to himself large bodies of land — compelling the latter to cultivate it for him, and requiring him to use not only *his* land, but *his* mills, and *his* machinery of every description, whenever he sought to effect changes, whether in the places, or in the forms, of matter.

At times, the former has compounded with his tax-payers for certain portions of the produce, taking sometimes three-fourths, two-thirds, or one-half; but even then has generally required that when they needed to convert their grain into flour, they should pay for the privilege of so doing; that another tax should be paid when they desired to convert it into bread; and a still further one when they sought to exchange their bread, or their grain, with their neighbors for other commodities required for their purposes. If they wished to change their wool into cloth, they were obliged to pay for that privilege in the form of excise, or other duties. If the people of the town and country sought to maintain commerce, the permission so to do was to be paid for in the shape of duties of *octroi*, as in France; or if, as in Spain, they desired to make any species of exchanges, those who performed the duties of government claimed a tenth on every transfer of property, as *alcavala*. The right to labor has been held to be a privilege, the exercise of which required a patent, to be paid for at a heavy price. In every form, the few who were strong and enabled to live by virtue of the exercise of their power of appropriation, have sought to prevent the many, who, individually, were weak, from combining their efforts — except on conditions dictated by themselves. Slavery has existed in a variety of forms, sometimes more, and at others less, oppressive; but it has, in all cases, resulted from the efforts of those who were strong of body, or of mind, to deprive those who were weak, of the power to determine for whom they would work, or what should be their reward—and thus to prevent the growth of commerce.

As, however, population has increased, men have been more and more enabled to combine together for the acquisition of power over their own actions, and over the natural forces by which their efforts might be so much aided — building towns, or local centres, in which the artisan and the trader could associate for self-defence. The more they could associate, the more individuality became developed; and therefore is it that we see freedom to have grown so rapidly in the towns and cities of Greece and Italy, in those of France and Germany, the Netherlands and England.

Power thus resulted from association and combination, but its acquisition has but too generally been accompanied by a selfish desire for securing to the associates monopolies of its exercise, to be enjoyed at the expense of their fellow-men. The Phœnicians carefully guarded the secret of their dyes; and the Venetians were so jealous of their secrets, that they reduced their artisans to a condition approaching that of slavery, by prohibition of their emigration. The Flemings, in their turn—having succeeded in establishing among themselves the diversity of employments required for the development of intellectual force, for economizing human labor, and for utilizing the products of the earth — exercised, during a long period of time, the power of association to an extent then unparalleled in any part of Northern or Central Europe. Even here, however, the spirit of monopoly made its appearance, bringing with it regulations tending to give the trader advantages over the workman on the one hand, and over the producer of raw materials on the other — and thereby producing an emigration of the former, and a war of tariffs on the part of the latter; and in due season Flemish power followed in the wake of that of Carthage and of Tyre. The Dutch, profiting by the difficulties of their Flemish rivals, became the most extensive manufacturers of Europe; but they, in their turn — while enlarging in all directions their dominion—gave to various bodies monopoly powers, having for their object the prevention of any intercourse between important portions of the world, except by means of their own ships, their own ports, their seamen, and their merchants. The oppressive character of this system forced both France and England to measures of resistance, exhibited in the navigation act of Cromwell, and the tonnage duties, and tariff, of Colbert; and the power of Holland commenced from that period to pass away, as that of Venice and of Genoa had already done. In all these cases, the object in view had been that of preventing circulation abroad, with a view to produce increase of motion at home, and to foster centralization by compelling commerce to pay extra taxes in the form of transportation, for their emolument; and in all, the results, as we see, proved to be the same — failure and decline, even where not ending in absolute ruin.

§ 7. Among individuals, selfishness generally defeats itself; and as it is with them, so is it with nations. All the communities above referred sought to obtain strength and power, not in company *with* other — not by commerce *with* them, based upon the extension of commerce among themselves — but by carrying on trade *for* them, with a view to enrich themselves at others' expense. The natural rights of all were equal; and, had that principle been fully recognised, all might have grown rich, strong, and free together; but, as it was, they, each and all, first impoverished their weaker neighbors, and then found themselves, in turn, impoverished by means of the very measures to which they had looked for increase of wealth and power. The perfect harmony of all real interests, and the *advantage* of sound international morality, are lessons taught in every page of history; and yet, after so many centuries of experience, the leading nations of the world are, even now, acting as if the road to prosperity for themselves was to be found only through the adoption of measures tending to the injury of all around them.

That the power to control the forces of nature should be beneficial to mankind, it is *indispensable* that the knowledge by which it is acquired should be extensively diffused. Give to a single member of a community the secret of gunpowder, and enable him to monopolize it—and he will enslave his neighbors. In time, the latter may, perhaps, obtain the knowledge how to make it; but this they will do, if ever, in despite of all the resistance that can be opposed by the monopolist — already become so powerful as to be enabled to prohibit combination among his poor dependants. So is it, too, with nations. Limit to a single one the command of steam, or the power to convert wool into cloth, coal and ore into iron, or grain into flour, and it would assuredly become the tyrant of the world, to the injury of all, itself included. Centralization, find it where we may, looks to poverty, slavery, and death —and so entirely is this the case in regard to scientific knowledge, that *it would be better that the power of steam had no existence, than that the command of such a force should be limited to any single community of the world.* For a time, that community might be, itself, enriched; but with slavery there, as everywhere, the damage to the slave would recoil upon the master. Exhausting all the surrounding communities, it would itself speedily find arising the disease of "over-population" — tending to the production at home of the same slavery of which it had been the cause abroad.

Trade had built up, among the Flemings, large fortunes, the possession of which but stimulated the appetites of their owners for further acquisition — while increasing their power for controlling the movements of other nations, with a view to the accomplishment of their selfish objects. To that end, they sought monopoly at home and abroad; but the effect proved widely different from their expectations — their measures producing resistance both within and without. Workmen, flying to England, found in Edward III. a monarch fully sensible of the advantages which must result from enabling the farmer and the artisan to take their places by each other's side—and one, too, able and willing to grant them all the protection they required. Not only were franchises granted to them, but all restrictions upon domestic commerce, so far as related to the making of cloth, were at once repealed; while by an act of Parliament, of 1337, the export of wool and the import of cloth were both prohibited. The selfishness of the Flemings, in their efforts to monopolize the knowledge they had acquired, with a view to convert the gifts of nature into machinery of oppression, had thus produced resistance, whose effects will be considered in another chapter.

# CHAPTER XVI.

## THE SAME SUBJECT CONTINUED.

§ 1. At the opening of the fourteenth century, the commerce of England was such as indicated a very rude condition of its people—wool, hides, and tin, with the latter of which it had for ages supplied the world, constituting the list of exports, and cloth the chief article of import. The custom of foreign nations, for these raw materials, was courted by means of grants of privileges to their merchants, while oppressive export duties threw upon the farmers of the country all the burden of the government. Sent abroad in their rudest state, their products came back to them in the form of cloth, and were then admitted on the payment of a merely nominal duty, of less than one per cent.* Raw produce was, consequently, very cheap, while manufactured commodities were very dear.

Commerce at home was impeded by countless restrictions, while all the domestic markets, in towns and fairs, were so freely opened to the Flemish and other manufacturers, that in reading the history of the Plantagenets it is difficult to avoid being struck with the identity of the English system of that day with the Turkish one of our own—that under which the Ottoman Empire has sunk to its present state of inanition. While enjoying privileges within the kingdom the exercise of which was denied to Englishmen, the foreign merchants were unsparing in their efforts to monopolize the purchase of the raw material on one side of the Channel, and the conversion of it on the other—and thus to maintain the largest difference between the prices of the wool they needed to buy and the cloth they desired to sell. To carry into effect these views

* The price of wool being fixed in the market of the world, was entirely unaffected by the division that might be made between the government and the people. Of that price the government claimed one-third — and this was purely and simply a direct tax.

was the object of the regulations of the Flemish cities to which reference has above been made.

The power of association — or commerce — then scarcely at all existed in England — diversity of employment being a thing but little known. As a consequence, although wool was low in price, all articles of food were yet, by comparison, greatly lower — their bulk being quite too great to admit of their exportation to distant countries, and there being little market for them at home. The former — representing food that had undergone a single process of manufacture — commanded, ton for ton, twenty times as much of the precious metals. The cost of transportation being, therefore, comparatively small, it could, with some facility, travel to a distance; whereas, food was often being wasted in one part of the kingdom when famine prevailed in others; and therefore it was that sheep and hogs constituted almost the entire capital of those who professed to farm the land.

The facts thus presented for consideration, by England of that day, are identical with those occurring in the purely agricultural countries of our own. The cotton of India can be sent to a distance, because it, like the English wool, is the representative of food that has undergone a single process of manufacture. The food of India cannot travel even from one part of the country to another; and therefore it is that famines prevail in one district, while corn perishes for want of demand in others. The Russian corn can, with difficulty, go abroad, but its wool can readily do so. The corn of Illinois and Iowa is to so great an extent absorbed on the road to market, that the farmer desires, wherever possible, to subject it to the first rude process of manufacture, and therefore passes it through the stomach of the hog — carrying it to market in the form of pork. That of Virginia is passed through the stomachs of negro men and women, and taken to market in the form of slaves. That of Carolina, after having been digested by men and women, finds its way to England in the shape of cotton.— In the latter, the necessity for effecting changes of place was—as it now is — felt to be the great obstacle to improvement; and, as that diminished with every diminution in the bulk of the commodities requiring to be transported, it is no matter of surprise that we find the common sense of the English people leading them to take the first step in the career whose advantage was afterwards so clearly exhibited by Adam Smith, when showing how great was the weight of corn and wool contained in a piece of cloth; and how easily the two could be transported when they had assumed that form.

Then, as now, distance from market was productive of great unsteadiness in the demand for, and the supply of, the bulky products of the earth—the laborer perishing at one moment for want of food; and the farmer, at the next, being ruined for want of people who required to eat, and were able to pay for the corn he desired to sell. From 1302 to 1317, the price of wheat rose steadily, until from 12*s.* in the first, it had attained £5 18*s.* in the last; and then, but a few years later, we find it down to 6*s.*, 10*s.*, and £1 7*s.** Cultivation was limited everywhere to the superficial soils—the richest lands of the kingdom being then, as for centuries afterwards they continued to be, so covered with wood, or so saturated with moisture, as to render them useless for any of the purposes of man. On the opposite side of the Channel, all was different. Combination of action, resulting from diversity of employment, having brought into activity the richest soils, agriculture had already attained a position higher, probably, than that occupied by any part of England, even at the opening of the eighteenth century. With every day, the people of Holland, and of Flanders, were then obtaining greater power over nature, and greater facilities for the accumulation of further wealth.

§ 2. Such was the state of things in England at the date of the passage of the act prohibiting the export of wool and the import of cloth. It was a measure of resistance, looking to the protection of the English farmer against the monopolies of the Flemish manufacturers; and, as such, tended greatly to the promotion of commerce.† In this proceeding, however, the usual error of refor-

* These prices are in money of the present time, as given by Adam Smith, *Wealth of Nations*, book 1, chap. xi.

† "Edward III., and others of our princes, incurred no little odium by the judicious protection which they afforded to the foreign manufacturers who took refuge among us."—McCulloch: *Discourse introductory to the Wealth of Nations*, p. xxv.

Mr. McCulloch is, nevertheless, an opponent of the system which looks to extending the same protection in the present time, even where the circumstances are precisely similar.

mers—that of going too far and fast—is clearly obvious. When nature works most beneficially for man, she works slowly; and what is true in the natural world, cannot be other than true in the social one. Man as rarely profits by violent changes in the societary edifice, as he does by earthquakes, or by water-spouts. The difficulty of the English corn and wool growers consisted in the absence of competition for the purchase of their commodities, consequent upon long-continued dependence upon a single and distant market. Its remedy was to be found under a system of alterative treatment looking to the creation of a domestic one—while leaving untouched the export of the raw material required for the supply of distant countries.

What was required for giving the producer a choice of markets, was the imposition of such a duty on foreign cloths as would have made it the interest of the foreign weaver to come to him and consume his bulky corn, while converting into cloth his more compact wool. Such a measure might have been fully and promptly carried into effect, and its adoption would have given all the advantages that could have been expected from the other, while unattended by any counterbalancing disadvantages. As it was, however, the nation being poor, and the ability to purchase foreign merchandise, consequently, very small, while the necessities of the king were very great, the latter needed, as far as possible, to retain all the accustomed sources of revenue; among which that afforded by the export of wool stood forth most conspicuous. The prohibition of the trade throwing it chiefly into his own hands, he continued largely to profit by it. The one great measure, however, the establishment of direct commerce between the producer of wool and corn and the consumer of cloth, was, in some degree, accomplished; and from that time forth there was a daily increase in the power of voluntary association, manifested by the building of new towns and enlargement of old ones; by the enfranchisement of serfs; and by the growing power of the Commons to direct the movements of the ship of state. Magna Charta provided for securing the privileges of the aristocracy; but the statute of 1347 laid the foundation of the liberties of the people, by providing for the diversity of their employments and the development of their various individualities; as a consequence of which the change of system was followed by a rapid increase in the amount of force at the command of the community itself.

§ 3. For centuries. nevertheless, England continued to be an importer of cloth, iron, and other manufactured commodities, and an exporter of raw materials — a course of things leading necessarily to the exhaustion of the soil, and to great waste of mental and physical force. That force represented the capital consumed in the form of food, the quantity of which required for the proper nourishment of the population was just as great as it could have been had all the time been profitably employed; but that it could not be, in default of the power to maintain commerce, the condition of whose existence is found in the rapidity of circulation resulting from diversity in the modes of employment. The mass of the force produced being wasted, the people remained poor — requiring laws providing for their compulsory support out of the produce of the land; and hence arose a necessity for establishing a forced circulation by means of poor laws, the commencement of which is found in the act of 43 Elizabeth.

The community continued poor and weak as compared with others across the Channel, in which employments were more diversified; and hence it is that we find the Dutch enjoying almost a monopoly of the privilege of managing the commerce of England with foreign countries. The period of the Protectorate brought with it, however, a successful effort at establishing direct commerce with distant nations, by means of navigation laws, that laid the foundation of British power on the ocean at the present day. For a still later one it was reserved to witness a similar effort for the promotion of commerce at home, by establishing direct intercourse between the producers of food on one hand, and the consumers of shoes and stockings, hats, caps, and bonnets, on the other—between the men who had labor to sell, and those who had corn or wool, cloth or iron, with which to buy it. The distinction of having been the first to suggest the measures that since have led to the manufacturing greatness of England, has recently been claimed for Andrew Yarranton, some extracts from whose work*

* *England's Improvement by Sea and Land. To Outdo the Dutch without Fighting. To pay Debts without Moneys. To set at work the Poor of England with the Growth of our own Lands, &c. &c.* By ANDREW YARRANTON. London, 1677.

will enable the reader to see what was the then position of the English farmer; and why it was that protection was deemed to be required:—*

"From France were imported 'canvases, lockrums, and great quantities of coarse cloths,' so much so, in fact, 'that it hath almost laid aside the making of linen cloth in England.' Twine and yarn were also imported to make sail-cloth and cordage, 'which hath taken off the labor of multitudes of people in Suffolk and thereabouts, and hath so lessened the trade that it is almost lost.' Narrow coarse cloths were imported from north Germany, 'the cheapness whereof hath beaten out the linen trade formerly made in Lancashire, Cheshire, and thereabouts, about forty years since, a very great trade.' Bed-ticking was also imported, which had 'almost destroyed that trade in Dorsetshire, and Somersetshire, so the spinners are idle, and the lands fall in price.' Yarns were imported from Germany. 'Formerly, the clothiers made use of linen yarn spun in that country, (the neighborhood of Kidderminster,) to make their lynsey-woolseys, but now the cheapness of the foreign threads hath put them upon making use of German yarn. Great quantities of thread (yarn) also are used at Manchester, Maidstone, and in other parts of England, to mix with woollen; with infinite other commodities; and all the benefit of the labor of these threads is applied to foreigners.'"

The remedy for this state of things was, according to Yarranton, to be found in *importing the skill*, to which end he gave the following advice:—

"'Send for one man from Friburgh, to put you in the true way and method of making the tape, and to bring over two engines—one to weave narrow tape, and the other to weave broad tape, with wheels to spin. (The German wheels were much superior to the English.)

"'Send for one man from Dort, in Holland, to put you in the true way of ordering the fine threads.

* The following passages are from a recent work—Dove's *Elements of Political Science*—in which are given copious extracts from Yarranton's remarkable book. They are here copied at some length, because the facts they record correspond so precisely with those of all other countries of the present day engaged in exporting raw materials and importing manufactured commodities. The difficulties now to be overcome by them are the same that then existed in England, and the remedial measures now pursued in the advancing countries of the world are the same that are here suggested.

" 'Send for a spinning-mistress out of Germany, to order and govern the little maids, and instruct them in the art of spinning.

" 'Send for a man from Harlem, in Holland, to whiten (bleach) your tapes and threads.' "

Regarding the iron manufacture as being, next to linen, of the first importance, he says —

" 'Consider how many iron-works are laid down' (abandoned) 'both in Kent, Sussex, and Surrey, and many more must follow. The reason is, the iron from Sweadland, (Sweden,) Flanders, and Spain comes in so cheap, that it cannot be made to profit here. * * *

" 'Now I have showed you the two manufactures of linen and iron, with the product thereof, and all the materials are with us growing; and these two manufactures will, if by law countenanced, set all the poor in England at work, and much enrich the country, and thereby fetch people into the kingdom, whereas now they depart;' (yes, honest Andrew, and *now* also they depart;) 'and thereby deprive the Dutch of these two great manufactures of iron and linen. I mean, iron wrought into all commodities, so vastly brought down the Rhine into Holland from Liege, Gluke, Soley, and Cologne, and by them diffused and sent all the world over. And these two trades being well fixed here, will help to beat the Dutch without fighting. I pray, consider the charge England is now at with the poor, and observe what they now cost the public; but, if employed in these two manufactures, what advance by their labor might the public receive! Admit there be in England and Wales a hundred thousand poor people unemployed, and each one costs the public fourpence the day in food, and, if these were employed, they would earn eightpence the day; and so the public, in what might be gained and saved, will advance twelvepence the day by each poor person now unemployed. So a hundred thousand persons will be to the benefit of the public, if employed, one million and a half yearly in these two manufactures of iron and linen. And as these two manufactures are now managed in Saxony, they set all their poor at work. I, travelling aworter and across Saxony, did not see one beggar there; and these two manufactures being prudently and by good laws, there supported and encouraged, they are become two parts in three of the revenue and benefit of that duke; and they are sent into

England at this time in great quantities, all paying customs in ten several places before they come here. * * * *

"'But there is something that may be of worse consequence than ordinary, if the iron manufacture be not encouraged. At present, most of the works in Sussex and Surrey are laid down, and many in the north of England, and many in other parts, must follow, if not prevented by enclosing commons to supply them with wood. And when the greatest part of the iron-works are asleep, if there should be occasion for great quantities of guns and bullets,'—(always guns and bullets,

> 'As if the metals were intended
> For nothing else but to kill men dead,')—

'and other sorts of iron commodities, for a present unexpected war, and the Sound happen to be locked up, and so prevent iron coming to us, truly we should then be in a fine case!'

"The next branch of industry to which Andrew directed the attention of his countrymen was the woollen trade; and this he proposes to improve by the adoption of the processes which enabled the foreigner to make a handsomer cloth than was made in England. Here his advice was, '*import the machinery.*' Two pieces of the same web of cloth may be so differently dressed, that the one shall be coarse, hard, unpleasant to the wear, unattractive to the eye, and comparatively unsuited to the market. The other piece, although made of the same wool, and woven in the same loom, may be so judiciously treated as to assume qualities of an entirely different character. Dressing, in fact, is the education of cloth—the woollen fabric, like the man who wears it, may grow up a boor or a gentleman. Andrew, then, tells his countrymen how they may dress their cloths, and make them of a superior quality; and this he does in a dialogue which would do no discredit to Izaak Walton. Before considering his method, however, we must notice one of his statements—so contrary as it is to the common supposition that manufacturers were flocking into England. This they *had* done a century before; but Andrew assures us that, in his day, the manufacturers were actually emigrating to Germany, Ireland, and Holland. His statements on this head, although concise, are quite explicit. We shall cite only one, premising that he is speaking of those practices which were calculated to injure the trade of England :—

"'Another trick there is of carrying fullers' earth from Woborne to Lynn in Norfolk, as they pretend; and then ship it to be carried to the clothiers in the west, and when at sea, a west wind blows the ship into Flushing, in Zealand. And we will have more fullers' earth carried from Arundel in Sussex to Portsmouth or to Chichester, and there shipped to secure the clothiers in the north of England; and when that ship is over against Hull, a west wind shall blow her over to the Brill, or into the Texel, into Holland. And these two ladings of earth, with a little that shall be brought over for ballast for ships, will do mischief enough, *for trade will go where it is most encouraged, and where the merchant and clothier can get most by it.*

"'*Draper.*—True, old friend, these tricks there are, and there are bad men enough that will be apt enough to leave the land where they were born; but let us see to help these matters, for if you should be one of them, all the poor of this country will be bound to curse you, and so will the rich too; *for we have had men bad enough of our own trade, (but it will not become me to name persons,) who have provoked many clothiers to sell their estates, and transport themselves into the Lower Palatinate, and other parts of Germany, and there set up the clothing trade, which hath already spoiled our coarse cloth trade eastward, and the trade at Hamborough too; for if their trade be spoiled in England, they must try if they can make it out somewhere else, as in Ireland, Holland, and Germany, &c.*'"

The folly of England in confining herself so almost exclusively to agriculture, had in those days become proverbial on the continent. "The stranger," as they said, "buys of the Englishman the skin of the fox for a groat, and sells him the tail for a shilling." Seeing that the system then existing tended towards the cheapening of all the raw materials of manufacture, labor included, Yarranton had little difficulty in arriving at the conclusion that a people wholly employed in tillage must remain poor, because of the waste of labor consequent upon the absence of that combination of effort which constitutes commerce. He, therefore, urged upon his countrymen the adoption of protective measures, by means of which they should, at once, incur the expense of bringing the machinery and the skill to the raw materials, and thus for ever relieve themselves from the necessity for sending the bulky corn and wool to the machinery and the skill. Were this done, it would, as he confidently assured them, lead to such improvements in the internal communications, and in commerce generally, that food could be cheaply supplied to all parts of the country — that rents would rise — that capital would so much increase, that interest would greatly fall — and that land would sell more readily at thirty years' purchase of the greater rent than it then could do at sixteen years' purchase of the lesser one. These were remarkable predictions, but they were made by a man who seems fully to have appreciated the advantages resulting from that rapidity of circulation which constitutes commerce; and their entire accuracy was verified by the great increase in the value of both land and labor which subsequently followed their emancipation from that heaviest of all taxes — the one resulting from a necessity for effecting changes of place, and constituting the great bar to progress.

In the advice thus given in regard to a great question in social science, this remarkable man only indicated measures similar to those we now see to be everywhere else pursued. When the chemist desires to diminish the centralizing force by means of which particles of matter are held together — and thus to produce individuality, and the consequent power of association among those particles — he does it by means of the establishment of a stronger counter-attraction in another direction; as when he immerses zinc and copper in acids, and thus develops electricity. So, too, with the occupant of our Western prairies, who always fights fire with fire — establishing local centres of attraction by means of which gravitation towards the great central fire is so much diminished, that the latter quickly ceases to exist. Flanders, Holland, and Germany had already attained to so great a perfection of manufacture, that the attraction of centralization was drawing in that direction not only all the raw materials of England, but many of the most valuable among her people; and Yarranton saw clearly, that the latter could never prosper until she should have established a system of counter-attraction sufficient not only to enable her to retain the skill she already had; but, also, to attract that which she required, and as yet had not. His advice was taken;

and from that time the statute-book of England became, from year to year, more and more filled with laws having for their object the bringing together of the farmer and the artisan, with a view to the production of association and combination—and thereby diminishing the necessity for exhausting the land by means of the exportation of its products in their rudest state.

§ 4. The insular position of England had given her security of person, and of property, so far as regarded the devastations of war, to an extent unknown in any part of Europe; and, in the days of Yarranton, she was waiting only the adoption of a system that should enable her people to combine together for the development of their various individualities. To effect a change in the movements of a nation requires, however, no inconsiderable time. The knowledge existed on the continent, but it was not to be found in England. In Holland, in the Netherlands, and in the manufacturing states of Germany, wealth abounded, and the loan of capital could be obtained at the rate of four or five per cent.; whereas, in the other it was with difficulty obtained for employment either in manufactures, or in agriculture. For centuries, the current of raw materials had been towards the continent, but now the course of that current was to be changed; and to accomplish this was a work requiring serious effort. Commerce, too, in England herself, was impeded by numerous restrictions, many of which had been created by law, while others had resulted from the anxiety of the existing manufacturers to discourage domestic competition for the purchase of raw products, as well as for the sale of finished commodities. Then, as now, they desired to buy cheaply and sell dearly; and the more they could prevent the extension of manufactures at home, the cheaper would be wool and the dearer would be cloth.

Time, however, brought the change, but not until the English farmer had experienced in its full effect the loss resulting from the necessity for depending on distant markets for the sale of the raw products of the earth. In the long and warlike period that closed with the treaty of Utrecht, the power of wheat to command money in exchange had been equal to 43*s.* 6*d.* per quarter, but with the return of peace, (1713,) the price fell to 35*s.*, and thereafter continued gradually to decline until, in the ten years ending 1755, the average was but 21*s.* 3*d.*; or less than half of what before had been obtained for it. The product exceeding the consumption, a small portion needed to go abroad; and that the price obtained for the surplus fixed that of the whole crop, will be obvious to all who remark the course of trade. A deficiency to the extent of even a hundred thousand bushels raises the price of all to the level of that at which that small supply may be brought from the distant market; while an excess to that extent reduces the whole to the level of the price at which this trivial quantity must be sold. How very slight was the excess to which was due the great reduction that had taken place, is shown by the following figures:—

| Ten years ending | Price. | Export, average. |
|---|---|---|
| 1725 ........ | £1 15*s.* 4*a.* ........ | 124,000 quarters. |
| 1735 ........ | £1 15*s.* 2*d.* ........ | 176,000 " |
| 1745 ........ | £1 12*s.* 1*d.* ........ | 276,000 " |
| 1755 ........ | £1 1*s.* 2*d.* ........ | 446,000 " |

At the low price of 21*s.* 2*d.*, the farmers of England obtained a market abroad for less than four millions of bushels — yielding scarcely two millions of dollars a year. The total product of wheat in Great Britain in this latter period must have been more than forty millions of bushels; and as that grain then entered little into consumption as compared with what it since has done, it would be, perhaps, fair to place the total production of food as being the equivalent of a hundred millions of bushels. Of this, about four per cent. constituted the surplus thrown upon the then regulating markets of the world, depressing the prices there, and in a corresponding degree depressing those obtained for the whole quantity produced; to the injury of the land and labor of the kingdom — to that of the artisan — and to that of all but those who were dependent upon fixed incomes for their support.

The population of England was then but six millions, of whom the land-owners — then numbering nearly two hundred thousand —and their families, must have been nearly one-sixth, or a million in number. Adding to them the laborers in husbandry, we have a large proportion of the community directly dependent upon the results of agriculture. The mechanic, however, was equally interested in the prosperity of the farming class, because, if they could sell at fair prices, they could buy the products of his skill and labor. The more *instant* the demand for food and wool, the greater was the ability of the agricultural laborer to purchase cloth — and that of the proprietor of land to effect improvement upon his property, with a view to the larger production of both food and wool. What England then needed, was the direct motion between the producer and the consumer at home — commerce — by help of which her farmers might be emancipated from the dominion of trade. In default of this motion, the latter were obliged to accept 21*s.* 2*d.* per quarter for the whole wheat crop, and corresponding prices for all other descriptions of food—while exporting but four millions of quarters, and importing, in the forms of cloth and iron, probably thrice that quantity.

Progress was, however, being made. With the middle of the century it came to be discovered that iron could be smelted by help of mineral coal; and thenceforward improvements tending to the diversification of the pursuits of men became numerous and rapid. The mighty power of steam was brought to supersede the labors of the human hand—the spinning-jenny was invented—and the processes required for the manufacture of iron continued to be improved — with rapid increase in the circulation of labor and its products—in the economy of human effort—in the accumulation of wealth—and in the power of further progress. The farmer being now freed from his dependence on the distant market, the price of grain rapidly rose—as a necessary consequence of the approximation of the consumer and the producer, and the extension of commerce. The power of wheat to command money in exchange increased in the ten years ending in 1765 to £1 19*s.* 3*d.*; and in those ending in 1775, to £2 11*s.* 3*d.*, at or near which price it remained in the twenty following years. Taking the average quantity, of food of all descriptions, consumed, as being the equivalent of twenty bushels of wheat, the total advance in the return to agricultural labor, consequent upon the increase in the rapidity of circulation resulting from the creation of a domestic demand, could thus be little short of twenty millions of pounds sterling, or a hundred millions of dollars. Agriculture, therefore, advanced rapidly—creating new demands for labor, and enabling the laborer to claim a constantly increasing *proportion* of the augmented quantity of things produced.*

§ 5. So far as protection had been resorted to with a view to enable the farmers to call to their aid the skill and the machinery already in use abroad, and to obtain command of the various natural forces required for finishing their products and fitting them for consumption, it was right. It relieved them from the heavy tax of transportation; it promoted the diversification of employments and the development of intellect; and it tended to give to society that natural form in which strength and beauty are most combined; and therefore is it that we see in the movements of the years immediately preceding the breaking out of the wars of the French Revolution, so strong a tendency towards a reform in the constitution of Parliament — looking towards a fairer representation of the various portions of which the society was composed.

Had that been the limit of the movement — had the British policy looked solely to the creation of a domestic market for the British farmers — had it been limited to *their own* emancipation from dependence on the casualties of distant markets — had British statesmen been governed by that great fundamental law of Christianity, which requires that we should respect the rights of others as carefully as we desire that they should respect our own — all would have been well; and the doctrines of over-population — of the necessity of a cheap and abundant supply of labor — of the expediency of expelling a kindred nation, with a view to supply its place by "one more mixed, more docile, and more serviceable," and one "which can submit to a master" † — the doctrines, in short, of modern political economy, would have remained unheard of.

Such, however, was not to be the course of events. Here, as

* How immense was the effect of the creation of a home market in making a demand for land and labor, is shown in the fact, that in the reigns of Anne and George I. — 1702 to 1751 — the whole number of enclosure acts obtained was 18, and the quantity of land embraced therein but 19,339 acres. From 1751 to 1760, the number was 226, and the quantity of land, 318,778 acres; but from 1760 to 1797, the former rose to 1532, and the latter to 2,804,197 — and nearly all of this in the period from 1771 to 1791.

† *London Times*, on the Exodus of Ireland.

everywhere else had been the case, there arose a disposition to monopolize within themselves the knowledge by means of which progress had been obtained; and the more free the people by whom the monopoly was desired, the more unscrupulous were certain to be the measures by aid of which it would be sought to be secured. Had it been otherwise, it would have been in opposition to all the lessons taught by the history of the world; and should, at any future time, the people of the American Union be so unfortunate as to have colonies, and they should then fail to prove themselves the most tyrannical and unscrupulous of masters, the fact would constitute the most remarkable one in history. It is, therefore, no matter of surprise that to the freest people of Europe we owe the invention of the system described in former chapters — of all that have ever existed, the most oppressive and exhausting.

Nothing comparable with it in its capacity for evil had ever been devised. Invasions by bodies of armed men are attended with waste of property, destruction of life, and temporary suspension of commerce; but with the return of peace men are enabled again to combine their efforts, and at the close of a few short years all is again as it before had been. Such, however, is not the case with invasions looking to the permanent substitution of trade for commerce; for under them, the power of association dies away, the intellect declines in its development, and man gradually loses all the power over nature that he before had gained. He, himself, then diminishes in value, while that of the commodities required for his support as regularly increases—and with every step in that direction he becomes more and more enslaved. The one is a sudden shock from which, with care, the patient may recover; whereas, the other consists in opening the veins and permitting the life's blood slowly to ebb away—rendering recovery from day to day more difficult, and closing at length in death. Of all the countries of Europe, none has so frequently been overrun — none has so much suffered from the evils of war — as Belgium; and yet it has at all times ranked among those most prosperous. Of all, the only ones that have for centuries been almost unprofaned by a hostile foot, are the British islands; yet, there was invented the Malthusian theory, and in one of them is found the great treasury of facts by means of which it is attempted to be supported.

France has suffered heavily from war; but she maintains a policy tending to promote the growth of commerce, and therefore does she advance in wealth and power. Portugal, except during the period from 1807 to 1812, has been in a great degree exempt from war; yet she declines in wealth and strength, because wholly subject to the exhaustive influences of trade.

§ 6. The more rapid the circulation in a community, the greater is the power at command, and the greater the tendency towards increase in its amount. Whether or not mankind shall profit by its acquisition of wealth and strength, is dependent wholly upon the spirit in which it is directed. Wrongly guided, its power for evil is as great as is its capacity for good; and therefore is it that we everywhere see the grievousness of the tyranny to be in the direct ratio of the freedom of those by whom the power is exercised. A people tyrant is an hydra-headed monster, compared with which an autocratic one is harmless. The knowledge of the Athenians gave them power, and when they became masters of the lives and fortunes of a thousand subject cities, they proved themselves the most oppressive of taskmasters—every man among them being a sovereign, whose revenue was to be increased by measures tending to the exhaustion of his subjects. The aristocracies of Carthage, and of Venice, and of Genoa, were less oppressive—the number of masters being not so great. The despotism of Charlemagne was light by comparison with that of the aristocracy which succeeded to it; as was that of Louis XI., when compared with the anarchy of Charles VI. and VII., when there existed no law but that of force — when kings and dukes had recourse to assassination with a view to free themselves from troublesome competitors—and when robbery and murder, in the persons of men like La Hire, Dammartin, and Saintrailles, claimed and received the high honors of the state. So was it with the despotism of Louis XIII., as compared with the anarchy of the League; and so with that of Frederick III., as compared with that of the many little despots who, until then, had disposed of the lives and fortunes of the Danish people. So is it now with the Russian government, as compared with that worst of all tyrannies maintained in Poland down to the day of its partition.

The more numerous the masters, the worse for both master and servant; in proof of which may be cited the fact that it is within the limits of the American Union, in which it was once proclaimed that "all men were born equal," that the assertion has first been made that "free society has proved an utter failure;" and that the natural condition of a large portion of the human race is that of slavery — involving the separation of husbands from wives, parents from children, and brothers and sisters from each other. Such being the case even here, it is no matter of surprise that to the freest people of Europe we owe the invention of the most oppressive despotism — of that system which, more than any that had preceded it, looked to the enslavement of man — that one, the supporters of which now publicly proclaim that for its maintenance there is required that the further increase of population should be "in the most serviceable — the most laborious — part," as "otherwise it will not be sufficiently at the control of capital and skill" — being precisely the doctrine taught in Carolina by men who hold that "slavery is the corner-stone of our institutions."

§ 7. The first and heaviest tax to be paid by man and land, and the great obstacle to the indulgence of the desire for association, is, as has been shown, that resulting from a necessity for effecting changes of place. The various portions of the earth are differently fitted for the production of commodities suited to satisfy the wants, or gratify the tastes, of man — the tropics yielding rice, cotton, sugar, and various fruits; while it is to the temperate zones we must look for corn, and to the arctic ones for furs and ice. International commerce is, therefore, provided for by natural laws; but, to its extension there is opposed the great amount of effort required for transporting commodities in the form in which they are yielded by the earth — the cotton in the seed — the raw wheat — or the cane from which the sugar has yet to be obtained. Looking, next, to the various divisions of the earth's surface, we find, in every little state, provisions almost precisely similar — one part of England being best fitted for yielding copper, and another iron; one yielding hay, and another hops; one producing coal, and another tin. Here, however, as in the case of international commerce, we are met by the difficulty attendant upon the necessity for transportation, for the removal of which we find every man intent upon reducing, as far as possible, the bulk of his commodity—smelting his ore, and thus converting coal and ore into copper or iron — grinding his wheat, and exporting the finer portions in the form of flour — or sawing his trees into planks, that he may save the expense of transporting those portions that are of little use. Elsewhere, other men are seen combining quantities of corn and wool into cloth ; or converting masses of coal and iron into steel ; and again reducing the bulk by converting large quantities of coal and of steel into knives, forks, and other instruments. The more perfectly they succeed in this — the more they can relieve themselves from the tax of transportation — the more rapid must be the circulation among themselves, the greater their power to improve the modes of transportation, so far as it is yet required ; and the greater must be their ability to maintain commerce with distant people.

The English system looked to the diminution of the bulk of *their own products ;* but it looked, also, to the prevention of any such diminution in the *products of other countries.* Directed to the extension of commerce at home, it was directed, also, to the annihilation of commerce among the people of other communities ; and here it was, as has been already said, that it went far beyond any other that had ever been devised. Irish cloths had been celebrated in the days when England exported all her wool and imported all her cloth ; and yet we find the latter availing herself of all the power at her command for the suppression of the Irish woollen manufacture, and for compelling all the wool of the country to pass through the mills of England, before the Irish people, themselves, could use it. Had she simply prohibited the manufacture—leaving the wool-growers to seek a market where they would — she would thus greatly have augmented the cost of transportation, while diminishing the power of association and promoting the exhaustion of the land ; but to this was added, Pelion upon Ossa, a prohibition of intercourse with the world except through the markets of England—and such was the policy afterwards adopted in reference to all the colonies.

Having acquired wealth and power, it was deemed desirable to carry out this policy in reference to independent nations ; and hence the passage, in the period from 1765 to 1799, of the various laws prohibiting the export of machinery and artisans; and the maintenance of those prohibitions until 1825. Their object was, so far as might be possible, that of compelling the rude produce of the earth to be sent to England, there to be subjected to those mechanical or chemical processes required for bringing it to the form in which it was fitted for consumption. Thence it might go abroad to be exchanged for sugar, tea, or coffee; but even these articles were, as far as possible, to be required to pass through English ports, and by means of English ships. So oppressive a system as this had never before even been imagined. It looked to making every country outside of England a purely agricultural one; but, were all the communities of the world reduced to that condition, each and every of them, and each and every of its parts, would be compelled to produce all the commodities required for consumption, as commerce there could be little or none, abroad or at home. To enable distant commerce to exist, the bulk of commodities must be reduced, and in the effort to accomplish that object, diversity of employment is necessarily produced. That diversity had arisen in England, and all her efforts were now given to preventing its appearance in any other part of the world — and thus to establish the entire supremacy of the trader and transporter over the producer.

§ 8. Commerce grows with the diminution in the necessity for transportation. The more the latter can be dispensed with, the more continuous and rapid becomes the societary movement; the more is muscular and mental effort economized; the more rapidly does the reappearance of capital follow its consumption; the greater is the power of accumulation; the greater the utility of all the materials of which the earth is composed; the less the value of the commodities required for the use of man; the greater the value of man; and the more rapid is the development of individuality and the growth of freedom.

That such is the case is everywhere felt, and therefore it is that the men who cultivate the earth so much rejoice in having the workers in iron and cloth — consumers of food and wool — come to occupy places in their neighborhood. To prevent this, and to produce a constantly intermitted motion — one that should cause a long interval between production and consumption — was the object of the British system. It sought everywhere to cause the wool and the cotton to travel thousands of miles in quest of the little spindle and the loom; and that, too, under the most disadvantageous circumstances—the bulk of all the commodities being preserved at its largest, and the aperture through which they were to pass contracted to the smallest size, as here is represented:—

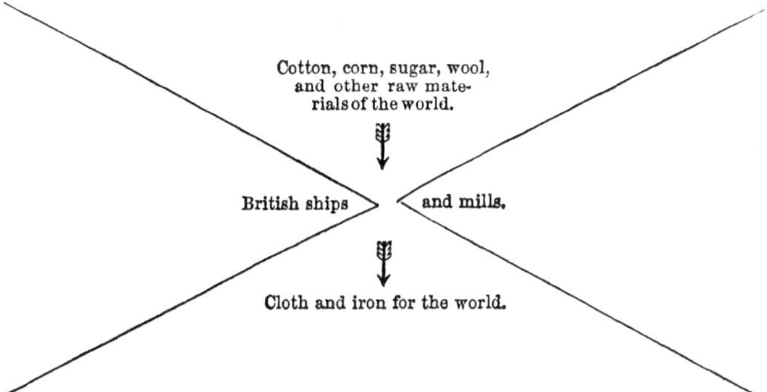


The quantity seeking to pass being great, and the aperture being narrow, it followed, necessarily, that the friction was immense, and that the greater part of the raw produce disappeared under the process to which it thus was subjected. The larger the crop, the greater was the mass to be transported, the higher became the freights, and the larger the charges for storage and insurance; but the smaller became the prices. It hence resulted—as a natural consequence of this most unnatural process—that the farmer and planter were forced to deprecate the extension of production, for to them it was fraught with ruin. Small crops—giving low freights, small charges for storage, and high prices in the distant market—were profitable; whereas large ones were injurious to all engaged in the development of the resources of the earth.

Until now, increase of population had been regarded as an element of strength, but as the British system came fairly into operation the modes of thought were changed, and growth of numbers came to be regarded as an evidence of weakness, and not of strength. How far an unsound and unjust system of policy tended to produce this change of doctrine, will be examined in another chapter.

# CHAPTER XVII.

## THE SAME SUBJECT CONTINUED.

§ 1. The *Wealth of Nations* was first published in 1776; and its chief object was the enforcement upon its author's countrymen of the consideration of the great truth that trade and manufactures were useful so far — and so far only — as they contributed to the advancement of agriculture, to the development of the treasures of the earth, and to the promotion of commerce. The tendency of the colonial system was, as he thought, decidedly adverse to the production of any of these effects, as—by preventing the colonists from working in the "more refined manufactures," and limiting them to those "coarse and household" ones usually carried on by a private family "for its own use"—it tended, certainly, to augment the quantity of raw materials sent to Britain—thereby discouraging British agriculture. That effect was, however, precisely the one sought by the trader and the manufacturer to be accomplished — the cheaper the raw material abroad, the higher being the freights of the one, and the profits of the other.

So far as the system tended to create a market for food, the British farmer profited; but, as regarded all other raw products, he was a heavy sufferer under what Dr. Smith denominated "the mean rapacity, the monopolizing spirit of merchants and manufacturers" — the class of men who thought that "England's treasure" was to be found "in foreign trade" alone. That that trade might prosper, they desired cheap raw material; and, that it might be cheapened, they sought to promote competition for the sale on the soil of England of all the rude products of other lands, as well as of the half-converted ones required for any of the processes of manufacture. "By encouraging the importation of cotton yarn," says Dr. Smith, "and thereby bringing it into competition with that which is made by our own people, they endeavor to buy the work of the poor spinners as cheap as possible.

They are," he continues, "as intent to keep down the wages of their own weavers, as the earnings of the poor spinners; and it is by no means for the benefit of the workman that they endeavor to raise the price of the complete work, or to lower that of the rude materials. It is the industry of the rich and powerful that is principally encouraged by our mercantile system. That which is carried on for the benefit of the poor and indigent is too often either neglected or oppressed."*

Looking, thus, almost exclusively to trade, the system tended, as he saw, unnaturally to increase the *proportion* of the British population employed in the work of exchange and transportation —thereby raising up a nation of mere shopkeepers, and breaking "that natural balance which would otherwise have taken place among the different branches of British industry." "Instead of running in a number of small channels, it had been taught to run principally in one channel"—thereby rendering "industry and commerce less secure," and "the body politic less healthful than it otherwise would have been." "In her present condition," as he thought, "Great Britain resembled one of those unwholesome bodies in which some of the vital parts are overgrown, and which, upon that account, are liable to many dangerous disorders, scarce incident to those in which all the parts are more properly proportioned." The dangers attendant upon this exclusive devotion to the supposed interests of trade, being clearly obvious to him, he cautioned his countrymen that "a small stop in that great blood-vessel, which has been artificially swelled beyond its natural dimensions, and through which an unnatural proportion of the industry and commerce of the country has been forced to circulate, is very likely to bring on the most dangerous disorders upon the whole body politic." * * * "The blood, of which the circulation is stopped in some of the smaller vessels, easily disgorges itself into the greater, without occasioning any dangerous disorder; but, when it is stopped in any of the greater vessels, convulsions, apoplexy, or death, are the immediate and unavoidable consequences. If but one of those overgrown manufactures which, by means either of bounties or of the monopoly of the home and colony markets, have been artificially raised up to any unnatural height, finds some small stop or interruption in

* *Wealth of Nations*, book 4, chap. viii.

its employment, it frequently occasions a mutiny and disorder alarming to government, and embarrassing even to the deliberations of the legislature. How great, therefore, would," as he thought, "be the disorder and confusion which must necessarily be occasioned by a sudden and entire stop in the employment of so great a proportion of our principal manufacturers!"*

Great as were the dangers even then so evident as resulting from an unnatural increase in the proportion of the population engaged in the works of trade and transportation, the people of England had at that time but entered upon the effort to reduce the world at large under the system which so long previously had existed in the colonies. The interdiction of the emigration of artisans was then but ten years old; and the British power was then but beginning to be established in Hindostan. The fifth year following the publication of the work of Dr. Smith witnessed the prohibition of the export of silk and woollen machinery; and before the close of the century the policy had been perfected by the extension of the prohibition to all other descriptions of machinery, as well as to artisans by whom it might be made, and to colliers.

§ 2. From 1750, when corn had been 21*s.* 3*d.* per quarter, to 1790, the population had increased about forty per cent., or from six, to eight and a half millions; but the supply of food had grown at a rate still more rapid — the production of the later years of the period having been at least one-half greater than that of the previous ones. The price, nevertheless, had more than doubled, as has been already shown; and thus had the farmer profited by his emancipation from the necessity for seeking a market in distant countries. Corn was then higher at home than abroad, as a consequence of which there had arisen a commerce of importation, for the prevention of which, and for thus securing themselves against the cheapening of the raw materials of life, the agricultural interest procured, in 1791, the passage of a law limiting the price at which it might be imported.

During all this period the tendency had been towards an increase in the *proportion* of the population engaged in consuming food, whether as artisans, soldiers, traders, or transporters. The system denounced by Dr. Smith was being, as the reader has seen,

* *Wealth of Nations*, book 4, chap. vii.

from year to year, more fully carried out. For almost half a century, India had been devastated by contending French and English armies, engaged in extending the dominion of trade at the expense of commerce. Trade had stirred up dissensions between the mother country and her American colonies, and had thus produced the war of 1776. The class living by appropriation, trade, and transportation, had increased in numbers and in power, but it was reserved for the war of 1793—a war largely due to the thirst for "ships, colonies, and commerce" — to see it attain to full dimensions. The demand for men and money for warlike purposes then limited the power to apply labor, or capital, to the improvement of the land, and greatly diminished the demand for the services of the laborer. Consumers increasing in number, while producers remained stationary, the price of food advanced, while that of labor fell—the effects of which were speedily seen in the rapid growth of the almshouse population.

Pauperism prevailed to an extent that before had been unknown; and then it was that Mr. Malthus furnished the world with the "*Principles of Population*," by help of which, as he told his readers, they might understand the causes of "that poverty and misery observable among the lower classes of people in every nation;" and of "the repeated failures in the efforts of the higher classes to relieve them." Dr. Smith had seen that the policy based upon cheap labor and cheap raw materials was itself the work of those "higher classes;" and *upon them* he had urged the abandonment of a system that, as he saw, looked to the enslavement of the people, and the weakening of the community. Mr. Malthus, on the contrary, found the cause of slavery in a great law of God, by means of which he relieved those "classes" from all responsibility for "that poverty and misery" which they had so unsuccessfully labored to "relieve"; and thus enabled them to close their purses, and even their hearts, against the commonest dictates of charity, by the reflection that if they should in any manner "stand between the error and its consequences" — if they should in any manner "intercept the penalty" affixed to the procreation of their species by those who had not already accumulated the means of support and education for their children — which penalty is poverty, wretchedness, and death — they would "perpetuate the sin,"* and become themselves participants in crime! In these two sentences may be found the real differences between the political economy of Adam Smith and that modern one since so generally received. The former looks to the extension of commerce—to the development of mind—and to the augmentation of the powers, and of the freedom of man; the latter to the extension of the dominion of trade—to the limitation of the mass of mankind to the works of cultivation and transportation—and to the ultimate enslavement of man by nature, and by his fellow-man.

§ 3. The mercantile system, so much reprobated by Dr. Smith, had for its object the cheapening of all the raw material of manufacture—wool, cotton, food, and labor. Thus far it had, as he saw, been productive of most injurious effects—having increased the dependence on machinery of trade and transportation—having produced a belief that the more widely men were separated from each other, and the greater the distance to be travelled over, the greater was the benefit to be derived from commerce—having fostered the warlike tendencies of the people—having caused an improper division of the population—and having tended greatly to promote the creation of large fortunes at the expense of those who had labor alone to sell. Such, as he told his countrymen, were the necessary consequences of the system; but it needed a further experience of twenty years for proving that such was certainly the case, and for giving occasion to the extraordinary discovery that although the demand for labor had become more steady as population had increased, and as men had more and more, from the days of the Plantagenets to those of George III., acquired wealth, and with its acquisition had obtained increased facility of combination; now, having in the last half century acquired an extraordinary increase of power—having began to utilize the great deposits of coal, and of iron and copper ores—having learned to command the wonderful force of steam—having learned to apply it to the conversion of wool into cloth—having obtained a great increase of wealth—having greatly facilitated the development of the latent faculties of man, and the latent powers of the earth—and having thus produced a vast increase in the move-

* *Edinburgh Review*, October, 1849: article, *Unsound Social Philosophy.*

ment of society — the demand for labor must become more unsteady, and pauperism must increase, in virtue of a great natural law, by which it had been provided that the more efficient the machinery of cultivation, the less must be the return to the labor employed in developing the resources of the earth.

This was a remarkable discovery, certainly; but, happily, it was a discovery of a fact that never had existed, and never can exist. The treasures of nature are boundless in extent; and they wait only for man to claim them. Unfortunately, however, the theory was precisely the one that was needed for the prevention of the adoption of any of the remedial measures proposed by Adam Smith. Proving, as it professed to do, that pauperism existed in obedience to the laws of God—that the natural rate of wages "was just so much as," and no more than, "was necessary to enable the laborers, *one with another*, to subsist and perpetuate their race, without increase or diminution" — that inequality of condition existed in obedience to divine laws — that the rich and powerful had therefore only rights to exercise, and not duties to perform — it proved, too, that they could safely and conscientiously "eat, drink, and make merry," though surrounded by poverty, wretchedness, disease, and death — solacing themselves with the reflection that the poor had their fate in their own hands, and that if they failed to exercise the "moral restraint" which should lead to abstinence from that regular association of the sexes which causes reproduction of the species, the fault was their own, and upon them must justly fall the penalty of transgression.

§ 4. The system which looked exclusively to foreign trade was, therefore, not only maintained in full, but with each successive year was more extensively carried out. From the days of Mr. Malthus to our own, the temple of Janus has rarely, even if ever, been closed, in testimony of the existence of peace throughout the British empire. The war in which Britain was then engaged was followed by one with this country, since the close of which there have been wars for the annexation of Scinde and Affghanistan—for the conquest of Ava and the Punjab — for the maintenance of the opium trade — for the extension of power in South Africa — for the development of new avenues for trade throughout the Turkish

Empire — and others — all looking to the one great object of cheapening the raw products of the earth, and thereby cheapening the labors of the men by whom the earth was being tilled.

For the accomplishment of that object, as the reader has seen, the union with Ireland was perfected, and her manufactures were annihilated. For its accomplishment, the people of India were required to receive the cotton goods of England free of duty, while deprived of the power to purchase more efficient machinery from abroad, and taxed to an unheard-of extent for the use of that which they already possessed. For its accomplishment, Gibraltar has been maintained as a smuggling depôt for Spain; while Heligoland, the Ionian Islands, and numerous other colonies, have been used for smuggling goods into Germany, the United States, and other countries — the smuggler being now regarded as "the great reformer of the age." For its accomplishment, it has been required that there should be combinations among masters for keeping down the price of labor — for limiting the hours in which machinery should be run, with a view to preventing the rise of raw materials — and for discouraging the growth of manufactures in other countries. That all of these are acts of war, and that they are properly so to be regarded, will be seen on a perusal of the following extract from an official document recently published by order of the House of Commons:—*

"The laboring classes generally, in the manufacturing districts of this country, and especially in the iron and coal districts, are very little aware of the extent to which they are often indebted for their being employed at all to the immense *losses* which their employers voluntarily incur in bad times, in order *to destroy foreign competition, and to gain and keep possession of foreign markets.* Authentic instances are well known of employers having in such times carried on their works at a loss amounting in the aggregate to three or four hundred thousand pounds in the course of three or four years. If the efforts of those who encourage the combinations to restrict the amount of labor and to produce strikes were to be successful for any length of time, the great accumulations of capital could no longer be made *which enable a few of the most wealthy capitalists to overwhelm all foreign*

* *Report of the Commissioner appointed to Examine into the State of the Population of the Mining Districts.* 1854.

*competition in times of great depression,* and thus to clear the way for the *whole trade* to step in when prices revive, and to carry on a great business before *foreign* capital can again accumulate to such an extent as to be able to establish a competition in prices with any chance of success. *The large capitals of this country are the great instruments of warfare* (if the expression may be allowed) *against the competing capital of foreign countries,* and are *the most* essential instruments now remaining by which our manufacturing supremacy can be maintained; the other elements — cheap labor, abundance of raw materials, means of communication, and skilled labor — being rapidly in process of being equalized."

The system here described is very properly characterized as "warfare;" and we may properly inquire for what purposes, and against whom, it is waged. It is a war, as the reader sees, for cheapening labor and raw materials — being precisely the objects sought to be accomplished by the "Mercantile System," whose error was so well exposed in the *Wealth of Nations.* It is a war for compelling the people of other lands to confine themselves to agriculture—for preventing the diversification of employments in other countries — for retarding the development of intellect — for palsying every movement elsewhere looking to the utilization of the metallic treasures of the earth — for increasing the difficulty of obtaining iron — for diminishing the demand for labor — for producing pauperism — for doing all these things at home and abroad — and for thus bringing about the state of things whose approach was predicted by Adam Smith.

To measures such as here described was due the closing of all the manufactories of India, followed by the exportation of cotton to England, there to compete with the products of Carolina and Alabama. The more perfectly the system can be carried out—the more the manufacture can be restricted to England — the cheaper will be the raw materials; but the greater will be the export of cheap labor to Texas and to the Mauritius, there to raise more cotton, sugar, and other raw materials; and thence to compete with each other for the reduction of prices, and for the more complete enslavement of the laborers of all those countries.

§ 5. It is claimed that the warfare above described is beneficial to the people of England. Were that so, it would establish the lamentable fact that war *could* be profitable — that nations and individuals *could* permanently thrive by the commission of acts of injustice—and that, such being the divine law, communities were warranted in so exercising their power as to prevent the growth of civilization where it did not as yet exist, and to annihilate it where it did. Happily, there exists no such law. Nations can permanently prosper only as they obey the golden rule of Christianity; and when they fail to do so, Nemesis never fails to claim her rights. That she has done so on this occasion, and that the pauperism of England is due to failure in this respect, the reader may, perhaps, be satisfied after a brief examination of the effect of the system upon her own laborers, whether engaged in the work of the factory, or of the field.

The manufactures of Ireland gradually declined from the date of the Union in 1801. As they ceased to demand the services of men, women, and children, the latter were forced to seek employment in the field; and thus was the production of food increased, while the home consumption diminished. The exports, consequently, rose from 300,000 quarters in the early years of the century, to 2,500,000 thirty years later—causing the price in England to fall from an average of £4 per quarter in the years from 1816 to 1820, to one of £2 12*s* in those from 1821 to 1835. At first sight, this reduction in the price of food might seem to be an advantage, but, unfortunately and necessarily, it was accompanied by still greater cheapness of labor—it being one of the characteristics of the system which looks to the cheapening of raw materials that it lessens the demand for human service. At the moment when corn was so cheap, millions of Irish people were totally idle, and seeking anxiously, yet vainly, for employment at sixpence a day, without clothing, or even food. As a consequence of this, Great Britain was, says one of the British journals,* "flooded with crowds of half-clad, half-civilized Celts, reducing the standard of living" among English laborers, and furnishing that "abundant supply of cheap labor" to which, says the *Times*, Britain is indebted for all her "great works." Man had, to quote again the words of that journal, "become a drug, and population a nuisance;" and had so become, because of the annihilation of com-

* *North British Review*, November, 1852.

merce among the Irish people. Labor, another of the raw materials of manufacture, having, therefore, fallen faster than food, the pauperism of England had so rapidly increased that no less than one-ninth of the population had become recipients of aid from the public purse; and the poor-tax had risen in thirty years from five to nearly nine millions of pounds, while the price of wheat had fallen nearly forty per cent. Food was low, but wages were so very low that the laborer could not purchase. Labor was low, but food was so cheap that the farmer was unable to pay rent and wages. Thus did both the land-owner and the laborer of England suffer from the want of that circulation of men and things throughout Ireland which would have resulted from the establishment in the latter of a system under which every man would have been enabled to sell his own labor, and to become a purchaser of that of his neighbors, their wives and children—a system under which Irish commerce could have grown.

The manufacturing population, however, it might be supposed, had gained by the cheaper food. On the contrary, they suffered, because the decline of wages in other pursuits was accompanied by a diminution in the power to purchase cloth — and with the decline in the price of food, the farmer had become unable to purchase machinery of cultivation. All thus suffered alike. The destruction of the home market for food and labor in Ireland, consequent upon the annihilation of her commerce, had produced the same effect in England.—The great manufacturer may, perhaps, have profited. On the contrary, his market in England had been lessened, while that of Ireland had almost totally failed —and thus had a nation been almost annihilated with no profit to those who had done the work; but, with the most serious loss to all, resulting from the fact that the standard of living and of morals had been greatly reduced; that the disease of over-population had far more widely spread; and that the gulf dividing the higher and lower classes of English society had greatly widened. Nowhere in the world is there to be found stronger evidence of the *advantage* to be gained in carrying out, in the management of public affairs, the strictest observance of the great fundamental law of Christianity, than is to be found in the history of the connection between England and Ireland in the present century.

§ 6. The power to purchase the labor of others is dependent altogether upon the existence of the power to sell our own labor. The power to purchase things is dependent upon the power to produce things with which to purchase. The man who cannot sell his own labor cannot buy that of others; nor can the man who is deprived of the power to produce things purchase the things produced by others. In annihilating the power of association among the Irish people, the manufacturers of England annihilated the power to purchase the products of English looms—the land-holders annihilated the power to consume the products of the earth—the laborers annihilated the power to consume Irish labor—and the society of Britain annihilated the motion of society—or commerce—of Ireland; the consequences of all of which were seen in the fact that the land and labor of England herself declined in value and in power, for the benefit of the classes dependent upon their powers of appropriation.

It might, however, be supposed that the other markets which had been acquired were of a character to make some amends for the losses by English land and labor resulting from the steady pursuit of a policy so entirely opposed to the enlightened views of Dr. Smith; and we will, therefore, turn to the trade with the hundred millions of the people of India. The export of cotton yarn and cloth to that country did not then amount to 70,000,000 of pounds, nor did the import of raw cotton amount to 200,000 bales, of 400 pounds each; and yet this constituted the only item of the trade with that country that was of any essential importance; or that was materially dependent upon the maintenance of the system above described. The quantity of cotton now converted into cloth in the little town of Lowell, with its thirteen thousand operatives, being 40,000,000 of pounds, it follows, that two such little places would perform all the labor required for the whole trade for which England is indebted to the destruction of the cotton manufacture and commerce of India—a measure attended with the production of an amount of misery and destitution "unparalleled in the annals of commerce."

For its accomplishment, it was needed that English children of the most tender age should be kept employed twelve or fourteen hours per day—that they should apply the Sunday morning hours to the cleaning of the machinery—and that men, women, and children should be brutified to an extent that can be imagined only by those who have studied the reports of the commissions that have at various times been instituted with a view to the correction of some of the many evils resulting from the system.* Need we wonder at the fact that the theory of over-population — which is the theory of centralization, slavery, and death — had its origin in the country which originated such a policy?

The student of Indian history is shocked when he reads the account of the invasion of Nadir Shah, closing, as it did, with the plunder of Delhi, the destruction of its buildings, and the massacre of a hundred thousand of its inhabitants — and yet, how utterly insignificant was the loss thus caused, compared with that which has resulted from the annihilation of a manufacture that, but half a century since, gave employment to the people of "whole provinces"—one, the account of whose progress included "no less than a description of the lives of half the inhabitants of Hindostan"! Utterly insignificant was it when compared with the

* "The crowd of low pot-houses in our manufacturing districts is a sad and singular spectacle. They are to be found in every street and alley of the towns, and in almost every lane and turning of the more rural villages of those districts, if any of those villages can be called rural.

"The habit of drunkenness pervades the masses of the operatives to an extent never before known in our country.

"In a great number of these taverns and pot-houses of the manufacturing districts, prostitutes are kept for the express purpose of enticing the operatives to frequent them, thus rendering them doubly immoral and pernicious. I have been assured in Lancashire, on the best authority, that in one of the manufacturing towns, and that, too, about third-rate in point of size and population, there are *sixty* taverns where prostitutes are kept by the tavern landlords, in order to entice customers into them. Their demoralizing influence upon the population *cannot be exaggerated;* and yet these are almost the only resorts which the operatives have, when seeking amusement or relaxation.

"In those taverns where prostitutes are not actually kept for the purpose of enticing customers, they are always to be found in the evenings, at the time the workmen go there to drink. In London and in Lancashire the gin-palaces are the regular rendezvous for the abandoned of both sexes, and the places where the lowest grade of women-of-the-town resort to find customers. It is quite clear that young men, who once begin to meet their friends at these places, cannot long escape the moral degradation of these hot-houses of vice.

"The singular and remarkable difference between the respective condition of the peasants and operatives of Germany and Switzerland, and those of England and Ireland, in this respect, is alone sufficient to prove the singular difference between their respective social condition.

"The village inn in Germany is quite a different kind of place to the village inn in England. It is intended and used less for mere drinking than as a place for meeting and conversation: it is, so to speak, the villagers' club." — KAY: *Social Condition of the People of England and of Europe*, vol. i. p. 232.

daily and hourly waste of capital now resulting from a total absence of demand for the exertion of physical or mental capacity—with the decline and death of commerce—the ruin of Dacca and other famous and flourishing cities—the abandonment of rich lands—the unceasing exhaustion of the soil—the resolution of society into a body of grasping money-lenders on the one hand, and wretched cultivators on the other—and the inauguration of famine and pestilence as the chronic diseases of a people inferior to none in moral and intellectual qualities, and embracing a tenth of the population of the world. The booty obtained by Nadir was estimated at five hundred millions of dollars; and yet, large as was its amount, very far greater is *that annual tax* imposed upon the people of Hindostan by a system that—by forbidding association—by forbidding combination of effort—by forbidding the development of the human faculties—and by forbidding the existence of that commerce by help of which alone capital is accumulated—converts the whole body of the people of that great country into candidates for admission into the public service, as the only possible means of advancement. Greatly superior as is the loss inflicted, as greatly inferior is the gain to those by whom the loss is caused. Nadir did obtain an enormous amount of plunder, but the English people have gained nothing but the privilege of employing themselves as transporters, spinners, and weavers of a trivial quantity of cotton; a privilege obtained at the cost of the sacrifice of the rights of a hundred millions of people abroad, and the establishment at home of the doctrine proclaimed by Mr. Huskisson, in 1825, that "to enable capital to obtain a fair remuneration, the price of labor must be kept down;" or, in other words, that to enable trade to thrive, men must be enslaved. The destruction of the temple of Ephesus by the torch of the incendiary Erostratus, animated thereto, as he was, by a desire to perpetuate the recollection of his existence, will probably appear to future ages to have been an act of the highest wisdom, when compared with the annihilation of commerce throughout immense communities under the mistaken idea that prosperity to any single one was to be obtained under a system like that denounced by Dr. Smith—looking solely and exclusively to the purchase of all the raw material of manufacture, labor included, at low prices, and the sale of cloth at high ones.

Turning to the West Indies, to Portugal, and to Turkey, we meet everywhere, as the reader has already seen, the same result — the power to purchase the products of English labor having perished with the loss of the power to sell their own. All of those countries are paralyzed. In all, circulation has so far ceased, that they more resemble dead than living bodies; and England now presents the extraordinary spectacle of a nation possessing, more than any other, the power to render service to mankind, yet surrounded by colonies and allies, all of whom are slowly, but certainly, passing towards entire inanition — while she, herself, is exhausting her energies in the ceaseless effort to extend throughout the world the system by means of which they have been so much reduced.

§ 7. In the natural order of things, the prices of all the rude products of the earth tend to rise, and for the reason, that as population increases, as the power of association becomes more complete, as individuality is more and more developed, and as circulation becomes more rapid, the men engaged in developing the resources of the earth are enabled more readily to maintain commerce with each other. In one country, silver or gold is mined; in another, corn, or cotton, is raised; and in a third, coal, iron, and other ores, are extracted from the earth; but, in their rude state, none of these can readily be transported. The gold-miner needs clothing, paper, books, and iron instruments — but he has no use for wool, rags, or iron ore; and until the producers of these latter obtain the means of diminishing the bulk of their commodities—compressing the rags and the food into paper — the wool and the food into cloth—or the food and the ore into instruments useful for the miner — there can be no direct intercourse between them.

That such intercourse may exist, it is, then, indispensable that employments become diversified—the producer and the consumer of corn taking their places by each other's side, in accordance with the idea so well expressed by Dr. Smith. As that idea is more and more fully carried out, commerce between the producers of corn and wool on the one hand, and of gold on the other, becomes more and more direct — the necessary result of constant diminution in the quantity of labor required for changing the placcs, or the forms, of the rude products of the earth. With every diminution in the obstacles to direct commerce, thus produced, the prices of raw materials and of finished commodities approximate more nearly to each other—those of the former tending *steadily to rise*, while the others tend *as steadily to fall;* and thus, while one obtains more cloth for his gold, another obtains more gold for his food and his wool — all, therefore, profiting by that increase in the power to command the services of nature which constitutes wealth.

That the facts are so, will readily be seen by those who study the gradual increase in the prices of wheat, corn, and oats throughout our Western States; or, the yet greater changes resulting from the creation of local centres of exchange, at which hay, potatoes, turnips, or other of the most bulky articles, are converted into cloth, or iron — the former rising in price as regularly as the latter decline; as is shown in the fact before referred to, that, whereas, thirty years since, fifteen tons of wheat were required, in Ohio, to pay for a ton of iron, a similar quantity may now be had in exchange for two, or, at most, three, tons. In England, in the ten years ending in 1750, the power of a quarter of wheat to command gold in exchange was only, as has been seen, 21*s.* 3*d.*; whereas, twenty years later, that power had become twice as great, because of the growing facility of intercourse with the gold-producing countries, consequent upon an increased control of the powerful forces of nature in the various processes required for changing the places, or the forms, of matter. The value of man steadily increased, for he could command more gold, more food, and more cloth in return for a given quantity of effort. The *value* of gold, in England, declined, because it would command less of the raw materials of manufacture — food, wool, and labor. To the gold-producer the *utility* of his commodity increased, because it would command in exchange a larger quantity of clothing and other commodities required for his consumption.

*Approximation in the prices of raw materials and finished commodities is the one essential characteristic of civilization* — it being the manifestation of a diminution of the obstacles standing in the way of association, and impeding the growth of commerce. As the mill comes nearer to the farm, there is a constant increase in the proportion borne by the price of a bushel of wheat to that of a barrel of flour; and that proportion still further increases as improvements are effected in the machinery of the mill itself. As the processes of converting hides are improved, the prices of leather, and of all commodities in the making of which it is required, tend steadily downward; but that of hides so steadily advances, that whereas, when certain kinds of leather sold for twenty cents, hides were worth but five cents a pound, now, when the same leather sells for fourteen cents, the price of the raw material is seven. In the last quarter of a century, rags have increased in price not less than fifty per cent., while paper has fallen thirty or forty per cent.; and whereas, it then required six pounds of the one to pay for a pound of the other, the same may now be obtained for less than three pounds. Five-and-twenty years since, raw silk was low in price, and silk goods were high; but since then, the first has advanced fifty per cent., while the last has so greatly declined, that silks have largely taken the place formerly occupied by cotton. The saw-mill lowers the price of planks; and the planing-machine does the same by that of doors and window-frames; but they increase the price of timber, and the farmer of the West is thus enabled to sell the trees that before he would gladly have seen destroyed. Look where he may, the reader will see that, in the natural course of things, the price of raw material of every kind — land, labor, cotton, wool, or corn — tends to rise with every increase in the facility of intercourse with the men employed in producing gold and silver. Everywhere around, he will find evidence of the truth of the proposition, that as population grows, as the power of association increases, as the faculties of man are more and more developed, and as wealth augments, the rude products of the earth tend to increase in their power to command the precious metals in exchange, while finished commodities tend as steadily to decline — thus enabling all, whether producers of corn or gold, wool or silver, to profit by, and to rejoice in, the constantly increasing power of their fellow-men to command the services of nature. Among communities, as among individuals, the harmony of all real and permanent interests is perfect.

The British system looks, however, in a direction exactly opposite to this—being based upon the idea of cheapening all the raw materials of manufacture, labor included. Examine it where we may, we find it promoting extension of the cultivation of cotton, wool, sugar, and corn, while limiting the commerce between the producers of those commodities and the consumers of cloth and iron, by requiring the whole to pass through the narrow strait afforded by ships and distant mills — and thus augmenting the obstacles that intervene between the growers of corn and cotton and the miners of silver and of gold. So long as the people of India converted their cotton, rice, and sugar into cloth, they could maintain direct commerce with the producers of the precious metals; as a consequence of which the exchanges were in their favor with every part of the earth, with constant tendency to rise in the price of raw materials of every kind. Since the prostration of the cotton manufacture, the difficulty of maintaining commerce has increased — the flow of the precious metals has been outward instead of inward — and cotton has fallen to three halfpence a pound; while the difficulty of obtaining cotton cloth has so largely increased, that its consumption does not probably exceed a single pound per head. So has it been in Ireland, Jamaica, Portugal, and Turkey — in all of which the obstacles to commerce have increased, with corresponding decline in the price of labor and of raw materials of every kind; *and that decline has been in the direct ratio of the increase in the facilities for reaching the great central market.* A quarter of a century since, the brown sugar of India would command in the market of England from 20*s*. to 30*s*. per hundredweight, whereas it will now commonly exchange for only 15*s*. or 20*s*. Forty years since, the cotton of Carolina commanded money in England at the rate of twenty pence a pound; whereas it now fluctuates between four and seven pence—and for the reason that the obstacles to direct intercourse with the world at large increase, when they should as regularly diminish. Forty years since, flour was exported from this country at eight dollars a barrel; whereas, in the years which immediately preceded the breaking out of the Crimean war, it had fallen to little more than half that price — and that, too, notwithstanding the wonderful increase in the supply of gold that had resulted from the discovery of the Californian mines.

§ 8. The reader may perhaps understand the working of the system above described after an examination of the following com parative prices of commodities that the people of England have to sell, and those that they need to buy :—

| | 1815. | | | | 1852. | | |
|---|---|---|---|---|---|---|---|
| Those they sell are— | | | | | | | |
| Bar iron, per ton | £13 | 5s. | 0d. | ......... | £9 | 0s. | 0d. |
| Tin, per cwt. | 7 | 0 | 0 | ......... | 5 | 2 | 0 |
| Copper, " | 6 | 5 | 0 | ......... | 5 | 10 | 0 |
| Lead, " | 1 | 6 | 6 | ......... | 1 | 4 | 0 |
| Those they buy are— | | | | | | | |
| Cotton, per lb. | 0 | 1 | 6 | ......... | 0 | 0 | 6 |
| Sugar, per cwt. | 3 | 0 | 0 | ......... | 1 | 0 | 0 |

While the principal articles of foreign produce have fallen to one-third of the prices of 1815, iron, copper, tin, and lead, the commodities that they supply to the world, have declined but about twenty-five per cent. It is more difficult to exhibit the changes of woven goods; but that the planters are constantly giving more cotton for less cloth, will be seen on an examination of the following facts in relation to recent years, in which the crop was large, as compared with the course of things a few years previously: From 1830 to 1835, the price of cotton here was about eleven cents, which we may suppose to be about what it would yield in England, free of freight and charges. In those years our average export was 320,000,000 of pounds, yielding about \$35,000,000; and the average price of cotton cloth, per piece of 24 yards, weighing 5 pounds 12 ounces, was 7*s*. 10*d*., (\$1.88,) and that of iron, £6 10*s*., (\$31.20.) Our exports would therefore have produced, delivered in Liverpool, 18,500,000 pieces of cloth, or about 1,100,000 tons of iron. In 1845 and 1846, the average price here was six and a half cents, making the product of a similar quantity, \$20,000,000. The price of cloth having been 6*s*. 6¾*d*., (\$1.57½,) and that of iron, £10, (\$48,) the result was, that the planters could have, for nearly the same quantity of cotton, about 12,500,000 pieces of cloth, or about 420,000 tons of iron, also delivered in Liverpool. Dividing the return between the two commodities, it stands thus :—

| | Average from 1830 to 1835. | | 1845–6. | | Loss. |
|---|---|---|---|---|---|
| Cloth, pieces | 9,250,000 | ......... | 6,250,000 | ......... | 3,000,000 |
| And iron, tons | 550,000 | ......... | 210,000 | ......... | 340,000 |

The labor required for converting cotton into cloth had been greatly diminished, and yet the proportion retained by the manufacturers had greatly increased, as will now be shown :—

| | Weight of Cotton used. | Weight of Cotton given to the planters. | Retained by the manufacturers. |
|---|---|---|---|
| 1830 to 1835..... | 320,000,000 ........ | 110,000,000 ........ | 210,000,000 |
| 1845 and 1846.. | 320,000,000 ........ | 76,000,000 ........ | 244,000,000 |

In the first period, the planter had thirty-four per cent. of his cotton returned to him in the form of cloth, but in the second, only twenty-four per cent. The grist-miller gives the farmer from year to year a *larger* proportion of the product of his grain, and thus the latter participates in the advantage of every improvement. The cotton-miller gives the planter from year to year a *smaller* proportion of the cloth produced. The one miller comes daily nearer to the producer. The other goes daily farther from him, because he is himself compelled to exhaust his land, and remove from year to year further from his market.

How this operates on a large scale will now be seen on an examination of the following facts :—

The declared or actual *value* of exports of British produce and manufactures in 1815, was........................................... £51,632,971
And the *quantity** of foreign merchandise retained for consumption in that year was........................................... £17,238,841

This shows, of course, that the prices of the raw products of the earth were then high by comparison with those of the articles that Great Britain had to sell.

In 1849, the *value* of British exports was......................... £63,596,025
And the *quantity* of foreign merchandise retained for consumption was no less than........................................... £80,312,717

We see thus that while the value of exports had increased only *one-third*, the produce received in exchange was *almost five times greater;* and here it is that we find the effect of that *unlimited* competition for the sale in England of the raw products of the world, and *limited* competition for the purchase of the manufactured ones, which it is the object of the system to establish.

* The returns of imports into Great Britain are given according to an official value established more than a century since, and thus the sum of the values is an exact measure of the quantities imported.

Look where we may, we see that while, under a natural system, the prices of the raw products of the earth, and those of finished commodities, tend constantly to approximation — leaving a diminished *proportion* for the parties engaged in the work of transportation and conversion — directly the reverse is the case in all the countries subject to the British policy, the *proportions* of those parties tending constantly to increase, and the power of the producer to command the services of money tending as constantly to decrease. The lower the price of cloth, and the higher the price of food and cotton, the greater will be the tendency towards freedom. The higher that of cloth, and the lower those of food and cotton, the greater will be the tendency towards slavery. The British system tends to cheapen the raw materials of cloth, and to enhance the difficulty of obtaining cloth itself; and thus does it look in a direction precisely opposite to that of advancing civilization. Retrograde always, and everywhere, the facts occurring under it could be explained only by means of a theory of over-population, by help of which the ultimate slavery of man could be made a part of the divine law.

§ 9. The higher the price of raw materials, and the lower the price of finished commodities, the less will be the proportion of the total product of labor absorbed by the persons engaged in the work of transportation and conversion; and the less, necessarily, will be the *proportion* borne by those classes to the mass of which society is composed. The nearer the mill to the farmer, and the more perfect its machinery, the more nearly will the price of wheat and flour approximate to each other—and the smaller will be the *proportion* borne by the labor required for carrying the raw product to the mill, for converting it into flour, and for carrying the flour back again to his home, to that which had been given to the improvement of the land required for the production of the wheat itself. In the natural course of things, therefore, the *proportion* of the labor of man given to augmenting the quantity of raw products should be a constantly *increasing* one, and that given to changing them in place, or in form, a constantly *decreasing* one.

Directly the reverse of this, however, is the effect produced by the system which looks to the building up of trade upon the ruins of commerce. The men of India who raised cotton and rice could formerly exchange directly with their neighbors who converted it into cloth; and all could give *the whole* of their time to the work of producing wool and food on the one hand, and cloth on the other. Now, all are obliged to send, or carry, their rice and their wool to a place fifteen thousand miles distant, and to do this by aid of oxen, horses, ships, canal boats, and other machinery; as a consequence of which the *proportion* of the labor given to transportation and conversion has largely increased, while that given to production has as constantly decreased. The result of this is seen in the fact, that after having annihilated the Indian manufactures, the total quantity of cotton now supplied to England is not more than could be converted in a little town containing twenty thousand operatives. So has it been in Ireland, where so large a *proportion* of the labor was required to be given to effecting changes in the place of things and people, that little remained to be given to production, and the market for British manufactures proved to be more and more worthless the more perfectly it had been secured.* So has it proved in Jamaica, Portugal, and Turkey, in which, as the *proportion* of labor required to be given to those purposes has increased, the consumption of British manufactures has decreased. The process is exhaustive; and hence the constantly increasing necessity for seeking new and more distant markets, with daily augmenting tendency to increase in the *proportion* of the British population given to the carriage, the conversion, and the exchange of the products of distant lands.

That this effect is steadily being produced is shown by the following facts, furnished by the several recent censuses of the people of Great Britain:—

* The power of Ireland to pay for British manufactures is dependent upon her ability to furnish commodities with which to pay for them. How entirely insignificant the latter has become, will be seen by the following table of exports for the year ending January 5, 1854:—

| | | | |
|---|---|---|---|
| Oxen, number | 180,785 | Oats, quarters | 1,552,917 |
| Calves " | 5,281 | Bacon and hams, cwts | 530 |
| Sheep, " | 224,550 | Beef and pork, barrels | 472 |
| Swine, " | 101,396 | Butter, cwts | 17,944 |
| Wheat, quarters | 76,495 | | |

From the value of this trivial export was to be deducted the amount required to be paid to the absentee owners of land, and to the government, and it seems difficult to imagine how there should remain any thing to be applied to the payment for articles required for consumption.

| Year. | Engaged in agriculture. | In trade and manufacture. | Others.* | Total. |
|---|---|---|---|---|
| 1811 | 35·2 | 44·4 | 20·4 | 100 |
| 1821 | 33·2 | 45·9 | 20·9 | 100 |
| 1831 | 28·2 | 42·0 | 20·8 | 100 |
| 1841 | 25·17 | 44·64 | 30·19 | 100 |

We have here a gradual decline in the proportion of persons employed in augmenting the *quantity* of things requiring to be converted or exchanged, until from $\frac{7}{20}$ it has fallen to $\frac{5}{20}$, and that in the short space of thirty years; and the change thus indicated is hailed by British economists as evidence of growing civilization! Directly the opposite of this, however, is what we had a right to look for—the power of steam having been substituted for that of man, to the extent of hundreds of millions of hands; and all the force thus gained having been given to the work of changing the places, and the forms, of the raw products of the earth. The effect should have been that of *setting free* the labors of millions of men, to be applied to the augmentation of the quantity of things susceptible of being converted or exchanged; whereas, so far the reverse has it been, that the *proportion* of people engaged in the works of transportation, conversion, and exchange has increased from $\frac{13}{20}$ to $\frac{15}{20}$—and that in only thirty years. The more that nature is made to supersede the labor of men in these departments of employment, the larger is the proportion of their labor *absorbed* by them. The movement here, as everywhere, is a retrograde one; and, being so, may, perhaps, enable us to account for the invention of the Ricardo-Malthusian theories.

The flour-mill is useless unless there is corn to be ground—and the cotton-mill is idle where there is no wool to be spun and woven. The less the labor required for grinding the one, or spinning the other, the less is the necessity for increasing the number of mills, *unless* the time and mind thus set free be applied to the work of developing the powers of the earth, and thus augmenting the quantity of raw material requiring to be converted. If the labor that is economized be thus applied,

* Embracing—I. Capitalists, bankers, and professional and other educated men; II. Laborers employed in labor not agricultural; III. Male servants, 20 years of age and upwards; IV. Navy, army, and seamen in merchant service; V. Persons of independent income; VI. Alms-people.

then more mills will be needed; and then the quantity of labor applied to the work of conversion, or transportation, may advantageously be increased; but not otherwise. In the case before us, the *proportion* of the labor given to conversion increases in the direct ratio of the diminution of the necessity for it; and the *proportion* given to production diminishes in the ratio of the increase in the machinery used for the conversion of the things produced. There is, therefore, a constant increase in the number of people requiring to be fed and clothed, accompanied by as constant a decrease in the number of persons employed in furnishing the raw material to be used by those who need supplies of food and clothing.

One-fourth only of the people of England being engaged in increasing the quantities of things, while three-fourths are either entirely unoccupied, or are occupied in effecting changes in their places, in their forms, or in their ownership, it follows necessarily that the major part of the things produced is absorbed in its passage from the place of production to that of consumption. That such is really the case, we learn from a leading British journal,* which tells its readers that "the number of retail traders and shopkeepers is out of all proportion to the requirements of society, or the numbers of the producing classes. There are in many places," as it continues, "ten shopkeepers to do the work which one would suffice for—such at least is Mr. Mill's estimate. Now these men, industrious and energetic as they are, do not add to the production, and therefore not to the wealth, of the community; they merely distribute what others produce. Nay more, in proportion as they are too numerous, do they diminish the wealth of the community. They live, it is true, many of them, by 'snatching the bread out of each other's mouths;' but still they *do* live, and often make great profits. These profits are made, it is obvious, by charging a per-centage on the article they sell. If, therefore, there are *two* of these retailers to be supported by a community when *one* would suffice to do the work, the articles they sell must cost that community more than needs to be the case, and so far the country is impoverished by supporting an 'unproductive laborer' too many. Any one who examines into the subject is surprised to find how small a portion of the

* *North British Review*, November, 1852.

price paid by the consumer for any article goes to the *producer* or importer, and how large a portion is absorbed by the distributor.*"

We have here the real difficulty of British society, and the source to which we are indebted for the suggestion of the extraordinary theory of Mr. Malthus. The system tends unnaturally to increase the proportion of consumers, and to cause the absorption of so large a portion of the product of labor on its passage from the field in which it is produced, to the mouth that needs to eat it, or the back that needs to wear it, that its producer finds it difficult to obtain the means of supporting life. The man who labors in the field upon land yielding thirty or forty bushels to the acre, receives but six shillings, or the price of a single bushel, for his week's work; and yet, the product of his year's labor is probably but little short of a thousand bushels. His share is, therefore, six, eight, or ten, per cent., while ninety, or more, per cent. is absorbed by those who own the machinery with which he works —by those who control its management—by those who direct the government, those who carry arms, those who live in almshouses — and those who, in a thousand other ways, stand between the production of the food and its consumption.

The poor man of the west of Ireland is glad to get five *pence* for a pair of chickens that will sell in London for as many *shillings;* and thus does he receive *eight per cent.* as the price of his labor—the remaining *ninety-two per cent.* being absorbed by the class of middlemen.† When, however, he desires to invest the

* "I think any one who has had occasion to inquire, in particular cases, what portion of the price paid at a shop for an article really goes to the person who made it, must have been astonished to find how small it is. It is of great importance to consider the cause of this." * * * "It does not arise from the extravagant remuneration of capital. I think it proceeds from two causes: one of them is, the very great, I may say *the extravagant, portion of the whole produce of the community which now goes to the mere distributors;* the immense amount that is taken up by the different classes of dealers, and especially by retailers. Competition has, no doubt, some tendency to reduce this rate of remuneration; still, I am afraid that, in most cases, and looking at it as a whole, the effect of competition is, as in the case of the fees of professional people, rather to divide the amount among a larger number, and so diminish the share of each, than to lower the scale of what is obtained by the class generally." * * * "If the business of distribution, which now employs, taking the different classes of dealers and their families, perhaps more than a million of the inhabitants of this country, could be done by a hundred thousand people, I think the other nine hundred thousand could be dispensed with." — J. S. MILL: *Evidence before a Committee of the House of Commons*, June 6, 1850.

† See page 332, *ante.*

proceeds in sugar, he pays five pence for that which had not yielded to its original producer as much cloth as could be purchased with a farthing — and thus is more than nine-tenths of the product of labor absorbed by intermediate men, who live by means of the exercise of their powers of appropriation. The poor Hindoo sells his cotton for three halfpence a pound, of which the government takes one-half, and the money-lender half of the remainder; and when, after the lapse of years, it comes back to him in the form of cloth, he pays for it twelve, fifteen, or twenty pence—being forty or fifty times more than it had yielded him. What goes with all the difference? It is absorbed on the road from the land on which it has been produced to the house, perhaps on that same land, in which reside the people by whom it is to be worn. The farmer of Iowa sells his corn at ten cents a bushel, but by the time it reaches the consumer in Manchester, it has so much increased in value that it pays for several days of labor. That labor yields hundreds of yards of cotton cloth, but by the time the latter reaches Iowa, it has, in its turn, so much increased in value that a bushel of corn is given in exchange for a single yard — not less than *eighty per cent.* of the whole having been absorbed in the process of making the exchanges.

The system tends to increase the disproportion between the price of the rude product of the earth and the finished one — to produce cheap raw materials and dear manufactures; and that is the road towards barbarism. It seeks to augment the difficulties lying between the consumer and the producer, while building up the fortunes of those who stand between them; and hence it is that it gave birth to the idea of over-population — an idea inseparably connected with that of the ultimate enslavement of man.*

* "When Mr. McCulloch tells us to look at the success of our large properties and larger farms, let us look at the whole population — let us look at the fact that, at the very moment of his writing, *about every tenth person in England* was a pauper—let us look at our prisons, our poor-laws, our union workhouses, our poisonings for the sake of burial-fees, our emigration, as if our people were flying like rats, helter-skelter, from a drowning ship. Let us sum up the whole, and then perhaps we should find that our boasted system of social distribution was no more successful than the muster of one regiment, when we should find, on the one hand, order and competence; on the other, rags and tatters, wives abandoned, parents neglected, children left to the hazard of casual charity, and too often a dark shadow of vice and wretchedness, following in the train of our vaunted institutions." — *Hugh Miller.*

## CHAPTER XVIII.

### THE SAME SUBJECT CONTINUED.

§ 1. In the natural order of events, the necessity for the services of the trader and transporter tends towards diminution; and with every increase in the power of man to maintain direct commerce with his fellow-man, the circulation of society tends to acceleration — enabling each and every one to find a purchaser, on the instant, for his time and talents, and thus to become a competitor for the purchase of those of others. Capital then accumulates rapidly, with constant tendency to further development of the various faculties, and constant increase in the facility of combination, and in the tendency to further progress. Whenever, and wherever, the reverse is seen — wherever the necessity for the services of the trader and transporter is an increasing one — the opposite effects are seen — the circulation becoming more and more languid—the waste of power increasing—and commerce gradually declining, until at length it ceases to exist.

Stoppage of circulation — as fatal to the social as it is to the physical body — is the natural tendency of the British system. Hence it is that we have been called upon to remark the total disappearance of so large a proportion of the negroes imported into the West India islands; and the almost total waste of power among those who still exist. Hence, too, it is that the marks of approaching dissolution are now so clearly obvious in Ireland and in India. To the same cause was due the growth of pauperism in the days of Mr. Malthus; as well as in those later days when England was inundated with crowds of Irishmen, eager to sell their labor at any price — causing her poorhouses to become so filled as to threaten to swamp the land and its owners by the taxation required for their support.

Such being the facts, the question arose, as to what was the cause to which they were to be attributed; and, most naturally, the advocates of the system which looked to the cheapening of raw materials, ascribed them all to the scarcity, and consequent high price, of food. The land-owners — believing, with Adam Smith, that "if the whole produce of America in grain of all sorts, salt provisions, and fish," were "forced into the market of England," it would be "a great discouragement to agriculture" — had endeavored, as the reader has seen, to shield themselves against the operation of the mercantile system, by the passage of laws preventive of the importation of food except under certain circumstances; and to the existence of those laws was now ascribed a state of things that was only the natural product of the policy whose error had been so fully exposed in the *Wealth of Nations*.

The people were, however, assured that if they wished to find the cause why two laborers had so long been seeking employment when only one could find it, they must look for it in the laws above referred to; and this assurance came from the selfsame persons to whose opinions expression had been given by Mr. Huskisson, twenty years before, when declaring that "to give capital a fair remuneration, the price of labor must be kept down." Now, however, they professed to move in an opposite direction — seeking to raise wages at the expense of capital; not, however, their own capital. Repeal the corn laws, said they, and there will be two employers seeking one laborer, and the price of labor will rise; and then money will be abundant, while *corn* will be cheap. The laws were repealed, but the effect has been directly the reverse of what was promised — the circulation of society having diminished when it should have increased. Instead of men having been enabled to come nearer to each other, and more and more to dispense with the services of the trader and transporter, they have been constantly receding from each other — emigration from the British islands having far exceeded any thing that had before been known. Instead of tending to restore society to its natural proportions, the repeal has increased the disproportion that before existed — the rural population having fled from the land, and thus created demand for ships and sailors.* Instead

* "The wheel of 'improvement' is now seizing another class, the most stationary class in England. A startling emigration movement has sprung up among the smaller English farmers, especially those holding heavy clay

of diminishing centralization, and thus establishing a motion in the direction of freedom, it has rendered centralization more complete, with daily diminution in the power of the laborer to determine for whom he will work, and what shall be his reward; and this it has done, too, despite the counteracting tendencies of the gold discoveries of California and Australia.

§ 2. The recent census shows that of the total increase in the population of the United Kingdom — less than a single million — more than half has been absorbed by London; while Manchester, Birmingham, Liverpool, Glasgow, and other towns and cities, have taken much more than all the balance. The rural population of the country has, therefore, largely diminished, while the town and city one has largely increased — the whole mass being thus from year to year more and more converted into mere traders in, and transporters of, the produce of the lands and labor of other countries. Commerce, therefore, declines, with steady tendency to deterioration in the condition of the yet remaining agricultural population, as is shown by Mr. Cobden, who advises his readers to "take a rural walk on the downs, or the weald, or the fens" — doing which "they will find the wages of agricultural laborers averaging, at this moment, under twelve shillings a week." "Let them," he continues, "ask how a family of five persons, which is below *their* average, can live with bread at $2\frac{1}{2}d.$ a pound. Nobody can tell; but follow the laborer, as he lays down his spade or mattock, and settles to his dinner in the nearest barn or shed, and peep into his wallet, or drop in at his cottage at twelve o'clock, and inquire what the family dinner consists of; — bread, rarely any thing better, and not always enough of that, with nothing left out of his earnings for tea, or sugar, or soap, or candles, or clothes, or the schooling of his children, and with his next year's harvest-money already mortgaged for shoes; and this is the fate of millions, living at our very doors, who con-

soils, who, with bad prospects for the coming harvest, and in want of sufficient capital to make the great improvements on their farms which would enable them to pay their old rents, have no other alternative but to cross the sea in search of a new country and of new lands. I am not speaking now of the emigration caused by the gold mania, but only of the compulsory emigration produced by landlordism, concentration of farms, application of machinery to the soil, and introduction of the modern system of agriculture on a great scale." — *Correspondence of the New York Tribune.*

stitute the vast majority of the 'agriculturists' of whose great prosperity we now hear so much. Never within the recollection of living man was the farm laborers' condition so bad as at present." *

This is the condition of millions of Englishmen,† and it is so, because the system looks to the annihilation of commerce, and the substitution of trade — and to the cheapening of raw material of every description, land, labor, food, cotton, and wool; while maintaining the value of cloth and iron. Instead of looking to the approximation of the prices of the raw material and the finished commodity—always an evidence of advancing civilization—it seeks to widen the difference between the two — always an evidence of the approach to barbarism.

* COBDEN: *What Next? and Next?* p. 45.

† "Our village peasantry are jostled about from cottage to cottage, or from cottage to no cottage at all, as freely, and with as little regard to their personal tastes and conveniences as if we were removing our pigs, cows, and horses from one sty or shed to another. If they cannot get a house over their heads, they go to the union, and are distributed—the man in one part, the wife in another, and the children again somewhere else. That is a settled thing. Our peasantry bear it, or, if they can't bear it, they die, and there is an end of it on this side of the grave; though how it will stand at the great audit, we leave an 'English Catholic' to imagine. We only mean to say that in England the work has been done; cotters have been exterminated; small holdings abolished; the process of eviction rendered superfluous; the landlord's word made law; the refuge of the discontented reduced to a workhouse; and all without a shot, or a bludgeon, or a missile being heard of." — *London Times.*

"The miserable character of the houses of our peasantry is, of itself, and independently of the causes which have made the houses so wretched, degrading and demoralizing the poor of our rural districts in a fearful manner. It stimulates the unhealthy and unnatural increase of population. The young peasants from their earliest years are accustomed to sleep in the same bed-rooms with people of both sexes, and with both married and unmarried persons. They therefore lose all sense of the indelicacy of such a life. They know, too, that they can gain nothing by deferring their marriages and by saving; that it is impossible for them to obtain better houses by so doing; and that in many cases they must wait many years before they could obtain a separate house of any sort. They feel that if they defer their marriage for ten or fifteen years, they will be at the end of that period in just the same position as before, and no better off for their waiting. Having, then, lost all hope of any improvement of their social situation, and all sense of the indelicacy of taking a wife home to the bedroom already occupied by parents, brothers, and sisters, they marry early in life — often, if not generally, before the age of twenty—and very often occupy, for the first part of their married life, another bed in the already crowded sleeping-room of their parents! In this way the morality of the peasants is destroyed; the numbers of this degraded population are unnaturally increased, and their means of subsistence are diminished by the increasing competition of their increasing numbers." — KAY: *Social Condition of Europe*, vol. i. p. 472.

The repeal of the corn laws having diminished the rapidity of circulation, the consequences have been seen in the fact that the waste of labor has increased; in proof of which may be adduced the fact that a recent writer — Mr. Mayhew — informs his readers that, in thirteen weeks, "no less than eleven thousand vagabonds were ascertained to have passed through a little town" of less than double that amount of population. The same fact, however, is obvious in all the English books; and particularly in those of Mr. Dickens. Two laborers are everywhere seeking the single employer; and a dozen shopkeepers are always on the watch for the single purchaser. That measure was but another step in the path of centralization — the terminus of which is always found in slavery, depopulation, and death. The real remedy was to be sought in the direction of a system looking to the restoration of society to its natural proportions, and to the reproduction of the circulation that had so long been stopped. Had the people of Ireland, in 1846, been reinvested with the right of managing their own affairs in their own way, a market would have been made among themselves for all their labor-power; and then the laborers of England would have found themselves no longer overwhelmed by a torrent of "half-fed and half-civilized Celts, reducing the standard of living and of comfort" everywhere — forcing them to accept diminished wages, and aiding in giving support to the doctrine that "the natural rate of wages is that which will enable men, *one with another*, to subsist and perpetuate their species, without increase or diminution." Had they been permitted so to do, the competition for the hire of land, in both England and Ireland, would have been less, and the landlords would have been unable to demand so large a *proportion* of the product; and yet the *quantity* of their rents would have been greater, because prosperous tenants would have been enabled more rapidly to improve the land, and the crops would largely have increased. Had they been permitted so to do, agriculture would have absorbed a larger proportion of English labor, while Irish mining and manufactures would have taken up that of the sister isle; and the competition among English artisans would have been less—enabling the workman to claim larger wages, and to become himself an employer. Directly the reverse of this, however, was the policy commenced by Mr. Huskisson, and perfected by Sir Robert Peel, who urged the necessity for cheap food, as a means of enabling the manufacturer to lower the wages of labor; and thus still further to carry out the system under which there had been produced an almost total cessation in the motion of society throughout all the countries subject to it.*

What is needed in all those countries, and in England herself, is a restoration of the circulation — a restoration of commerce; and until that shall have been effected, the disease of over-population must be an ever growing one.

§ 3. With the growth of commerce, the labor of the present acquires a constantly increased control over the accumulations of the past: with its decline, and consequent increase in the supremacy of trade, the past acquires increased power over the present. With the one, the circulation increases and becomes more steady; whereas, with the other, it decreases and becomes more fitful. Based on the single idea of extending the dominion of trade, the tendency of the English system is towards the arrest of motion everywhere; and the more it is arrested, the greater becomes the power of the trader to carry into effect the doctrine which teaches that to cheap raw materials of every kind — cotton, food, and labor — England is to be indebted for the maintenance of her supremacy in the trading world. The less rapid the circulation of cotton — the more it accumulates in warehouses — the more is the dealer in cotton goods enabled to dictate the prices at which he will buy, and those at which he will sell. The more unsteadiness in the price of cotton goods, or iron, the less is the danger of domestic competition for the purchase of labor, for the employment of capital, or for the rent of mines; but the higher is the price of cottons, and of iron, and the greater the power of the already wealthy to carry on that "warfare" recommended by Messrs. Hume and Brougham, and now regarded as so essential for destroying "foreign competition;" and for gaining and keeping "possession of foreign markets."

The more perfectly this system is carried out, the greater, necessarily, becomes the centralization at home. The number of persons who can afford, "voluntarily," to make large sacrifices for obtaining possession of foreign markets, is small, and those who

* See extract from *North British Review*, p. 240, *ante*—note.

cannot make them are forced to keep aloof from the trades in which they are likely to be required — as is the case with all the important branches of English manufacture. The opportunity for employing small capitals is, therefore, constantly diminishing —land becoming daily more and more consolidated, and trade as steadily becoming monopolized. In former times, small properties were numerous, and the little capitalists found in them little savings banks to be managed by themselves, in which they could deposit all their spare hours and half hours — thus accumulating little fortunes. From day to day there is a diminishing power of direct intercourse, attended by an increasing necessity for the services of middlemen; and hence the enormous mass of capital invested in life insurance offices, savings funds, &c. &c.—yielding little to the owners, but enabling the few who control their movements to accumulate fortunes for themselves. Under other circumstances, the real capitalists would manage their own affairs, and would thus diminish the competition for the loan of capital, while increasing the competition for the purchase of labor; and through the laborer, increasing the demand for the food and other raw materials yielded by the earth. The tendency of the English policy, injurious abroad, is not less so at home, for it looks to the conversion of the nation into a mass of traders, surrounded everywhere by a population regarded as mere instruments to be used by trade.

§ 4. With the growth of the power of association, or commerce, the proportion of the product going to the middleman — to the class which stands between the producer and the consumer — tends to decline, and that of the laborer to rise; with constant tendency towards equality in the conditions of men. With the decline of commerce, and increasing power of the trader, the opposite phenomena are everywhere observed — the inequality of conditions increasing steadily, and the laborer losing power over himself, while the trader as regularly acquires power over him.

The latter phenomena are those presented to view on an examination of English society. In the days of Adam Smith, the landholders of that country numbered two hundred thousand, whereas they are now but thirty-four thousand. The remainder have disappeared, and in their place we have everywhere the hired laborer.

Looking to the manufacturing districts, they are seen throughout, says a recent writer, to "present the peculiar spectacle of a small and very wealthy class standing apart on a great height, far above the level which is occupied by the rest of the population. The connection between the two consists wholly of those harsh and pecuniary ties which have never yet had time to become clothed with the soft and warm interlacement of affectionate moral association. The work carried on by the two parties is," as he continues, "essentially one of co-operation; but their moral attitude towards each other is much more one of hostility than of friendship." *

The gulf dividing the higher and lower classes of society is an ever widening one—the immensity of fortune acquired by successful bankers and traders being in the direct ratio of the poverty of the agricultural class so well described by Mr. Cobden. The accumulations of the past acquire daily more and more control over the labor of the present; and such must continue ever to be the case, so long as it shall be held that the welfare of the country requires "a cheap and abundant supply of labor."† This is the doctrine of the slavery of man as required by the exigencies of trade; and hence it is that it more and more obtains as land becomes more and more consolidated — and as the great capitals engaged in the several branches of trade are more and more en-

* Lalor: *Money and Morals*, p. 12.

† "A great miners' strike has just ended in Scotland—the men giving in, dead beat, after horrible sufferings, and going back to their work with rage in their hearts. A pretty human relation this, between man and man! Mutual defiance—that is the common attitude of employer and employed in these walks, especially in Scotland, where the feeling of personal independence is stronger and keener than it is here. The rise of the great Scottish manufacturers is one of the most marked features of our times. The iron-masters are buying lands everywhere, from the Tweed to the Orkneys — clearing away those old gentle houses which have produced so many able men—ay, and sent them to America, too—as your James Buchanan is there to testify, and as Judge Haliburton in Canada testifies likewise! One iron family, the Bairds, has bought the Closeburn of the Kirkpatricks, the Stitchell of the Pringles, and other famous spots. It is the age of iron, with a vengeance. But how comes the working man, who produces all this 'greatness,' to fare so ill? It may be all very fine that a McBuggins has bought out a Graham or a Lindsay, is toadying Buccleuch, and swears a little in broad Scotch in the presence of ladies in a drawing-room. But how about the poor McB., grimy, sweaty, and sad, with a little, half-fed family growing up heathens in the land of Knox? I want to see something done for him — before he tries to do something irregular for himself." — *Correspondence of the New York Tribune*, June, 1856.

abled to carry on that "warfare" which looks to securing them in a monopoly of the privilege of purchasing raw materials abroad, and labor at home.

"The peasant knows," says a recent English writer,* "that he must die in the same position in which he was born." Elsewhere he says, "the want of small farms deprives the peasant of all hope of improving his condition in life." The London *Times* assures its readers that "once a peasant in England, the man must remain a peasant for ever;" and Mr. Kay, after careful examination of the condition of the people of Continental Europe, assures his readers that, as one of the consequences of this state of things, the peasantry of England "are more ignorant, more demoralized, less capable of helping themselves, and more pauperized, than those of any other country in Europe, if we except Russia, Turkey, South Italy, and some parts of the Austrian Empire." †

Under such circumstances, the middle class tends gradually to pass away, and its condition is well expressed by the term now so frequently used, "the uneasy class." The small capitalist, who would elsewhere purchase a piece of land, a horse and cart, or a machine of some kind that would double the productiveness of his labor and increase its reward, is, as has above been shown, forced to make his investments in savings banks or life insurance offices, to be by them lent out on mortgage at three per cent.; whereas, he could earn fifty per cent. could he be permitted to use his capital himself. There is, therefore, a perpetual strife for life, and each man is, as has been said, "endeavoring to snatch the piece of bread from his neighbor's mouth." The atmosphere of England is one of gloom. Every one is anxious for the future, for himself or his children — and this is a necessary consequence of the system that looks to increasing the difficulties standing in the way of commerce.

§ 5. The more perfect the power of association, the greater is the tendency towards equality of condition, resulting from the development of the mental faculties — and towards having the chain of society perfect in all its links. The less that power, the greater is the tendency towards inequality, resulting from the development of mind in a single portion of society, and the sub-

* Kay: *Social Condition of England and of Europe*, vol. i. 70. † Ibid. 359.

stitution, in the other, of brute force for mind; and towards having the laborer become a tool in the hands of those who desire to profit by his efforts. Mere animal power is, as we are told, what is required in the English system; and hence it is, that there so little progress has been made in the development of the artistic faculty, while everywhere throughout the continent of Europe it is seen to be so rapid.* Centralization is destructive of the mental power, for it looks to cheapening labor abroad and at home, and to diminishing the ability to purchase things requiring taste and skill in their preparation. The market for such commodities afforded by Ireland, by Portugal, by Jamaica, or by India, is not now one-tenth as great as it was half a century since; and, small as it is, it declines from year to year — thus affording proof conclusive of the *disadvantage* of the system, leaving moral considerations altogether out of view. The difficulty now complained of in the English journals is but the necessary result of a policy which requires low-priced labor—that being always the labor of a slave.

§ 6. The more rapid the circulation of the blood throughout the human body, the greater is the tendency to have each and every part thereof attain its full development, and the more harmonious is the action of the whole. The more languid the circulation, the greater is the liability to disease and death. So is it with societary bodies. The rapid circulation of Greece was shown in the creation of numerous local centres, and in the existence of a spirit of association for all useful purposes that had never before been known; but when, in later times, Athens had made herself the sole centre of a system of subject towns and cities, the rapidity of the circulation declined, and though the great city itself became from day to day more splendid, its splendor was but the evidence of growing slavery — producing disease that was to end in death.

In earlier times, the British isles presented to view numerous local centres — London, Edinburgh, and Dublin being the seats of the English, Scottish, and Irish parliaments; while local

* "We are perpetually trying to separate the workman and the work. We like one man to think, and another to do; but the two will never really flourish apart: thought must govern action, and action must stimulate thought, or the mass of society will always be as it is now, composed of 'morbid thinkers and miserable workers.' It is only by labor that thought can be made healthy, and only by thought that labor can be made happy." —*North British Review*, May, 1854. See note to page 239, *ante*.

authorities throughout the several kingdoms controlled the management of the affairs of the various counties into which they were divided, and towns and cities which so much abounded. One by one, however, they have disappeared — Edinburgh and Dublin having long since ceased to be more than mere provincial towns, and smaller towns and cities having found the direction of their affairs gradually passing into the hands of government commissioners, directing all the local operations from the immediate neighborhood of the sole Parliament of a consolidated kingdom.

Charged, as is this central legislature, at one moment with the decision of questions vitally affecting the interests of the hundred millions of the people of India — at a second, with others of high importance to the people of Canada, Australia, or the Ionian Islands — and at a third, with the regulation of the lodging-houses, or the hackney fares, of London, or the sewerage of towns and villages throughout the kingdom—it is scarcely matter of surprise that legislation now, as we are told, "involves an amount of drudgery which many men, best qualified in other respects for the duties of Parliament, cannot, and will not, undertake."* Under such circumstances it is, that Parliament is besieged by applicants for railroad and other privileges, the grants of which are to be obtained only by aid of consummate skill and management, by the possession of which qualities agents now accumulate enormous fortunes; so that the middleman system, which always attends the decline of local centres, is thus extended to the affairs of legislation. Thus far, the expenditures preliminary to the making of roads have amounted, as it is said, to more than a hundred millions of dollars; and the result of the system is seen in the establishment of powerful combinations, "versed in all the dodges of the committee-rooms, and possessed of funds and agencies sufficient for any contest" — giving them "full command of the lands and property of only quiet respectability and limited means." "For nineteen men out of twenty

* "Our legislators are bound to spend half their time in unriddling the mysteries of the Puddle Dock Company against Jenkins about the upper corner of a two-acre field, in detecting the glosses which would mislead them in respect of a turn in a road, the height of a bridge, or the outfall of a drainage; and then we expect them to go straightway to just determinations on our colonial administration, the government of India, the conservation of our own constitutional principles, or the general policy of Europe."— *Westminster Review*, January, 1854: article, *Constitutional Reform.*

to oppose such a body in the costly litigation of Parliament, is," as we are told, "entirely out of the question, the even balance of right being," as the writer adds, "as effectually clogged as if Dame Justice herself were unhoodwinked, and held it according to the greatest fee." *

While India or Ireland, Canada or Australia, with difficulty obtains a hearing, strictly local affairs are almost entirely neglected. Therefore it is, that the management of the affairs of the country passes gradually under the control of commissions which are being created from year to year—superseding the local authorities by whom they before had been administered.† Centralization grows, thus, on every hand. But recently it was proposed to make of the government a great life insurance office — taking into its hands all the property now administered by the numerous private companies. This, however, would be only another step in the same direction in which England so long has walked. The existence of those companies, on their present extended scale, is due entirely to an erroneous policy, based on the idea of cheap raw materials and cheap labor — that policy which consolidates the land, fills the poor-houses, and enables a few people of great wealth so to control the movements of trade as to drive from it all the people whose means are moderate, and who cannot afford to waste hundreds of thousands of pounds in the effort to annihilate competition at home and abroad.

§7. Man is ever a creature of progress, either upward or downward. He is never stationary. Every step towards centralization is but the preparation for a new and greater one; and therefore

* *Westminster Review*, January, 1854.

† "The land of twenty neighbors wants common drainage or a common road. Nothing but an act of Parliament, to be obtained at vast cost, and three hundred miles from the spot, can effect the improvement. The improvement is therefore never made, and even the dream of it is repressed as a dream; and then come centralizers and *doctrinaires*, with all kinds of vituperation of local authorities and local owners for their want of knowledge and interest in such matters: straightway, a great metropolitan department is set up to supply—to pump artificially—to the provinces the energy which the system of Parliament itself has repressed at its natural fountain. On this follow differences between provincial feeling and metropolitan dictation, and on that a new contraction of whatever interest was felt in the subject before. Thus, as alternate cause and effect, compact bureaucracy tends constantly to firmer establishment; and, but for causes yet too strong for it, we should verge rapidly to the chilling and dangerous system of Austria and France, any merely electoral reform notwithstanding."—*Ibid.*

is it that there has been more progress in that direction in the last twenty years than had been made in the preceding century.*

Much was hoped for from the passage of the Reform Act, but it has failed to accomplish the good that was to be expected; and for the reason, that the whole policy of the country looks towards the aggrandizement of trade at the expense of commerce. Instead of putting "the actual franchise in the hands of the most independent and the most intelligent class of the community — the artisan class"— it has, says Mr. Toulmin Smith, put it into those "of a class which, though most mistakenly and unwisely, is actually and increasingly, owing to the growing influence of centralization, the least independent of any—namely, that of small traders and retail shopkeepers." †

The remedy having failed, we are now told, and by a distinguished writer, that the constitution of Parliament must be so radically changed as to enable the ministry for the time being to "command a majority"—and thus avoid the necessity for making troublesome explanations in the House of Commons. "A strong government," as we are assured, is the one thing needful; and that it may exist, a number of new seats should be created, to be filled, not by the people, but by those who are, or should be, the people's servants. Nothing has yet occurred that so clearly marks the growing centralization of England as the publication of the pamphlet here referred to.‡

§ 8. "The more imperfect a being," says Goethe, "the more do its individual parts resemble each other, and the more do those parts resemble the whole. The more perfect a body, the more dissimilar become the parts. In the former case, the parts

* "Here we see the greatest danger to English society: the evil is far from being so great as it is with the continental nations; but England has already arrived upon the fatal slope. It is time for her statesmen to be well aware that the universal and immoderate desire of public employment is the worst of social maladies. It spreads through the whole body of the nation a venal and servile temper, which does not, however, exclude, even in the case of those best provided for, the spirit of faction and of anarchy. It creates a posse of starvelings capable of any extravagance in the desire to satisfy their appetite, and fit for any meanness as soon as its cravings are appeased. A people of solicitors is the lowest of people—there is no humiliation that it may not be brought to submit to." — MONTALEMBERT: *De l'Avenir Politique de l'Angleterre*; quoted in *Blackwood's Magazine*, May, 1856.

† *Local Self-Government*, p. 242.

‡ W. R. GREG: *The Way Out*, London, 1855.

are more or less a repetition of the whole; in the latter, they are totally unlike the whole." Tried by this standard, English society is becoming more and more imperfect, as it becomes from year to year more and more a mere body of traders, surrounded everywhere by men who work for wages. The little landed proprietor has disappeared. The little capitalist becomes an annuitant. The little daily journal yields place to the gigantic *Times*. Centralization increases steadily, and with every stage of its increase the parts more and more resemble each other, and the more does the whole resemble its parts—trade and transportation becoming, from year to year, more and more the objects of all the aspirations of a government whose policy is "determined by considering what is for the moment Expedient, without admitting the previous inquiry whether there was a claim of Right."*

The higher the organization—the more perfect the development of the various faculties of the man—the more complete is the power of self-government. This is as true of societies as we see it to be of individuals. The more perfect the power of association, and the more complete the development of the various faculties of its various members, the more entire is its power to control its own action; and the less is it liable to outside influence.

In England, as we see, the power of association declines, and local self-government tends to disappear—centralization certainly

* "The English government is encroaching and tyrannical where it is strong, as in Asia and in the colonies, but is cringing and complaisant to tyrants in Europe, where it is weak. Those who have defended the opening of Mazzini's letters by Sir James Graham, will never convince us that the English cabinet was providing for English interests. The belief that this was done to gratify the hateful governments of Naples and of Austria, and that it occasioned the death of the brothers Bandiera, has never been refuted. When Austria, in 1846, invaded and overthrew the Republic of Cracow — a republic established and guaranteed by the treaty of Vienna—Lord Palmerston refused even to protest against it, and has since continued to prate of the sacredness of that treaty as often as it is convenient to the despotic powers against the liberties of the nations. What is meant by 'protection,' was once more manifested. But what was this, compared to our destruction of the liberties of Portugal in 1847, while Lord John Russell, too, was prime minister? Of *Right*, he made no more account towards Portugal, then ten years previously towards Canada. The sole question was, 'Is it *convenient* to us to allow a just revolution to succeed in Portugal?' and the reply was, 'No; for the kingdom of Sardinia is in process of reformation; Switzerland is excited by internal movements; Prussia, having at length got a parliament, is pushing its advantage against the king; moreover, there is a reforming pope at Rome; and if revolution succeeds in Portugal, the example will be followed in many other places: therefore, right or wrong, it must be suppressed.'"—*Westminster Review*, July, 1855; article, *International Immorality*.

and rapidly taking its place. Hence it is that we are called to remark a constantly growing weakness, indicated by an increased necessity for modifying her policy, in obedience to the dictation of other nations. The change in the navigation laws was forced upon her—first, by the resistance of the United States, and then, by that of Prussia and other powers.

So, too, was it with regard to the question of protection. For seventy years, and even down to 1819, the duties on foreign manufactures had steadily been increased. In that and the five following years, several of the communities of Europe adopted measures looking to resistance, while in the last of them was passed the first American tariff based upon the idea of bringing the farmer and the artisan nearer together — and thus approximating the prices of raw materials and manufactured commodities. To this was due the change of measures commenced by Mr. Huskisson in 1825—a change, however, looking steadfastly towards the accomplishment of the one great object, that of cheapening all the raw materials of manufacture, whether corn, cotton, or labor. The successful resistance of Russia—the formation of the German *Zoll-Verein*—and the American tariff of 1842, were the causes of the total change of policy that occurred in 1846. So, likewise, was it with the sugar duties. The emancipated negroes of Jamaica had been assured of protection against slave-grown sugar, yet Brazil compelled a violation of the well-understood agreement. The Crimean war is scarcely to be regarded as having been a voluntary act on the part of the government — any more than is the peace that has recently been made. Turning to India, we find the government making the most unjust of wars, because it "cannot afford" to let it appear, even for a moment to let it be doubted, that its hold on India rests "upon the might of the conqueror."*

* "*From Lord Dalhousie's Minute of February* 12, 1852:—

"The British power in India cannot *safely afford* to exhibit *even a temporary* appearance of inferiority. Whilst I should be reluctant to believe that our empire in India has no stay but the sword alone, it is vain to doubt that our hold must mainly rest upon the might of the conqueror, and must be maintained by that power. The government of India cannot, consistently with its own safety, *appear for one day* in an attitude of inferiority; or hope to maintain peace and submission among the numberless princes and people embraced within the vast circuit of the empire, if, *for one day*, it give countenance to a doubt of the *absolute* superiority of its arms, and of its continued resolution to assert it."—*Blue Book, presented to Parliament June* 4, 1852, p. 66: quoted in *Westminster Review*, for July, 1855, p. 35.

The removal of restrictions upon trade, and the repeal of the navigation laws, are said, however, to have been a consequence of improved modes of thought, and to have been made in deference to the advancing spirit of the age. Were this really so, a similar spirit might be manifested in other directions; but such, unhappily, is not the case. Nothing could be more unjust than the taxation imposed upon all the correspondence between America and the continent of Europe; yet is it persisted in, in spite of all remonstrances. The people of the West India islands have, for years, and in vain, petitioned for such an alteration of the duties as would enable them to refine their own sugar. The British colonies of the continent and the West Indies but recently determined to establish between themselves a perfect reciprocity — abolishing all duties upon their respective productions; and in so doing only desired to carry into full effect the views so strenuously urged upon the government of the United States in reference to the — so-called — Reciprocity Treaty, then just made with Canada. Upon submitting the question, however, to the consideration of the home government, the answer was, that her Majesty's government trusted that they would "not be asked to submit for her Majesty's approval acts or ordinances giving effect to measures of that character," as "it would be inconsistent with the imperial policy of free trade"! *

The Spanish people find themselves greatly aggrieved by the use of Gibraltar as a smuggling depôt, yet is there manifested no disposition to make a change in that respect; although, when the place was ceded, it was made a part of the treaty stipulations that it should never be used for such a purpose. Spanish commerce is thus sacrificed to the promotion of British trade.

The people of China being forced, despite of all opposition on the part of their government, to receive from fifteen to twenty millions of dollars' worth of opium annually, the result is seen in growing intemperance — in an enormous waste of life — and in a tendency towards the resolution of Chinese society into its original elements, to be followed by universal anarchy; yet is Hong Kong retained as a necessary appendage to the Indian Empire, because "expediency" requires the carrying out of measures utterly unjustifiable on the ground of "right." Such being the course of

* *Despatch of Sir William Molesworth to the Governor of Barbadoes.*

proceeding towards the weaker communities of the earth, the adoption of any other towards the stronger ones can be attributed only to a diminution of power to pursue that which had so long been practised.

§ 9. Action and reaction are equal and opposite—the ball that stops another in its course finding itself retarded, if not entirely arrested, in its own motion towards the point to which it had been directed. So is it with communities. Whatever movement of France tends to stop the circulation of Germany or Italy, tends equally to produce the same effect at home; and Frenchmen suffer when the armies of France destroy the commerce of her neighbors. So is it, too, with England, in reference to Ireland, India, the West Indies, Spain, and all other countries. The real interests of each and every community are to be promoted by the adoption of measures tending to produce increase of commerce in the bosom of each and every other — thereby increasing the value of man—diminishing the value of all the commodities required for his use — facilitating the development of intellect — and thus enabling men more and more to combine their efforts with those of their neighbor-men for obtaining that power over nature which constitutes wealth; and therefore is it that an enlightened self-interest would prompt each and all to carry into the management of public affairs the same spirit that should animate every Christian man in his dealings with his fellow-men.

Such, however — and most unhappily — has not been the spirit in which the English policy has been directed. Purely selfish, it has sought to annihilate commerce everywhere, and everywhere to substitute trade—thereby lessening the value of man — increasing the value of all the commodities he needed for his purposes — arresting the development of his intellect — preventing him from obtaining command over the forces of nature — and thus keeping him in that state of poverty which makes him a mere instrument in the hands of the soldier and the trader. For the accomplishment of these objects, the world has been belted round with colonies—alliances have been made and broken—thousands of millions of pounds have been spent on ruinous wars* — millions upon

* "Every rock in the ocean where a cormorant can perch is occupied by British troops — has a governor, deputy-governor, storekeeper, and deputy-

millions of lives have been sacrificed; and the result is seen in the fact that she now stands emphatically alone among the ruins she has made.

Having stopped the motion of society in Portugal, her old and faithful ally now hangs upon her hands, useless even for the purposes of trade. So is it with Turkey, and so, too, with the Indies of the West and of the East, both of which are causes of anxiety, and not sources of profit. Coming nearer home, Ireland —a country abounding in all the elements of wealth—presents to view, and for the first time in the history of the world, a nation gradually disappearing from the earth in the midst of the profoundest peace. Looking into Scotland, we see the land becoming consolidated, and its occupants being everywhere expelled to make room for sheep—while almost hundreds of thousands of people around are in constant danger of starvation.* Turning

storekeeper, and will soon have an archdeacon and a bishop; military colleges with thirty-four professors, educating seventeen ensigns per annum—being half an ensign for each professor—with every species of nonsense, athletic, sartorial, and plumigerous. A 'just and necessary' war costs this country about one hundred pounds a minute; whip-cord, fifteen thousand pounds; and tape, seven thousand pounds; lace for drummers and fifers, nineteen thousand pounds; a pension for one man who has broken his head at the Pole—to another who has shattered his leg at the Equator; subsidies to Persia; secret-service money to Thibet; an annuity to Lady Henry Somebody and her seven daughters, the husband being shot at some place where we never ought to have had any soldiers at all, and the elder brother returning four brothers to Parliament—such a scene of extravagance, corruption, and expense as must paralyze the industry and mar the fortunes of the most industrious, spirited people that ever existed."—*Sidney Smith.*

* "Recent inquiry has discovered that even there, in districts once famous for fine men and gallant soldiers, the inhabitants have degenerated into a meagre and stunted race. In the healthiest situations, on hillsides fronting the sea, the faces of their famished children are as thin and pale as they could be in the foul atmosphere of a London alley. Still more deplorable are the scenes exhibited in the Western Highlands, especially on the coasts and in the adjoining islands. A large population has there been assembled, so ill provided with any means of support, that during part of almost every year from 45,000 to 80,000 of them are in a state of destitution, and entirely dependent upon charity. Many of the heads of families hold crofts from four to seven acres in extent, but these, notwithstanding their small size, and the extreme barrenness of the soil, have often two, three, and sometimes even four, families upon them." * * * *

"Of course, they live most wretchedly. Potatoes are the usual food, for oatmeal is considered a luxury, to be reserved for highdays and holidays, but even potatoes are not raised in sufficient abundance. The year's stock is generally exhausted before the succeeding crop is ripe, and the poor are then often in a most desperate condition, for the poor-law is a dead letter in the north of Scotland, and the want of a legal provision for the necessitous is but ill supplied by the spontaneous contributions of the land-owners."—THORNTON: *Over-Population and its Remedy*, pp. 74, 76.

from the land to the great trading city, Glasgow, we meet there with the people who have been expelled — living in a state of destitution not exceeded even in Ireland.* Arriving in England herself, we find an overgrown metropolis and a great trading city, between which points is to be found nearly all the circulation of the empire. Such are the unhappy consequences of mistaking trade, ever warlike and exhausting, for the always peaceful and invigorating commerce.

§ 10. Adopting as her motto, "ships, colonies, and commerce," England has glorified the former, and has, therefore, sought everywhere to magnify the obstacles standing in the way of her own improvement and that of the world. To increase the number of her ships, she required colonies, and to obtain colonies she has involved herself in almost endless wars.† To find employment for ships, she made herself the contractor for supplying negro slaves to the Spaniards; and to enable herself to obtain supplies of slaves, she stirred up wars in every part of Africa. As Portugal, Turkey, and Ireland became more and more impoverished and exhausted, she became more and more dependent upon India; and as India became more and more exhausted, it became more and more necessary to deplete China by help of opium — and hence the opium war. As her earlier India possessions became more and more impoverished, troops were more

* "The *wynds* in Glasgow comprise a fluctuating population of from 15,000 to 30,000 persons. This quarter consists of a labyrinth of lanes, out of which numberless entrances lead into small square courts, each with a dunghill reeking in the centre. Revolting as was the outward appearance of these places, I was little prepared for the filth and destitution within. In some of these lodging-rooms (visited at night) we found a whole lair of human beings littered along the floor, sometimes fifteen and twenty, some clothed and some naked; men, women, and children huddled promiscuously together. Their bed consisted of a layer of musty straw intermixed with rags. There was generally little or no furniture in these places — the sole article of comfort was a fire. Thieving and prostitution constitute the main sources of the revenue of this population. No pains seem to be taken to purge this Augean pandemonium — this nucleus of crime, filth, and pestilence—existing in the centre of the second city in the empire." — SYMONDS: *Report on the Hand-loom Weavers.*

† "The history of the colonies for many years is that of a series of loss, and of the destruction of capital; and if to the many millions of private capital which have been thus wasted, were added some hundred millions that have been raised by British taxes, and spent on account of the colonies, the total loss of wealth to the British public which the colonies have occasioned, would appear to be quite enormous." — *Parnell.*

readily obtained for carrying war into Scinde, Affghanistan, the Punjab, and Burmah. As Jamaica declined, the cooley trade was established. Trade and war thus travel always in company with each other — always exhausting the earlier fields of action, and always compelled to seek for new ones, with constant increase in the necessity for effecting changes of place, and constant decline in the condition of man; whereas, commerce tends always towards diminution of that necessity, with constantly accelerated improvement in his condition.

Centralization in both the material and social world is destructive of the power of motion. Annihilate the local attraction of the planets, and the splendor of the sun would for the moment be increased, but that splendor would be but the precursor of ruin, and of the total destruction of the individuality of the sun himself; and so precisely must it be in the affairs of nations. That centralization grows with the extension of empire, is a fact proved by all the chapters in the world's history; and therefore was it most justly said by one of England's greatest writers, that "extended empire, like extended gold, exchanges solid strength for feeble splendor" — centralization bringing in its train depopulation, slavery, and death; and producing a necessity for inventing a theory of over-population, whereby the rich and powerful may be enabled to comfort themselves with the belief that the poverty and wretchedness with which they find themselves surrounded, are to be traced to the blunder of an all-wise, all-merciful, and all-powerful Creator.

# CHAPTER XIX.

## THE SAME SUBJECT CONTINUED.

§ 1. By help of association and combination with his fellows, man obtains power over nature — substituting steam, electricity, and other forces, for the human hand, and passing from the cultivation of the poor soils of the hills to that of the rich ones of the river bottoms; with constant increase in the facility of obtaining the food, clothing, and shelter required for his nourishment and support.

To enable them to associate and combine, there must be diversity in the modes of employment—developing the various faculties of individual men, fitting them for association, and producing that wealth of intellect by means of which they are enabled to direct those forces to their service. Commerce grows with the development of intellect and the growth of wealth. The more rapid its growth, the greater is the tendency towards having matter take upon itself the forms in which it is best fitted for the purposes of man — the more regular and abundant is the supply of food and clothing — the longer is the duration of life, and the more continuous and regular is the motion of society; and the greater is the tendency towards diminution in the power of those who live by trade and transportation, and towards increase in the freedom of man.

Such are the facts observed in every country of advancing civilization.

---

Looking, next, to those of advancing barbarism, we find that all the facts are directly the reverse — the power of association declining with the diminishing diversity of employments — men becoming more and more limited to the single pursuit of scratching the earth in quest of food — the rich soils being more and more abandoned — food becoming more scarce, and famines and pestilences more frequent—commerce declining — trade becoming more and more the master of the fortunes of the poor cultivators — population diminishing — the chain of society becoming more and more deficient in its connecting links—and society itself tending more and more to take upon itself a form similar to that now seen existing among savage tribes, by whom the disease of over-population is most experienced.

§ 2. In the first of the cases above described, the tax of transportation steadily declines, with constant increase in the *utility* of the rude products of the earth, and as constant diminution in the *value* of commodities required for the uses of man. In the last, that tax as regularly increases, with constant decline in the utility of the raw material, and increase in the value of food, clothing, and other necessaries of life.

In the first, land becomes more and more divided, with growing tendency to its cultivation by the man who owns it, and to the creation of local centres—facilitating the combination of men with their fellow-men, and increasing the demand for their various faculties. In the last, the land becomes more and more consolidated, with constantly increasing tendency to having the work of cultivation performed by hired laborers — towards the creation of a body of absentee proprietors — and towards the disappearance of local centres, and the establishment of a single centre of action — thus lessening the facilities of association, and diminishing the demand for the exercise of mental power.

In the first, the prices, or money values, of the rude products of the earth, and those of finished commodities, tend steadily towards closer approximation — with constant increase in the productiveness of labor, and in the laborer's *proportion* of the augmented product; and constant decrease in that remaining for the persons who stand between the men who produce and those who need to consume. In the last, those prices tend to recede from each other, with decline in the productive power, and diminution in the laborer's share of the diminished product.

In the first, the labor of the present is obtaining a constant increase of power over the accumulations of the past. In the last, the accumulations of the past are obtaining greater power over the labor of the present.

In the first, the forces of nature become centred in THE MAN, whose value increases from year to year, and who becomes from day to day more free. In the last, nature acquires power over man, whose value diminishes from day to day, as he becomes more and more enslaved.

In the first, the circulation is rapid, with constant tendency to have society assume that form in which strength and beauty are most combined — that of a cone, or pyramid. In the last, the circulation becomes from day to day more languid, and society tends to assume that form which is least consistent with either strength or beauty — that of an inverted pyramid.

§ 3. Looking to Greece, in the days of Solon, we observe the first of the sets of phenomena above described — a rapid circulation of society, accompanied by division of the land—by the creation of local centres — by a constant growth in the power of association and combination — by a wonderful development of intellectual power—and by the enfranchisement of man. Looking to it, next, in the days of Pericles and his successors, we find the circulation becoming more languid — the land becoming consolidated—the local centres diminishing in importance, while a great central city rises on their ruins — the demand for intellectual faculty declining — pauperism increasing from year to year, and producing a necessity for colonization — and free citizens being re-enslaved.

Turning next to Italy in the days when the Campagna afforded food to the inhabitants of its numerous cities, we see a reproduction of the facts of early Greece. Studying it in the days of Pompey and Cæsar, we find property in land to have become everywhere consolidated, and its owners to have become absentee proprietors, residents of a great city filled with paupers and owned by traders in men and money; the local centres to have so far diminished in importance that they almost cease to be known to history; the circulation of society almost to have disappeared; the demand for intellectual faculty to have been superseded by that for mere brute force, to be employed in extending the field of operation — and thus replacing the already exhausted Italy and Sicily by the yet unexhausted fields for plunder presented by Asia and by Africa.

Looking next to the British islands, we see, during a long course of centuries, facts similar to those observed in early Greece and Italy—the circulation of society increasing with the gradual increase in the variety of employments—the local centres growing in number and in importance—the land becoming more and more divided—the power of association and combination steadily augmenting—and man becoming everywhere more free.

Turning thence to the British empire of the present day, we see landed property becoming more and more consolidated—its owners more and more becoming absentees—and its cities becoming more and more crowded with paupers, and more and more becoming the property of traders in men and money; while everywhere the local centres are declining in importance—everywhere the circulation of society becomes more languid—everywhere the demand is made for those additions to population which consist in the mere brute force required to serve the purposes of those who live by the exercise of their powers of appropriation—and every day exhibits an increased necessity for new fields of action to take the place of the ruined Portugal, the almost extinct Turkey, the exhausted Ireland, and the now rapidly perishing Indies of the East and of the West.

In all the cases of advancing civilization above presented for the reader's consideration, the facts were one and the same. In all those of declining civilization, the evidences of such decline are precisely similar. In all, absenteeism and over-population are seen growing in due proportion to each other. In all, the accumulations of the past acquire an increased control over the labors of the present.* In all, the proportion of society engaged in the work of simple appropriation is a constantly augmenting one. In all, the form of society is seen passing from the beautiful and stable one of the true pyramid to that of the inverted one. Will the end in all prove to have been the same? In answer, we can only say that the prosperity of a community based upon trade has always proved to be a very fleeting one; that its foundations

* See *ante*, p. 420, for the assertion, that the workman is "indebted for being employed *at all*" to the losses incurred by his employer. The effect of an unsound system in corrupting the modes of thought was never more clearly exhibited than in the document from which that extract was made. The reasoning, throughout, in reference to the relation of employer and employed, is precisely the same with that we find in the journals of Carolina; and yet that document was published by order of the British House of Commons!

have always thus far proved to have been laid "in gold-dust and sand" — and that there exists no reason for believing that which has always been true in the past can be otherwise than true in the present, or will prove false in the future.

§ 4. The theory of over-population having originated in England, and thence, too, having been derived the supporting one of Mr. Ricardo, in relation to the occupation of the earth, it has been deemed just and proper to study carefully the English system, with a view to ascertaining to what extent the peculiar policy there attempted to be established has tended to production of such serious error on the part of her economists. If the doctrines taught in the English school are right, then has the Creator made a serious blunder—having established slavery as the ultimate condition of a vast majority of the human race. If, on the contrary, they are wrong, then is freedom the ultimate lot of man, and then are there found throughout the natural laws regulating the social system, the same order, beauty, and harmony of arrangement we see prevailing everywhere else throughout the organic and inorganic world. One of these things is absolutely and universally true, and the other as absolutely and universally false. Either an all-wise Deity has made a mistake, or man has made one, and has invented a theory by help of which to gloss it over.

That slavery is the ultimate tendency of the Malthusian system, will be obvious to the reader after a moment's reflection upon the proposition, that in the natural course of things population tends to outrun subsistence—men tending to increase in geometrical proportion, while food can be made to increase only in an arithmetical one. This being so, then the man who owns the food-producing machine *must* become the master of those whose necessities require that they should use it. The one holds the key of the great granary of nature, and the other must pay for the privilege of entering therein, be the price of admission what it may. The doctrine of over-population is, therefore, one of centralization, slavery, and death.

That this, in fact, was Mr. Malthus's own view of the case, is proved by the passage in which he tells his readers, that as, "by the law of our nature which makes food necessary to the life of man, population can never actually increase beyond the lowest nourishment capable of supporting it, a strong check on population, from the difficulty of obtaining food, must be *constantly in operation*. This difficulty must fall somewhere, and must necessarily fall in some or other of the various forms of misery, or the fear of misery, by a larger portion of mankind." * Mankind are thus subjected to a constant pressure, forcing their numbers up to that point at which it is impossible to obtain "the lowest nourishment;" and at which misery is required to step in, and—by thinning them off—keep them within the limits of the supply of food. Under such circumstances, there can be no law but that of force—the man who is strong of arm, or of intellect, enslaving his neighbor who is weak in these respects; and doing so in virtue of the laws of God!

The over-population theory originated in England, in the midst of an appalling state of pauperism, and it finds its chief support in the facts furnished by the British empire. Why should this be so? Because the English policy has so long looked steadily to the augmentation of that great obstacle to the progress of man which results from the necessity for effecting changes in the place of matter. Wherever that obstacle most exists the supply of food is least, and population is most superabundant. As it diminishes, the supply of food increases, man acquires a higher value, and it comes more and more to be recognised that the treasures of nature are infinite in extent — waiting only the demand for their production.

It is precisely as that obstacle is removed that the prices of raw materials and of finished commodities tend more and more to approximate—thus furnishing the most perfect evidence of advancing civilization. As they come more and more together, the power of the laborer over nature, and over himself, increases, but the power of other men over him as steadily declines; and thus does he pass from the condition of slave to that of freeman. The English system having for its base the idea of cheap land, cheap labor, cheap cotton, cheap corn, and dear cloth and dear iron, the more it is carried out, the greater is the tendency towards a decline in the power of man over nature—towards his subjection to the will of his fellow-man — and towards the verification of the Malthu-

* *Essay on the Principle of Population,* book 1, chap. i.

sian theory, in virtue of which man becomes necessarily the hewer of wood and the drawer of water for his fellow-man.

§ 5. The one great characteristic of the laws of nature is, that they act always in one direction. Having ascertained that the law of gravitation is true in regard to the apple now falling from the tree, it becomes safe to assume that it is equally so in reference to all the planets of which our system is composed, and that it has governed the movements of all the apples that have ever fallen, and will govern all that ever will fall, however long may be the duration of the earth. Admitting the case to be the same with the laws controlling the movements of man, and seeing that in the earliest periods of society he is very poor and miserable, while in later ones he becomes stronger and more able to command supplies of food, it follows, necessarily, that his power to command the services of nature must steadily increase, as he becomes more enabled to combine his efforts with those of his neighbor man.

That such is the tendency in the early ages of society, is admitted by all — food then becoming more abundant as men increase in numbers, and are more and more enabled to work in combination with each other. Having, however, reached some certain point, the law, according to Mr. Malthus, turns round, and, with every step in the further progress of population and of wealth, food becomes more scarce—requiring that a portion of the occupants of the land should "regularly die of want;"* as the savages of the early period had done.†

This, as the reader will now observe, exactly represents what *has been* the course of events in Ireland, in Jamaica, in India, in Portugal, and in Turkey; and also, that which was the course in England at the date of Mr. Malthus's work, when property in the land was just beginning to be consolidated; and when the pro-

* MILL: *Elements of Political Economy*, p. 16.

† "After a certain, and not very advanced, stage in the progress of agriculture; as soon, in fact, as men have applied themselves to cultivation with any energy, and have brought to it any tolerable tools; *from that time*, it is the law of production from the land, that in any given state of agricultural knowledge, by increasing the labor, the produce is not increased in an equal degree; doubling the latter does not double the former; or, to express the same idea in other words, *every increase of produce is obtained by a more than proportional increase in the application of labor to the land*."—J. S. MILL, *Principles*, vol. i., p. 212.

perism that has since become so frightful had begun to show its head. Seeing these things, it would seem to be obvious that his theory is merely to be regarded as *descriptive* of what had been, and what were bound to be, the effects of an unsound course of human action, but erroneously regarded as the necessary consequence of divine laws.

§ 6. So, too, is it with the Ricardo-Malthusian law of the occupation of the earth, in virtue of which man commences with the rich lands, and then obtains food in abundance, but in course of time finds himself compelled to resort to soils yielding less and less in return to labor — and enabling the land-owner to claim a constantly increasing *proportion*, under the name of rent. Such being the law, the laborer becomes of necessity the bond slave — the hewer of wood and drawer of water — to the man who claims to own the land. That such is the inevitable result, cannot for a moment be doubted by any one who believes, with Mr. McCulloch, that, "from the operation of fixed and permanent causes, the increasing sterility of the soil is sure, in the long run, to overmatch the improvements that occur in machinery and agriculture" — man thus becoming more and more the slave of nature, whose representative — the land-owner — holds the key by help of which alone her gifts can be obtained.

Man becomes more free as the labor of the present acquires power over the accumulations of the past — and less free as they acquire power over him. If the Ricardo theory is true, then is slavery provided for by the laws of God, and then must every effort at the enfranchisement of man prove to have been made in vain.

That theory involves, necessarily, the separation of men from their fellow-men, in search of distant and fertile lands; and yet, separate as they may, the original curse still follows them — "the increasing sterility of the soil being sure to overmatch" any improvements they may make. The utility of the materials of which the earth is composed *must* diminish — the value of the commodities required by man *must* increase — and the value of man himself *must* decline; while the necessity for the service of the trader and transporter must be a constantly augmenting one. The more their services are required, the greater must be the differences between the prices of raw products and finished commodities; and the greater must be the tendency towards that state of things in which might makes right — that one in which barbarism takes the place of civilization. Look to the doctrine from what point we may, it carries man so certainly towards slavery, that, were it true, it would be folly to undertake resistance.

§ 7. Happily for man, history tells a story widely different from that of Mr. Malthus. All that is by him depicted as a consequence of increase of numbers, is precisely what we see to have existed in the past, when population was small, and when men could occupy at will either the lands of the hills, or those of the valleys — when no man had property in either — and when none could demand rent; but when all-powerful nature forbade the occupation of the lower and richer lands, and limited the labors of man to those of the poor ones of the hills. Such having been the case, and man having steadily acquired power as the result of that combination which could come only with increase of numbers, it would seem very clear that these theories could be entitled to no consideration whatsoever; unless, indeed, it were possible for us to conclude that the Creator had instituted laws that were to work at one time forward, and at another backward—at one time up, and at another down — while instituting, in relation to all other matter, laws which work so invariably in one direction, that having once determined what it is, man feels himself entirely safe in assuming that such it has been in all the times that are past, and that such it will be in all that are to come. That the Creator *could* have instituted such a system — that he *could* so have acted towards the being he had placed at the head of creation — is an idea so absurd as almost to warrant us in hesitating to credit that those by whom it was first suggested could really themselves have believed therein; and yet not a doubt that they really and honestly did so can now be entertained. What, however, could have been the cause of the error into which, men of high intelligence as they undoubtedly were, they fell? To obtain a reply to this question we must here briefly review the tendencies of the system as exhibited in the several countries to which reference has above been made.

What, in the first place, were the objects sought by it to be accomplished? Did it look to the promotion of association and combination? Did it look towards the development of the powers of man? Did it look to the development, or even to the maintenance, of the powers of the earth? Did it seek to lessen that greatest of all the obstacles standing in the way of commerce, the tax of transportation? Did it, in any manner, tend to increase the utility of the matter of which the earth is composed — to diminish the value of the commodities required for the uses of man—or, to increase the value of man himself? If such were its objects, then did it tend towards civilization.

That it did none of these things we know. It sought to prevent association. It prohibited diversity of employments, and thus forbade the development of mind, and the growth of the power of combination. It reduced the people subject to it to the condition of mere tillers of the soil — while enforcing the exhaustion of the land. All of these phenomena are those which attend the early ages of society — those ages that we denominate barbaric — those in which food is obtained with greatest difficulty — those in which famines and pestilences abound — and those in which the disease of over-population most exists. The system tended towards the reduction of the supply of the necessaries of life; and therefore is it that we find in Ireland, India, and Jamaica the most conclusive evidences of the truth of the doctrines of the English school. It was a retrograde policy, tending to cause a return of society to that state of barbarism from which it had emerged; and therefore was a retrograde theory required to enable those who sought to profit by it, to account for the diseases of which it was itself the cause. That theory was supplied by Messrs. Malthus and Ricardo, who gave us laws of God by help of which to account for famines, pestilences, and slavery, that were but the necessary result of the misconduct of man.

Such was the origin of that modern political economy which so entirely repudiates the ideas of Adam Smith, and finds in trade the substitute for commerce. Retrograde throughout, it requires that we should at once, and for ever, ignore the existence of an all-wise and all-benevolent Deity, and put our trust in a Being by whom had been instituted great natural laws in virtue of which men should necessarily, and "regularly, die of want."

Retrograde throughout, it teaches—

That, in the early stages of society, as the first miserable tools are obtained, by means of which to work, men are enabled to compel the earth to yield *larger* rewards to labor; but, that, as soon as they "have applied themselves to cultivation with any energy, and have brought to it any tolerable tools,"* a new law supervenes, in virtue of which the return to labor becomes yearly *smaller* than before.

That, although the progress towards civilization has everywhere been marked by an increase in the power of man over matter, there exist "fixed and permanent causes" why matter must everywhere, and under all circumstances, obtain greater power over man.

That, although the value of man had everywhere increased, as the value of the commodities required for his use has diminished, the true road of progress is to be found in the direction of increased use for ships and wagons, because in their use is to be found the greatest *increase* in the value of those commodities.

That, although men have everywhere become more free as employments have become more diversified, and as the utility of the various kinds of matter has become more and more developed, the road of progress lies in the division of nations into agricultural and manufacturing ones—the single workshop being thousands of miles distant from the places at which the materials are produced.

That, although man has always thriven in the precise ratio in which the price of the raw material has approximated that of the commodity manufactured from it, his further progress is to be increased by the adoption of a policy looking to cheapening the raw materials and increasing the quantity thereof required to be given for the finished article.

That, although he has always acquired value with the growth of commerce, and with decline in the necessity for trade and transportation, his condition must be improved by establishing the supremacy of trade.

That, although progress had always been marked by increase in the power of labor over capital, it is now required that "labor should be abundant and cheap," in order that it may be kept "sufficiently under the control of capital."

* J. S. MILL: *Principles of Political Economy*, vol. i. p. 212.

Such being the tendency of all its teachings, it is no matter of surprise that modern English political economy sees in man only an animal that *will* procreate, that *must* be fed, and that *can be made* to work — an instrument to be used by trade; that it repudiates all the distinctive qualities of man, and limits itself to the consideration of those he holds in common with the beast of burden or of prey; that it denies that the Creator meant that every man should find a place at his table, or that there exists any reason why a poor laborer, able and willing to work, should have any more right to be fed than the cotton-spinner has to find a market for his cloth; or that, as the reader has already seen, it assures its students that "labor is a commodity," and that if men *will* marry and have children without having previously made provision for them, it is for them to take their chance — and that "*if we stand between the error and its consequences, we stand between the evil and its cure*—if we intercept the penalty, (where it does not amount to positive death,) we perpetuate the sin." *

§ 8. Adam Smith knew nothing of any such "dismal science" as that above described. Having full faith in the advantages of commerce, he held in great contempt the system based upon the idea of converting a whole nation into a mass of mere traders in the products of other lands. Believing that "the one thing needful was, obviously, to make land yield the largest possible surplus," he favored its division, because "small farms," as he saw, could "afford a greater surplus than similar portions of a larger one;" and because his eyes had not been opened to the imaginary fact, that consolidation of landed property "raises universally the standard of competence, and gives force to the springs which set industry in motion."† Had that idea been suggested to him, he would probably have inquired why it had been that, in all other countries, such consolidation had been the companion of depopulation, slavery, and moral and political death.

A firm believer in the equal rights of man, he was as little able to see the justice of prohibition of commerce among the colonists,‡

* *Edinburgh Review*, October, 1849.

† McCulloch: *Principles*, p. 259.

‡ "To found a great empire for the sole purpose of raising up a people of customers may at first sight appear a project fit only for a nation of shopkeepers. It is, however, a project altogether unfit for a nation of shop-

as he would now be to discover the propriety, or the advantage to England herself, of a "warfare" on the part of great capitalists at home, with a view to the destruction of competition at home and abroad. Having a confident belief in the existence of the being known to him as MAN — a being possessed of feelings and affections — he held in great admiration the "small proprietor who," knowing "every part of his little territory, views it with all the affection which property, especially small property, naturally inspires; and who, on that account, takes pleasure not only in cultivating, but in adorning it;" and he would, with scorn, have rejected the idea of the modern politico-economical man—a being that sleeps, eats, and procreates, and must have so much wages as will enable him to supply the lowest wants of his nature, and those alone. Seeing clearly that "the most advantageous employment of the capital of the country to which it belongs, is that which maintains the greatest quantity of productive labor, and increases most the annual produce of the land and labor of that country," he held in small respect the opinions of those who saw in "foreign trade" the only index to prosperity; and in as little respect would he, were he now living, hold those of the men who see in the import of

"The wealth of climes, where savage nations roam,
Pillaged from slaves to purchase slaves at home,"

any compensation for the establishment of a system under the action of which "man" becomes "a drug, and population a nuisance." Holding to scarcely a single opinion in common with that modern political economy which since has emanated from the school of England,* it is little matter of surprise that we find in his great work no evidence of his belief that the "misery" described by Mr. Malthus had its existence in virtue of any of the laws of God

keepers; but extremely fit for a nation whose government is influenced by shopkeepers." — *Wealth of Nations*, book 4, chap. vii. Of the measures that had been adopted with a view to carry out this idea, and to magnify trade at the expense of commerce, as is still being done, Dr. Smith gave his opinion in the following words: — "To prohibit a great people, however, from making all they can of every part of their own produce, or from employing their stock and industry in the way that they judge most advantageous to themselves, is a manifest violation of the most sacred rights of mankind." — *Ibid.*

* The chief point of agreement between Dr. Smith and his followers is to be found in his chapters on Money, where he was most in error.

—that that great and beneficent Being had provided no place at his table for important portions of the human family—or that he believed a nation was to be enriched by such an extirpation of

"A bold peasantry—their country's pride"—

as has since taken place in every portion of the United Kingdom.

Appreciating fully the advantages—pecuniary and political, moral and social—resulting from commerce, Dr. Smith saw clearly that it increased as the necessity for the services of the transporter diminished—as the men engaged in effecting those mechanical and chemical changes in the form of matter required to fit it for man's consumption, more and more took their places by those engaged in developing the treasures of the earth, and in augmenting the quantity of raw materials requiring to be converted; and that every step in that direction was attended with diminution in the value of commodities, and an increase in the value and in the freedom of man.*

§ 9. The reader may now readily comprehend the simple and beautiful law in virtue of which society tends gradually to assume the form described in a former chapter.†

Among savages, raw material is low in price, while finished commodities are dear. Among civilized men, the reverse of this is true—raw material being dear and finished commodities cheap. The former give skins that have cost them days, in exchange for

* In the notes to Mr. McCulloch's edition of the *Wealth of Nations*, that gentleman tells his readers that "it would be inexcusable" to waste their time "by endeavoring to prove, by argument, the advantage of having supplies of food at a low price. To facilitate production," as he continues, "and to make commodities cheaper and more easily obtained, are the principal motives which stimulate the inventive powers, and which lead to the discovery and improvements of machines and processes for saving labor and diminishing cost."—p. 520. The words "price" and "cost" are here treated as if they referred to the same idea; whereas, the one refers to the value of corn in money, and the other to its value when measured by labor. It is precisely as "the inventive powers" become stimulated, that the former rises, as may be seen by a comparison of Poland with France, or England of the days of George I. with the same England of the time of George III. It is then, however, that the latter falls, as may be seen by a comparison of France of the present time with France of the days of Louis XV., or England of the present day with the England of those of the Plantagenets. The more numerous the discoveries and "improvements of machines," the less will be the "cost" of food, the greater will be its tendency to a rise of "price;" and the more rapid the improvement in the condition of man.

† See *ante*, p. 223.

knives produced by the labor of little more than minutes. The latter receive from the neighboring miller in the form of flour nearly all that they had given him in that of wheat.

Between these two conditions of society there are many stages, for whose illustration we give the following figures: —

| | | | | | | | | | |
|---|---|---|---|---|---|---|---|---|---|
| Finished commodity | 10 | 10 | 10 | 10 | 10 | 10 | 10 | 10 | 10 |
| Cost of transportation and conversion | 9 | 8 | 7 | 6 | 5 | 4 | 3 | 2 | 1 |
| Raw material | 1 | 2 | 3 | 4 | 5 | 6 | 7 | 8 | 9 |

We have here a rapid increase in the proportion retained by the producer, accompanied by corresponding decrease in that going to the payment of the various persons engaged in the works of trade, transportation, and conversion. In the first, the latter's share pays for the labor of nine times as many persons engaged in the work of cultivation — who are, of course, slaves both to nature and to their fellow-men. In the last, it pays for the labor of only one-ninth as many men; as a natural consequence of which, the slave of the earlier days is represented by the freeman of the later ones.

Admitting, now, that all were equally paid — that wages in all employments were the same — society would tend gradually to take the forms that here are indicated: —

| | | | | | | | | | |
|---|---|---|---|---|---|---|---|---|---|
| Employed in trade, transportation, and conversion | 900 | 800 | 700 | 600 | 500 | 400 | 300 | 200 | 100 |
| Employed in developing the resources of the earth | 100 | 200 | 300 | 400 | 500 | 600 | 700 | 800 | 900 |
| | 1000 | 1000 | 1000 | 1000 | 1000 | 1000 | 1000 | 1000 | 1000 |

The form of society thus gradually changes from the top-heavy and unstable one of an inverted pyramid, to the beautiful and stable one of a true pyramid — the mass of the physical and mental power of the community being, in the last, given to effecting those *vital changes in the forms of matter*, which result in augmentation of the quantity of things to be consumed; while but little of it is required for effecting changes in the places, forms, or ownership, of the things produced. With every stage of this progress, agriculture becomes more and more a science — the men employed in developing the resources of the earth rise in the scale of being—the various utilities of matter are more and more called into activity — local centres are created — food and clothing are more and more readily obtained—and man becomes more happy and more free. With each, mind is more and more stimulated into action — the feelings and affections are more and more developed — and man becomes from year to year more fitted for occupying the place for which he was intended — that of master over nature, and master of himself.

Such, under a natural system, are the results of an increase of population. That they are so, is shown by every page in the history of improving nations. That Mr. Malthus should so have misrepresented the action of the Creator — that he should have made slavery, instead of freedom, the ultimate condition of mankind — was due to the fact, that he lived in the midst of an artificial system, whose tendency to produce the enslavement of man is being, with each successive day, more clearly demonstrated.*

* In a recent debate in the House of Commons, it was stated that in the bleaching establishments of both England and Scotland, men, women, and children were obliged to work from sixteen to twenty hours per day, and under a temperature so high that, not unfrequently, "the nails in the floors became heated, and blistered the feet of those who were employed in the rooms — usually called 'wasting shops,' because of the extraordinary destruction of life of which they are the cause." To remedy these evils, and to protect the work-people — especially those whose tender age forbids that they should protect themselves, and whose lives are now, as was said by one of the speakers, "being expended just like those of cattle on a farm" — it was proposed to limit the hours of employment; but the bill for that purpose was rejected after a speech from Sir James Graham, in which, as the reader will here see, the laborer is regarded as a mere instrument to be used by trade:—

"It is admitted that the bleaching trade is exposed to the most severe competition with foreign rivals, and that it requires all the skill and energy of the British manufacturer successfully to contend against that competition. Just as in a race where two horses of exactly equal powers are to run—if you put three pounds extra on one of them, his defeat is certain: so it is with regard to this trade. Mr. Tremenheere admits the keenness of this competition, but, while he states most distinctly that if you follow his advice, the additional cost of production will be 10 per cent., and the addition to the selling price 1 per cent., he maintains that this is a very trifling matter indeed. That is so astounding a proposition in a matter of trade, that I, for one, cannot consent blindly to follow Mr. Tremenheere as a guide. If the effect should be as he states — to add 10 per cent. to the cost of production—I predict at once that by such hasty, wild, and extravagant legislation, you would insure the success of our foreign rivals in this branch of trade."

END OF VOL. I.

www.ingramcontent.com/pod-product-compliance
Lightning Source LLC
LaVergne TN
LVHW020916110826
845150LV00004B/687

* 9 7 8 1 4 2 5 5 5 5 7 4 0 *